Spain in an International Context, 1936-1959

Spain in an International Context, 1936–1959

Edited by

Christian Leitz

and

David J. Dunthorn

Berghahn Books
New York • Oxford

First published in 1999 by

Berghahn Books

Editorial offices:
55 John Street, 3rd Floor, New York, NY 10038, USA
3 NewTec Place, Magdalen Road, Oxford OX4 1RE, UK

Library of Congress Cataloging-in-Publication Data
Spain in an international context, 1936-1959 / edited by Christian
  Leitz and David Joseph Dunthorn
  p. cm.
  Includes bibliographical references and index.
  ISBN 1-57181-956-8 (alk. paper)
  1. Spain—Foreign relations. 2. Spain—Foreign relations—
  1939–1975. 3. Spain—Foreign relations—1931–1939. 4.
  Spain—Foreign relations—Europe. 5. Spain—Foreign relations—1939–1975—Europe. 6. Spain—Foreign relations—
  1931–1939—Europe. 7. Europe—Foreign relations—Spain.
  8. Europe—Foreign relations—1945– . 9. Europe—Foreign
  relations—1918–1945.   I. Leitz, Christian.   II. Dunthorn,
  David Joseph.
  DP85.8.S62   1999   99-31903
  327.46—dc21   CIP

British Library Cataloguing in Publication Data
A catalogue record for this book is available
from the British Library.

Printed in the United States on acid-free paper

Contents

List of Abbreviations

AA	German Foreign Ministry
AAN	Archive of the French National Assembly
ADAP	Documents on German Foreign Policy
AFD	Alliance of Democratic Forces
AGA	General Spanish Archive for Administration
AGK	Export Association for War Material
AHN	Spanish National Historical Archive
AN	French National Archive
ANCOM	Archives Nationales Centre d'Outre-Mer
ANMAE	Archive of the French Ministry for Foreign Affairs
APG	Archive of the Presidency of the Spanish Government
AMAE	Archive of the Spanish Ministry for Foreign Affairs
AuA	Australian Archive
BA/MA	German Federal Archive/Military Archive
BA/Pots	German Federal Archive (Potsdam)
BE	Bank of Spain
CAB	British Cabinet Papers (PRO)
CCR	Central Council of Resistance
CEDA	Spanish Confederation of Autonomous Right-Wing Groups
CGE	Compagnie Générale de l'Electricité
CIA	(U. S.) Central Intelligence Agency
CNT	Spanish National Confederation of Labour (anarcho-syndicalist)
CNT-FAI	Spanish anarchist movement
Cominform	Communist Information Bureau
Comintern	Communist International
CPSU	Communist Party of the Soviet Union
CSG	Conseil Supérieur de la Guerre
CTE	Compagnies de Travail des Etrangers
DBPO	Documents on British Policy Overseas
DDF	French Diplomatic Documents

DDI	Italian Diplomatic Documents
DEFE	British Defence Ministry Records (PRO)
DGFP	Documents on German Foreign Policy
DSB	U.S. Department of State Bulletin
DVP	Soviet Documents on Foreign Policy
EC	European Community
ERP	European Recovery Programme
FAO	Food and Agriculture Organisation (of the UN)
FCO	British Foreign and Commonwealth Office Library
FET	Spanish Falange
FFI-MOI	Forces Françaises de l'Intérieure-Main d'Oeuvre Immigrée
FO	British Foreign Office
FRUS	Foreign Relations of the United States
HC	House of Commons Debates
HISMA	Sociedad Hispano-Marroqui de Transportes
IBRD	International Bank for Reconstruction and Development
IEME	Spanish Foreign Exchange Authority
IMF	International Monetary Fund
INI	National Institute of Industry
IWM	Imperial War Museum
IPC	International Press Correspondence
JCS	Joint Chiefs of Staff
JEL	Junta Española de Liberación
JIC	Joint Intelligence Chiefs
JONS	Juntas de Ofensiva Nacional Sindicalista
MAE	Spanish Ministry for Foreign Affairs
MOI	Main d'Oeuvre Immigrée
MP	Member of Parliament
mts	metric tons
NA	U.S. National Archives
NATO	North Atlantic Treaty Organisation
NCOs	Non-commissioned Officers
NIA	Non-Intervention Agreement
NIC	Non-Intervention Committee
NKVD	People's Commissariat of Internal Affairs
OEEC	Organisation for European Economic Co-operation
OKM	German Navy High Command
OKW	German Armed Forces High Command
PA/AA	Archive of the German Foreign Ministry
PCE	Spanish Communist Party

PCF	French Communist Party
POUM	Spanish Workers' Party for Marxist Unification
POW	Prisoner of War
PPUS	Public Papers of the President of the United States
PRO	Public Record Office
PSOE	Spanish Socialist Party
pta.	Pesetas
RLM	Reich Air Ministry
RM	Reichsmark
ROWAK	Rohstoff-Waren-Kompensation Handelsgesellschaft
RTsKhIDNI	Russian Centre for the Preservation and Study of Documents Relating to Contemporary History
RWM	Reich Economics Ministry
SFIO	French Socialist Party
SHAA	Archive of the Historical Service of the French Air Force
SHAT	Archive of the Historical Service of the French Army
SHM	Archive of the Historical Service of the French Navy
SNCF	French National Railway Company
SOE	Special Operations Executive
UGT	Spanish General Workers Union
UN	United Nations
UNESCO	United Nations Educational, Scientific and Cultural Organisation
UNGA	United Nations General Assembly
USSR	Union of Soviet Socialist Republics

Preface

The essays in this collection emerged from a major international conference commemorating the sixtieth anniversary of the outbreak of the Spanish Civil War on 17 to 18 July 1936. Intending at first to focus on the international aspects of the Civil War years alone, the conference eventually became a forum for contributions on 'Spain in an International Context' during the period of the 'first Franco-ism'. This proved to be an apt expansion of the original more limited chronological framework. After all, following the Spanish Civil War – a truly internationalised conflict – the Franco regime continued to be closely connected to and affected by international developments. During the Second World War Spain never joined either of the belligerent camps, yet it still became embroiled in the conflict, usually in favour of the Axis. So much so that after the war most of the international community temporarily ostracised the Franco regime – not just because it was 'founded on fascist principles',[1] but also for the support it had given to the defeated fascist powers. Finally, from the late 1940s onwards another international development, namely the emergence and heightening of the East-West conflict, helped to ease Spain back into the international community, at least into its Western part.

This international historical 'chalk line' runs very clearly through all the essays in this collection, which has been arranged in near-chronological order. Yet, the conference was not simply an accumulation of summaries of the most important aspects of Spain's foreign relations during the period mid-1930s to late 1950s – nor are the essays. Rather, the conference brought together a mixture of specialised and more general contributions from both historians of Spain as well as international historians. Much original research from archives in many countries, including not just Spain but also Britain, France, Germany, Russia and the United States, found its way into the essays which, for the purpose of this collection, have been expanded and revised by their authors.

To enable the reader to put the individual essays into the general context of the emergence and the establishment of the Franco dictatorship an introductory overview of Franco's foreign policy until the 1950s is provided in the first chapter. By looking at the foreign policy of the regime Paul Preston establishes the central theme of all subsequent chapters, namely the crucial influence of the international context. Preston shows that on a number of important occasions the 'fate' of the regime was not determined by its actions alone, but rather by decisions taken abroad.

The pre-history of the Spanish Civil War, the developments from the victory of the *Frente Popular* in February 1936 to the rebellion of 17 to 18 July 1936 is traced by David W. Pike in the second chapter. Rather than provide a general history of events in Spain, which has been done abundantly elsewhere,[2] Pike examines the road towards the conflict from the angle of France's south-western press. More than any other country, France was affected by developments in Spain, particularly as, in May 1936, the country had experienced the electoral success of its own Popular Front. Moreover, France came to suffer from a similar ideological cleavage. This is vividly reflected in the left, right and liberal newspapers whose distributive coverage reached as far as the Spanish border.

While Pike provides a taste of domestic developments in Spain from a foreign perspective, the next three chapters take the reader straight into the international repercussions of the Spanish Civil War. Whether to intervene or not was the question which came to occupy various governments. Both Hitler and Mussolini, independently of each other, rapidly answered the question in the affirmative. From the end of July, Nazi Germany and Fascist Italy were to provide General Franco with crucial supplies (and troops).[3] While the insurgents were thus successful in obtaining urgently needed aid, the legally elected government of Spain ran into unexpected difficulties.

Decisive and immediate support by Britain would undoubtedly have given the Republican Administration a clear advantage. Yet, the noninterventionist attitude of Stanley Baldwin's government, which was continued under his successor Neville Chamberlain, favoured the insurgents. In his contribution to this collection, Enrique Moradiellos makes this point very clear. Moreover, he shows that Chamberlain's government in particular was strongly influenced by very widespread sympathies for Franco within the Prime Minister's Conservative Party.

That support was not forthcoming from the British Government – notwithstanding the various forms of aid provided by other sections of British society – was less surprising than the lack of support which the Spanish Popular Front government received from its 'sister' government in France. The initial supplies provided by Léon Blum's government ceased in early August to be replaced by an official policy of non-intervention. Yet, the situation across the border, in particular the possible outcome of the conflict, continued to preoccupy the French government as well as the French military – as clearly demonstrated in Chapter 4, Peter Jackson's paper on French strategy and the Spanish Civil War.

By early August 1936 the Spanish Republic thus found itself deprived of support from the two states which – considering their affinity to the Spanish political system – should have been expected to intervene. Owing to this and growing Italian and German support for Franco the Republic's initially favourable military position was reversed. In autumn 1936, Madrid seemed about to fall to the insurgents' offensive. It was the intervention of the 'other' totalitarian power which helped to save Madrid and the Republic and contributed to the prolongation of the Civil War. In October 1936, the Soviet Union, which had kept itself on the sidelines of the conflict, stepped in by sending urgently required war material. In Chapter 5 Geoffrey Roberts offers a new interpretation of Stalin's motives and his attitude towards the Civil War in Spain.

Ultimately, Soviet aid did not save the Republic, in fact, supplies were wound down months before Franco's victory in March 1939. Nazi Germany and Fascist Italy, on the other hand, kept up their support for the insurgents until success was ensured. Yet, peace in Europe was to last only for five months. By September France and Britain, who had allowed the Spanish Republic to be obliterated, were at war with the State that had actively contributed to the Republic's demise, Nazi Germany. At least for France, however, the Spanish Civil War had not really come to an end with Franco's official declaration on 1 April 1939. In the last months of the war, hundreds of thousands of desperate Spaniards had fled across the Pyrenees into the perceived safety of France. How the French government under Daladier as well as other French institutions, including the trade unions, reacted to this influx, first under conditions of peace then during the first months of the Second World War, is critically highlighted in Martin Alexander's paper (Chapter 6). Clearly, far too little was done to integrate such a large quantity of manpower into the French war effort.

Ironically, many of the Republicans in France, who would have willingly helped their host country, were soon forced to contribute to the war effort of Nazi Germany.[4] Yet, Adolf Hitler anticipated Spanish help of a different kind when, during the second half of 1940s, he bargained with Franco about Spain's entry into the war. That both sides, despite their keenness to achieve an entry, did not come to agree on the issue is well known. An overview of these unsuccessful negotiations is provided in Norman Goda's chapter, though his paper (Chapter 7) is particularly focused on Germany's strategic plans for the situation 'post-entry'.

Strategic considerations, which relate directly to those discussed in Goda's paper, are also at the forefront of Chapter 8. As pointed out by Goda and Preston, French Morocco was the linchpin of Franco's imperial dream, and therefore his main condition for entry into the war. Although the dictator's dream was never to be fulfilled, until the success of Operation Torch France had to reckon with the possibility of some hostile action against its north-west African possessions. The reaction of the regime of Marshall Pétain and the French Administration in Morocco during the crucial period 1940 to 1942 is examined in Martin Thomas's contribution.

Not surprisingly, the defeat of the Axis in North Africa and at Stalingrad influenced Franco's view of the war. His temptation to take Spain into the war all but disappeared, yet he continued to maintain close relations with Nazi Germany. These relations are highlighted by Christian Leitz in Chapter 9, where the emphasis is placed on their most important aspect, the economic, and in particular on the role of German arms exports to Spain.

How did relations between the Allies and Spain develop during the Second World War? It is clear that, after the defeat of France, Britain did its utmost to prevent Spain's entry into the war. An initially fairly weak (though successful) defensive action, in which the British Government made particular use of the economic weapon, was gradually transformed into a more aggressive effort to convince Franco not only to abandon any idea of becoming a belligerent, but also to scale down any support given to Germany. Particularly after December 1941, the British Government could count on crucial help from the United States. Ultimately, however, pressure by the Allies worked only in combination with their growing superiority in the war. Even so, it took until May 1944 before Franco reluctantly agreed to make written concessions to the Allies.

It is in this context that Glyn Stone's contribution examines the evolving relationship of the British government to the Franco regime during the Second World War. A particular concern of the chapter is to highlight the stance of the British government towards the Spanish Republicans in exile and the question of whether to work actively towards a restoration of democracy in Spain. Although largely concerned with Winston Churchill's war-time coalition, Chapter 10 also leads over into the first years of Clement Attlee's premiership and thus into the post-war international position of Franco Spain.

In a near-seamless transition we arrive at Qasim Ahmad's contribution (Chapter 11), which looks at Franco Spain's international isolation after 1945 and the country's eventual emergence from it. Ahmad provides a detailed examination of Anglo-Spanish relations under Attlee's Labour Government. Despite its opposition to the Franco regime the British government took insufficient action to remove the Spanish dictatorship. The Spanish Republicans in exile, who had reason to hope for move decisive support from a Labour administration, were to be disappointed.

Geoffrey Swain, in the subsequent chapter, provides the counterpoint to Ahmad's contribution. Swain's examination of Soviet policy towards 'the Spanish problem' shows Stalin adopting a harsher approach towards the Franco regime (than his Western Allies). In particular, the communist opposition to Franco was able to count on Soviet support, at least up to a point. Ultimately, however, the Spanish Republicans' position did not benefit from Stalin's ideological whims.

Franco remained in power, a fact which was soon acknowledged by the United States. From a tacit *rapprochement* in the late 1940s under Truman, close relations emerged in the 1950s under the Eisenhower administration. In a brief survey Boris Liedtke traces this 'compromising with the dictator' up to the 1953 economic and military agreements, the 'key achievement of all foreign policy efforts under Franco' (Viñas).

How did the Franco regime itself handle this period of isolation and subsequent gradual return into the (western) international community? José Luis Neila Hernández's examination of the development and role of Franco's foreign policy administration (Chapter 14) demonstrates clearly the extent to which Spain's Ministry for Foreign Affairs and its policies were subject to Franco's personal views and beliefs. This theme is continued, indeed heightened in the last chapter.

Franco's powerful personal influence is starkly exposed in Chapter 15 by Angel Viñas whose essay takes the collection up to 1959, the end of the 'first Francoism'. Angel Viñas pulls no punches in this scathing criticism of Franco's (and Luis Carrero Blanco's) mismanagement of Spain's economy and foreign policy. As demonstrated in Chapters 1, 7 and 8 Franco's dreams of empire never left the drawing-board. Autarky, another dream, was taken beyond the planning stage with the regime desperately trying to make the impossible true. Only in the late 1950s did a reluctant Franco abandon his regime's miserable attempts at copying Nazi Germany's (unsuccessful) policy. Again the 'international context' played an important role in this change of direction.

The essays in this collection clearly demonstrate how turbulent the 1930s, 1940s and 1950s proved to be for Spain. The development of the country was frequently influenced and affected by international factors and protagonists. This 'international contextualisation' in which Spain evolved is at the heart of this collection. After 1959 the international context ceased to have the same decisive impact, though events in Franco Spain continued to be keenly observed abroad. Owing to the nature of the regime, a full normalisation of Spain's international relations had to wait until after Franco's death in 1975. In the 1980s it was symbolised by membership of the EC and NATO and normal diplomatic relations to the (then) Eastern bloc countries. Spain had finally moved out of the limelight that it had attracted during the period with which this edited collection is concerned.

Without the help of a number of people and institutions the conference and therefore this edited collection would not have been possible. First and foremost, the editors would like to thank the Faculty of Humanities at the University of the West of England in Bristol. Important financial support was granted by the Dean, Professor Geoffrey Channon, while the work done by Vicky Madden and Janet Garland proved to be invaluable. The editors are also indebted to the 'Gang of Four', Glyn Stone, Geoffrey Swain, Martin Thomas (and Christian Leitz) who hatched the original plan for the conference and continued to give a helping hand thereafter. For their crucial financial support given to the conference the editors would like to express their gratitude to the British Academy, Records and Historical Services of the British Foreign and Commonwealth Office (in particular Heather Yasamee), the British Council in Barcelona and Madrid, and the Spanish Embassy in London (in particular Dr Dámaso de Lario). Finally, we would like to thank the anonymous reader for his valuable comments and Marion Berghahn for her patience and commitment.

Christian Leitz (University of Auckland)

Notes

1. Comment by U.S. President Roosevelt, cited in Glyn Stone's contribution to this present volume.
2. See, *inter alia*, P. Preston, *The Coming of the Spanish Civil War: Reform, Reaction and Revolution, 1931-1936*, 1st edn, London, 1978 ; idem, *Franco: A Biography*, London, 1993; R.A.H. Robinson, *The Origins of Franco's Spain: The Right, the Republic and Revolution, 1931-1936*, Newton Abbot, 1970; R. Carr (ed.), *The Republic and the Civil War in Spain*, London, 1971.
3. See P. Preston, 'Mussolini's Spanish Adventure: From Limited Risk to War', and C. Leitz, 'Nazi Germany's Intervention in the Spanish Civil War and the Foundation of HISMA/ROWAK', both in *The Republic Besieged; Civil War in Spain 1936-1939*, eds P. Preston and A.L. Mackenzie, Edinburgh, 1996, pp. 21-52 and 53-86.
4. From late 1941, for instance, Spanish Republicans were used to build fortifications on the Channel Islands; C. Cruickshank, *The German Occupation of the Channel Islands*, Oxford, 1975, p. 181.

1

Franco's Foreign Policy
1939–1953

Paul Preston (London School of Economics)

DURING the Spanish Civil War, Franco seized a crucial advantage for the Nationalist uprising by swiftly establishing himself as the recipient of help from Germany and Italy. In doing so, he showed an awareness of the international dimension of his own fate and acquired an interest in foreign policy that he was to cultivate well into the 1950s. He overcame Benito Mussolini's initial doubts about helping him by convincing the Italian authorities in Tangiers to support his request for transport aircraft. The history of the negotiations for Italian aid shows Franco seizing the initiative and pursuing it with dogged determination until Mussolini unequivocally placed his bets on Franco rather than on Mola. His case was a skilfully aimed appeal to Mussolini, offering flattery, certain success, future subservience and a bargain price. Franco declared that his objective was to establish 'a republican government in the fascist style adapted for the Spanish people'. He claimed that success would be assured if his Italian transport aircraft was granted. Finally, he promised that if Italy smiled on his cause, 'future relations will be more than friendly' (*più che amichevoli*).[1] In Germany too, Franco's contacts prospered more than those of Mola. While Mola's various emissaries got entangled in a bureaucratic web in Berlin, Franco secured the backing of energetic Nazis resident in Morocco and his decision on 22 July to send them directly to Adolf Hitler to request transport aircraft was a bold initiative which would make him the beneficiary of German assistance and constitute a giant step on his path to absolute power. Thereafter, throughout the war, Franco took a special interest in relations with Hitler and Mussolini.

In the wake of his victory in the Spanish Civil War and given his imperial ambitions, there could be no doubt where Franco's sympathies lay when Hitler unleashed his war against the hegemony of the Western democracies. In the last resort, however, the *Caudillo's* instinctive anti-democratic inclinations in foreign policy were restrained by two overriding considerations, his own domestic survival and Spain's economic and military capacity for war. In both of those areas, he was obliged to pay considerable heed to the views of the Army High Command. The Army was the most powerful player within the complex game of power rivalries between the component groups of the recently victorious Nationalist coalition.[2] At the beginning of the world war, military conviction of an inevitable German victory was virtually unanimous. However, the likelihood of Spanish generals acting on the basis of that conviction was diminished both by their awareness of Spain's shattered economic and military capacity and by their monarchist sympathies. From the autumn of 1940 onwards, the generals showed increasing scepticism about the ultimate Axis triumph. The Falange was a different matter. In its ranks could be found an unrestrained sympathy for German military exploits that was to remain undiminished until the last days of the war. Ideological affinities with the Third Reich immeasurably strengthened the Falange in the internal power struggle within Spain. The military and the Falange were to be the two major influences on Franco in the making of his foreign policy during the Second World War.

The views of all the Nationalist groups, with the exception of the most hard-line Falangists, would inevitably evolve in relation to the shifting fortunes of war. Franco, always sensitive to the moods of his most powerful supporters, would similarly adapt his responses to changing wartime developments. At the same time, he was careful always to hide behind his ministers. In foreign affairs, as in many other areas, Franco followed the tactic of *dejar hacer* (rather more than *laissez faire*, it also has the connotation of giving enough scope for a subordinate to compromise himself). Of course, in foreign policy, he hid behind his ministers only when it suited him for foreign affairs were a matter of the first concern to him. Foreign policy was crucial to his survival, gave him a sense of his own importance on the international stage and was rather more interesting than many domestic issues. Officially, Franco did not deal with specific departmental affairs and this was used as an excuse for him to decline to receive ambassadors or chargés d'affaires, other, of course, than his favourites of the day – the Germans and Italians during the Second World War, the Americans during the Cold War. Beigbeder, Jordana and Lequerica, all Ministers for Foreign Affairs at different points during the Second World War, made identical claims that the *Caudillo* made policy while they simply dealt with issues of detail and implemented his instructions. From 1945 onwards, Franco's propagandists worked hard to present Ramón Serrano Suñer as the exclusive architect of pro-German policy. That is nonsense. It is inconceivable that Franco passively let his brother-in-law make foreign policy.

At the beginning of the Second World War, flushed with success in the Civil War, fired by solidarity with the Axis allies who had played such a crucial role in achieving his victory, Franco was anything but cautious. Indeed, he was very nearly to take Spain into war on the Axis side in the course of the summer of 1940. By the autumn of that year, the unexpected survival of Britain had helped Franco's natural caution to reassert itself. However, even then, had it not been for the off-hand way in which both Hitler and Ribbentrop treated him and Serrano Suñer, Spain could easily have slid into war. Moreover, after the most acute danger of Spanish belligerence had passed in late 1940, Franco was to go on experiencing what might be called the Axis temptation, most intensely after the German invasion of Russia in the summer of 1941.

Accordingly, it understates the case to say that, in the course of the first year of the Second World War, Franco made less use of his characteristically careful ambiguity with regard to international relations than he was later to do. As early as 20 February 1939, the *Caudillo* had agreed to join the Anti-Comintern Pact, a secret act of solidarity with the Axis made public on 6 April.[3] On 8 May, he pulled Spain out of the League of Nations. When Hitler and Mussolini signed the Pact of Steel at the end of May 1939, Franco, in a further gesture of virile bellicosity, sent troops to the Gibraltar area. The Spanish dictator's relations with Hitler were cordial, informed by gratitude for German aid during the Civil War but tinged too with the caution provoked by the *Führer*'s brutal arrogance. With Mussolini, there were no reservations but rather an effusive warmth and sympathy.[4]

Both Mussolini and his Foreign Minister, Count Galeazzo Ciano, felt that Serrano Suñer was 'undoubtedly the strongest Axis prop in the Franco regime'.[5] There is little doubt about Serrano Suñer's enthusiasm for Fascist Italy. However, Serrano Suñer should not be made the scapegoat for the pro-Axis activities of the

Francoist establishment in these years. There were few senior figures in civilian or military life who did not participate in a general-
ized enthusiasm for the new political order that seemed to be in the
process of being forged. Franco told the Italian Ambassador, Count
Viola, on 5 July 1939 that Spain needed 'a period of tranquillity to
devote herself to internal reconstruction and the achievement of the
economic autonomy indispensable for the military power to which
she aspired'. At the same time, he asserted that he planned to keep
a large army mobilized to prevent Spain being imposed upon by the
British and the French. Such a force would 'permit him to make
Spain's weight be felt in the unfolding of events and possibly to take
advantage of circumstances'. France, he boasted, 'would never be
able to feel easy with regard to Spain'.[6]

When Ciano visited Spain in July 1939, Franco told him that he
needed five years of peace for economic and military preparation
before he could identify completely with the totalitarian states. In
the event of war, he would prefer neutrality but would be on the
Axis side because he did not believe that his regime could survive a
victory by the democracies in a general war. Accordingly, with
apparent lack of concern about Spain's bankruptcy, he speculated
about a major rearmament programme for both the navy and the
air force.[7] Franco was in fact worried that, if the Axis won the coming war without his participation, the world would be reconstructed
without respect for his ambitions.

Franco's awareness that war was imminent found an immediate
reflection in the cabinet changes of 9 August 1939 in the replacement of the Anglophile Minister for Foreign Affairs, General Francisco Gómez, Conde de Jordana y Souza by Colonel Juan
Beigbeder Atienza, an early adherent of the Falange. A keen
Africanista, Beigbeder shared Franco's imperial ambitions in
Morocco.[8] After hostilities had begun, the German Ambassador in
Madrid, Baron Eberhard von Stohrer, tended to by-pass Beigbeder
and to liaise with Serrano Suñer who promised to influence the attitude of the Spanish press completely in favour of the German
cause.[9] This was done with the acquiescence of Franco and done so
effectively that it became an important Axis propaganda weapon in
Spain. The willing Falangist press apparatus was supplied by the
German embassy with Nazi propaganda material which was then
relayed as news. Pro-Allied material virtually never appeared except
in response to specific diplomatic protests.[10] In fact, German influence over the press was just one of the many ways in which Spain
was heading towards becoming an informal German satellite.[11]

When war did break out on 3 September, Franco, like Mussolini, lamented the fact that it had happened too soon. The best that either could do was to proffer surreptitious help and take advantage where possible. Officially, Franco announced that 'the most strict neutrality' would be required of Spanish subjects.[12] In private, his attitude was far from neutral. Both he and Serrano Suñer believed that Spain had been kept in humiliating subjugation by the arrogance of Britain and France. Accordingly, they were looking for any opportunities provided by the war to help Spain achieve her place among the European powers.[13]

As eager spectators of the phoney war, Franco and Mussolini were drawn together even more. The warmth of their relations was underlined by Italian generosity in the settlement of Spain's war debts. Eventually, the *Duce*, ever restless and unwilling, as he put it, to sit on the sidelines while history was being written, decided to enter the war. He had given Franco two months notice of his plans, on 8 April 1940. After her exhausting enterprises in Abyssinia, in Spain and in Albania, Italy was barely in better shape than Spain for a military escapade. Serrano Suñer and Beigbeder both told Stohrer in the first half of April that Spain was on Germany's side and that Italy's imminent entry into the war would ensure that Spain would be 'automatically drawn in'. Despite the parlous state of Spanish reserves of fuel and grain, both Franco and Serrano Suñer were sorely tempted by the prospect of Spanish belligerence leading to the acquisition of Gibraltar and Tangiers.[14]

In the spring of 1940, Franco was confident of an early German victory.[15] As the British withdrew from Dunkirk after their defeat in France, the *Caudillo* watched with excitement. He sent his Chief of the General Staff, General Juan Vigón, to Berlin on 10 June with an effusive letter of congratulation for Hitler.[16] In fact, Hitler kept Spain at arm's length, rebuffing Vigón when he saw him at the Castle of Acoz on 16 June 1940, merely acknowledging Spain's Moroccan ambitions. At that stage, Hitler had no intention of paying a high price for services which he believed would not be needed since he expected the British to surrender at any moment. The fact that Spain did not ultimately join in the war on the Axis side has been the basis of claims from apologists of Franco that, with immense statecraft and sheer guile, he outwitted Hitler and Mussolini in favour of the Allies.[17] In 1940, in fact, Franco was seriously committed to entering the war and was held back only by his inability to negotiate acceptable terms with Hitler. Franco would certainly approach the question of joining the German war effort with more circumspection than did Mussolini. Nevertheless, in the early summer of 1940, the spectacular success of Hitler's drive to the West impelled the *Caudillo* to uncharacteristic impetuosity. He knew that an economically prostrate Spain could not sustain a long war effort but, on the other hand, he could not bear the thought that France and Britain might be annihilated by a new Hitlerian world order and Spain still not get any of the spoils. Accordingly, fully convinced that German victory was inevitable, Franco sought to make a last-minute entry in order to gain a ticket for the distribution of the booty. His attitude was, however, conditioned by the troubled legacy of his economic relations with Hitler during the Civil War. Ultimately, the common desire of both dictators for cooperation against Britain was to run aground on the inability of Hitler to stop underestimating Franco's dogged meanness and inflated sense of destiny. If the *Führer* had been able, as Mussolini was, to make a virtue of enforced generosity over Civil War debts, or if he had lied more daringly over his readiness to give away French North Africa, the outcome would certainly have been different.

Until he ran into German arrogance and intransigence, Franco's first chosen moment for Spanish entry into the war was shortly after the fall of France when Britain seemed also on the verge of surrender. The second was in the autumn of 1940 when he believed that Operation Sealion was about to be launched and the collapse of England was imminent. On the first of these two occasions, the Germans brushed off the Spanish offer with a cavalier disdain convinced that they did not need it. On the second, when they did need it, they were indifferent to Franco's sensibilities and in particular to his African ambitions. After a cabinet meeting on 12 June, Franco changed Spain's official neutrality to the much more pro-Axis position of non-belligerency. Franco told the Italian chargé d'affaires in Madrid that 'the present state of the Spanish armed forces prevented the adoption of a more resolute stance but that he was nonetheless proceeding to accelerate as much as possible the preparation of the army for any eventuality.'[18] Enthusiastic about German triumphs, Franco was soon to take the reins of Spanish foreign policy from Beigbeder and give them to Serrano Suñer.[19] Franco permitted German submarines to be provisioned in Spanish ports; German reconnaissance aircraft to fly with Spanish markings, a radio station at La Coruña to operate for the *Luftwaffe* and German destroyers to be secretly refuelled at night in bays on Spain's northern coast.[20]

With France on her knees and Britain with her back to the wall, Franco felt all the temptations of a cowardly and rapacious vulture.

Despite his professed friendship with Pétain, on 14 June, as the Germans poured into Paris, Spain occupied Tangiers having assured the French that their action was necessary to guarantee its security. Hitler was delighted, all the more so because Franco 'had acted without talking'.[21] On the day following the French plea for an armistice, Franco asserted that the further existence of the French empire in North Africa was impossible and demanded French Morocco, the Oran region of Algeria and the expansion of Spanish Sahara and Spanish Guinea. In the event of England continuing hostilities after the surrender of France, the *Caudillo* offered to enter the war on the Axis side in return for 'war materials, heavy artillery, aircraft for the attack on Gibraltar, and perhaps the cooperation of German submarines in the defence of the Canary Islands'. He also requested foodstuffs, ammunition, motor fuel and equipment from the French war stocks.[22]

After keeping the Spaniards waiting for nearly a week, the AA rebuffed their offers with a dry acknowledgement of Spain's territorial desires in North Africa.[23] Hitler had responded coolly to Vigón three days earlier, suspicious, in the aftermath of Mussolini's last-minute attack on France, of more unwanted last-minute volunteers for a war which he was convinced was already won. He was not about to prejudice the armistice negotiations with France in order to give gratuitous satisfaction to Spain. Franco was obsequious towards the Third Reich, constantly seeking means of currying favour with Berlin. On 23 June, an offer was made to the Germans to detain the Duke and Duchess of Windsor who were passing through Madrid *en route* to Lisbon. Throughout the summer of 1940, Serrano Suñer and Franco were willing collaborators in German machinations to prevent the Duke of Windsor taking up the post of Governor of the Bahamas in order that he might be used against 'the Churchill clique' in peace negotiations with England.[24]

In contrast to the Spanish efforts at ingratiation with the Third Reich, Franco's urgent requests for food were simply dismissed out of hand on the grounds of the greater needs of Germany and Italy.[25] Although Franco was upset by the *Führer*'s offhand response to his offer, he remained anxious to negotiate Spanish entry into the war. Franco declared on 18 July 1940 that Spain had two million warriors ready to fight to revive her past imperial glories and to pursue the mission of retaking Gibraltar and expanding Spanish Africa.[26] The general staff was drawing up plans for an attack on French North Africa and on Gibraltar. Moreover, during this period, Hitler was gradually being forced to adjust his priorities for Spanish entry into the war. The unexpected obstinacy of British resistance and the defeat of the *Luftwaffe* in the Battle of Britain put paid to his invasion plans, Operation Sealion. German thoughts turned to the idea of bringing down Britain by means other than frontal attack. On 15 August, General Jodl had suggested the intensification of U-boat warfare and the seizure of the nerve centres of her empire, Gibraltar and Suez, in a bid to give the Axis control of the Mediterranean and the Middle East. Already on 2 August, Ribbentrop had informed the Ambassador in Madrid that 'what we want to achieve now is Spain's early entry into the war'.[27] German officials began the process of ascertaining what exactly were Spain's essential civilian and military needs in terms of fuel, grain and other vital goods. The figures produced for civilian uses alone were enormous.[28]

The acute problems of supplying a war machine were skated over in Madrid because of a widely held conviction in official circles that the conflict would be short and the Third Reich swiftly victorious. Franco told Vigón that he regarded an early entry into the war as useful since, as a result of the British blockade, 'Spain already had one foot in the war'. He also said that he could reconcile himself to a war of longer duration.[29] The *Caudillo* also wrote a letter, on 15 August, to Mussolini from Madrid, in which he declared that Spain was 'preparing to take her place in the struggle against our common enemies'.[30]

In the early summer of 1940, enthusiasm for Spanish entry into the war had come entirely from Madrid. Since it was blatantly obvious that Franco and Serrano Suñer planned for Spain to take part after the worst of the fighting was over but before the division of the spoils, their offers had been brushed aside ungraciously by the Germans. In the autumn and winter, the situation was to change slowly as Franco gradually came to appreciate the strength of British resistance and as Spain's economic position deteriorated. Although he was never to admit it and always to resent it, Franco was, from the autumn of 1940, to become ever more vulnerable to Anglo-American pressures and blandishments. The German view was that, in return for the Reich supplying the necessary military equipment and foodstuffs, Spain would undertake to recognize her Civil War debts to Germany and pay them off through future deliveries of raw materials. French and British mining properties in Spain and Spanish Morocco would be conceded to Germany. Spanish territory on the Gulf of Guinea was to be transferred to Germany. The Spanish economy would be integrated into a German-dominated European economy. Spain would play only a subordinate role, her activities being confined to agriculture, the production of raw materials and industries 'indigenous to Spain'. The *Führer* also wanted one of the Canary Islands for a German base, and further bases at Agadir and Mogador with 'appropriate hinterland'.[31] The harsh demands made by Hitler and Ribbentrop in their meetings with Serrano Suñer in Berlin on 16, 17 and 24 September clinched Franco's determination to enter the war only if he was paid in advance.[32]

On 18 October 1940, Franco replaced Beigbeder as Minister of Foreign Affairs with Serrano Suñer.[33] No reconciliation was effected at the historic meeting between Hitler and Franco at Hendaye on 23 October 1940. Always keen to profit from Hitler's successes but determined not to have to pay for the privilege, Franco opened the Hendaye meeting with rhetorical assurances – 'Spain would gladly fight at Germany's side', but because of difficulties being made by the United States and Britain, 'Spain must mark time and often look kindly toward things of which she thoroughly disapproved'. More than a conversation, there were opposing monologues. Hitler explained laboriously and rather obliquely why Spain's Moroccan ambitions were problematic given his need for cooperation with the French. Hitler had thought to deceive Franco over French Morocco by the seemingly frank admission that he could not give what was not yet his, implying that he would indeed give it when it was in his power to do so. He was, of course, confident of being able to dispose of the French colonial empire as he wished but had no intention of giving it to Franco. That was his 'grandiose fraud'. Serrano Suñer suggested years later that he had not told a sufficiently big lie. According to the *cuñadísimo*, Franco's *Africanista* obsession with Morocco was such that, if Hitler had offered it, he would have entered the war.[34]

Franco's offers to join in the war in the early summer of 1940 had been rebuffed by Hitler as gratuitous. The *Führer*'s efforts to get Franco to join the Axis in the autumn of 1940 failed because Hitler did not feel that he had to pay the going rate for the *Caudillo*'s services. Thereafter, in the entire course of the Second World War, Spain came no nearer than she had in 1940 to joining the Axis. That is not to say that Franco was working hard to keep out of Hitler's clutches, as some of his admirers have suggested. There is little doubt that the *Caudillo*'s sympathies continued to lie with Germany and Italy. If Hitler had met the asking price, Franco would almost certainly have joined him. Nevertheless, his own survival was always Franco's paramount ambition and, in addition to the fact that Hitler seemed to be seeking Spanish aid on impossible terms, after the cancellation of Operation Sealion, the possibility of Axis defeat made the *Caudillo* ever more circumspect. Moreover, the tensions between the Army and the Falange precisely over whether or not to go to war also gave Franco pause. The most obvious example of that circumspection and its link with domestic issues was his noninterference during Operation Torch, which took place less than two months after the dismissal of Serrano Suñer. Yet between Hendaye and Torch, there was plenty of evidence that Franco still hankered after being part of a victorious Axis coalition.

In mid-February 1941, the *Caudillo* met Mussolini at Bordighera.[35] Franco told the *Duce* of his continued conviction of an ultimate Axis victory. He admitted quite candidly 'Spain wishes to enter the war; her fear is to enter too late' and stated dryly that 'Spanish entry into the war depends on Germany more than on Spain herself, the sooner Germany sends help, the sooner Spain will make her contribution to the Fascist world cause'. Mussolini was inclined in consequence to stop trying to persuade Franco to join the Axis war effort in the short term. Instead, he believed that Germany and Italy should confine their Spanish efforts to keeping the hesitant *Caudillo* in the Axis political sphere.[36] At about the same time as the *Duce* informed Hitler about the Bordighera meeting, the German Department of Economic Planning reported that Spanish demands could not be met without endangering the Reich's military capacity.[37]

When finally Hitler contemplated forcing the issue, he had already committed his military machine to rescuing Italy from its disastrous involvement in the Balkans.[38] In fact, Bordighera showed that Franco was, for the moment, immune to the Axis temptation. He would not entirely put it behind him until late in 1944 but equally he was never again to be drawn by it unequivocally. Hitler simply did not have kingdoms enough to offer. Nevertheless, for a brief moment in mid-1941, with a swift victory over the Soviet Union apparently possible, the *Caudillo* was once more sorely tempted. His pro-Axis enthusiasm was inflamed anew by the Nazi invasion of the Soviet Union on 22 June 1941. On being officially informed of the German attack on Russia, Serrano Suñer expressed great enthusiasm and informed Stohrer that Franco wished to send volunteer units of Falangists to fight, 'independently of the full and complete entry of Spain into the war beside the Axis, which would take place at the appropriate moment'.[39]

On 17 July 1941, the fifth anniversary of the outbreak of the Spanish Civil War, Franco addressed the *Consejo Nacional* of the Falange and expressed his enthusiasm for Hitler's Russian venture at 'this moment when the German armies lead the battle for which Europe and Christianity have for so many years longed, and in which the blood of our youth is to mingle with that of our comrades of the Axis'. During the summer of 1941, Franco's government continued to display an increasingly pro-German attitude. The controlled press frequently attacked Britain and the United States and glorified the achievements of German arms.[40] However, shortages of coal, copper, tin, rubber and textile fibres presaged a breakdown of Spanish industry within a matter of months. Franco was forced to be more circumspect and to seek some rapprochement with the western powers.[41] This reflected in part the fact that a significant section of the military now believed that Britain and the U.S. would win the war and were already taking their economic revenge on Spain. Moreover, the most senior generals, and even Franco himself, could not avoid the alarming conclusion that Hitler had got himself into serious trouble in Russia. Franco's second flowering of pro-Axis enthusiasm withered in the winter of 1941, along with the fortunes of the German armies in Russia. The entry of the United States into the war and with the British victorious in North Africa, the *Caudillo* seems finally to have accepted that there were no territorial compensations which could justify the risks now involved in going to war.

The unavoidable realisation that U.S. involvement meant that the war would be a long and titanic struggle obliged Franco to postpone Spanish entry into the war indefinitely. The precise moment of his so-called *chaqueteo* (or change of coat) is difficult to locate for the simple reason that it was never definitive. Speaking to high-ranking army officers at the Alcázar of Seville in February 1942, Franco declared 'if the road to Berlin were opened then not merely would one division of Spaniards participate in the struggle but one million Spaniards would be offered to help.'[42] Since Franco's own readiness to declare war still depended on guarantees both that British power was irrevocably finished and that prizes from Hitler would be forthcoming, Spain remained at peace. Neutrality then, far from being the result of brilliant statecraft or foresight was the fruit of a narrow pragmatism and what Serrano Suñer called the 'good fortune' that Germany would not or could not pay the price demanded for entry into the war.

In the autumn of 1942, when the preparations for Operation Torch showed that an eventual Axis triumph was far from assured, Franco reacted, not with prophetic awareness of ultimate Allied victory, but rather with an entirely reasonable short-term caution. The massing of force on his borders was hardly the best moment to cross swords with Perfidious Albion, particularly in the wake of Rommel's failure to conquer Egypt. Franco was intensely conscious of the Allies' power of retaliation. In any case, Allied successes in North Africa were so spectacular as immediately to inhibit any Spanish thoughts of hostile action. When Anglo-American forces entered precisely those French Moroccan and Algerian territories that he coveted, Franco was enough of a realist to instruct his ambassador in London to start a *rapprochement* with the Western Allies. That did not mean that he had lost his belief in an ultimate Axis victory. The *chaqueteo* was to be gradual and to leave options open.

Nevertheless, there could be discerned the beginnings of a slow move back to neutrality, visible for instance in the signing in December 1942 of the *Bloque Ibérico* agreement with Portugal. By the spring of 1943, it was obvious that the international panorama in which Franco operated had changed dramatically. 'Torch' had shifted the strategic balance, but throughout most of 1943, certainly up to the fall of Mussolini in the summer, Franco remained convinced that the Allies could not win and that their successes in Africa were of marginal importance. On 3 December 1943, Franco told the new German ambassador, Hans Heinrich Dieckhoff, that his own survival depended on an Axis victory and that an Allied triumph 'would mean his own annihilation'. Accordingly, he hoped with all his heart for German victory as soon as possible. It is significant that he never made a similar statement of sympathy with the Allied cause to any British or U.S. diplomat. By the beginning of 1944, with the tide of war clearly turning, North Africa secure and Italy out of the war, the United States were altogether less inclined to be patient with Franco. The U.S. military staff was furious about continued Spanish wolfram exports to Germany. Wolfram was a crucial ingredient in the manufacture of high quality steel for armaments in general and particularly for machine tools and armour-piercing shells. A crisis was reached when Franco sent a letter of congratulation to José P. Laurel on his installation by the Japanese as puppet governor of the Philippines. The consequence was that the United States precipitately curtailed petroleum exports to Spain.[43] Eventually, Franco was obliged to close down the German consulate in Tangiers, withdraw all Spanish units from Russia and promise to expel German spies and saboteurs from Spain. In fact, German observation posts and radio interception stations were maintained in Spain until the end of the war.[44]

In 1945, Franco knew that he could not survive on repression alone if the international situation was adverse. He placed his hopes on the Allies seeing him as a better hope for anti-communist stability in Spain than either the Republican opposition or the pretender to the throne, Don Juan de Borbón. Goodwill towards America was publicly exaggerated while in private, however, Franco spoke of his deep unease about becoming dependent on 'America's political hysteria', by which he meant changes of government based on popular electoral choice. It was a revealing indication of his contempt for democracy in the United States which he regarded as a hotbed of dangerous freemasonry. The plain-speaking U.S. President, Harry S. Truman, loathed Franco's deviousness, his repressive regime, his religious bigotry and his denunciations of freemasonry, liberalism and democracy. Accordingly, Franco was obliged to rewrite the history of his role in the Second World War. For foreign consumption, he began to emphasise the Catholic and monarchical elements, and play down the fascist ones, in his political system. For foreign consumption, he introduced the conservative Catholic Alberto Martín Artajo as Foreign Minister. As he had done during the Second World War, the *Caudillo* maintained an iron control over foreign policy, using Martín Artajo as the acceptable face of his regime. Artajo told José María Pemán that he spoke on the telephone for at least one hour every day with Franco and used special earphones to leave his hands free to take notes. Pemán cruelly wrote in his diary 'Franco makes international policy and Artajo is the minister-stenographer'. On 21 July, in the first meeting of the new cabinet team, Franco told his ministers that concessions would be made to the outside world only in nonessentials and out of convenience.[45]

The central objective was simply that Franco remain in power. After nearly a decade of exposure to daily adulation, he could see no contradictions between his own political needs and those of Spain. He dismissed foreign criticism of himself as the work of a masonic conspiracy against Spain. He saw himself as the divinely inspired steersman navigating the beleagured ship of Spain. The only tactic available to him was to ride out the international ostracism until the natural antagonism between the communist and capitalist blocs crystallised. Then the geopolitical advantages of Spain would buy him out of his original sin of friendship with Hitler and into the Western bloc. It was to be a much easier task than Franco expected, but he made it more difficult by his obsessive hatred of freemasonry. During the period from 1945 to 1950, Franco talked as if he and Spain were under deadly siege from what he called 'the masonic offensive', although the Allies were unlikely, as he knew, to take action to remove him.

Franco denied that he had ever supported the Axis, despite the publication in 1946 of the captured German documents which proved the contrary and of UN reports that, since the closing stages of the war, his regime had given asylum to 2,000-3,000 escaped Nazis, Italian fascists and supporters of Vichy France. Franco saw this international criticism as the work of a communist-masonic conspiracy dedicated to destroying Spain. His arguments were bizarre and feeble yet, paradoxically, effective. In September 1945, he told the religious advisers of the *Sección Femenina* that the Civil War had been undertaken to combat the 'satanic machinations' of perverted freemasons and now Spain was coming under attack from 'the masonic superstate' which controlled the world's press and radio stations as well as the key politicians in the Western democracies.[46]

The propaganda campaign to present him as the champion of a beleagured Spain eventually paid off. The disastrous economic performance of his corrupt and incompetent autarchic system was blamed on a nonexistent economic blockade. In early December 1946, the Franco regime was denounced by the UN as fascist, unrepresentative and morally repugnant. Franco mounted a massively choreographed display of public support, haranguing 700,000 people in the Plaza de Oriente with civil war rhetoric. His personal reply to the UN resolution was the publication in *Arriba* of a series of articles attacking freemasonry in general and denouncing the leaders of the UN as freemasons at the orders of Moscow. The articles, published under the pseudonym Jakim Boor (the two pillars of the masonic temple), ran until May 1951. Their central thesis was that freemasonry, which Franco saw as consubstantial with liberal democracy, was conspiring with communism to destroy Spain.[47]

In fact, the *Caudillo* survived the worst. The UN Resolution of December 1946, the peak of the international ostracism, had failed.[48] The communist take-over in Czechoslovakia in February 1948 was followed by the Berlin blockade from June 1948 to May 1949 and by the successful explosion of a Soviet atom bomb in August 1949 all of which intensified pressure within the United States for a *rapprochement* with Spain in order to secure both air and naval bases. At the beginning of October 1949, Mao Tse-Tung had established the Chinese People's Republic. The anti-Francoist Truman was obliged to capitulate before the growing Congressional demand for a *rapprochement* with Spain.[49] Franco continued to write in *Arriba*, naïvely thinking that the pseudonym Jakim Boor permitted him to denounce freemasonry as an evil conspiracy with communism while publicly expressing admiration for America. The White House received thousands of telegrams of protest. Washington was fully aware that the articles were the work of the *Generalísimo*.

Nevertheless, the *Caudillo* escaped the consequences of his pro-Axis past and his antidemocratic present because of concern in the United States and Europe about the advances and activities of world Communism. One after another, the abandonment of the December 1946 resolution on Spain, the return of ambassadors to Spain, the conclusion of the Pact of Madrid in 1953 were all hailed in Spain as colossal victories for Franco against a vicious siege. In fact, there had never been a full-scale *cerco internacional* and, when Franco was welcomed to the bosom of the Western allies, it was because they wanted him not because he had manipulated them. Thereafter, Franco left the direction of foreign policy to his ministers.[50]

Notes

1. DDI, 8ª serie, Rome, 1993, vol. IV, p. 652, Luccardi to Ministero della Guerra, 21 July 1936.
2. On the military in this period, see Carlos Fernández Santander, *Tensiones militares durante el franquismo*, Barcelona, 1985.
3. Galeazzo Ciano, *Diario*, 2 vols, Milan, 1946, vol. I, pp. 43-4; DGFP, series D, 13 vols, London, 1951-1964, vol. III, pp. 880-1.
4. Ciano, *Diario*, I, pp. 112-13; Ramón Serrano Suñer, *Entre Hendaya y Gibraltar*, Madrid, 1947, pp. 91-118.
5. DGFP, D, vol. VI, pp. 695-7; Ciano, *Diario*, I, p. 110 and pp. 114-15.
6. DGFP, D, vol. VI, pp. 830-2; ibid., vol. VIII, p. 24; *The Times*, 17 and 21 June 1939; Marc Ferro, *Pétain*, Paris, 1987, pp. 51-2; Javier Tusell and Genoveva García Queipo de Llano, *Franco y Mussolini: la política española durante la segunda guerra mundial*, Barcelona, 1985, p. 37.
7. Galeazzo Ciano, *L'Europa verso la catastrofe*, Milan, 1948, pp. 439-46; Tusell, *Franco y Mussolini*, pp. 38-9. See also Christian Leitz's contribution to this present volume.
8. See Martin Thomas's contribution to this present volume.
9. DGFP, D, vol. VII, pp. 501-2; Maurice Peterson, *Both Sides of the Curtain*, London, 1950, pp. 191-2.
10. Samuel Hoare, *Ambassador on Special Mission*, London, 1946, pp. 54-5; Serrano Suñer, *Entre Hendaya y Gibraltar*, 132; Javier Terrón Montero, *La prensa de España durante el régimen de Franco*, Madrid, 1981, 41-54.
11. Paul Reynaud, *Au coeur de la Mêlée 1930-1945*, Paris, 1951, 919; Peterson, *Both Sides*, 191-5.
12. *Boletín Official del Estado*, 4 September 1939. Cf. Serrano Suñer, *Entre Hendaya y Gibraltar*, p. 89.
13. Serrano Suñer, *Entre Hendaya y Gibraltar*, pp. 133-5 and 142-3.
14. DGFP, D, vol. VIII, pp. 190-2.
15. Ibid., vol. IX, p. 396.
16. Ibid., vol. IX, pp. 509-10.

17. See, *inter alia*, Brian Crozier, *Franco: A Biographical History*, London, 1967, pp. 313-75; José María Doussinague, *España tenía razón (1939-1945)*, Madrid, 1949, *passim*; George Hills, *Rock of Contention: A History of Gibraltar*, London, 1974, pp. 428-32.

18. ABC, 13 June 1940; DDI, 9ª, Rome, 1965, vol. V, pp. 14 and 24, Zoppi to Ciano, 13 and 15 June 1940.

19. DGFP, D, vol. IX, p. 542; Serrano Suñer, *Entre Hendaya y Gibraltar*, pp. 159-60.

20. DGFP, D, vol. IX, pp. 449-53; ibid., vol. XI, p. 445.

21. Ibid., vol. IX, pp. 585-8; Reynaud, *Au coeur de la Mêlée*, pp. 855-6.

22. DGFP, D, vol. IX, pp. 620-1.

23. Ibid., vol. X, pp. 15-16.

24. Ibid., vol. X, pp. 2, 9, 187-9, 199-200, 276-7, 283, 290-1, 317-18, 366-7, 376-9, 397-401 and 409-10; Walter Schellenberg, *The Schellenberg Memoirs: A Record of the Nazi Secret Service*, London, 1956, pp. 126-43; Mariano González-Arnao Conde-Luque, '¡Capturad al duque de Windsor!', *Historia 16*, no. 161, September 1989; Michael Bloch, *Operation Willi: The Plot to Kidnap the Duke of Windsor July 1940*, London, 1984, *passim*.

25. DGFP, D, vol. IX, pp. 605-606 and 608-11.

26. Hoare, *Ambassador*, pp. 48-9.

27. DGFP, D, vol. X, p. 396; Hoare, *Ambassador*, p. 44; Serrano Suñer, *Entre Hendaya y Gibraltar*, p. 65; Winston S. Churchill, *The Second World War*, 6 vols, London, 1948-1954, vol. II, *Their Finest Hour*, p. 463.

28. DGFP, D, vol. X, pp. 466-7, 499-500 and 521; André Brissaud, *Canaris*, London, 1973, pp. 191-4; Macgregor Knox, *Mussolini Unleashed 1939-1941: Politics and Strategy in Fascist Italy's Last War*, Cambridge, 1982, p. 184.

29. DGFP, D, vol. X, pp. 514-15 and 521.

30. Ibid., vol. X, pp. 484-6; Ciano, *Diario*, I, p. 302; Serrano Suñer, *Entre Hendaya y Gibraltar*, pp. 103-104.

31. DGFP, D, vol. XI, pp. 83-91; Serrano Suñer, *Entre Hendaya y Gibraltar*, pp. 165-71. See Norman Goda's contribution to this present volume.

32. Denis Smyth, 'The Moor and the Money-lender: Politics and Profits in Anglo-German Relations with Francoist Spain 1936-1940', in *Von der Konkurrenz zur Rivalität: Das britische-deutsche Verhältnis in den Ländern der europäischen Peripherie 1919-1939*, ed. Marie-Luise Recker, Stuttgart, 1986, pp. 171-4.

33. DGFP, D, vol. XI, pp. 331-4.

34. Heleno Saña, *El franquismo sin mitos: conversaciones con Serrano Suñer*, Barcelona, 1981, p. 193. See also the polemic between Serrano Suñer and Antonio Marquina in *El País*, 19, 21, 22, 26, 28 and 29 November 1978.

35. DDI, 9ª, Roma, 1986, vol. VI, pp. 568-76, verbale del colloquio tra Mussolini, Franco e Serrano Suñer; Serrano Suñer, *Entre Hendaya y Gibraltar*, pp. 262-3.

36. Serrano Suñer, *Entre Hendaya y Gibraltar*, pp. 261-4; Ciano, *L'Europa verso la catastrofe*, pp. 629-43; Roberto Cantalupo, *Fu la Spagna. Ambasciata presso Franco. Febbraio-Aprile 1937*, Milan, 1948, pp. 279-94.

37. DGFP, D, vol. XII, pp. 96-7 and 131-2.

38. Charles B. Burdick, *Germany's Military Strategy and Spain in World War II*, Syracuse, 1968, pp. 103ff.

39. DGFP, D, vol. XII, pp. 1080-1.

40. FRUS 1941, Washington, 1959, vol. II, pp. 913-25.

41. Ibid., pp. 924-9.

42. Hoare, *Ambassador*, p. 140.

43. *Churchill & Roosevelt: The Complete Correspondence*, 3 vols, Princeton, 1984, vol. II, pp. 725-6, 728 and 751; Sir Alexander Cadogan, *The Diaries of Sir Alexander Cadogan 1938-1945*, ed. David Dilkes, London, 1971, pp. 602-3; Edward R.Stettinius Jr., *The Diaries of Edward R.Stettinius Jr., 1943-1946*, eds Thomas M. Campbell and George C. Herring, NewYork, 1975, pp. 28-9; Hoare, *Ambassador*, pp. 257-62.

44. *Churchill & Roosevelt: Correspondence*, III, pp. 66-8, 99, 106-108 and 114; Cadogan, *Diaries*, pp. 622-3; Hoare, *Ambassador*, pp. 262-8.

45. Javier Tusell, *Franco y los católicos: la política interior española entre 1945 y 1957*, Madrid, 1984, pp. 84-94 and 118; Florentino Portero, *Franco aislado: la cuestión española (1945-1950)*, Madrid, 1989, pp. 106-10.

46. Francisco Franco, *Textos de doctrina política: palabras y escritos de 1945 a 1950*, Madrid, 1951, pp. 334-5.

47. Jakim Boor [pseudonym of Francisco Franco Bahamonde], *Masonería*, Madrid, 1952.

48. See Quasim Ahmad's contribution to this present volume.

49. See Boris Liedtke's contribution to this present volume.

50. See Angel Viñas's contribution to this present volume.

2

Reaction in France to the Frente Popular (January to July 1936)

David Wingeate Pike (American University of Paris)

Spain is less a country of light than a country of night. Like a wild beast, it sleeps in the daytime and awakes at dusk. Its history is an enigma: the darkness of the caves at Altamira, the half-light of the Andalusian harems, the opacity of its Middle Ages eternally prolonged. Its whole tragic destiny has unfolded in the shadows. Only the Romantics were taken in by its cafe lights and its midday sun.[1]

Introduction

IT may well be that 1936 will be looked upon in the future as the most important year of the twentieth century. Everything that happened from that year to 1990 seemed to flow out of it. It opened with the democracies facing, in the Rhineland, their last chance to stop the march of fascism without a general war. Four months later the world's searchlight had moved to Spain, and in Spain, as nowhere else in the world at any other time, every political ideology that ever was now entered the arena, from ochlocracy to theocracy, from nihilism to the police state and the divine right of kings. Even worse, it was the year in which the centrist and moderate elements failed the test, with catastrophic consequences for Spain, democracy and the world.

The year 1936 will also be remembered for the advent of radio into war and for the unprecedented importance of the press as a conduit of propaganda. Never before had so many famous figures inside and outside the world of politics contributed so frequently to the press. Never before and never since do we find the press so diverse in its ideological leanings, and rarely has it been so engaged. More than a few times newspapers carried nothing on their front page than the news from Spain. If, therefore, it would be presumptuous today to measure public opinion by the study of the press alone, it was not true for the period in question, and as far as Spain is concerned, the press of Toulouse, by its quality and its ideological diversity, formed a microcosm of the French press in general. Toulouse, the largest city in the Midi west of the Rhone, remained the best observation point on Spain, and as the capital of the Southwest (a region primarily rural) its press was distributed virtually everywhere in the Midi. Its leading daily, *La Dépêche*, on sale in Paris and abroad, was of world quality, with some 2,000 correspondents and a whole legion of famous contributors who wrote articles exclusively for that journal; these included Julio Alvarez del Vayo, Clement Attlee, Julien Benda, Yvon Delbos, Guglielmo Ferrero, Salvador de Madariaga, Heinrich Mann, Thomas Mann, Herbert Samuel, Count Sforza, Albert Thibaudet, and Emile Vandervelde. Its editorial position was liberal and moderate, its analysis precise, its counsel prudent. While *La Dépêche* represented the Radical Socialists, the essential parliamentary support of Léon Blum's *Front Populaire*, the Left and the Right (but not their extremes) both had their organs. The absence of a communist organ and a fascist organ was of small account in covering the news from Spain, given the relative unimportance in the period under study of both the PCE and the Falange. For the Left, the daily *Le Midi Socialiste* served as a southern auxiliary of *Le Populaire*, the central organ of the SFIO, whose editorials were regularly reproduced in *Le Midi*. As for the Right, it was represented by a clerico-monarchist, not to say pro-fascist, daily, *L'Express du Midi*, supported by the weekly *Journal de Toulouse*. While the latter remained a very modest journal, *L'Express du Midi*, with offices in Paris, figured among the most important of French provincial journals. Like so many of the French right-wing journals of the time, *L'Express*, which called itself the organ of social and religious defence, tried its best to reconcile conflicting points of view.[2]

The Orientation of the Toulouse Press

As the year opened, a black mood seems to have taken hold of the Toulouse press, the consequence of the deteriorating socio-political panorama in the year before. 'On the threshold of the new year,' wrote Léon Hudelle in *Le Midi Socialiste*, 'I certainly hope it won't look anything like the last one.'[3] On the contrary, 1935 was to be the happiest in what was left of the 1930s. That was more and more evident to *La Dépêche*, which in February published a cartoon entitled 'Optimism' with the caption: 'A clairvoyant, in looking at her crystal ball, exclaims, "In 1936, everything will go better. Better than in 1937".'[4]

As François de Tessan, Undersecretary of State, wrote in *La Dépêche*, what was needed above all else in Spain was solidarity around the Republic. As the year opened, he said, it was the duty of all Republicans to overlook their disagreements and to regroup in a powerful bloc, in a sort of Popular Front.[5] When precisely this came into existence, *La Dépêche*, while wishing the *Frente Popular* well, advocated caution. Paul Bastid remarked that new regimes needed, in order to win acceptance in a country whose ancient traditions they were overturning, a great deal of patience and tact.[6] It was to be hoped, added Paul-Marie Masson, that the far-left parties were not planning to implement their entire programme overnight. By the same token, the right-wing parties had to yield to the inevitable concessions whenever the time came.[7] In the midst of all the difficulties, brought about by the Spaniards' lack of training in the democratic and liberal tradition, it was to the *Frente Popular* that *La Dépêche* looked for the most reliable friends of France, and it took care not to throw any stones at the unhappy Republic. The right-wing elements, in Bastid's opinion, far from being in a position to provide forces of law and order and of social construction, were merely elements of dispersion, violence and impotence. In spite of the indisputable mistakes made by the leaders of the *Frente Popular*, to bank on the right seemed to *La Dépêche* the worst of errors. If Spain was ever to emerge from the chaos in which it was plunged, it would come only with the Left acting wisely; outside of that, Bastid saw no hope for Spain.

Some of the contributors to *La Dépêche* fell into a facile optimism. For Masson, the Spanish Republic was solid and durable, and Spain had a particular advantage, that of being protected geographically from any immediate risk of war:

Spain is thus in a position to carry out its political and social experiments in total freedom, in a cocoon so to speak, without having to worry that the attainment of its ideal can be hampered by foreign concerns.[8] May the Spanish Republic avoid the double danger which has caused the downfall of so many nations: civil war and dictatorship.[9]

Spain preserved from foreign intervention, from civil war, from dictatorship? The irony would be bitter. And to carry optimism to its apogee, Heinrich Mann, six weeks before the military insurrection in Spain, wrote in *La Dépêche*:

Just as the Front Populaire has gained the upper hand in France, and has done the same in Spain, just as everywhere it is on the march and looks set to become an overwhelming majority in all of Europe, it is hard to see how the Hitlerian empire can long delay the day of liberation.[10]

As for the socialist journal, *Le Midi Socialiste* was an official organ of the SFIO, and as such it protected the party's ideological purity against those socialists who would align it with the parties of the bourgeois Left or those who wished to close ranks with the communists. That policy was guided by its director Vincent Auriol and sustained by almost daily editorials by Léon Blum. As for its attitude towards the Church, *Le Midi* made it clear at the time it reported the statement of Pope Pius XI in regard to communism: 'that force whose programme is social ruin, the same social ruin that we knew in centuries past, with the Crescent.' *Le Midi* replied: 'We respect religion, being as it is a private matter. But we do not recognise the right of any church to interfere in political life. What is that old gentleman meddling in?'[11] The respect shown by *Le Midi* towards religion seems genuine; where it did make a distinction was between the Church and the doctrine of Christ.[12]

The conservative and even reactionary character of Pius XI could not fail to arouse strong resentment among the socialists. 'It is the present Pope who has inspired the CEDA's programme in Spain,' *Le Midi* declared in May, adding, hyperbolically, that 'he stamped his foot with joy when the Asturian massacre was announced.' In the same way, André Leroux denounced the custom of Pius XI of putting the communist label on every voice of opposition and every attempt at reform: '"Communism" the struggle of the Mexican peasants against clerical feudalism, "communism" the hunger for land of the Andalusian peasant, "communism" the stirring of the people's conscience against the white terror of the Lerroux-Gil Robles régime in Spain and of the Vargas dictatorship in Brazil.' In André Leroux's opinion, what preoccupied the Pope was the proliferation of popular fronts that were drawing the masses into the struggle for bread, for peace, for freedom. It was indeed the *Front Populaire*, and not simply communism, that the Pope was targeting in his latest address. 'He prefers to denounce both as neo-paganism.'[13]

That *Le Midi Socialiste* was sincere in its desire to preserve peace is beyond all question, and no one was more so than Léon Blum, who provided the editorial on New Year's Day. Blum presented in it his view of the two poles of political thought in contemporary France:

> All of France has been witness for thirty years to the struggle waged between those who consider war as the natural state, inevitable and eternal, and those who believe it possible to educate all peoples into wanting a better direction. France knows which are the parties, groups and individuals that detest war as the worst of errors and the worst of crimes, and which are those that exalt war as a salutary test, a crucible into which the manly virtues can be poured.

On the right, *Le Journal de Toulouse* was a literary and socio-political weekly whose ideology was pro-monarchy, pro-Church, and anti-socialist. It was ready to accept anything, 'anything at all, anyone at all, but not the *Front Populaire*.'[14] It was the excesses and the errors of socialism, said *Le Journal*, which gave birth to fascism, as could be seen in Poland with Pilsudski and in Hungary with Béla Kun: 'fascism is a reaction against the impotence and malfeasance of socialism.'[15] *Le Journal* linked the events in Spain to the Revolution of 1789. The fate of Madero, of Kerensky, and of the Kuo-Min-Tang was the repetition of the fate of the Girondists. 'Poor, poor Spain!' *Le Journal* concluded. 'This is where we are led by the brutality, the violence, the sacrilege, the expropriations, the rapine and the excesses of every sort. Is this the pretty end that the *Front Populaire* wants to bring us to in France?'[16]

As for *L'Express du Midi*, in its first issue in 1891 it defined its purpose. 'We create this journal,' wrote its editor, 'in order to defend what we cherish: religion, nation, freedom.'[17] 'Dieu et Patrie' was its epigraph, but from the start, in the decade that produced the Dreyfus Affair, its deity was anti-Jewish and its France pure of foreign contagion. With *Le Journal de Toulouse*, *L'Express* championed the cause of unity among the Latin people and called for sympathy for Italy's aspirations. 'Who is looking for war?' asked F. Mazelié. 'France and Italy bound in an indissoluble alliance and co-rulers of the Mediterranean is enough to guarantee the peace of Europe.'[18] *L'Express* suggested that the British Home Fleet, engaged in the spring of 1936 in grand manoeuvres in the Mediterranean, would do better to attend to its business in the Baltic and leave the Latin lake in peace.[19]

For *L'Express*, enemy number one was bolshevism; number two, pagan National Socialism; number three, agnostic liberalism. As for the first, *L'Express* deemed it expedient to remind its readers how communism defined religion, quoting from Anatoli Lunacharsky's address to the Congress of Primary School Teachers in 1925:

> We hate Christians as we hate Christianity. Even the best of them must be considered our worst enemies. They teach us to love our neighbours and to show compassion, which is contrary to our principles. Christian love is an impediment to the development of revolution. Down with loving our neighbours! What we need is hate![20]

In associating all socialism of the left with murder, pillage, theft, and the collapse of law and order,[21] *L'Express* kept its distance even from the Radical Socialists.

The growing threat from Nazi Germany, enemy number two, was not lost on *L'Express*'s editor, Gaston Guèze, who moved from a relative indifference at the time of Hitler's accession to a genuine concern by the time of his remilitarisation of the Rhineland: 'When Hitler says that Nazism, unlike communism, is not an export commodity, he is lying.'[22] As for enemy number three, some of *L'Express*'s writers advocated a return to theocracy. Judex denounced France, and by extension the Spanish Republic, as atheistic and materialistic, 'a veritable dictatorship of immorality, longed for by the Freemasons and tolerated by the State.'[23] The journal's director, the Marquis de Palaminy, denounced his compatriots for having a 'deformed brain: they see nothing in humanity except the individual.'[24] For Paul Mathiex, France was the source of too many pacifists, feminists, and avant-garde literati,'[25] while for G. d'Adhémar, the most dangerous poisoners were the humanist intellectuals.[26]

Confronted by anarchy and dictatorship, the two monsters which had emerged at the same time, *L'Express du Midi* found no safe refuge in democracy. Democracy, it insisted, merely served as the prelude to the one or the other, preparing its bed. Charles Maurras deplored in *L'Express* the right of democracy to commit suicide at will:

> All our fortune, all our moral treasure of civilisation and tradition, all now thrown in question by the threat from the barbarism of Berlin or by these hordes of Muscovy, which latter we can call the barbarism of the nether world – all this is to be decided in the ballot-box, by a throw of the dice.[27]

24

L'Express was equally perturbed by the return to the old system of alliances. But since the trend of events was calling on everyone to align with one side or the other, *L'Express* held to its preference for the Italian model. What *L'Express* found particularly admirable in Mussolini was the blossoming in Italy of the will to empire. Given the Latin character, explained the journal, its warmth of feeling and its penchant for rebellion, it needed an outlet. Imperialism was the natural solution. What counted most was to overcome the prejudice that had built up against it, and to free the white conscience from all sense of guilt. The death at that moment of Rudyard Kipling, the bard of empire, served *L'Express* as the paragon to follow. 'The real death,' wrote Jean Douyau in his eulogy, 'is mediocrity.'[28] *L'Express* saw its champion in the clerico-authoritarian regime of Dollfuss in Austria and to a large extent in Gil Robles, his disciple in Spain. It was up to him to construct the clerico-corporatist state in Spain. However, the esteem in which *L'Express* held him would be amplified and total only if Gil Robles put an end to his ambiguous attitude towards the Church and the monarchy. It was his editorship of the Madrid Jesuit review *El Debate*, the organ of his party *Acción Popular*, and the rather liberal opinions which he expressed in it, which had provoked Pedro Cardinal Segura, Archbishop of Toledo and Primate of Spain, to censure the publication.[29] The attitude of Gil Robles towards the Republican Constitution was even more ambiguous. Even as Minister of War in the cabinet of Alejandro Lerroux, he was opposed to the use of force to overthrow the Republic. He had declared neither for the Republic nor for the monarchy, which remained after all a monarchy alive and intact: King Alfonso XIII had not abdicated but had merely suspended his prerogative 'until the nation speaks'.

For *L'Express* there was no question. Only the doctrines of the monarchist Right could serve to dissipate the fog of this all-encompassing confusion of having to choose between fascism and communism.[30] It was from the Gospels and from the Church that the monarchy derived its philosophy and its moral force. And a nation such as Spain, threatened as it was by separatist movements, needed more than any other a monarchy capable of holding it together. All that stood against the monarchist idea, added *L'Express*, was the irrational prejudice against it. 'The sacrosanct dogma of the "Rights of Man" and the principles of 1789 are now shown to be nothing more than a frightful chimera. The only way to restore to France its glory of old and provide it with a better social order resides in hereditary monarchy.'[31] And if *L'Express* considered this good for France, *a fortiori* it considered it good for Spain.

The Situation at the Beginning of 1936

The year opened, ominously, with the bifurcation of the centre. The *Partido Radical* drew further and further apart from its natural ally, the left of centre, and the ground between the two was becoming a veritable chasm. When the parties of the former majority withdrew their support of the caretaker government of Manuel Portela Valladares, Portela resigned, only to form a new government of technocrats formed of the left of centre. In *Le Midi Socialiste*, Leroux saw in the move the fear on the part of the President, Niceto Alcalá Zamora, that the Right had decided to repeat the Austrian experiment and install a clerico-fascist state.[32] In *La Dépêche*, François de Tessan added that the President had little trust in the sincerity of Gil Robles's loyalty to the Republic.[33]

The battle was thus joined between the two wings of the Spanish political spectrum, a battle which put the Constitution itself at risk, since it was nothing less than a struggle for or against the survival of the Republic. While the Right tried to reconstitute the anti-Marxist front of 1933, the Left began to build a *Frente Popular* to include all parties between the national republicans of Felipe Sánchez Román and the anarcho-syndicalists of Angel Pestaña. This they achieved on 13 February.[34] While François de Tessan appealed to all Republicans to rally to the defence of the Republic,[35] *L'Express du Midi* claimed that if the Constitution was at risk, it was the revolutionary Left, and not the right-wing bloc, that was intent on overthrowing it.[36]

The government of Portela Valladares proceeded to arrange the new legislative elections set for February. At first, neither *L'Express du Midi* nor *Le Midi Socialiste* found any cause to reproach the government for showing favour. But a few days before the elections, the socialist André Leroux reported that the government was entering into more and more compromises and collusion with the Right. In *La Dépêche*, Salvador de Madariaga, then Spain's permanent delegate to the League of Nations, expressed his concern over the extremist character of both the worker and the clerical sectors and concluded that 'reason requires the creation of a powerful centre.'[37] Far from such a centre reviving, it was visibly in its final dissolution. On 13 February, Leroux noted in *Le Midi* that almost every centrist candidate in Portela's government was included on the ballots of the Right. The moment had indeed arrived to choose one or other of the extremes. Gil Robles's plan was clear, wrote Leroux: 'attain power by hook or by crook, take back the Ministry of War, and prepare the coup d'état which would put an end to the Revolution of 1931.'[38] As for the Church, the reservations it had felt towards Gil Robles were now forgotten: it offered him all its help, and he accepted with alacrity. The forces of the Church were mobilized to the full, and the Catholic labour unions, recently constituted, entered the fray.

For the *Frente Popular* to win the elections, wrote *Le Midi Socialiste*, it was essential that the electoral temperature reach a very high degree, that the masses recover the enthusiasm of the 1931-1932 period, and that they fully overcome the trauma they had suffered from the failure of the Asturian rebellion. For Leroux, the key element in the struggle was the PSOE. If it could free itself from all sectarianism, if it kept an absolutely tight cohesion, and if it threw all its strength into the struggle, it was certain that the masses would follow. 'And the flag they would be rallying to would be the flag of the Republic itself, a Republic saved from fascism, which would then become, without stepping backward anymore, the "Republic of the workers" which the Constitution of 1931 had promised.'[39]

Despite its desire to see the socialist party attain hegemony in the *Frente Popular*, *Le Midi* worried about the *Frente*'s need to expand its base. On this score, the decision of the anarchist CNT-FAI to allow its huge membership to vote if they so wished was of supreme importance; the only other time the authorisation had been granted, in April 1931, it contributed heavily to the fall of the monarchy. However little gratitude was expressed in the socialist press, the help of the anarchists in Catalonia was now the decisive factor.

All three of the Toulouse dailies published their predictions, even though the general feeling was one of uncertainty. *Le Midi* moved from anxiety to cautious optimism. In early January, André Leroux thought that the two sides were evenly balanced.[40] A week before the elections he thought the outcome still uncertain: 'It is generally believed that there will be a slide to the left, but without the Left attaining the majority it won in 1931.'[41] Four days before the elections, Leroux almost predicted a victory of the Right: 'The new Cortes will be born in confusion and equivocation. The Right is a hybrid in which traditional monarchists and fascists rub elbows with Radicals and Catalan autonomists.'[42] In the same journal, Pamplona, on the eve of the elections, wrote with greater confidence: 'The *Frente Popular* must win for the dignity and future of the Republic. It will win. And its victory will be the magnificent prelude to the triumph of the *Front Populaire* in France.'[43]

One of the reasons given by Pamplona to explain the imminent victory of the Left was the popular reaction to the suppression of civil rights. More than 30,000 workers were still languishing in the prisons of Spain.[44] Among them was Lluis Companys, the former president of the Generalitat of Catalonia, and as *La Dépêche* put it, 'in a people as sensitive as the Catalans, that carries weight'.[45] The voice of the liberal centre added this warning: 'If the Whites triumph in Barcelona and if the Reds win in Madrid, there is a risk that the people will turn to arms.'[46]

As for *L'Express du Midi*, it brimmed with confidence in the victory of the Right.[47] The leader of the Right, for his part, did not take victory for granted. 'Success is certain,' he said, in the final run-up, 'but we must struggle as if it weren't.'[48] On the day of the election, *L'Express* reported that never had an electoral campaign opened under better auspices for the advent of the 'Good Republic,'[49] that is to say a clerico-monarchist republic. It quoted *L'Osservatore Romano*, which was following with deep sympathy 'the great efforts of the Spanish people in their struggle against the enemies of social well-being', and the organ of the Vatican expressed the wish that Catholic Spain would 'regain the path of salvation and peace'.[50]

In the Toulouse press, in résumé, *Le Midi Socialiste* yearned for the victory of the Left and did its best to believe in it. *L'Express du Midi* yearned for the victory of the Right and certainly believed in it. *Le Journal de Toulouse* had withdrawn from the issue and showed no interest in the elections at all. And *La Dépêche* represented the position of the majority of the French: hope in the victory of the Centre or of the Left of Centre, and fear of the victory of the Right.

The fatal day arrived. On the morning of 16 February, Paul Bourniquel, a correspondent of *La Dépêche* newly arrived in Barcelona, described the Catalan capital as 'calm'. But this calm, at a time when excitement would seem so natural, worried other observers, among them the correspondent of *Le Petit Parisien*: 'The calm reassures no one. On the contrary, it gives rise to sombre predictions, to dreadful prophesies.'[51]

The February Elections

Contrary to the hopes of President Alcalá, and to his supporters on *La Dépêche* and throughout France, the elections were a sharp defeat for the centre and the right of centre. Even centrist leaders such as Portela Valladares and Lerroux lost their seats. The landslide victory of the Left took the whole French press by surprise. It was now said on all sides that the victory of the Left was attributable to the women's vote, especially in Catalonia, and *La Dépêche* was of the opinion that the women, no longer under the thrall of the clergy, who had taken advantage of them in the confessional, now voted their resentment and their conscience.[52] Alvarez del Vayo, again in *La Dépêche*, shared this opinion: 'The women knew, even better than the men, the catastrophic results of the policies of the Right. The low wages, the rise in unemployment, the hope of amnesty for the imprisoned all worked like a stimulant.'[53] In *Le Midi*, Andrée Marty-Capgras referred to the concrete hopes that drew the women to vote Left. If, as she admitted, women had sold their vote in 1933 for 10 pesetas or a mattress or a large portion of lard, this time the promise of bread for all, the reenactment of social legislation, and the abolition of the death penalty excited them passionately.[54]

As for the Right in France, the result was taken as a warning to resist any attempt to introduce universal suffrage into the elections set for 9 May. *L'Express du Midi* quoted André Corthis, writing in *La Revue des Deux Mondes*: 'The Spanish woman neither asked for nor wanted the right to vote, she is in no way educated enough to exercise it, but from the moment she was given the right she became furiously jealous of her triumph.'[55] Again in *L'Express*, G. d'Adhémar was less gallant in his assessment of the motives of the Spanish women supporters of the Left, who, he saw, included the bourgeoisie as well as the working class: 'The latter voted so that the rich would be poor and the poor rich, nothing else. Using this vulgar but irresistible enticement, reminding them endlessly about their needs, about their abject misery, dangling golden wonders before their eyes, their women leaders, commanded in turn by the instigators of world revolution, drag them into the chaos they need in order to carry out their abominable purposes.' As for the middle-class women who voted Left, they did so 'either out of snobbery or from reading Marx, or even Kropotkin, so that, on the ruins of Christian civilisation, they could remake humanity, a humanity which, when its little four-hour workday is done, can indulge itself without let or hindrance.'[56] Nevertheless, *L'Express* conceded that the Left had won because it had a well-articulated and uncompromising programme,[57] and, as Roger Parant wrote, because it had campaigned with energy, while their adversaries lacked stomach for the fight.[58] That the Right lacked an articulated programme was the opinion also of André Leroux in *Le Midi*. The Right, he wrote, had become an 'anti' bloc: anti-revolutionary, anti-marxist, anti-socialist, 'but all these antis could not take the place of a programme.'[59]

Parant later offered another explanation for the rout of the Right. Against all the evidence, he claimed that the campaign of the Right had run short of funds. He complained that the monied class, which had the most to lose in the elections, had given nothing, or almost nothing, to the coffers of the parties defending them. At the same time, he added, the poorest of the revolutionaries were paying every week into the treasury of their labour union or of their local cell; as a result, the *Frente Popular* could put out magnificently illustrated posters, while those of their opponents seemed to be printed on wrapping paper.[60] The enormous poster of Gil Robles displayed in the Puerta del Sol hardly buttressed Parant's argument, nor did he stop to consider that any gift, however small, paid in by an Andalusian peasant from his salary of one peseta a day was an enormous personal sacrifice. *L'Express*'s purpose, in fact, was to frighten the rich in France into giving more to the party coffers in preparation for the May elections.

It had been well said that peace in Spain would depend not on those who won the February elections but on those who lost them. The problem now, as Paul Bourniquel wrote in *La Dépêche*, was how to live together, when in Catalonia there was so little in common even between Republican allies such as the anarchists and the Esquerrra.[61] While Leroux in *Le Midi* offered a toast to 'Spain, liberated from the clerico-fascist danger,'[62] Guèze in *L'Express* was hardly induced to accept the result gracefully. And to the cry of the Left, '*Viva la Republica!*', Guèze had a question. 'Do they not have a republic already? The answer is no, not the one they want. The republic they dream of is sung to the music of the *Internationale*.'[63] As a result, added *L'Express*, on the day that the results were announced a state of alarm was proclaimed throughout the country, and on the next day it reported that warrants had been issued for the arrest of Generals Goded and Franco.

The hopes of the Right now focused on the possibility of a disintegration of the Left. 'How could anything so disparate possibly govern?' asked Guèze in *L'Express*.[64] *Le Midi* carried Calvo Sotelo's prophetic warning to the Republican Left of the danger from the proletarian parties, 'whose first victims they would be,' and Leroux, equally prophetically, remarked that such a schism on the Left would open, in Spain as elsewhere, the way to fascism.[65] *L'Express* carried the speech of Azaña, broadcast on radio, which was a reply to the statement of Gil Robles when interviewed by the Catholic daily *Ya*: 'If the monarchists are outside the régime, so too are the socialists and the communists.'[66] 'Our motto,' said Azaña, 'is defence of the Republic, restoration of law and order, prosperity, freedom, justice. Under this flag Republicans and non-Republicans can unite.'[67] For *L'Express* these were empty words: 'The *Frente Popular* will not be content with that.'[68] Among those not content was Marcel Cachin, director of *L'Humanité*, who had apparently not yet received, or well understood, the new signal from Moscow calling for reconciliation with the bourgeois Left. 'A will of iron will still be needed,' wrote Cachin, 'to complete the rout of the class enemy and ensure the final victory of the proletariat.'[69]

'Two great factions,' wrote Lucien Romier in *Le Figaro*, 'are now pitted against one another in Spain, each as negative as the other. Each hurls itself at the other, then steps back, in a compromise that is over in a day.'[70]

The Return of the Azaña Administration

What was to be, first of all, the attitude of the new government towards the press? At the beginning of 1936, press censorship had been in full operation. Now Joan Moles, the new president of the Generalitat of Catalonia, issued a statement published in *La Dépêche*: 'We intend to show goodwill and indulgence to the press, but we expect the press, for its part, to refrain from publishing reports which are uncorroborated and unnecessarily alarmist, as indeed too many are in the press.'[71] A few days later, Moles added a warning directed at the French press in particular: 'The French people have for too long been misled in regard to Spain by journalists too much in search of local colour which sometimes they fabricate at home when they cannot find it here.'[72]

Between mid-February and May, the French press devoted virtually all its attention to the elections in France. The image it formed of the *Front Populaire* would nevertheless be based largely on that it had formed of the *Frente Popular*. The importance of giving the new administration a fair chance was not lost on the Paris daily *L'Instransigeant*, which, though conservative, published an article by Jean Antoine, its special correspondent in Spain: 'We know that a part of the French press warns Spain every day of the threat it faces from Stalin's iron hand. For the sake of our own domestic policy, we do not hesitate to wage the most unfriendly campaign against a country engaged in working out its future as a republic.'[73]

Other Paris journals of the Right saw things differently. 'If the *Front Populaire* wins,' groaned *L'Action Française*, 'it will turn France into a cemetery.'[74] The weekly *La Production Française* warned, 'The same ordeals will fall on us if we allow the *Front Populaire* to win.'[75] In Toulouse, *L'Express* became more and more alarmist as the May elections approached: 'It must be cried out everywhere: the *Front Populaire* means war.'

Unsurprisingly, *L'Express* complained that the Azaña government had reinstated censorship, 'in order to hide,' as André Nicolas put it, 'as far as it could, the tragic events which continue to bathe the Peninsula in blood.'[76] *L'Express*, however, had no correspondent in Spain. *La Dépêche* did, and did not complain of censorship.

The Azaña government, with its majority increased, wasted no time in resuming the work it had had to abandon in 1933. This time, the pressure from the socialists weighed upon it more and more. Before mid-April, the press could judge the extent of the new reforms. *L'Express* could only deplore the government's programme of nationalisation and the confiscation of the wealth of the Church. On the vital question of education, Pamplona in *Le Midi* wrote that the leftist government of the First Biennium had, between 1931 and 1933, opened more than 2,500 schools; in the two years that followed under Lerroux, only 333 schools had been created.[77] Now, in the two years ahead, the Azaña government decreed the creation of another 10,600 schools. Herein probably lay the essential cause of the disorder that followed. The suspension by the Bank of France of lines of credit to the Spanish Republican Government, the so-called 'silver wall', deprived Azaña of the means of carrying out his project. In the absence of capital, the government began to requisition the convents and all the colleges run by the Church. *L'Express* shuddered at the thought that at Avila the government had seized the College of Santa María de Gracia, where St Teresa of Avila was educated and where nuns had taught for fifteen centuries.[78] While the socialist press did not deny the burning of certain convents and churches, 'a manifestation of the people's lingering rancour',[79] the incidents were magnified to the maximum by *L'Express*. Azaña himself, in an address to Cortes, described the acts of arson as 'a Spanish tradition from the time of the Inquisition. In times gone by, they burned heretics, today they burn saints, at least in effigy.'[80] But the Prime Minister denounced the practice, calling it 'shameful and futile'. The campaign posters of the *Frente Popular*, it was recalled, had appealed for law and order: in one of them, below the scales held by the goddess of justice, was the caption: 'Not one crime more, not one more act of theft.'[81] Even in May, Paul-Marie Masson in *La Dépêche* expressed his hope in a more or less peaceful transition, in which the Spanish revolution could follow its course without spilling the blood that marked its forerunners in other countries.[82] In *L'Express*, on the other hand, André Nicolas accused the Azaña government of seizing upon the unrest which its policies inevitably provoked in order to raise the cry of fascism. The word 'fascist' was excluded from *L'Express*'s vocabulary for months on end. Even when the complicity of fascists was well established by the most reputable and impartial organs of the press, *L'Express* reported that 'evidence is lacking.'[83] The attempt upon the life of Luis Jiménez de Asua, the socialist professor of law who was the author of the Constitution of the Second Republic, was attributed by *L'Express* to 'a group of persons unknown'.[84] On 14 March *L'Express* described his funeral, even though Jiménez was still alive and would later become president of the Cortes in exile. At this supposed funeral, a major of the *Guardia de Asaltos* (the Republican defence corps) was attacked and savagely beaten; far from attributing the crime to the fascists, *L'Express* imputed it to 'rioters who, it is said, belong to the anarcho-syndicalist movement'.[85] Or, 'the finger points to a socialist crime.'[86] The incident on 14 April in Madrid, resulting in one death and six wounded, all socialists, was attributed to 'certain individuals'. Only now did the word 'fascists' appear in *L'Express*, which still put the term in quotation marks and did not accuse them of the crime: the 'fascists' merely intervened.[87] The next day it was a case of the 'fascists' taking legitimate action: '"Fascist" elements reacted resolutely against the disorders provoked by the communists.' The terrorists of the Right remained 'drunks and persons unknown'.[88] It was only with the killing of Lieutenant de los Reyes, and the incidents that took place at his funeral, that *L'Express* began to speak of 'the Spanish tragedy'.[89]

Countdown to the Cataclysm

On 7 April, the Cortes forced the resignation of the President of the Republic. In *Le Midi Socialiste*, André Leroux, without an ounce of generosity, reported that the Cortes had 'thrown out the traitor to the Republic'.[90] It remained for Paul Bastid in *La Dépêche* to assess the situation fairly. It was, after all, the first time in history that an elected lower house had forced out a Head of State. 'The Spanish Republic,' wrote Bastid, 'has been deprived of an experienced President at the moment it needs him most. As was to be expected, the political disarray has magnified the social disorder which had given birth to the political disarray.'[91] His replacement by Azaña created a vacancy in the prime ministership. In *La Dépêche*, Rieu-Vernet saw no leader in the Republican Left strong enough to resist the growing pressure from the communists who were eager to speed up the reform programme of the *Frente Popular*; he therefore regretted that Azaña had left the post which counted most.[92] In an exclusive interview granted to *Le Midi Socialiste*, the new President revealed the vanity that was among his weaknesses: 'If I move into the presidency, it is to endow it with new ideas. I shall not live at home; I shall live in the National Palace [formerly of Alfonso XIII] in the grand suites on the first floor, and I shall open all the staterooms to Republican society. I do not view the office of President in a paltry manner, and no one can have a clearer view of it than the Head of State. The policy adhered to up to now has not been in the interests of the Republic.'[93] As for Azaña's choice of the liberal Santiago Casares Quiroga to succeed him as Prime Minister, it was received by the Left in France with considerable satisfaction, and by the Right, initially, with reserve. This attitude changed soon enough. A few days later, the new Prime Minister left nothing in doubt. In the fight against fascism, he said, 'the government cannot remain neutral. The government is a belligerent. It will not lack in daring, but neither will it let itself be directed from the street.'[94]

In order not to be 'directed from the street,' the Casares government proceeded to put its powers to use, wherever the violence erupted and whatever the ideology of its perpetrators. In accordance with their ideological position, the press of the Left and Right minimized and maximized the incidents of violence. *L'Express du Midi*, which had still not sent a single reporter to Spain, attributed every disorder to communists or anarchists, 'resulting in a strong reaction from elements on the Right.'[95] The policy of *L'Express* was simple: exaggerate the extent of the disorder and deplore it at the same time. This led *L'Express* into open self-contradiction. It now conceded that the government intended to apply the law with vigour,[96] and a day later went so far as to say that the government was 'beginning to keep its promises', but in the same issue it accused the Spanish Government (and the French Government too) of only pretending to put an end to the disorder while in reality they were elevating violence to the level of an institution. *Le Journal de Toulouse* chimed in with a claim that, in five years of republic, there had been 'more deaths than in several centuries of monarchy'.[97] As the violence mounted, Leroux in *Le Midi Socialiste* wrote that the Spanish far Right was pushed towards terrorism precisely because it knew it was defeated politically.[98] When fascists were shown to be the principal instigators of the violence, Guèze in *L'Express* placed the blame solely on the programme of the *Frente Popular* and added a sinister warning: 'The bell could soon be tolling for Monsieur Blum as well as for Señor Azaña.'[99]

Nothing, however, put an end to the strikes and the violence, and violence reached its apogee with the twin murders that would set Spain ablaze: the first, of José Castillo, a lieutenant in the Republic's Assault Guards, on the night of 12-13 July; and the second, obviously in reprisal, of José Calvo Sotelo, leader of the Alphonsist party (*Renovación Española*), on the night of 13-14 July.

In its reaction to the assassination of Castillo, *L'Express* did not publish the news until 14 July, and even then it did not impute it to the fascists. Again, the same issue contained conflicting ideas. On the one hand, *L'Express* showed at this terrifying moment an unwonted restraint. Certain departments of the state, it wrote, were not functioning as they should: 'If officials can act like this, it will be difficult to prevent private persons from taking the law into their own hands.'[100] Conversely, it accused the left-wing press of hypocrisy in its alleged tardiness to report crimes committed by the Left. In fact, *Le Midi Socialiste* reported the death of Calvo Sotelo on the morning after, but now, as the two funerals were celebrated, the press in Toulouse (like that in Paris and elsewhere) was swept along, separated into two virtually hostile camps. While *Le Midi Socialiste* reported only the funeral of Castillo, *L'Express* described only that of Calvo Sotelo. Its coverage included the highly provocative funeral oration of Antonio Goicoechea, who had led the *Renovación Española* up until February 1936 when he lost his seat in the elections and was replaced by Calvo: 'Before God who hears us speak, I swear to follow your example and to avenge your death. Our duty is to save Spain, and we shall.'[101]

The oration of Goicoechea was, as much as anything else, the battle-cry that announced the opening of the Civil War. While *L'Express* ignored the death of Castillo, *Le Midi Socialiste* showed no sympathy for the fate of Calvo. 'The clerico-monarchist reactionaries,' it wrote, 'will be wiped out with him from the political life of Spain.'[102] *Le Midi* clearly underestimated the force of the right-wing reaction, even if it understood that most of Gil Robles's young supporters had deserted him to enter the ranks of the fascists. On the eve of the military insurrection, André Leroux wrote:

> We do not believe that the Right constitutes an immediate danger to the Republican regime. The situation is nevertheless quite tense,

and the decision of the workers' parties and labour unions to rally around the government is most timely. Now that that is announced, it will be enough perhaps to dispel any fancy on the Right to embark on adventure.[103]

Conclusion

The two killings, of Castillo and Calvo Sotelo, had the effect of electrifying the press in France which seemed to have become satiated with the constant accounts of violence in Spain. *L'Express* especially was so laconic as to give the impression that it knew all about the imminent *coup d'état*. When it first reported the insurrection, it did so with a reserve that suggested it doubted its chances of success. The organ of conservatism nevertheless threw all its support to the rebellion, and threw its weight into the apotheosis of Calvo Sotelo. André Nicolas described the monarchist leader as irreplaceable: 'As Finance Minister under General Primo de Rivera, he had restored the economy to balance, ushering in prosperity and putting an end to unemployment, and in 1933, when the Left had been ousted, this man of unquestioned competence had stepped forward again.' Nicholas added that the monarchist leader had been warned by a friend, two days before the crime: 'With the bodyguards that you've been given, you'll wind up dead,' to which Calvo allegedly replied, 'I accept this, if my blood is needed to save Spain.'[104] This account is at variance with the known facts. Calvo went to great lengths to avoid arrest, keeping his door bolted, trying his best to identify from the window the guards who had come to take him, and placing phone calls to ascertain their orders. But accuracy in reporting was now less in demand than ever. Words now took on new meanings: those in arms against the elected government were the 'patriots', never the rebels, and those defending the Republic were 'communists' or 'revolutionaries'. It was left to *La Dépêche* to uphold the principles of a journal responsive to the truth. Civil wars, wrote Edmond Haraucourt in the great Toulouse daily, are unleashed by 'the collision of two certainties'.[105] It was all so bitterly reminiscent of another civil war, fought in Greece and described by Thucydides:

> New extravagances of zeal, elaborate methods of seizing power, and unheard-of atrocities in revenge. Fanatical enthusiasm was the mark of the real man. Nothing was barred. Party leaders were always ready to satisfy the hatreds of the hour. As for the moderates, they

were destroyed by both extremes. As a result, a general deterioration of character was visible throughout the Greek world. The simple way of looking at things, so much the mark of a noble nature, was regarded as a ridiculous quality and soon ceased to exist.

And so the moderate centre, which should be serving as the meeting ground of the extremes, turns into a no-man's-land, where men and ideas are mown down in the withering crossfire of the guns. Well might the exiled Italian anti-fascist Guglielmo Ferrero write in *La Dépêche* that Europe was divided and plunged 'into the greatest intellectual and moral confusion in all its history'.[106]

Notes

1. Paul Morand, *Le Figaro*; reproduced in *La Dépêche*, 20 October 1936.
2. For an analysis of the Toulouse press, see David Wingeate Pike, *Les Français et la Guerre d'Espagne*, Paris, 1975, pp. 52-4. This work begins at the point (July 1936) where the present article ends.
3. *Le Midi Socialiste*, 1 January 1936.
4. *La Dépêche*, 22 February 1936.
5. Ibid., 11 January 1936.
6. Ibid., 19 April 1936.
7. Ibid., 6 May 1936.
8. Georges de Marsilly, in *Le Petit Bleu de Paris*, another journal of the Republican Left, was equally optimistic: 'The Spaniards are unquestionably the only people in the world who, in the game of politics, risk nothing more, if one may say so, than internal death; they do not risk a foreign yoke'; reproduced in *L'Express du Midi*, 23 April 1936.
9. *La Dépêche*, 6 May 1936.
10. Ibid., 6 June 1936.
11. 'Le Pape contre le Front Populaire', *Le Midi Socialiste*, 13 May 1936.
12. For example, in its reporting on the dismissal of Monseigneur Dubois de La Villerabel as Archbishop of Rouen and Primate of Normandy; ibid., 18 May 1936.
13. 'Le Pape Pie XI part en guerre', ibid., 19 May 1936.
14. *Le Journal de Toulouse*, 26 April 1936.
15. Ibid., 3 May 1936.
16. Ibid., 26 July 1936.
17. Ibid., 23 January 1938.
18. *L'Express du Midi*, 13 February 1936.
19. Ibid., 11 March 1936.
20. Ibid., 5 May 1936.
21. Ibid., 7 February 1936.
22. Ibid., 14 March 1936.
23. Ibid., 26 May 1936.
24. Ibid., 11 November 1936.
25. Ibid., 16 September 1936.

26. Ibid., 26 May 1936.
27. Ibid., 29 March 1936.
28. Ibid., 20 January 1936.
29. Cardinal Segura's hatred of the Republic was such that he had been driven into exile in 1931. From the pulpit of the cathedral of Rheims, Segura greeted Christmas 1936 with the thundering cry: 'Let the wrath of God crush Spain to pieces, if the Republic endures!'
30. *L'Express du Midi*, 4 March 1936.
31. Ibid., 3 April 1936.
32. *Le Midi Socialiste*, 2 January 1936.
33. *La Dépêche*, 11 January 1936.
34. But without the two wings. Sánchez Román dissolved his party on 15 February, while the anarchist CNT-FAI remained outside the *Frente Popular*.
35. *La Dépêche*, 11 January 1936.
36. *L'Express du Midi*, 7 January 1936.
37. *La Dépêche*, 8 February 1936.
38. *Le Midi Socialiste*, 13 February 1936.
39. Ibid., 2 January 1936.
40. Ibid.
41. Ibid., 10 February 1936.
42. Ibid., 13 February 1936.
43. Ibid., 17 February 1936.
44. Ibid.
45. *La Dépêche*, 15 February 1936.
46. Ibid.
47. *L'Express du Midi*, 17 February 1936.
48. Ibid., 18 February 1936.
49. Ibid.
50. Ibid.
51. *Le Midi Socialiste*, 14 February 1936.
52. *La Dépêche*, 20 February 1936.
53. Ibid., 1 March 1936.
54. *Le Midi Socialiste*, 27 February 1936.
55. *L'Express du Midi*, 29 April 1936.
56. Ibid.
57. Ibid., 18 February 1936.
58. Ibid., 13 April 1936.
59. *Le Midi Socialiste*, 19 February 1936.
60. *L'Express du Midi*, 13 April 1936.
61. *La Dépêche*, 19 February 1936.
62. *Le Midi Socialiste*, 19 February 1936.
63. *L'Express du Midi*, 18 February 1936.
64. Ibid., 20 February 1936.
65. *Le Midi Socialiste*, 8 March 1936.
66. *L'Express du Midi*, 18 February 1936.
67. Ibid., 21 February 1936.
68. Ibid.
69. *Le Midi Socialiste*, 22 February 1936.
70. Ibid.
71. *La Dépêche*, 19 February 1936.

72. Ibid., 23 February 1936.
73. *Le Midi Socialiste*, 10 April 1936.
74. *La Dépêche*, 19 April 1936.
75. Ibid.
76. *L'Express du Midi*, 5 May 1936.
77. *Le Midi Socialiste*, 17 February 1936.
78. *L'Express du Midi*, 24 May 1936.
79. *Le Midi Socialiste*, 18 March 1936.
80. *La Dépêche*, 6 May 1936.
81. *La Dépêche*, 16 February 1936.
82. Ibid., 6 May 1936.
83. *L'Express du Midi*, 10 March 1936.
84. Ibid., 13 March 1936.
85. Ibid., 15 March 1936.
86. Ibid., 22 March 1936.
87. Ibid., 15 April 1936.
88. Ibid., 16 April 1936.
89. Ibid., 19 April 1936.
90. *Le Midi Socialiste*, 9 April 1936.
91. *La Dépêche*, 19 April 1936.
92. Ibid., 11 May 1936.
93. *Le Midi Socialiste*, 5 May 1936.
94. Ibid., 21 May 1936.
95. *L'Express du Midi*, 10 March 1936.
96. Ibid., 14 July 1936.
97. *Le Journal de Toulouse*, 26 July 1936.
98. *Le Midi Socialiste*, 16 July 1936.
99. *L'Express du Midi*, 15 July 1936.
100. Ibid., 14 July 1936.
101. Ibid., 15 July 1936.
102. *Le Midi Socialiste*, 20 July 1936.
103. Ibid., 16 July 1936.
104. *L'Express du Midi*, 26 July 1936.
105. *La Dépêche*, 23 August 1936.
106. Ibid., 9 August 1936.

3

The British Government and General Franco during the Spanish Civil War

Enrique Moradiellos
(University of Extremadura, Cáceres)

FROM July 1936 to April 1939, throughout the Spanish Civil War, both contending parties shared the view that the policy of the British authorities towards the conflict was of fundamental importance. The president of the Republic, Manuel Azaña, from the very beginning held the opinion that the result of the war 'was dependent, in the last resort, on what the British government could do or wanted to do'. General Franco's Foreign Minister also acknowledged privately on several occasions that 'the English government has in its hands the key to peace (by promoting a Francoist victory)'.[1]

This unanimity reflected an undeniable and, indeed, proven reality: the attitude of the British Government to the conflict had a decisive influence on its course and final outcome. This was the result of two parallel factors: Britain's economic and strategic interests in Spain and her position as a leading European and imperial power.[2]

As regards British interests in Spain, three points should be borne in mind. First, that the naval base in Gibraltar was crucial to Britain's control of the Mediterranean with its security dependent on Spanish goodwill; second, Britain was Spain's most important trading partner, accounting for 25 percent of Spanish exports and providing 10 percent of her imports; third, British capital accounted for 40 percent of foreign investments in Spain, largely concentrated in the iron and pyrites mining industries.

Given the extent of those interests, the FO followed with attention the critical situation in Spain from 1931, when the oligarchic monarchy was peacefully toppled by a democratic Republic bent on a programme of social reform. The persistence of social and political upheavals, particularly after the narrow victory of the Popular Front in the general elections of February 1936, convinced the British authorities that Spain had entered a process of prerevolutionary crisis, probably fostered by the Comintern, which the Republican government was unable to contain or resolve. So, by June 1936, the FO had all but given up any hope of a constitutional solution in Spain, and expected either a military intervention to restore order and avoid anarchy, or some sort of leftist social revolution.[3]

Such a perception of the Spanish crisis ran parallel to the beginnings of the British policy of *rapprochement* towards Fascist Italy after the Abyssinian War, as part of the general policy of appeasement in Europe.[4] The origins of this policy lay in the difficult dilemma which the British authorities were at the time confronting in their strategic and diplomatic planning. Since the start of the economic depression, an overextended and enfeebled British Empire was threatened in three different and distant points by powers hostile to the *status quo*: Japan in the far east; Nazi Germany in central Europe; and Italy in the Mediterranean. Britain had neither the economic nor the military resources to confront alone the three potential dangers simultaneously. Nor could it rely on the support of a debilitated France, an isolationist United States or a socially disturbing Soviet Union. In such conditions, appeasement was a diplomatic strategy designed to avoid war and the hostile convergence of the three powers by reducing tensions with the weakest (Italy) and nearest (Germany).

Therefore, from June 1936, the main objective of British diplomacy was to restore harmonious relations with Italy in order to stabilize the Mediterranean situation and to arrest an Italian alignment with the potentially hostile powers of Germany and Japan. Strategic considerations alone seemed to demand such a course, but there was also the strong desire to prevent an arms race whose financial demands would endanger the economic recovery and the social and political stability of Britain and its empire. In addition, there was also British suspicion of hidden Soviet intentions and the conviction that any war would provide ample opportunities for the expansion of communism.

It is clear, then, that prior to the eruption of the Spanish Civil War, the antirevolutionary preoccupation about Spain and the search for a Mediterranean entente with Italy, were twin considerations at the FO. They were to set the basic framework for the British reaction to the conflict, which began on the 17 July 1936 with a large military insurrection against the Republican government. The partial failure of the coup in many areas, including Madrid and Barcelona, transformed it into a bloody civil war. Since neither side had the means to wage a full-scale war, both were immediately obliged to look for foreign support. General Franco, soon to be head of the insurgent army, asked Mussolini and Hitler for help. The Republican government, hampered by total dislocation of the state apparatus, sought support from the new Popular Front government in France. Both sides tried to gain indirect help from the British government. Yet the subsequent process of internationalisation of the Civil War had very different results for each side.

Before the end of July 1936 Hitler and Mussolini had decided secretly to send a small amount of aid to Spain. They were convinced that this would not provoke a dangerous reaction in Britain and France where conservative quarters were terrified at the prospect of a bolshevik-style revolution in Spain. These decisions were taken without mutual consultations but based on a similar rationale; the rapid supply of aid could help Franco win the war and, as a result, alter the political-strategic balance of power in the western Mediterranean in favour of Germany and Italy and against the democratic powers at low cost and with minimal risk. In fact, it would be the rapid coordination of this aid to Franco which would originate the collaboration between both dictatorships and the formation of the Italo-German Axis.[5]

In contrast to the success of Franco in gaining Fascist and Nazi support the Republic's efforts in Europe ended in failure. The French government, which was initially in favour of sending aid, had to step back in the face of the reaction of conservative opinion and the more moderate sectors within the Popular Front coalition, who were fearful of provoking a civil war in France or a confrontation with Germany and Italy. Moreover, Britain, France's key ally, made her disapproval clear, and this attitude had great weight in Paris given France's vulnerability in the face of the hostile continental powers and her dependence on the defensive alliance with Britain.[6] Nor did the Republic at first receive direct aid from the Soviet Union. Stalin was trying to fashion a common front with the democracies in order to defend against the double threat of Germany and Japan on the borders of the USSR. For this reason, fearing Franco-British complicity in a plan of German aggression, the Soviet government was careful not to intervene and, instead, limited itself to proclaiming diplomatic solidarity with the Republic's anti-fascist struggle.[7]

Britain's official response to the Spanish crisis was to adopt a policy of tacit neutrality (that is, never formally proclaimed) which was clearly benevolent towards the military insurgents. The essential aims of that policy were to avoid giving any direct or indirect help to the government side, whose legality was held to conceal a revolutionary purpose, and to avert any possibility of a confrontation with rebel forces of counter-revolutionary persuasion. Not in vain, British diplomats in Spain had warned from the beginning of the war that 'no government existed today' and that 'there were military forces in operation on the one hand, opposed by a virtual Soviet on the other'.[8] The extent of the anti-revolutionary feeling created by the Spanish crisis among the British authorities is clearly revealed by this statement by Sir Maurice Hankey, Cabinet Secretary: 'In the present state of Europe, with France and Spain menaced by Bolshevism, it is not inconceivable that before long it might pay us to throw in our lot with Germany and Italy.'[9]

Therefore, the Conservative-dominated British government preferred a victory by the military insurgents over the Republican government forces both because of its effect on British interests in Spain and because of its possible consequences in Europe. This was recognised in private by an official in the FO who noted:

> that this memorandum (on expropiation and collectivisation of British firms in Republican Spain) shows quite clearly that the alternative to Franco is communism tempered by anarchy; and ... further believed that if this last régime is triumphant in Spain it will spread to other countries, and notably to France.[10]

This barely concealed preference for a rebel military victory, either through the Francoists' own devices or through foreign aid, was based on the certainty that it would always be possible to maintain a friendly relationship with a future Spanish government. The reasons could not be more firmly based: in order to carry out the difficult post-war reconstruction of the country, Spain would be dependent on the British financial and commercial market. And in a worst case scenario, if the power of attraction of the diplomacy of pound sterling should fail, there still remained in full operation the power of deterrence of gun-boat diplomacy: the superiority of the Royal Navy and its capacity to implement an economic blockade.

Faced with the danger that the Civil War would escalate into a European war, the British authorities enthusiastically accepted a French proposal that all the European powers sign a Non-Intervention Agreement (NIA) thereby imposing a collective embargo on the sale of arms to Spain. France's aim on making this proposal was to confine the war to Spain and put a stop to Italo-German aid to the rebels given her own inability to supply the Republic. The British quickly took up the proposal, which seemed the ideal means to maintain its official neutrality with the support of public opinion as a shield against Labour accusations of pro-rebel bias.

Indeed, the signing of the NIA by all European governments in late August 1936, together with the establishment of a supervisory committee in London, gave the FO the diplomatic instruments necessary in order to safeguard her principal diplomatic objectives in the conflict: the restriction of the war to Spain, restraining the intervention of her French ally, avoiding any alignment with the Soviet Union, and any confrontation with Italy and Germany over their support for the rebels. In this respect the Prime Minister, Stanley Baldwin, had on 26 July given a clear instruction to his Foreign Secretary, Anthony Eden, 'that on no account, French or other, must he bring us into the fight on the side of the Russians'.[11]

Hence, there is no doubt that, from the beginning, for the British authorities the multilateral policy of nonintervention contained a hint of fraudulence, in that its real end was not the one declared (the avoidance of foreign participation in the war) but rather the safeguarding of the established objectives by its mere existence and apparent efficacy. An internal FO memorandum recognised this fact in the following words: 'We have considered the continued existence of the Agreement and of the supervising Committee as of more importance than the actual efficacy of the embargo itself.'[12]

The British Cabinet's Spanish policy lent itself very easily to the diplomatic strategy pursued by General Franco from the outset of the war. The rebel leaders had constantly sought the abandonment of the Republic by the great democratic powers while at the same time ensuring this did not reduce their capacity to receive foreign aid. A memorandum by Franco's Ministry for Foreign Affairs in 1939 defined the major coordinates of the rebels' diplomatic activity as follows:

Our principal and almost exclusive task had to be to localise the war in Spanish territory, avoiding in this way by all means an international war out of which we would have little to gain and much to lose. At the same time, however, we had to ensure that we would still be able to obtain the aid we needed from our foreign friends while ensuring at all costs that our enemy received no aid or at least that this aid was minimised.[13]

In this way there was a basic coincidence between the objectives of British foreign policy and the diplomatic aims of the rebel authorities. Both General Franco and the British government opted to localise the war and to uncouple it from tensions in Europe. And while Franco hoped to isolate the Republic while maintaining Italo-German aid, the British Cabinet was primarily interested in the achievement of Anglo-French neutrality independent of whether this policy was imitated by Italy and Germany. There was, however, one worry. The possibility that the Spanish conflict would become interwoven with divisions on the European continent, thereby leading to an alignment between the insurgents and those powers whose expansionist policies most endangered the British Empire.

In order to allay British fears, from the first Franco gave London repeated assurances that his was a purely national and anti-communist movement, that there were no revisionist objectives with respect to Gibraltar, and no intention of cementing a long-term alliance with Italy and Germany. The British authorities decided to accept these guaranties and to confine their diplomacy to that of the pound sterling while saving the Royal Navy for the future. As a high official of the FO noted in private:

> We have all along been inclined to discount the permanence of any German or Italian influence in Spain. Franco has had to lean on those two Powers because no help was forthcoming from any other quarter; but he obviously must have feared the consequences of this assistance from the outset, and the manners and methods of his allies have inevitably led to further friction and dissension. ... German and Italian activities in Spain are not in the long run going to favour good relations with the future government of that country.[14]

In these circumstances relations between Britain and the insurgents were basically calm and friendly during the first six months of the war. The opposite was the case with respect to British relations with the Republican government, which were dominated by British fears regarding the revolutionary situation within the Republican zone, and by Republican suspicion, fuelled by Britain's barely concealed hostility to the Republican cause. Three additional factors contributed to the difference in Britain's relations with the two sides. First, the rapid advance of Franco's troops towards Madrid and the concomitant collapse of Republican resistance reinforced the general belief that the war would end in an insurgent victory in the very near future. Second, the work of the NIC proved essentially favourable to the insurgents' interests, for while it prevented the Republic from securing arms in continental markets, it did not interrupt continued military supplies from Italy and Germany. Finally, Franco's political elevation during the autumn of 1936 quietened British fears for the future because it demonstrated military hegemony over the Nationalist coalition and guaranteed the military's control over the fascist Falange. In brief, Franco did not appear to be either a dangerous doctrinaire politician (like Hitler) or an unpredictable fascist demagogue (like Mussolini), but a good Spanish military man, who was prudent, conservative and nationalist, and who had risen up only to combat chaos and the spectre of social revolution.[15]

On the rebel side, there were occasional complaints at the lack of any direct British aid. Nevertheless, the insurgents fully understood the importance of the British position and the difficulties the British government faced in maintaining it. In July 1937 this was recognised by General Franco's Secretariat in the following revealing words: 'The attitude of England is most difficult because of the pressure exercised by Labour and the difficult [situation] in France, and if it were not for England France's aid to the reds would have been greater and more effective, and even of a different order.'[16]

However, Anglo-insurgent relations began to cool from the end of 1936 as a result of three simultaneous factors. In the first place, the Republicans were able to withstand the Nationalist onslaught on Madrid in November 1936 thanks above all to the arrival of Soviet aid and the entry into action of the International Brigades (composed of between 35,000 and 60,000 volunteers over the course of the war). Second, Hitler and Mussolini responded to the Soviet initiative and greatly intensified their support for Franco, conscious of the fact that his victory now required more than some limited and secret aid. The result was the dispatch of the German Condor Legion (totalling 16,500 men) and the Italian expeditionary force (with 79,000 troops in all). In Britain, this open and massive intervention on the part of the Axis powers reinforced popular sympathy for the Republic and accentuated Labour criticisms at the passivity of the Conservative government.

As a result of these three parallel processes the Civil War became a long war, and moreover, it became fully integrated into the European tensions which would lead to the Second World War. Indeed, it had become a mini European civil war, which aroused the passions of public opinion on the continent whether it was considered as the antechamber of the inevitable conflict between the West and communism or the prologue to an imminent struggle between fascism and democracy.

The events of late 1936 provoked a deep split in the British Cabinet regarding the policy which should be followed. Eden and various analysts in the FO, who were worried by the Axis' expansionist policies and the consequent threat to British interests wanted to pursue a vigorous nonintervention policy in order to favour international mediation and so preclude the victory of a fascistic military regime allied to the Axis. However the majority of the Cabinet, presided over by Neville Chamberlain from 1937, did not share his concerns. Chamberlain in particular believed that in order to preserve the peace in Europe it was necessary to tolerate Italian intervention during the war and rely on the diplomacy of the pound sterling after it had finished. This could be seen in a declaration by Chamberlain to the Cabinet in March 1937 in opposition to a proposal by Eden that the British navy impose a blockade on Spain:

> It had to be remembered that we were dealing not only with the Spanish Insurgents, but, behind them, with the Germans and Italians. General Franco was not a free agent. No doubt he hoped to win, but hardly without assistance from the Germans and Italians. .. To insist up to the point proposed in the Secretary of State's Memorandum therefore, was not only useless but must lead to a very serious situation with Germany and Italy. If and when General Franco had won the Civil War, however, the situation would be very different, and no doubt he would be looking round for help from other countries besides Germany and Italy. That would be the moment at which to put strong pressure upon him ... that would be the time for action.[17]

Due to these underlying tendencies, the Spanish policy of the British Cabinet during 1937 showed ambigous and contradictory features. On the one hand, there were initiatives clearly inspired by the policy of stiff measures advocated by Eden: the establishment of a land and naval control of nonintervention; the nonrecognition of the Francoist blockade of Bilbao; and, foremost, the Nyon Conference which stopped the piratical attacks in the Mediterranean against international merchant ships (which had been the work of Italian submarines trying to blockade the Republic by sea). On the other hand, following Chamberlain's view, there was continuous tacit tolerance of Italo-German aid to Franco, a firm negative to condone any French help to the Republic and a persistent search for a way to ameliorate Anglo-Italian relations.

By February 1938, with the Nazi *Anschluss* of Austria on the horizon and Mussolini offering to begin the negotiations for an Anglo-Italian agreement, the difference of opinion between Eden and Chamberlain reached a climax. Eden, forced to resign, was replace by Lord Halifax as Foreign Secretary. From then on, the British Cabinet reinforced its pro-Francoist policy in the pursuit of a quick reconciliation with Italy. Clear proof of this was given by the fact that there was only one meeting of the NIC during the whole year. Furthermore, in order to facilitate the agreement with Italy, the British authorities actively promoted the end of the Civil War by a victory for Franco, primarily by pressing the French government to close their frontier to the transit of Soviet war material for the Republic. Mostly as a result of such pressure, by mid-June 1938 France closed its Spanish frontier and cut off the last and only channel of war supplies to the beleaguered Republic.

The Francoist authorities during the whole of 1937 and 1938 tried to ensure that Britain maintained the favourable policy of nonintervention, despite the massive intervention of the Axis powers. To do this they attempted to allay fears regarding Italo-German influence and the growing power of the Falange within the Nationalist regime. In July 1937 the Duke of Alba, well liked in British official and conservative circles partly because he possessed the title of Duke of Berwick, was sent to London as Franco's diplomatic agent. The instructions he received from Franco, which were immediately passed on to a host of official contacts (including George VI), reveal this policy:

> We have no compromise with anyone. The national character of the Movement renders absurd the idea of the cessation of part of our national territory, a feeling which the reds lack because they feel no love for the fatherland. We no longer have imperial ambitions. We only wish to reconstruct Spain with the help of England, with whom we wish to maintain our old and good friendship. ... Dividends in Spain will be good. ... There will be no concessions regarding naval bases or the passage of troops. The national character of our Movement also rules this out. ... As has always been the case every help will be given for the export of pyrites, iron, minerals, etc. ... Spain has no quarrel with England. If Bolshevism were to triumph in Spain (and then no doubt extend to Portugal) it would be as a result of Russia. In the struggle between the two ideas one has to be victorious.[18]

In similar fashion in July 1938 after British pressure had obtained the closure of the French frontier and the definitive isolation of the Republic, Franco sent a confidential personal message to Chamberlain expressing his gratitude. The conveyor of the note was Lord Phillimore, and the main point was:

> His Excellency wishes me to salute Mr. Chamberlain in his name and sincerely thank him for the friendship he has shown towards Spain, and to remind him that with his policies he is defending the same ideals and principles as us and working in the interests of world peace and civilisation.[19]

British doubts regarding the character of Francoist foreign policy were temporarily submerged during the crisis of September 1938, which would lead to the Munich Agreement and the partition of Czechoslovakia. By then the only hope of military salvation for the Republic was to link its cause to those of the Western democracies if the latter decided to confront Germany in defence of Czechoslovakia. In order to guard against this contingency, which could have snatched victory from his hands, Franco decided to anticipate events and, in a desperate attempt to separate the Spanish war from the Czech question and Nazi expansionism, proclaimed Spanish neutrality in the case of a European war. In fact, the Nationalist authorities had already concluded that the alternative of fighting on the side of the Axis against the democracies would be suicidal:

> It is enough to open an atlas to convince oneself of this. In a war against the Franco-English group one can say, without exaggerating at all, that we would be surrounded by enemies. From the first moment they would be surrounding us, on all our coasts and all our borders. We could contain them in the Pyrenees, but it would be highly impossible to prevent an invasion across the Portuguese frontier. ... Germany and Italy would only be able to offer insufficient aid to a weak Spain, and nothing they could offer us would make up for the risk of fighting on their side.[20]

Fortunately for Franco, diplomatic negotiations and the Franco-British concessions avoided the outbreak of war at the cost of the dismemberment of Czechoslovakia. Nevertheless, the Francoists' decision to declare neutrality comforted the leaders in London and Paris and accelerated the abandonment of the Republic. At the beginning of October 1938 the Duke of Alba telegraphed 'literally' the following declaration made by Lord Hailsham, Lord President of the Council:

Offer of neutrality was received with great satisfaction being communicated at the most critical moment, strengthened the position of the Prime Minister particularly in his dealings with France. That it should arrive at this time was almost a miracle.... . Cabinet would love to see the earliest possible victory for General Franco, would round off peace in Europe.[21]

In these circumstances on 27 February 1939, after the collapse of Republican military resistance in Catalonia, the British and French governments jointly recognised Franco's Administration as the legitimate government of Spain. Barely a month afterwards, the political breakdown of the Republic gave Franco an unconditional victory and put an end to the Civil War.

There is no doubt as to the decisive impact British policy had on the outcome of the Spanish conflict. Along with Italo-German aid it was one of the key factors making possible the Francoist victory and the defeat of the Republic. This was recognised by Pedro Sainz Rodríguez, a prominent monarchist leader and first Minister of Education of General Franco, in his memoirs:

Many Spaniards, disorientated by the anti-English propaganda of the Franco regime, honestly believe that we gained our victory exclusively through Italian and German aid; [I] am convinced that, though this did contribute, the fundamental reason for our winning the war was the English diplomatic position opposing intervention in Spain.[22]

Within official British circles, Sir Robert Vansittart, Chief Diplomatic Adviser to the FO, fully endorsed this assessment stating: 'the whole course of our policy of Non-Intervention – which has effectively, as we all know, worked in an entirely one-sided manner – has been putting a premium on Franco's victory'.[23] The confidential final report of the British assistant military attaché in Spain confirmed this impression without any hesitation. His words may be regarded as a fitting epitaph on the effects of British conduct during the Civil War:

It has become almost superfluous to recapitulate the reasons (for Franco's victory). They are, firstly, the material superiority throughout the war of the Nationalist forces on land and in the air, and, secondly, the qualitative superiority of all their cadres up to nine months or possibly a year ago. ... This material inferiority (of the Republican forces) is not only quantitative but qualitative as well, being also the result of multiplicity of types. However impartial and benevolent the aims of the Non-Intervention Agreement, its repercussions on the armament problem of the Republican forces have been, to say the least of it, unfortunate and, no doubt, hardly what they were intended to be. The material aid of Russia, Mexico and Czechoslovakia has never equalled in quantity or quality that of Germany and Italy. Other nations, whatever their sympathies, have been restrained by the attitude of Great Britain.[24]

Notes

1. The quote by M. Azaña is taken from an article written in 1939, in *Causas de la guerra de España*, Madrid, 1986, p. 39. General Jordana's judgement in AMAE, serie 'Archivo Renovado', file 833, box 17 (AMAE 833/17), *Apunte para la entrevista con el representante inglés*, 17 March 1938.
2. On Anglo-Spanish relations before and during the Civil War, there are two basic studies: J. Edwards, *The British government and the Spanish Civil War*, London, 1979; E. Moradiellos, *La perfidia de Albión. El gobierno británico y la guerra civil española*, Madrid, 1996.
3. E. Moradiellos, 'The Origins of British Non-Intervention in the Spanish Civil War: Anglo-Spanish Relations in Early 1936', *European History Quarterly* 21, no. 3, 1991, pp. 339-64.
4. N.H. Gibbs, *Grand Strategy*, London, 1976, vol. 1 (*Rearmament Policy*); L.W. Pratt, *East of Malta, West of Suez. Britain's Mediterranean Crisis, 1936-1939*, Cambridge, 1975; G. Schmidt, *The Politics and Economics of Appeasement. British Foreign Policy in the 1930s*, Leamington Spa, 1984; P. Kennedy, *The Realities behind Diplomacy. Background Influences on British External Policy*, London, 1981.
5. J. Coverdale, *Italian Intervention in the Spanish Civil War*, Princeton, 1975; I. Saz, *Mussolini contra la Segunda República*, Valencia, 1986; P. Preston, 'Mussolini's Spanish Adventure: From Limited Risk to War', in *Republic Besieged*, eds Preston and Mackenzie, pp. 21-52; C. Leitz, 'Nazi Germany's Intervention in the Spanish Civil War and the Foundation of HISMA/ROWAK', in *Republic Besieged*, eds Preston and Mackenzie, pp. 53-86; D. Smyth, 'Reflex Reaction: Germany and the Onset of the Spanish Civil War', in *Revolution and War in Spain, 1931-1939*, ed. P. Preston, London, 1984, pp. 243-65; R.H. Whealey, *Hitler and Spain. The Nazi Role in the Spanish Civil War*, Lexington, 1989.
6. P. Renouvin, 'La politique extérieure du premier gouvernement Léon Blum', in *Léon Blum, chef de gouvernement, 1936-1937*, ed. Fondation Nationale des Sciences Politiques, Paris, 1967, pp. 329-53; J.B. Duroselle, *La politique étrangère de la France. La décadence, 1932-1939*, Paris, 1979.
7. See Geoffrey Roberts' contribution to this present volume.
8. PRO FO371/20523, W6575, telegram from the commercial secretary at the Madrid Embassy, 21 July 1936.
9. PRO FO371/20475, W11340, *The Future of the League of Nations*, 20 July 1936.
10. PRO FO371/20570, W15925, minute by Gladwyn Jebb, 25 November 1936.
11. Quoted in T. Jones, *A Diary with Letters, 1931-1950*, Oxford, 1954, p. 231.
12. PRO FO371/20585, W15624, minute by E. Shuckburgh, 16 November 1936.
13. AMAE R834/31, memo by Ginés Vidal (Director of the European Section, MAE), 28 January 1939.
14. PRO FO371/21288, W6244, minute by Sir George Mounsey, Assistant Under-Secretary in the Foreign Office, 3 April 1937.
15. See E. Moradiellos, 'The Gentle General: The Official British Perception of General Franco during the Spanish Civil War', in *Republic Besieged*, eds Preston and Mackenzie, pp. 1-20.

16. AMAE R1061/1, note, 10 July 1937.
17. PRO CAB23/87, cabinet minutes, 3 March 1937.
18. AGA (Madrid), serie 'Asuntos Exteriores' (archivo de la Embajada española en Londres), file 7.198 (AGA 7.198), nota mecanografiada, May 1937.
19. PRO FO800/323, 12 July 1938.
20. AMAE R834/31, memo by Conde de Torrellano, *Consideraciones sobre la futura política internacional de España*, 20 May 1938.
21. AGA 6.782, telegram from Alba to General Jordana, 7 October 1938.
22. P. Sainz Rodríguez, *Testimonio y recuerdos*, Barcelona, 1978, pp. 234-5.
23. PRO FO371/24115, W973, memo by Sir Robert Vansittart, 16 January 1939.
24. PRO FO371/22631, W16269, report by Major E.C. Richards on offensive strategy in the Spanish War, 25 November 1938.

4

French Strategy and the Spanish Civil War[1]

Peter Jackson (University of Wales, Aberystwyth)

THE impact of the Spanish Civil War on France has received considerable attention from historians of the inter-war period. Scholars have explored the differences and similarities between the French and Spanish Popular Fronts;[2] they have demonstrated how the Civil War in Spain exacerbated the great ideological divide between Right and Left in France;[3] and they have traced the evolution of the French policy of nonintervention in the Spanish conflict from its beginnings in the summer of 1936 to the final recognition of the Franco regime as the official government of Spain in February of 1939.[4] What is absent from this impressive body of scholarship, however, is a thorough consideration of the impact of the Spanish Civil War on French strategy.[5]

The Civil War played an important role in the evolution of French strategic policy. It magnified concerns about France's strategic vulnerability and intensified the ideological dimension to French military planning. A visceral hostility towards the politics of the Spanish Republic, exacerbated by the fear that the Spanish revolution might spread to France, underpinned a widespread sympathy for Franco within the French general staff. This sympathy led military planners to take an unrealistic view of the potential for *rapprochement* with Nationalist Spain. On another level, the Civil War also deepened suspicions of Soviet motives and made France's military leadership more resistant than ever to political pressure to negotiate a military alliance with the USSR. The army high command clung instead to the vain hope of reviving a military alliance with Italy as a means of deterring German aggression. A gulf emerged between the views of the army leadership and the increasingly hostile attitude adopted by the government, the Foreign Ministry and the navy towards Italy. The war in Spain was thus an important factor in France's failure to respond to the international challenges of 1936-1938.

I

Any study of French strategy during the 1930s must begin with the revolution in French defence policy during the late 1920s.[6] In the decade following the Great War, French security rested on three central pillars. The first was a French military presence in the Rhineland; the second was a system of alliances with the 'successor states' of eastern Europe; and the third was a decisive military superiority over Germany. By the mid-1930s all of these foundations had either collapsed or been badly eroded. Between 1927 and 1929 the French army was reduced in size and reorganised to constitute a training cadre for the nation in arms. In 1929 France began an early evacuation of the Rhineland and a French military presence in Germany was replaced by the ramparts of the Maginot Line. Finally, the recrudescence of German military power under the Nazi regime overturned the existing balance of power. The alliances with the 'successor states' were no longer sufficient. France required a Great Power ally in order to force Germany to wage a two-front war.

But neither Britain nor the United States, France's erstwhile allies, were willing to make any commitment to fight Germany. The remaining candidates for an alliance were therefore Italy and the Soviet Union. Italy could function as a 'bridge' linking France to its allies in the east in a vast front that would encircle Germany on three sides. The Soviet Union, conversely, possessed a massive demographic and industrial base which could prove decisive in a long coalition war. Mutual assistance agreements were fashioned with both states during the mid-1930s. For the French military, however, Italy was the more attractive ally. Native hatred of Bolshevism, heightened by the antimilitarist subversion of the Communist Party in France, made the military establishment profoundly suspicious of Soviet motives. Consequently, both the army and air force embraced a full-blown military alliance with Italy but opposed high-level conversations with the Red Army. In the summer of 1935

French and Italian military leaders engaged in detailed joint planning for a war against Germany. But there was no military corollary to the Franco-Soviet Mutual Assistance Pact of 1935.

Yet after 1935 the military arrangements with Italy became increasingly divorced from reality. Mussolini's desire to establish a Mediterranean Empire led to a re-orientation of Italian policy away from France and towards Germany. This trend was hastened first by the Italian invasion of Abyssinia and then by Italian intervention in the Spanish Civil War. After 1936 the emerging Rome-Berlin Axis became the central pillar of Italian foreign policy. Franco-Italian relations, conversely, went into a prolonged decline. The Soviet Union, meanwhile, stepped up its efforts to forge an anti-German military arrangement with France. Beginning in the summer of 1936 Soviet officials made repeated requests for staff conversations. At the same time the French Communist Party sponsored an anti-fascist political coalition which championed the cause of National Defence. The accession of a Socialist-led Popular Front government in France in May of 1936 appeared to reinforce the trend toward closer relations with the USSR and mounting tension with Italy. But the French defence establishment, in particular the army general staff (which dominated strategic planning), was loathe to abandon hopes for a *rapprochement* with Italy and even more averse to a close military relationship with the Soviet Union. In fact the high command remained unwilling to envisage real cooperation with the Soviets until the spring of 1939. By this time it was too late. The USSR had changed the orientation of its policies and initiated negotiations leading to the Nazi-Soviet Non-Aggression Pact of August 1939.[7]

The Spanish Civil War coincided with a period of crisis for the French military. Throughout 1936, a succession of French governments had failed to implement a serious land or air armaments programme to match the constantly expanding rearmament effort under way in Germany.[8] As a result, when the Popular Front finally instituted a massive reequipment programme in the autumn of 1936, France's armaments and aircraft industries were in a woeful state of disrepair and utterly unable to cope with the large orders placed for material of all kinds. Huge backlogs developed and crippled the rearmament effort. All the while the gap between French and German military power widened. To make matters worse, French intelligence consistently overestimated the pace of German rearmament. The result was an atmosphere of pessimism within the French military establishment that prevailed right up to the final months of peace.

This was the strategic context when France's military leadership learned that Civil War had erupted in Spain. The attitude of the other European powers was therefore a key consideration in the formulation of French policy. Britain, true to form, assumed a position of neutrality and made its opposition to intervention by any state very clear to French officials.[9] But by the end of July it was also evident that both Germany and Italy would aid the military insurgents. In fact, the day after Mussolini decided to support Franco, French intelligence reported that the Italians were preparing aircraft to help transport the Spanish Army of Africa across the straits to the Spanish mainland.[10] Two days later the *Deuxième Bureau*, the intelligence section of the French general staff, reported the arrival of 'at least two dozen' German aircraft in Spanish Morocco on the morning of 1 August. Several weeks later the high command was informed that a new Soviet ambassador had arrived in Madrid accompanied by a military delegation.[11] In the ensuing six months the intelligence services provided detailed reports of increasing Italian, German and Soviet involvement in Spain – all in direct violation of the NIA signed by the powers in August. Military assessments of the situation warned repeatedly that the Civil War could swiftly escalate into a conflict between European Great Powers.[12]

Just as important to the evolution of policy was the dramatic impact of events in Spain on the political and social situation inside France. In July 1936, the country had just endured a bitterly contested election campaign and a wave of paralysing strikes. The elections of May 1936 had brought a Popular Front alliance of Socialists, Radicals and Communists to power under the leadership of France's first ever Socialist Premier, Léon Blum. Only days after the new regime assumed power, the country was plunged into the most intense period of social unrest since the days of the Paris Commune. Inevitable parallels were drawn with the situation in Spain. This confluence of events was particularly important in shaping the military perspective because, by 1936, the spectre of communist subversion had become an obsession for the army general staff. The wave of factory occupations in June and early July had created a revolutionary atmosphere in Paris at a time when the high command was already preoccupied with reports of an expanding network of communist cells within the army rank and file. Even more alarming were rumours of a plot to murder a select group of high-ranking soldiers as a prelude to a proletarian *coup d'état*.[13] The atmosphere was so charged that even the relatively moderate daily *Le Temps* referred to the 'revolutionary situation' in Paris and suggested that the Popular Front was 'merely a screen for the establishment of a dictatorship of the proletariat in France.'[14] Fear of imminent revolution further radicalised politics on the Right, creating reactionary tremors that reverberated within the corps of professional soldiers. It was in 1936 that an important portion of the officer corps abandoned the traditional political neutrality of the French military caste and turned their backs on the parliamentary regime of the Third Republic.[15] A network of illegal right-wing cells emerged within the officer corps. These *Corvignolles* were an antirevolutionary action group organised nation-wide to take immediate action at the first indication of a communist coup. Its membership was alleged to have exceeded 10,000 officers, all committed to using illegal means to fight 'Bolshevik subversion.'[16]

The military reaction to the war in Spain must be interpreted within the context of this antirevolutionary hysteria. It is difficult, however, to identify a 'military' point of view. Because of the ostensibly apolitical status of the army within the French State, career soldiers were reluctant to express political views either in public or in official documents. As a result, frank assessments of the situation in Spain by military officials are less common in the existing documentation. Scholars have cautioned that we remain 'short of information on the state of mind of the army' and have noted that the Chiefs of Staff were not even consulted officially before the Blum government formulated its Spanish policy.[17] Yet, while it is true that one should avoid sweeping generalisations about the attitudes of the officer corps, it is also clear that the military did have a reasonably well-defined and consistent position on the Spanish conflict. The general staff viewed the entire situation as disastrous, desired a swift resolution of the war in favour of the military *junta* led by General Francisco Franco, and was thus opposed to any intervention whatsoever on behalf of the Republic.

On 30 March 1936 General Maurice Gamelin, Commander in Chief designate of France's armed forces, received a bleak report on French army morale. In this report General Gaston Billotte lamented the disturbing lack of patriotism among incoming conscripts and stressed the alarming extent of Communist subversion among the army rank and file. These conditions were linked to a wider crisis in French society. 'Billotte is right,' Gamelin minuted on a copy of the report forwarded to Minister of Defence Edouard Daladier, 'does France want to become another Spain?'[18] Gamelin's comment, composed before the military revolt in Spain, is highly revealing. From the perspective of the homogenous and overwhelmingly conservative French officer corps, the Spanish *Frente Popular* was a revolutionary regime devoted to the complete overthrow of the existing social order in Spain. The journals and newspapers most widely read among the officer corps, *France militaire*, *Le Jour* and *L'Echo de Paris*, all openly supported the rebels. There were long-standing ties between General Franco and the French army. Franco had visited the *Ecole Militaire* at St. Cyr in 1927 and in 1928 had been awarded the *Légion d'Honneur* for his part in combined Franco-Spanish operations against Moroccan rebels.[19] It is hardly surprising, therefore, that the military press, along with the rest of the French right, hailed Franco and the Nationalists as defenders of Christian civilisation. Hundreds of articles and pamphlets, many by retired members of the high command such as Generals Curières de Castelnau, Henri Niessel and Maurice Duval, raged against atrocities committed in the Republican zone.[20] Soviet involvement on behalf of the Republicans only confirmed the prevailing view that the revolution in Spain was the first stage of a world-wide Bolshevik revolution planned and orchestrated by Moscow.[21] The insidious hand of Moscow was detected everywhere in the Republican zone. Largo Caballero was demonised as a 'Spanish Lenin' and the outbreak of the Spanish revolution was attributed to 'the arrival of sixty Jews from Moscow'.[22] Franco, conversely, was praised for having 'raised the standard of revolt against Soviet slavery'.[23] French and Spanish Communists were accused of conspiring to foment a general European war which would deflect Hitler's attention away from Russia and prepare the way for the workers' revolt.[24]

This interpretation of events in Spain was by no means limited to retired officers. There were unofficial ties between the Nationalists and active officers on Marshal Philippe Pétain's personal staff.[25] More importantly, a careful reading of contemporaneous staff appreciations reveals that these views were also common currency within the army and naval general staffs. Assessments of the situation in Spain betray a systematic bias in favour of the military insurgents. Naval intelligence judged that the Spanish Popular Front had 'fallen under the domination of extremists' who had 'installed a reign of terror in Catalonia and throughout the governmental zone.' Therefore it characterised the 'Spanish Crisis' as 'the understandable reaction of those who believed in the principle of authority against the Marxist policies of the present government.'[26] The army *Deuxième Bureau* estimated that 'the real struggle is between leftist extremists and the military which seeks to restore order in Spain.'[27] General Franco was highly regarded in both army and naval intelligence summaries as 'a dedicated and clear-headed professional' and a 'Francophile' possessed of 'immense intelligence and energy.'[28] Even the rabidly anti-French Ramón Serrano Suñer was characterised as a 'sober man of politics' who understood 'the necessity of a military action that would throttle the communist revolution.'[29] Assessments of the situation on the Republican side were similarly distorted. Although the Republican troops were praised for displaying 'courage and determination worthy of a better cause', intelligence reports and general staff appreciations characterised the Republican government as a revolutionary cabal dominated first by anarchist and later communist extremists.[30] Army intelligence judged Largo Caballero a 'revolutionary fanatic' and concluded that his successor, Juan Negrín, was 'a cipher for the Communist Party and for Moscow'.[31]

The extent of military preoccupation with imminent revolution, and the Spanish dimension to this fixation, is apparent in the 'Spanish Document Affair' in 1937. In February copies of a leaflet of instructions for staging a military putsch, translated from what was supposed to be a Russian original, was circulated to all divisional and regimental headquarters in France by Deputy Chief of Staff General Paul Gérodias. This document, which had been obtained through the clandestine ties that existed between Marshal Pétain's staff and Nationalist Spain, caused a wave of panic in military garrisons across France. There was no coup and the origins of the document, which was communicated to Gérodias by the staff of Pétain's Chief of Staff, remain mysterious. When the affair was leaked to the Press, however, it generated a predictable furore in the Chamber of Deputies, led to Daladier's decision to reassign Gérodias and created tension between Gamelin and the Defence Minister.[32]

The military attitude towards Spain was no secret. Nor should the fact that the high command was not consulted on the question of intervention surprise. There was no need to consult the military because its views were already well-known. Indeed, the intensity of these views was such that Blum feared that France was 'on the eve of a military *coup d'état*' in the summer of 1936.[33]

II

A keen awareness of France's vulnerable military situation combined with sympathy for the Nationalist rebels and fear of revolution to shape the military perspective on policy towards Spain. The military leadership viewed the coming of the Civil War as an unequivocal disaster and opposed any intervention whatsoever on behalf of the Republic. Underpinning this position was the expectation that Italian and German assistance would ensure a victory for the Nationalists and restore order to the Spanish mainland.

From the outset military observers in Spain and intelligence analysts in Paris predicted victory for Franco. The best informed French official in Spain during the Civil War was Military Attaché Lieutnant-Colonel Henri Morel. Morel was well connected within the Republican camp. He was a daily visitor to the offices of the army general staff and was also received with regularity by the highest ranking civilian leaders of the Spanish Republic, Indalecio Prieto, Largo Caballero and Juan Negrín.[34] But close ties with the Republicans did not prevent Morel from consistently forecasting their defeat. As early as 31 July Morel predicted that the material superiority of the nationalists would eventually be decisive. Once the Germans and Italians began providing substantial aid, Morel was unequivocal that the Republic could not win.[35] The *section midi* of the *Deuxième Bureau* (responsible for analysis of the situation in Spain) concurred and the strategic overviews of the army, air force and naval general staffs, as well as the Secretariat of the *Conseil Supérieur de la Défense Nationale*, were based on the hypothesis of a Nationalist victory.[36]

Despite its sympathies for Franco's cause, the high command was predictably concerned about the consequences of the anticipated Nationalist victory for France. Its chief preoccupation was not a military threat from Spain. The consensus among the attachés and intelligence departments of both the army and navy was that, once the Civil War ended, Spain would need a long time to recover its strength and would be 'absolutely incapable of supporting an external war for years to come'.[37] The real danger was that Franco would be coerced into granting the Germans and Italians air bases in the Canaries and the Balearics. Rumours that these agreements had been concluded began in early August.[38] Operating from these islands German and Italian air power could attack the vital communications between France and its African possession and seriously compromise naval operations in the Mediterranean. The strategic position of France would be gravely compromised.[39]

The Blum government had two realistic options in dealing with the Spanish problem. One possibility was to support the Republican government. This was the course favoured by an important group (initially a majority) of ministers within Blum's Cabinet and by left-wing opinion in France. The second option was a policy of absolute neutrality and strict non-intervention. This was the approach championed by the military along with the centre and the right of the French political spectrum. Intervention on behalf of the Nationalist rebels was never a realistic consideration.

From a strategic perspective, intervention, either direct or in the form of massive material assistance to the Republic, would, if successful, ensure a friendly state on France's southern flank and check the spread of fascism in Europe. But the general staff raised two important arguments against such a course of action. The first was the danger that intervention would touch off another general European war.[40] France would enter such a war deeply divided and without being able to count on the assistance of the British. Neither the French army nor the air force were in any condition to undertake a major war. Indeed, the years 1936-1938 were a period of crisis for the French military. Sharp cutbacks in military spending between 1932 and 1936 had hamstrung efforts to modernise France's land and air forces and left the defence industry in a state of utter disarray. The situation was so grave that the army's field manoeuvres were cancelled from 1935 to 1938 owing to equipment shortages and a lack of funds. The air force was in even worse shape. When the government considered war with Germany and Italy over Spain in the spring of 1938, Air Chief of Staff General Joseph Vuillemin predicted that French air power would be destroyed in a matter of days.[41] Although the pessimism of France's military leadership was based on an exaggerated assessment of German and Italian military power, it reflected the debilitating sense of vulnerability with which they viewed the prospect of a major war during this period. The danger of escalation was a powerful argument in favour of non-intervention that was emphasised repeatedly in staff appreciations throughout the course of the Civil War.[42]

To ensure that the government was absolutely clear as to the general staff's views, Army Chief of Staff Louis Colson met with Daladier on 26 July 1936. Colson left the meeting confident that he had persuaded the Defence Minister against the 'madness' of sending war material to Spain. He was right. In cabinet meetings thereafter Daladier consistently opposed large scale arms shipments to Spain.[43] Indeed, along with fears that support for the Republic would tear France apart, the danger of a general war was a central consideration in the decision for non-intervention. In mid-1936 Blum and Foreign Minister Delbos both feared that Europe was 'on the brink of war'.[44] In defending non-intervention during his famous discourse at Luna Park that September, Blum asserted that non-intervention had prevented a Franco-German war. A war, he added, in which Germany, the greater industrial power, 'would have every prospect of winning'.[45]

The second argument in favour of non-intervention developed by the army staff rested on an unduly optimistic assessment of the Nationalist attitude toward France. The high command operated on the assumption that a vibrant xenophobia would emerge in the aftermath of the Civil War to undermine foreign influence in Spain. It assumed, moreover, that this xenophobia would be directed principally against the foreign states who had intervened and profited from Spain's suffering. Intelligence assessments consistently predicted that German and Italian influence would dwindle rapidly once the rebels secured victory. According to this line of reasoning, France was actually strengthening its future position in Spain by standing aside.[46] This assumption was central to the relatively sanguine view which the general staff adopted towards the prospect of a Nationalist victory. It also underpinned the deep chagrin with which the high command viewed the policy of *non-intervention relâchée* adopted by the Blum government in the autumn of 1936.[47] A general staff assessment prepared for Daladier stressed that 'non-intervention is our best course, but to be effective it must be real.'[48] Beginning in the middle of 1937, the army went one step further to advocate a *'prise de contact'* with the Nationalists. A lengthy study of the Spanish problem at this juncture stressed that Franco and his entourage were not real fascists and that there was no evidence that any territorial concessions had been made to either Italy or Germany. The note argued that 'the situation will be grave for us only if we do not possess a means of exercising our influence when the affair is finally liquidated' and that 'what is essential is that [Franco] has expressed a desire to enter into relations with France.' The same overview lamented that these overtures had met with no response from the French government. It warned that 'with each day that the war continues German influence in Spain increases.' In order to ensure that French interests would be represented, the report concluded, 'it appears necessary to put aside our pride and make contact, by different means than those employed up to now, before it is too late.'[49] Support for such an action increased in Paris as the war dragged on. By the autumn of 1938 even the Foreign Ministry was urging the Daladier government to send official representation to Burgos.[50]

Whatever the relative merit of these arguments, ideology was at the heart of the military perspective on the Spanish Civil War. Simply put, Franco and the Nationalists were much more palatable neighbours than a regime dominated by anarchists, revolutionary socialists or communists. The growing influence of the USSR with the Republic only strengthened this conviction because the general staff was convinced that the Soviets intended to dominate Spain through the ascendant influence of the Spanish Communist Party.[51] In early 1937 the *Deuxième Bureau* reported that the Soviets had installed an extensive secret police network in Republican Spain. Communist attacks on the trotskyists and anarcho-syndicalists in Catalonia in May of 1937 appeared to confirm the impression that the Negrín government was controlled by Moscow. Another intelligence report concluded that a victorious Republican government would 'subordinate Spanish foreign policy to that of the USSR.' Spain would become 'the centre of Comintern activity in western Europe.'[52] In the view of the army general staff, intervention on behalf of the Republic would only further the cause of revolution in Europe and therefore the interests of the Soviet Union.

Just as significantly, intervention would consolidate the division of Europe into two ideologically opposed camps. It would alienate France's conservative allies in eastern Europe and, more importantly, drive Italy into the arms of Nazi Germany. France would be left on the same side of the barricades as the Soviet Union and without any guarantee of British support. The general staff viewed such a development as an unmitigated disaster. Colonel Maurice Gauché, head of the *Deuxième Bureau*, warned Daladier and the high command that Germany was using the rhetoric of anti-Bolshevism to drive a wedge between France and Italy. If this policy was successful, he warned, it would be a grievous blow to France's strategic position and would create favourable conditions for the expected German *Drang nach Osten*.[53] The irony was that, by this time, there was little French policy could do to prevent the consolidation of the Rome-Berlin Axis. Italy and Germany were determined to overthrow a system that France was equally committed to preserve. Under these conditions the 'ideological' division of Europe was all but inevitable.

The high command's opposition to intervention, and its hopes to forge a working relationship with the Nationalists once the Civil War ended, meant that no dramatic changes were made to French war plans as a result of events in Spain. Only two significant measures were adopted to envisage the possibility of war with Nationalist Spain. The first was a strengthening of the contingent along the Franco-Spanish frontier in the autumn of 1936.[54] The second was an addition to the new mobilisation *Plan E* (implemented in January 1938 to replace *Plan Dbis*) which considered a possible offensive into northern Spain.[55] Although Spanish historian Jaimé Martínez Parilla has attributed great significance to this contingency plan (*Hypothèse E*), an invasion of Spain was never a serious consideration for the French high command. In fact, before *Plan E* was even in place the operations bureau of the general staff had concluded that such an operation was unfeasible because it would require troops and equipment that could not be spared from either the German or Italian fronts.[56] Plans for an offensive into Spain were effectively abandoned. *Hypothèse E* was not even included among any of the general staff exercises conducted between 1936 and 1939.[57] Detailed plans did exist, conversely, for a move into Spanish Morocco and for simultaneous attacks on the Canary and Balearic Islands. But these measures were envisioned only within the context of a general European war in which Nationalist Spain lined up alongside the Axis.[58] In sum, plans to fight Nationalist Spain were contingencies which the general staff hoped would never be implemented. The hope was instead that the Nationalists would win the Civil War and then come to some kind of satisfactory arrangement with France. The net effect of the Civil War on French war plans, therefore, remained secondary.

From the perspective of the general staff, the policy of nonintervention was not a failure. It prevented the conflict from spreading over Europe and ensured that the revolutionary *élan* of the Spanish left was contained south of the Pyrenees. The foremost of the concerns of the high command was Franco-German military balance. By the summer of 1936 the perception was that this balance had shifted decisively in Germany's favour. Avoiding war with Germany over Spain was therefore crucial and non-intervention was successful in this regard. But events were to reveal the flaws in the general staff's view of the situation in Spain. Hopes for a swift end to the war and for *rapprochement* with Franco were to come to naught. The Civil War dragged on through 1937 and 1938. Germany became ever more deeply involved in the exploitation of Spain's natural resources. When fighting finally ceased in early 1939, the Franco regime proved haughty and little interested in improving relations with France.[59] In fact, on the eve of war in 1939 French intelligence predicted that Franco would permit the Axis to use Spanish coastal bases for naval operations against France.[60] The French army's sympathy for the Nationalist side counted for little in Franco's calculations of Spanish national interest. French planners were forced to consider the possibility of a hostile Spain throughout the period from 1936 to the liberation of France in 1944.

III

It was in the realm of grand strategic planning, however, that the Spanish Civil War had the greatest effect on French policy. Events in Spain heightened suspicions of Soviet motives and made the army leadership more reluctant than ever to renounce the possibility of resurrecting the military arrangement with Italy. From 1936 to 1938 the army continued to advocate an amelioration of relations with Italy despite clear evidence of Italo-German collusion. At the centre of this reluctance to let go of Italy was the general staff's refusal to accept the division of Europe along ideological lines. The result was a major divergence between the policies advocated by the army and those put forward by the rest of the defence establishment. The Blum government, and Air Minister Pierre Cot in particular, wanted to jettison the Italian alliance and explore the Soviet option. The Quai d'Orsay and Navy, meanwhile, wanted little to do with either the Soviets or the Italians but focused instead on the importance of British support.

The general staff had resisted the trend towards closer military ties with the Soviets from the beginning. Shortly before the government signed a mutual assistance pact with the USSR, the *Deux-ième Bureau* produced an overview which openly opposed a military corollary to this agreement. The USSR was termed 'incapable of playing a significant military role at the outset of hostilities'. The study also suggested that the first priority of Soviet policy was to foment a general European war:

> We would certainly give more than we would receive in such a contract, concluded with an unreliable partner who would be liable to involve us in an adventure and then abandon us. ... Under these conditions an alliance is scarcely tempting.[61]

The army staff used these arguments to resist increased pressure from the new Popular Front government to enter into high-level military conversations with the Soviets during late 1937 and early 1938.

The USSR's involvement in the Spanish Civil War only reinforced military preconceptions about the insidious nature of Soviet policy. The predominant view within the army general staff was that the overriding objective of Soviet policy in Spain was to incite a war between

France and Germany.[62] This is clear from the celebrated report of Deputy Chief of Staff General Victor Schweisguth in the autumn of 1936. Upon his return from representing the French army at the Red Army manoeuvres in September, Schweisguth warned that the chief objective of Soviet policy was to incite a war between liberal and fascist capitalism. The Soviets were therefore 'exploiting events in Spain, pushing France toward dangerous provocations *vis-à-vis* Germany' with the hope that another world war would erupt. The USSR could then stand aside from such a conflict and emerge 'the arbiter of a drained and exhausted Europe'.[63] Schweisguth's report received wide distribution within the foreign policy and defence establishment and became the centrepiece of the arguments raised by the Ministry of Defence against high-level staff talks with the USSR.

The conviction that the Soviets were interested only in fomenting another world war endured through 1938. An intelligence summary circulated to the entire high command at this juncture (when Soviet interest in Spain was in reality waning) asserted that 'in order to understand the motives for Soviet involvement in Spain one must remember Lenin's principle that "the Soviet regime cannot subsist without developing its influence abroad."'

The *Deuxième Bureau* also warned that the USSR was behind the Negrín government's attempts to turn the Civil War into a Europe-wide conflict and that:

> The defeat of General Franco would open the door to communism in Spain. ... Will [the communists] be able to retain power? No. But it would take only a few months for such a regime to precipitate a general European war.[64]

The refusal of the French general staff to accept the ideological division of Europe is nowhere better illustrated than in these assessments. There is little difference between these estimates and the propaganda campaign mounted against the Spanish Republic by Italy and Germany. Significantly, this interpretation was contradicted by the assessments forwarded to Paris by the military attaché. Morel doubted Spain would ever serve as a bulwark of the international communist revolution. 'The Spanish are not ideologues,' he argued in May of 1937, 'ideology is only a façade. They are a people of instinct who will grow weary of the Red Flag and of Bolshevik demagoguery.'[65] But Morel's views failed to have any influence on the general staff. The conviction that world revolution was the foremost objective of Soviet foreign policy was too firmly entrenched within the high command to be dislodged by attaché reports.

Assessments of Italian intentions were sanguine by comparison. Army officials, in particular, were reluctant to accept the slow death of the Franco-Italian alliance and the emergence of the Rome-Berlin Axis. In September of 1936, for example, the *Deuxième Bureau* stressed that fundamental differences remained in the way of a full-blown military alliance between Germany and Italy. It judged that 'Italy remains attentive to the danger of a German push into central Europe and will retain complete freedom of action.' Hence the necessity to limit the damage done by French sanctions and by the Spanish Civil War to Franco-Italian relations. 'The timing appears propitious,' the study concluded, 'for a *rapprochement*.'[66]

The military was deceiving itself in its hope to revive the military alliance with Italy. Refusal to accept the division of Europe into ideological blocs had imbued army staff assessments with an air of unreality. Franco-Italian relations deteriorated steadily from 1936 to the spring of 1939 while at the same time the Rome-Berlin Axis emerged as a force in international politics. A steady stream of reports of meetings between German and Italian military officials arrived from Berlin and from Rome.[67] From November 1936 to October 1938 there was neither a French ambassador in Rome nor an Italian ambassador in Paris. During this period repeated violations of the NIA (in particular the 'pirate' submarine campaign during the summer of 1937), Mussolini's visit to Germany in September and, most importantly, his placid acceptance of the *Anschluss* in March of 1938, all suggested that Italy had moved into the German orbit.[68]

Any hope of reversing this trend would have required tacit cooperation in Mussolini's efforts to destroy the Spanish Republic. Whatever the views of the high command, this was a price the Popular Front governments of Blum, Chautemps and Daladier refused to pay. Instead a vibrant Italophobia emerged within the Foreign Ministry to reinforce the hard-line adopted by the government. The NIA had been conceived within the Quai d'Orsay and Delbos, along with the Secretary-General, Alexis Léger, and the Political Director, René Massigli, bitterly resented Mussolini's open mockery of this accord. Hence while the Foreign Ministry advocated a resolutely neutral stance toward the war in Spain, it also sponsored a hard-line attitude in the Mediterranean. Delbos, Léger and Massigli pressed for an Anglo-French seizure of Minorca as a bulwark against the further extension of Italian power into the western Mediterranean.[69]

This policy received enthusiastic support from the naval staff. The navy was less sensitive to the implications of a military arrangement with the Soviets and more concerned with the consequences of Italian naval rearmament for French power in the Mediterranean. Under the direction of Admiral Darlan French naval policy had assumed a distinctly anti-Italian orientation.[70] Advocates of a hardline against Italy gained an important adherent in Defence Minister Daladier. In meetings of the *Comité Permanent de la Défense Nationale* in November and December 1937, Daladier emphasised the danger of Italian expansionism and argued that the Mediterranean theatre must become a central factor in French strategic planning. Noting that Italy was the vulnerable half of the Rome-Berlin Axis, he argued that 'France must be prepared to pursue the defeat of Italy as a matter of first urgency.'[71]

Yet through 1937 and 1938 the army continued to cling almost pathetically to the hope that Italy could be detached from Berlin. Secret intelligence work against the Italians resumed only in August of 1937 – long after it became clear that Italy was spying on France.[72] In the spring of 1938 an eloquent plea for the resurrection of the Franco-Italian alliance emanated from the Military Cabinet at the Ministry of Defence. Colonel Buisson, former chief of the planning section of the general staff, warned that:

> There is only one way to halt [Germany] militarily and that is to reforge the circle of friendly states from England to Poland passing through Italy ... WE MUST RECREATE THE PARIS-ROME AXIS ... No matter what the price of an accord with Rome, it will never be too expensive.[73]

It was not until late 1938, when Italy officially renounced the Franco-Italian accords and launched a violent campaign of territorial claims on French Somaliland, Tunisia, Corsica, and even Nice, that the army planning staff finally relinquished its hopes to reconstitute the military alliance with Italy.[74]

The army was reluctant to take this step because Italy was central to its plans for war against Germany. In April 1936, for example, a strategic overview characterised Italian support as 'indispensable' to any plans to oppose German *Drang nach Osten*.[75] Italian involvement in the war against Spain made little difference to this conviction. In December of 1936 the planning section of the general staff bluntly observed that:

> Italian hostility, or even doubtful neutrality, makes it impossible for France to intervene effectively in central Europe to cement an inter-allied front on the eastern and southern borders of Germany.[76]

This conviction was behind the high command's frustration with the slow deterioration in Franco-Italian relations. This frustration is clearly evident in one of General Schweisguth's lectures to the *Collège des Hautes Etudes Militaires* in November 1936 and April 1937. Discussing the possibility of direct French support for France's allies to the east Schweisguth observed that 'everything depends on the attitude of the Italians'. He lamented, however, that this was a reality 'that statesmen and journalists who talk enthusiastically about "collective security" and "mutual assistance" do not wish to comprehend.'[77]

This interpretation of the relative merits of an Italian versus a Soviet alliance endured through the autumn of 1938. In the spring of that year, Blum returned to power and reopened the debate over intervention in Spain at a time when Czechoslovakia was threatened with military aggression from Germany. In policy discussions at this critical stage, the army high command consistently played down the potential contribution of the USSR to an anti-German coalition and emphasised the strategic importance of Italy. According to the *Deuxième Bureau*, the execution of Marshal Tukhachevski and the bulk of the Russian officer corps had left the Red Army 'no more than a decapitated corpse'. Nor was the Soviet air force judged capable of effective intervention in a European war.[78] Behind these analyses of the effectiveness of the Soviet armed forces was the same deep mistrust of Soviet motives. Daladier expressed this suspicion clearly during the debate over intervention in Spain in March of 1938:

> Such an intervention, not motivated by new developments, risks leaving us alone before Germany and Italy without any assurance of British assistance and with only the mediocre aid of a Russia that is far off and weakened.[79]

Significantly, at the same juncture, General Gamelin stressed that the prospective attitude of Italy must be 'decisive' to any French decision for war.[80]

It was not until December of 1938 that this view of the relative importance of Italy and the USSR came under serious reconsideration within the army staff. By this time Soviet involvement in Spain had all but ceased and the victory of the Nationalists was virtually assured. This is an important point which further demonstrates the links between internal politics and French military attitudes towards an alliance with the USSR. In the autumn of 1938 the Daladier government, in an effort to 'restore the authority of the state', had destroyed the Popular Front coalition and moved decisively to the right of the political spectrum.[81] With the possibility of a revolutionary regime south of the Pyrenees removed and danger of communist subversion at home less acute, the army general staff was more amenable to the 'realist alternative' of an alliance with the Soviet Union. In a wide-ranging survey of the European balance of power in late 1938, intelligence chief Colonel Gauché observed that the USSR was 'the sole military power capable of intervening effectively in the east'.[82] This conviction underlay the urgency with which French officials sought to obtain Soviet participation in an eastern front during the spring and summer of 1939. In war plans drafted in the spring of 1939, the USSR was to function as the arsenal of the projected *barrière à l'est*. It was to supply the Poles, Romanians, Yugoslavians and Turks with the war material they desperately required but could not obtain from France.[83] These efforts to include the Soviets in France's new eastern policy was to end in frustration and failure in Moscow the following August with the signing of the Nazi-Soviet pact of nonaggression.

IV

The prevailing view within the military towards events in Spain was perhaps best summarised by Gamelin when he admitted that 'in their hearts and their heads our soldier's sympathies favoured Franco.'[84] A closer look at the role of the Spanish war in the making of French policy illustrates the central place of ideology in French military planning during this period. Fear of revolution, hatred of the Comintern and mistrust of the Soviet Union were greatly exacerbated by events in Spain. These attitudes were central to the military's perspective on the international situation and underpinned the general staff's opposition to intervention in Spain as well as its refusal to explore the option of a Soviet alliance.

The course of French strategic policy from 1936 to 1939 marked a slow evolution away from reliance on Italy and towards a military alliance with the Soviet Union. The war in Spain acted as an important brake on this process and opened up a gulf between the positions assumed by the army on the one hand and the rest of the defence establishment on the other. The resulting disarray ensured that, when Hitler implemented the aggressive phase of his foreign policy, France was without a coherent strategic plan to resist German aggression. Decision-makers felt compelled to cleave to Britain, to embrace appeasement and to take the road that led to humiliation at Munich.

Notes

1. The author would like to thank Martin Thomas and Larry Black for their helpful comments on this essay.
2. See, for example, the excellent collection of essays in Martin Alexander and Helen Graham (eds), *The French and Spanish Popular Fronts: Comparative Perspectives*, Cambridge, 1989; and Helen Graham and Paul Preston (eds), *The Popular Front in Europe*, London, 1987; see also David W. Pike's contribution to this present volume.
3. See especially David W. Pike, *Les français et la guerre d'Espagne, 1936-1939*, Paris, 1975; José Borrás Llop, *Francia ante la guerra civil española: burguesia, interés nacional e interés de clase*, Madrid, 1981; and Joel Colton, *Léon Blum: Humanist in Politics*, New York, 1966, pp. 234-69.
4. The best accounts of the decision for nonintervention are in Julian Jackson, *The Popular Front in France: Defending Democracy*, Cambridge, 1988, pp. 201-209; Pierre Renouvin, 'La Politique extérieure du premier gouvernement Léon Blum', in *Léon Blum: Chef du gouvernement*, eds René Rémond and Pierre Renouvin, 2nd edn, Paris, 1981, pp. 329-62; Jean-Baptiste Duroselle, *Politique étrangère de la France: la décadence*, Paris, 1979, pp. 301-305 and 315-21; Daniel Cordier, *Jean Moulin: L'inconnu do Panthéon*, vol. II, *Le choix d'un destin*, Paris, 1989, pp. 41-57; and John Dreifort, *Yvon Delbos at the Quai d 'Orsay: French Foreign Policy during the Popular Front*, Kansas, 1973, pp. 31-54.
5. Jaime Martínez Parilla, *Las fuerzas armadas francesas ante la guerra civil Española (1936-1939)*, Madrid, 1987, focuses on French military policy towards Spain but does not consider the relationship between the Civil War and French preparations for war. Nor is this question addressed in either Charles Bloch 'Les relations franco-allemandes et la politique des puissances pendant la guerre d'Espagne', or Hans-Henning Abendroth, 'Deutschland, Frankreich und der spanische Bürgerkrieg, 1936-1939', both in *Deutschland und Frankreich, 1936-1939*, eds Klaus Hildebrand and Karl Ferdinand Werner, Munich, 1981. For limited discussions of Spain in French policy-making, see Martin Thomas, *Britain, France and Appeasement. Anglo-French Relations in the Popular Front Era*, Oxford, 1996, chap. 3, pp. 89-114; Henry Dutailly, *Les problèmes de l 'armée de terre française, 1935-1939*, Vincennes, 1980, pp. 25-114; Robert J. Young, *In Command of France: French Foreign Policy and Military Planning,1933-1940*, Cambridge, MA, 1978, pp. 138-9; Anthony Adamthwaite, *France and the Coming of the Second World War*, London, 1979, pp. 42-5; and Nicole Jordan, *The Popular Front in Central Europe: Dilemmas of French Impotence, 1918-1940*, Cambridge, 1992, pp. 309-310.
6. On French strategy and diplomacy during the 1920s, see Maurice Vaïsse (with Jean Doise), *Politique étrangère de la France: Diplomatie et outil militaire, 1871-1991*, Paris, 1992, pp. 324-62; and Judith Hughes, *To the Maginot Line: The Politics of French Military Preparation in the 1920s*, Cambridge, MA, 1971.
7. See also Geoffrey Roberts's contribution to this present volume.
8. On the politics of rearmament in France during the 1930s see Robert Frankenstein, *Le prix du réarmement français, 1935-1939*, Paris, 1982; and Martin Alexander, *The Republic in Danger: Maurice Gamelin and the Politics of French Defence, 1935-1940*, Cambridge, 1993.
9. See Enrique Moradiellos's contribution to this present volume.

10. SHAT, Carton 7N 2521, Compte-rendu des renseignements, 27 July 1936. On Mussolini's decision see Paul Preston, 'Mussolini's Spanish Adventure: From Limited Risk to War', in *Republic Besieged*, eds Preston and Mackenzie, pp. 21-50.

11. SHAT, 7N 2757, 'Liaisons journalières avec les Affaires Etrangères: 1936 – Guerre d'Espagne', 29 August 1936.

12. See the weekly intelligence reports in cartons 7N 2513 and the *comptes-rendus* in 7N 2521 and 7N 2757. See also military attaché reports for this period from Spain (7N 2753-2754), Italy (7N 2907-2908) and Germany (7N 2597-2598). See also Glyn Stone, 'Britain, France and the Spanish Problem, 1936-1939', in *Decisions and Diplomacy: Essays in Twentieth Century International History*, eds D. Richardson and G. Stone, London, 1995, pp. 129-52.

13. AN, *Papiers Schweisguth*, 351 AP 3, Dr. 9, 'Mémento', 25 June 1936, and Dr.10, 'Mémentos', 22, 30 October and 21, 30 November 1936. See also Maurice Gamelin, *Servir*, vol. II, *Le prologue du drame, 1930-août 1939*, Paris, 1946, pp. 220-1; and Martin Alexander, 'Soldiers and Socialists: The French Officer Corps and leftist goverment, 1935-1937', in *The French and Spanish Popular Fronts*, eds Alexander and Graham, p. 76.

14. *Le Temps*, 5 June 1936 cited in Paul-Marie de la Gorce, *The French Army: A Military-Political History*, London, 1963, p. 169.

15. On this question see P.C.F. Bankwitz, *Maxime Weygand and Civil-Military Relations in Modern France*, Cambridge, MA, 1967, pp. 267-89; de la Gorce, *The French Army*, pp. 241-68; and Jacques Nobécourt, *Une histoire politique de l'armée*, vol. I, *De Pétain à Pétain 1919-1942*, Paris, 1967, pp. 231-69.

16. On the *Corvignolles* see Georges Loustanau-Lacau, *Mémoires d'un Français rebelle*, Paris, 1994 reprint, pp. 89-124; J.R. Tournoux, *L'histoire secrète*, Paris, 1962, pp. 25-110 and Bankwitz, *Weygand*, pp. 267-72. Loustanau-Lacau was Pétain's Chief of Staff and the central organiser of the *Corvignolles* network.

17. Jean Lacouture, *Léon Blum*, Paris, 1977, p. 357. This conclusion is endorsed by Martin Alexander in 'Soldiers and Socialists', p. 72 and Martínez Parilla, *Las fuerzas armadas francesas*, pp. 91-2. On the failure to consult the Chiefs of Staff see Young, *In Command of France*, pp. 138-9.

18. SHAT, 7N 4034-1, 'Etat d'esprit de l'armée', 1 April 1936. I am grateful to André Lambelet of the University California at Berkeley for drawing my attention to this document.

19. Paul Preston, *Franco: A Biography*, London, 1993, pp. 56 and 65.

20. There is a good discussion of the attitudes of retired officers towards affairs in Spain in Borrás Llop, *Francia ante la guerra civil española*, pp. 213-22; and Martínez Parilla, *Las fuerzas armadas francesas*, pp. 91-114. See also Charles Micaud, *The French Right and Nazi Germany*, New York, 1943.

21. On Soviet intervention in the Spanish Civil War see Geoffrey Roberts's contribution to this present volume.

22. Cited in de la Gorce, *The French Army*, pp. 238 and 240-1.

23. *L'Echo de Paris*, 26 August 1936.

24. H. Haywood Hunt, 'The French Radicals, Spain and Appeasement', in *The French and Spanish Popular Fronts*, eds Alexander and Graham, p. 46.

25. On this question see Martínez Parilla, *Las fuerzas armadas francesas*, pp. 119-23 and 184-91; Pike, *Les Français et la guerre d'Espagne*, 296-7; and Preston, *Franco*, p. 312.

26. SHM, Carton 1BB2, 91, *Bulletin de renseignements*, 21 July-4 August 1936.

27. SHAT, 7N 2762-2, 'L'influence soviétique en Espagne', 10 March 1938.

28. SHAT, 7N 2759-3, 'Situation en Espagne nationaliste', 17 September 1936; and SHM, 1BB2, 91, *Bulletin de renseignements*, 21 July-4 August 1936.
29. SHAT, 7N 2761-l, 'Personalités du nouveau ministère nationaliste espagnol', 9 February 1938 and 'La situation politique en Espagne franquiste et la constitution d'un veritable Ministere par le General Franco', 16 February 1938.
30. SHM, 1BB2, 91, *Bulletin de renseignements*, 4-18 August 1936.
31. SHAT, 7N 2759-2, *section midi* synthesis of 13 November 1936 and 7N 2761-4, 'Rapport sur M. Negrín', 22 February 1937 [erroneousy dated 1936]. The latter report referred to 'Soviet technicians' who controlled the secret services of the Negrín government and excercised a reign of terror throughout the Republican zone.
32. See Gamelin, *Servir*, II, pp. 259-61; Bankwitz, *Weygand*, pp. 267-8, Martínez Parilla, *Las fuerzas armadas francesas*, pp. 120-3; and Dutailly, *Les problèmes de l'armée de terre française*, pp. 277-8.
33. Blum in *Le Populaire*, 15 October 1945 and 19 July 1950, cited in Joel Colton, *Léon Blum*, pp. 264-5.
34. On Lieutnant-Colonel Morel see Dominique de Corta, *Le rôle de l'Attaché militaire français pendant la guerre civile espagnole*, Paris, 1981; and Martínez Parilla, *Las fuerzas armadas Francesas*, pp. 66-8 and 93-7.
35. See DDF, 2ème série, III, doc. 54, Morel to Paris, 31 July 1936 and 350, Morel to Paris, 14 October 1936. See also SHAT, 7N 2754-3, Morel to Gauché [Chief of the *Deuxième Bureau*], 8 August 1936, Morel to Gauché 18 September 1936 and 'Conséquences possibles d'un victoire des rebelles', 26 September 1936. Morel's reports through 1939 are in SHAT, 7N 2759-2760. See also Thomas, *Britain, France and Appeasement*, chap.3.
36. See, for example, SHAT, 7N 2522-1, 'La situation politique et militaire de l'Europe', 4 June 1937; 1N 43-3, 'Note sur la situation militaire actuelle dans la monde', 29 March 1938; 2N 224-1, 'Répercussions de la situation internationale', Daladier to Premier Chautemps, 1 February 1938 and 2N 224-1, 'Note sur l'évolution du problème militaire français', 27 July 1938. On the naval side see SHM, 1BB2, 203, 'Note pour le Ministre', 4 November 1936; 1BB2, 180, 'Politique Navale', 20 January 1938. For a sampling of air staff appreciations see SHAA, Carton 1B 5, *Conseil Supèrieur de l'Air*, 7, 9 and 15 March 1938.
37. SHAT, 7N 2755-2, Morel to Paris, 11 June 1938. See also 7N 2761-1, 'Armée nationaliste espagnole', 15 March 1938; 7N 2761-1, 'Situation financière en Espagne nationaliste', 24 January 1938; 7N 2758-3, 'Note sur les possibilités de l'armée nationaliste à la date du 5 février 1939'.
38. French Naval Chief of Staff François Darlan alluded to these rumours repeatedly in his interview with British First Sea Lord Alfred Chatfield in London on 5 August. The *compte-rendu* of this meeting is in DDF, 2ème série, III, doc. 87, 'Entretiens franco-britanniques du 5 août 1936'.
39. For a sampling of army general staff concerns see SHAT, 7N 3421, 'Note sur les conséquences possibles des événements d'Espagne au point de vue des opérations', 10 September 1936; 7N 2757-2, 'Note au sujet des conséquences stratégiqes d'un succès du Général Franco', 15 March 1938 and 2N 227- 1, 'Note sur l'importance stratégique de l'Espagne', 24 April 1938. For the perceptions of the naval planning staff see SHM, 1BB2, 184, 'Note pour le Ministre', 13 February 1937 and 1BB2, 180, 'Politique navale', 20 January 1938. See also Martínez Parilla, *Las fuerzas armadas francesas*, pp. 131-99; Young, *In*

Command of France, pp. 137-9; René Sabatier de Lachadenède, *La Marine française et la guerre d'Espagne*, Vincennes, 1993, pp. 87-94; and Glyn Stone, 'The European Great Powers and the Spanish Civil War, 1936-1939', in *Paths to War*, eds R. Boyce and E.M. Robertson, London, 1989, pp. 220-2.

40. See, for example, SHAT, 7N 2513, *Rapport hebdomadaires* for 21 July-4 August and 11-17 August 1936; 7N 2513, 'Note sur les événements en Espagne (semaine de 3 au 10 août)'; 7N 2521, 'Résumé des principaux événements politiques du mois de juillet 1936', 5 August 1936; SHM, 1BB2, 91, *Bulletins des renseignements* for 21 July-4 August and 4-18 August 1936; 7N 3421, 'Note sur les conséquences possibles des événements d'Espagne au point de vue des opérations', 10 September 1936.

41. On French rearmament and military effectiveness before the Second World War see especially Frankenstein, *Le prix du réarmement français*; Alexander, *The Republic in Danger*; and Vaïsse, *Diplomatie et outil militaire*, pp. 363-414.

42. See the docments cited in note 39 above as well as SHAT 7N 2522-1, 'Note au sujet de la possibilité d'un conflit en Europe', January 1937; 7N 2522-1, 'Réflexions sur un conflit éventuel en Europe', 9 March 1937; and Martínez Parilla, *Las fuerzas armadas francesas*, pp. 96-137.

43. For Daladier's views on the Spanish question see Elisabeth Du Réau, *Edouard Daladier*, Paris, 1993, pp. 192-7 and Angel Viñas, 'Las relaciones hispano-franceses, el Gobierno Daladier y la crise de Munich', in *Españoles y franceses en la primera mitad des siglo XX*, Madrid, 1986, pp. 161-201.

44. Cited from the exposé by Delbos to the Chamber Foreign Affairs Commission in AAN, Commission des Affaires Etrangères, Seizième Législature, Delbos audition, 3 February 1937.

45. Cited in Renouvin, 'La politique extérieure du premier gouvernment Léon Blum', *Léon Blum*, eds Rémond and Renouvin, p. 331; and Bloch, 'Les relations franco-allemandes', pp. 433-4.

46. SHAT, 7N 2754-3, 'A propos des troupes étrangères en Espagne', 12 December 1936; 'Conséquences possibles d'une victoire des rebelle', 26 September 1936; 7N 2756-1, 'Note au sujet de la situation politique', 22 June 1938 and 'Note au sujet de l'influence soviétique en Espagne', 7 October 1938.

47. The policy of 'elastic' nonintervention was adopted after it became clear that the Germans, Italians and Soviets were intervening with impunity. The best account is in Cordier, *Jean Moulin*, II, pp. 43-62.

48. SHAT, 7N 2758-3, 'Note concernant l' évolution de la politique des National-istes espagnols à l'égard de la France et de l'Allemagne', no date but certainly spring or summer 1937; see also 7N 2755-2, Morel to Paris, 11 June 1938.

49. SHAT, 7N 2758-3, 'Note concernant l'évolution de la politique "National-istes" espagnols à l'égard de la France et de l'Allemagne', no date but certainly May-June 1937. This argument was taken up again on two further occasions in general staff summaries of the Spanish problem which appeared in 1938 and 1939; see 7N 2758-3, 'Note sur la situation en Espagne', 10 October 1938 and 7N 2761-2, 'Propagande en Espagne', undated but certainly early 1939.

50. ANMAE, *Papiers 1940: Cabinet Bonnet*, vol. 1, 'Espagne: le retrait des volon-taires et l'octroi de la bélligerence', 19 November 1938. This document is also in SHAT, 7N 2757-3. The memo noted that France, Lithuania and the USSR were the only three states without plans to send official representatives to Franco. See also Viñas, 'Las relaciones hispano-francesas', pp. 198-9.

51. SHAT, 7N 2521, 'Résumé des principaux événements politiques du mois d'Août 1936', 3 September 1936; 7N 2762-2, 'Ingérence russe en Espagne', 11 August 1936; 'Le parti communiste espagnol et les événements d'août', 8 September 1936.

52. For the (accurate) conclusion that the Soviets dominated internal security within the Republic see SHAT, 7N 2762-2, 'Organisation du service de renseignements russe à Barcelone', 22 December 1936; 7N 2762-2. 'Influence russe en Espagne gouvernementale', 13 January 1937; 7N 2762-2, 'Action soviétique: officielle et occulte', 21 January 1937. For assessments of the events of May 1937 see 7N 2762-2, 'Influence et attitude soviétique vers les événements de mai', 11 June 1937 and 7N 2760-1, 'Situation intérieure en Espagne gouvernementale', 22 June 1937.

53. SHAT, 7N 2522-1, 'Note au sujet de la possibilité d'un conflit en Europe', January 1937 and 'Reflexions sur un conflit éventuel en Europe', 9 March 1937.

54. SHAT, 7N 3603, 'Nos plans d'après guerre: Plan D*bis*', no date; Dutailly, *Les problèmes de l'armée de terre*, pp. 102-107; and Martínez Parilla, *Las fuerzas armadas francesas*, pp. 159-72.

55. SHAT, 7N 3714, 'Note sur le Plan E', 10 January 1938; see also 7N 3714, 'Note sur les bases du Plan E', 25 August 1937 and Dutailly, *Les problèmes de l'armée de terre*, pp. 102-107.

56. SHAT, 1N 47-2, 'Note sur les opérations offensives en Espagne', 29 September 1937. For the place of these plans in French grand strategy see SHAT, *Fonds Georges*, 1K 95-4, 'Réflexions concernant la politique de guerre de la France', 20 November 1937 and 2N 224-l, 'Mémento sur la conduite générale de la guerre', Gamelin to Daladier, 15 March 1938.

57. The staff excercises for this period can be consulted in SHAT, 1N 59-62; 1N 68-70 and 1N 76. See also Dutailly, *Les problèmes de l'armée de terre*, pp. 105-106.

58. These operations would be undertaken by colonial forces primarily from French Morocco. See SHAT, 7N 3421-l, 'Note sur la défense du Maroc en cas d'hostilité espagnole', 18 December 1936; 7N 3909, 'Instruction personelle et secrete pour le cas "Plan opération Maroc"', 22 March 1937. The question of operations against various Spanish territories was also discussed at length in the *Conseil Supérieur de Guerre*. See, for example, SHAT, 7N 3909, 'Problème espagnol', 30 January 1937. For the views of the naval planning staff see SHM, 1BB2, 170, 'Mémento', 16 November 1937.

59. For French anxieties over German economic activity in Spain see SHAT, 2754, 'Emprise allemande en Espagne', 17 December 1936; 7N 2758-3, 'Note concernant l'évolution de la politique des Nationalistes espagnols a l'égard de la France et de l'Allemagne', no date; SHM, 1BB2, 91, *Bulletin de Renseignements*, 8 October-8 November 1937. On German economic relations with Spain see Christian Leitz, *Economic Relations between Nazi Germany and Franco's Spain, 1936-1945*, Oxford, 1996; and Robert H. Whealey, *Hitler and Spain. The Nazi Role in the Spanish Civil War*, Lexington, 1989. For the Nationalist attitude towards France in the spring and summer of 1939 see Preston, *Franco*, pp. 327-35. See also Martin Alexander's contribution to this present volume.

60. SHAT, 7N 225-2, 'Procès-verbal de la réunion des Chefs d'Etat-Major Généraux', 11 April 1939.

61. SHAT, 7N 2520-2, 'Note sur les avantages et les inconvenients de l' alliance russe', 24 April 1935. The attitude of Britain strengthened this opposition. The British Government was clearly opposed to a Franco-Soviet military alliance

and warned of the damage such an agreement would do to Anglo-French relations; see Martin Thomas, *Britain, France and Appeasement*; and Alexander, *The Republic in Danger*, pp. 296-7.

62. On Stalin's intentions see Geoffrey Roberts's contribution to this present volume.

63. The original Schweisguth report is in Daladier's papers: AN, 496 AP 7, Dr. 5, sdr b, 'La rapport Schweisguth', September 1936. Excerpts of the report are published in DDF, 2ème série, VIII, doc. 343. For further discussion of the role of this report in the evolution of Franco-Soviet relations see Dutailly, *Les problèmes de l'armée de terre*, pp. 54-6; Young, *In Command of France*, pp. 146-7; and Duroselle, *La décadence*, pp. 140-1.

64. SHAT, 7N 2762-2, 'L'influence soviétique en Espagne', 10 March 1938.

65. SHAT, 7N 2755-1, 'Situation militaire fin mai', 29 May 1937. See also 7N 2754-1, 'Les influences étrangères en Espagne', 26 September 1936; 7N 2754-2, Morel to Paris, 12 December 1936; 7N 2756-1, 'Note au sujet de la situation poliaque', 22 June 1938 and 'Note au sujet de l'influence soviétique en Espagne', 7 October 1938.

66. SHAT, 7N 2598, 'Note sur l'attitude actuelle de l'Italie', September 1936. See also SHAA, 2B83-2, 'Note sur la situation de l'armée italienne', 26 September 1936.

67. AN, *Papiers Schweisguth*, 351 AP 3, 10 June 1936; SHAT, 7N 2514, *Rapport hebdomadaire*, 1-14 February 1937 and 7N 2599, 'Note sur l'attitude actuelle de l'Italie', September 1936.

68. Standard accounts of Franco-Italian relations during this period are in Duroselle, *La décadence*; William Shorrock, *From Ally to Enemy: the Enigma of Italy in French Diplomacy*, Ohio, 1985; and Robert Young, 'French Military Intelligence and the Franco-Italian Alliance, 1933-1939', *Historical Journal* 28, no. 1, 1985: 143-68. On French military reactions to the 'pirate' submarine affair see de Lachadanède, *La Marine française*, pp. 133-45.

69. ANMAE, *Papiers Massigli*, vol. 17, Massigli to Léger, 20 September 1937: 'Conversation de M. Yvon Delbos et de M. Eden de 20 septembre 1937'; DDF, 2ème série, VI, doc. 465, 'Analyse d'une conversation entre MM. Eden et Delbos le 17 septembre 1937'; and ANMAE, *Papiers Massigli*, vol. 14, 'Mesures à envisagée en cas d'échec de la négociation avec l'Italie sur le retrait des volontaires', 7 October 1937.

70. On this question see the important article by Reynolds Salerno, 'The French Navy and the Appeasement of Italy, 1937-1939', *English Historical Review* 112, 1997: 66-104.

71. The *procès-verbaux* for these meetings are in DDF, 2ème série, VII, docs. 223 (3 November) and 325 (8 December).

72. AN, *Papiers Schweisguth*, 3S1 AP 3, 3,7,8,26 May and 4, 6 August 1937. For contemporaneous reports on closer ties between Germany and Italy see SHAT 7N 2530-2, 'Note sur l'attitude de l'Italie', 11 April 1937 annd 7N 2522, 'Compte-rendu des renseigements', 16 June 1937.

73. SHAT, 5N 579-1, 'L'Alliance France-Italie', 13 March 1938, (capitalisation in the original). See also 7N 2522-l, 'La situation politique et militaire de l'Europe', 4 June 1937; and Young, 'French Intelligence and the Franco-Italian Alliance', pp. 163-5.

74. See the following strategic overviews, SHAT, 7N 2524-1, 'Le problème militaire français', draft of an exposé given to the Senate Army Commission, 13 January 1939; 7N 3439-l, 'Etude du problème stratégique à la date du 10 avril

1939', 15 April 1939. See also 7N 3434-3, 'Etude des données et du problème stratégique d'ensemble', 31 March 1939.

75. SHAT, 7N 2521-6, 'Note sur les conséquences à tirer de la renunciation par l'Allemagne du traité de Locarno', 8 April 1936. The following month Gamelin, in fact, approved a plan to send an expeditionary force across Italy to the Balkans: 7N 3449-l, 'Note sur la composition du Corps expéditionnaire et ses conséquences pour l'armée des Alpes', 20 May 1936. See also an untitled note on this subject by *3ème Bureau* Chief Lieutnant-Colonel Buisson, 26 June 1936.

76. SHAT, 7N 3434-1, 'Note sur la situation militaire française face à une coalition de l'Allemagne et de l'Italie', 10 December 1936.

77. AN, *Papiers Schweisguth*, 351 AP 7, Dr. 3, 'Conférence au C.H.E.M.', 20 April 1937.

78. SHAT, *Fonds Gamelin Supplementaires*, Carton 7, Vuillemin to Gamelin, 29 August and 16 September 1938. These dossiers have not been released for public communication by the Ministry of Defence.

79. DDF, 2ème série, VI, doc. 446, *Procès-verbal* of the meeting of the *Comité Permanent de la Défense Nationale* of 15 March 1938.

80. SHAT, 5N 579-6, 'Information du Président', 15 March 1938.

81. On the shift to the right in the domestic policies of the Daladier government see du Réau, *Daladier*, pp. 254-354. See also the essays in René Rémond and Janine Bourdin (eds), *Edouard Daladier, chef du gouvernement* and *La France et les Français en 1938-1939*, Paris, 1977 and 1978 respectively.

82. SHAT, 7N 3056-2, 'Considérations sur la constitution d'un bloc oriental', 28 December 1938. Professor Duroselle has defined a military pact with the USSR as the 'realist alternative' to French policy in *La décadence*, pp. 91-2, 104-112. Significantly, the last period where the general staff considered seriously the possibility of an alliance with the USSR was under the conservative Doumergue government in 1934 (with ardent anti-communists Barthou and Pétain as Foreign Minister and War Minister respectively).

83. On the resurgent importance of an eastern front in French strategic planning see my 'France and the Guarantee to Romania, April 1939', *Intelligence and National Security* 10, no. 2, 1995: 242-72; and Talbot Imlay, 'How to Win a War: Britain and France Prepare for War with Germany, 1938-1940', (PhD diss., Yale University, 1997). Recent literature on negotiations for a Triple Alliance includes Michael Carley, 'End of the "Low Dishonest Decade": Failure of the Anglo-Franco-Soviet Alliance in 1939', *Europe-Asia Studies* 45, no. 2, 1993; and Geoffrey Roberts, 'The Alliance that Failed: Moscow and the Triple Alliance Negotiations, 1939', *European History Quarterly* 26, no. 3, 1996: 383-414.

84. Cited in Alexander in Alexander and Graham, eds, *The French and Spanish Popular Fronts*, p. 73.

5

Soviet Foreign Policy and the Spanish Civil War, 1936–1939*

Geoffrey Roberts (University College Cork)

History... is often simpler than the historians make it.[1]

Introduction

NO FOREIGN state was more involved in the Spanish Civil War than the Soviet Union. From the outset of the conflict, Moscow was the main international champion of the Republican cause. The USSR supplied food, medical supplies and arms[2] to the Republican Government. Some 2,000 Soviet 'volunteers' (combatants, as well as military advisers and security agents) served in Spain. In the NIC established by Britain and France, Soviet diplomats struggled valiantly for policies and agreements which would hamstring Italo-German aid to Franco. In a massive solidarity campaign, the Communist International mobilised its forces in support of Republican Spain, including the organisation of the nearly 40,000 volunteers who fought in the International Brigades.[3]

From autumn 1936 Soviet involvement in the Civil War rapidly grew into a pervasive political and military presence in Spain. One of the main conduits of Soviet involvement was the PCE, which with Moscow's aid quickly became a dominant force in the Republican camp. Although Soviet personnel in Spain were given strict instructions not to interfere in Spanish internal affairs, this admonition quickly broke down in practice, and as the war progressed and the Republican position worsened, Moscow itself took to playing a more and more direct role in decision making.[4] There were many negative effects of such interference – not least, Moscow's promotion of a civil war within the Civil War against leftist and anarchist groups – but without the backing of the USSR it is doubtful that the Republican regime would have survived for as long as it did.

The Historiography of Soviet Intervention in Spain

Historical treatments of the Soviet role in Spain fall into three main categories. First, works by writers from within the communist tradition whose main theme is a defence of Soviet policies and actions. Their argument is that Soviet support for the Republic was an act of democratic, anti-fascist internationalist solidarity. The context of this support was the Soviet Union's commitment to collective action against fascist aggression and expansionism and the politics of the popular front – the communist policy during the 1930s of defending democracy and constructing broad-based people's alliances for social progress and socialism. Both the Soviets and the communists, the argument goes, did what they could to defend the Spanish Republic, but in the end the balance of international forces – Italo-German intervention and Anglo-French appeasement – favoured Franco. Such arguments were, of course, the mainstay of the Soviet and communist standpoint while the Civil War was being fought.[5]

The views expressed in the second category of historical treatments of Soviet policy and Spain also derive ultimately from arguments current at the time. These are works, mainly focused on the domestic politics of the Civil War, which endorse one or other version of the contemporary left-wing critique of Soviet foreign policy. The common thrust of this argument is that Soviet policy was driven not by a disinterested internationalism, but by diplomatic and political calculations extraneous to the Civil War struggle.[6] Views differ as to the precise character of these calculations, but all critics emphasise the primacy of Soviet state interests in determining Moscow's policy towards Spain. Perhaps the most popular interpretation in this vein is that Soviet policy was heavily influenced by the desire to avoid antagonising Britain and France, with whom the USSR was seeking a united front against Hitler. Hence, it is said, there was a Soviet policy of giving just enough aid to keep the Civil War going but not enough to secure a Republican victory – which would have complicated relations with the Western powers. This view is sometimes linked to the suggestion that Stalin, in prolonging the Civil War, was hoping to precipitate an Anglo-French clash with Germany and Italy. Yet other historians emphasise the impact of Soviet domestic politics on Moscow's policy; for example, Stalin's fear that a successful revolution in Spain could threaten his own power in the USSR; the need to appease radical opinion in the communist movement at home and abroad; a split in the Soviet Communist Party between 'isolationists' and 'revolutionary internationalists'. In any event, the critics are united by the supposition that behind Soviet involvement in the Civil War lay sinister and machiavellian motives and manoeuvres, including a fundamentally counter-revolutionary orientation within Spain. It is a view popularised by Orwell's *Homage to Catalonia* and, more recently, in Ken Loach's film *Land and Freedom*.[7] It is also endorsed by some textbooks on the Civil War. For example, Martin Blinkhorn argues that the political price of Soviet aid was

> acceptance of Communist leverage within Republican Spain, and all that this proved to carry with it: interference in the composition of cabinets and the formulation of strategy; the reversal of social revolution; the persecution of political enemies; and steadily declining popular morale. Soviet aid was never intended in any case to equip the Republic for victory, so much as to enable it to resist until the Spanish war became part of a more general conflict in which Britain and France would join the Soviet Union in fighting European fascism. Once the Munich Agreement of October 1938 appeared to dash any such prospect, Stalin lost interest in Spain and help for the by then desperate Republic dried up. The Soviet Union proved an unreliable friend.[8]

More than one echo of this leftist-inspired critique may be found in the third category of historical works: the specialist literature on Soviet diplomacy during the Civil War.[9] However, while these detailed reconstructions of Moscow's policy show that the pro-Soviet interpretation of its Civil War intervention is too complacent and simplistic, they also demonstrate that those who accept the leftist version of events are at best ill-informed and at worst indulge in sheer fantasy. The picture drawn in these specialist works is that Soviet policy was complex, contradictory and uncertain, driven as much by circumstances as anything else, and contained elements of genuine idealism and altruism as well as self-interest.

The present article is located in this historical, as opposed to political-polemical, tradition. It will examine, first, the circumstances and motives of the Soviet commitment to Republican Spain; second, the strategic character of Soviet and Comintern policy in Spain; and, third, the general impact on Soviet foreign policy on the course and outcome of the Civil War as one of the critical events in pre-war international relations. A number of differences with other interpretations of Soviet policy and Spain will become apparent, but it may be useful to highlight here two general points of critique of much of the existing literature.

First, there is the neglect of the role and importance of ideology. This article emphasises that in this particular episode in the history of Soviet foreign policy, *ideology mattered*. By and large Soviet and Comintern policy towards Spain was what it was said to be and its ideological and political inspiration was transparent in public pronouncements on the subject. To give just one example, the repression of POUM and the murder of Nin cannot be understood outside of the belief and discourse that 'Trotskyism' in Spain really was part of an international fascist bloc and conspiracy directed against the USSR. Such a belief was, of course, fantastical, but very real was its effect of exacerbating local conflicts with POUM and the anarchists and encouraging murderous solutions to internal political problems within the Republican camp.

Second, there is a failure to appreciate, as A.J.P. Taylor (quoting Maitland) famously said, that events in the past were once in the future. The script of the story of Soviet intervention in Spain was written as it happened. How Moscow reacted to events was informed by various strategic purposes – anti-fascism, collective security, popular frontism, the priority of defending and building socialism in the USSR – but much of what it did was contingent, immediate and unconnected to as yet unformed motives in a developing and changing scenario. As David Cattell, the author of the still classic *Soviet Diplomacy and the Spanish Civil War*, argued 'a historian looking back over events encounters the danger of reading into facts future motives of which the participants were not yet aware.'[10] Of course, in succumbing to this temptation historians are only replicating what participants themselves typically do, i.e., read back their current motives and future intentions into the past. In the case of the Spanish Civil War Moscow's cumulative and retrospective account of its involvement in Spain was that it formed part of a grand struggle and strategy in defence of peace, democracy and collective security. There is much truth in this, but Soviet policy was also a series of improvisations and adaptations whose outcome was indeterminate and whose result could have been a radically different story. Historians, however, can only tell the story that actually happened.

Soviet Intervention: Beginnings and Motivation

The first reports on the military revolt in Spain began to appear in the Soviet press on 20 July 1936. While these reports were confused and contradictory, the overall impression was of a Republican government embattled, but not fatally threatened. This picture, which was reinforced by reports from other sources,[11] had a crucial bearing on the initial diplomatic response of the USSR to the outbreak of the Civil War. Believing that the Republican government had the resources easily and quickly to put down the military mutiny, Moscow's immediate concern was the potential impact on the internal balance of forces in Spain of foreign intervention on behalf of the fascist generals.

On 5 August Payart, the French Chargé in Moscow, approached the Soviet Government with a proposal for a non-intervention agreement between Britain, France, Germany, Italy and the USSR. Moscow agreed to the proposal the same day, demanding, in addition, that outside aid to the rebels should be stopped and that Portugal should also adhere to the agreement.[12] In a letter to Shtein, the Soviet Ambassador in Rome, on 7 August Krestinsky, Litvinov's deputy, made it clear that the reason for the USSR's adherence to the NIA was to deny the Italians and Germans a justification for their own intervention in Spain. However, Krestinsky was sceptical that the French initiative would come to anything and expected Italian and German aid to the rebels to continue.[13]

Two important points need to be made here. First, the view that Soviet participation in the NIA was motivated primarily by a desire to keep in step with French and British policy on Spain is inaccurate.[14] The immediate and continuing motive, and aim, was to help the Republic. Secondly, when Moscow agreed to the French proposal, it had no idea or expectation that Germany, Italy and Portugal would formally commit themselves to non-intervention. When this happened, a temporary tactical expedient began to assume a different character. Faced with the choice of breaking ranks on non-intervention – and thereby opening the way for even greater and more overt Italo-German aid to Franco – or with attempting to make the agreement work, the Soviets predictably chose the latter.

On 23 August the USSR reaffirmed its commitment to non-intervention[15] and in September joined the newly-established NIC, which began meeting in London on 9 September. In a telegram to Kagan in the Soviet embassy in London (Ambassador Maisky was on holiday in the USSR) on 2 September Litvinov stated that: 'guiding our relationship to the Spanish events is a striving in every possible way to impede the delivery of weapons to the Spanish mutineers and the necessity of strictly curtailing the activities of countries such as Germany, Italy and Portugal.'[16] A month later Kagan received a letter, from Krestinsky, reinforcing the prime directive that the NIA must be made to work in practice. In addition, Krestinsky was scathing about Britain and France which, he said, had established the NIA in order to provide a legal cover for denying aid to the Madrid government and had no intention of exposing the interventionist activities of Germany, Italy and Portugal. He also pointed out that the Republican government was not so much concerned with denying aid to Franco as with securing supplies for itself.[17]

In this letter Krestinsky was signalling an important shift in Soviet policy on non-intervention in Spain. On 7 October the Soviets stated to the NIC that, in view of continuing violations of the agreement by Germany, Italy and Portugal, the USSR would consider itself free of its own obligations under the agreement should these violations not cease.[18] On 23 October this was followed by a further statement – that the USSR would bind itself to non-intervention only to the extent that other parties to the agreement did so.[19]

By this time, of course, the USSR had begun supplying arms to the Republicans. Indeed, the timely arrival of Soviet weaponry (and the International Brigades) played a crucial role in saving Madrid from Franco's forces in November 1936. There were three staging posts on the road to Soviet military aid to the Republican government. First, the beginning in July 1936 of communist and Soviet political mobilisation in support of Republican Spain. This took the form of articles and editorials in the Soviet and communist press, anti-fascist demonstrations and declarations, and, particularly in the USSR, a mass campaign to collect money to buy food and medical supplies for Republican Spain.[20] There has been some speculation about the provenance of this solidarity campaign and its co-ordination (or lack of) with the drift of Soviet diplomacy towards non-intervention, but what happened was, in the Soviet context, perfectly natural and predictable and there is no convincing evidence that it constituted a challenge to the official state policy or revealed internal divisions over Spain. It was simply a case of the traditional dualism and division of labour in Soviet foreign policy. Narkomindel diplomacy, on the one hand; communist agitation, on the other. But with the common aim of bolstering the Republican position.

Second, there was the dispatch to Spain in August 1936 of various Soviet military and political representatives and agents. This included the establishment of Soviet diplomatic missions in Madrid and Barcelona and the appointment of Marcel Rozenberg as the first Soviet ambassador to Spain, who presented his credentials on 31 August 1936.[21] Until this point no Soviet decision on military aid had been taken – despite deep and open misgivings about the NIA in the Russian and Comintern press.[22] But that does not mean that the idea of military aid had not been under active consideration. Krestinsky had alluded to the possibility (and difficulty) of military aid in his letter to Shtein on 7 August and, as Litvinov reported to Rozenberg, 'the question of aid to the Spanish Government was discussed by us many times, but we came to the conclusion that it was impossible to supply such aid from here.'[23]

The third stage was a decision in September 1936 to commence military supplies to Spain. This decision, it seems, followed the receipt in mid-September by the Soviet politburo of a plan to aid Spain drawn up by the defence ministry and the NKVD. The plan was approved on 29 September 1936.[24] The first shipload of Soviet arms arrived in Spain aboard the *Komsomol* on 15 October.[25]

The specific reasons (and evidence) for this shift in Soviet policy remain opaque, but they are not hard to guess at. First, it was evident that Italo-German intervention in Spain was continuing apace and the NIA was going to do nothing to stop it. Secondly, military aid was what the Republican government wanted and needed. Thirdly, the logistical and financial feasibility[26] of such aid had been demonstrated. Fourthly, the timing of the decision must have been connected with the receipt of reports from newly arrived Soviet military and diplomatic personnel in Spain, and, also, with the return (at the end of September) to Moscow from vacation of Stalin and Molotov.

The decision to supply arms was not publicised and neither did the Russians ever directly admit that their aid to Spain went beyond food and medical supplies. But the USSR's new interventionist stance was clearly signalled by the publication of a telegram from Stalin to the central committee of the PCE on 15 October:

> The workers of the USSR are doing no more than their duty in giving the help they are able to give to the Spanish revolutionary masses. They are well aware that the liberation of Spain from the oppression of the

Spanish reactionaries is not merely the private business of the Spaniards, but the common cause of all advanced and progressive mankind.[27]

With the decision to send arms the main lines of Soviet state policy during the Spanish Civil War were established. On the one hand, to aid a Republican military victory over Franco; on the other hand, to work within the NIC to contain and curtail Italo-German support for Franco.

Where do collective security and relations with Britain and France fit into this policy picture? Obviously, the USSR had a strategic interest (as did France and Britain) in preventing the establishment of an Italian and German-sponsored fascist regime in Spain. Equally, Moscow would have dearly loved to co-operate with Britain and France against Franco, Mussolini and Hitler. Clearly, there was a danger that Soviet intervention in Spain would precipitate (as it did) a competition with Germany and Italy that the USSR could not hope to win. Undoubtedly, the Soviet leadership had no desire to see the Civil War expand into a full-scale international conflict. Their priority was building socialism at home, not military adventures abroad. All these factors were part of the influences and constraints that constituted the context of Soviet policy towards Spain. But to suggest, as many authors do, that maintaining good relations with Britain and France was an important factor in Moscow's strategic and diplomatic calculations is to completely misunderstand the character and orientation of Soviet foreign policy in this period.

When the Spanish Civil War broke out, the mid-1930s Soviet drive for collective security had already passed its peak. That had been reached in May 1935 with the conclusion of mutual assistance pacts with France and Czechoslovakia. However, these pacts were a second-best alternative to the all-embracing collective defence agreement in Europe which the Soviets hoped for when they embarked on their collective security crusade in 1933-4. In many ways the pact with France was a purely political device designed to avert a Franco-German alignment. Moscow strove to cement its political and military relationship with France, but with no success – despite the election in May 1936 of the Popular Front government. The Soviets also worked hard to improve relations with Britain, but again to no avail. Nor were the Russians impressed with the Anglo-French performance in the League of Nations during the Abyssinian crisis of 1935, or when Hitler remilitarised the Rhineland. The view from Moscow was dominated by signs of Anglo-French appeasement and the ever-present spectre of a four-power pact between Britain, France, Germany and Italy that would exclude the USSR from the counsels of European great power diplomacy.[28]

In truth, cuddling up to Britain and France was the last thing on the Soviet diplomatic agenda in summer 1936. Moscow was disillusioned with collective security, suspicious and hostile towards Britain and France, and, if anything, in an isolationist mood. This orientation in Soviet relations with the Western powers was radically reinforced by the Spanish events. Relations with Britain and France deteriorated even further as a result of Moscow's intervention in the Civil War and its obstreperous activities in the NIC. Moreover, apart from a desire to avoid a break with Britain and France that could have damaged the Republican cause, there were no signs in Moscow of any qualms about the negative diplomatic consequences of its Spanish policy. This much was evident from Litvinov's spectacular public mockery and denunciation of the policy of non-intervention – a major theme of his speeches in the period 1936-38.[29] In private there was the same talk of Anglo-French perfidy in relation to Spain and other countries. This is not to say that the Soviets were completely undiplomatic and tactless in their dealings with the British and French over Spain. Moscow pursued various courses of action designed to convince and persuade London and Paris to change their non-interventionist policies, and frequently urged Madrid to pursue similar tactics. But in general the Soviet stance in relation to Britain and France was critical and confrontational on the issue of Spain, with instances of conciliation and appeasement notable by their relative absence.

The counterpart of Moscow's cavalier concern for Anglo-French sensibilities was its attitude towards relations with Germany and Italy. Before the Civil War there were some signs and hopes for an improvement in Soviet relations with the two states – which were dramatically dashed in the summer of 1936.[30] But Moscow's willingness to sacrifice faint possibilities of a *rapprochement* with the Axis powers is of less significance than its predisposition to risk an escalating international conflict with them over Spain. The key point here was the Soviet belief that the way to deal with the fascist powers was to stand up to them. In the face of a strong stand and the deployment of countervailing power, said Litvinov and other Soviet spokesmen,[31] Germany and Italy would back away from their expansionist and aggressive aims and policies. In the context of this belief the risks of a confrontation with Germany and Italy over intervention in Spain were not as great as they appeared. Soviet confidence in this respect was reinforced by a firm conviction that the USSR was strong enough to defend itself from attack, if necessary alone.

But counterbalancing the triumphalism and intransigency of Moscow's Spanish policy were a series of practical considerations constraining the Soviet intervention in Spain. For a start there was the inhibiting effect of the NIA. Having adhered to the agreement and become enmeshed in the work of the NIC it was difficult for the Soviets to extricate themselves. Maisky and Kagan strove to turn the committee into a collective security agency – a mechanism of collective action to stop foreign intervention in Spain – but without success. The NIA was a voluntary agreement which depended on individual restraint and consent to commonly agreed policies. In this latter regard, the committee's record was a dismal one. All schemes to control foreign intervention collapsed. The Nyon agreements of September 1937, which did stop Italian attacks on neutral shipping, were negotiated outside the framework of the NIC. The same applied to the withdrawal of foreign volunteers, which, in any case, only took place (in mid- to late- 1938) when the committee had effectively ceased to function. Yet Moscow persisted with its participation in the NIC until the very end of the Spanish Republic in March 1939.[32] Apart from the hope that some good might come from the work of the committee, there was the reason given by Litvinov to the Soviet leadership in October 1937 for staying in: 'our participation in the London committee has from the very beginning caused France, and especially England, much embarrassment, preventing them from deceiving public opinion and making difficult an internal deal with Germany and Italy.'[33] This last point was underlined in a telegram from Maisky to Litvinov in March 1938. If the Soviet Union left the NIC, that would leave the way open for a four-power agreement on Spain excluding the USSR.[34]

A second practical constraint on Soviet intervention in Spain was that it was not the only item on Moscow's foreign policy agenda during this period. For a time in 1936-7 the Spanish events were the number one priority of Soviet foreign policy. But they were not the only priority and from the end of 1937 other developments pressed their claim for attention – further Japanese expansion into China, the *Anschluss*, the all-consuming Czechoslovakian crisis of 1938. This was of some significance given the centralised nature of Soviet foreign-policy decision making. According to M.T. Meshcheryakov, 'practically no question on Spain was decided without [Stalin's] participation'.[35] Moreover, until 1939 foreign policy was a matter of secondary concern for Stalin and the top Soviet leadership (of which Litvinov was not a member). Their priorities lay in the domestic sphere – with the five-year plans and with internal social and political problems. Although Stalin maintained a keen interest in Spanish affairs and contributed to many specific decisions on the political conduct of the Civil War,[36] it is likely that once a general policy and a level of intervention and aid were established, they were maintained on an everyday basis by a combination of inertia and neglect. From the Soviet leadership's point of view this was no crime. What consumed their time and attention was more important than anything else – for the USSR, for Spain, for the international workers' movement, for the whole of humanity. As Marcelino Pascua, the Spanish Ambassador in Moscow, observed:

> The present policy of the USSR is dominated by the idea of the socialist construction of this country... the socialist construction of the USSR absolutely predominates over everything else not only as the current task, but also as decisive for the future of socialism. This is ... the axis of the question as regards the Soviets.[37]

With their overriding commitment to building socialism in one country the Soviets had no compunction about making the Spaniards pay for their aid, even if that meant using up Spain's gold reserves.[38] Nor were they happy with the loss of vital war materials – whether it be because of capture or destruction by the Nationalists or wastage in pursuit of a lost cause.

A final restraint on Soviet intervention in Spain was not so much practical as ideological. The role of the Soviet state was conceived primarily in terms of countering Italo-German intervention and mitigating the deleterious effects of Anglo-French policy. Soviet state intervention, however, could not win the Civil War. That outcome would be determined by the internal military and political struggle. The most important contribution the Soviet Union could make to a Republican victory was not as a state but as a bastion of the revolutionary movement. In this role the USSR, together with the Communist International and the PCE, would intervene in the Civil War in the form of proposing, shaping and helping to implementing an appropriate political and military strategy for victory. From the Soviet and communist point of view no greater aid could be rendered to the Spanish people.

Soviet and Comintern Strategy in Spain

The main agency of Soviet and Comintern strategy in Spain was the PCE, whose policies were formulated in the organisational framework and under the guidance of the Communist International in Moscow. Soviet control (far from absolute and unilateral) of the policy of the Comintern was secured by CPSU representatives in the higher organs of the Communist International and by regular meetings and contacts between Dimitrov and Stalin and other Soviet and Comintern leaders.

The main lines of PCE policy during the Civil War are well known: to win the war against Franco; to maintain the Popular Front alliance between the Left and the Republican parties; to carry out a number of measures of democratic and social reform, but to resist attempts to implement a socialist revolution in Republican Spain; to strengthen communist leadership and representation of oppressed classes and groups; and to make a contribution to the international struggle against fascism, including the defence of the Soviet Union against capitalist-imperialist threats and aggression.

PCE strategy in Spain was a specific application of the popular front policy endorsed by the Seventh World Congress of the Comintern in July to August 1935.[39] Indeed, it was under the auspices of this policy that the PCE abandoned its sectarian and ultra-revolutionary policies of the early 1930s and agreed to enter a reformist electoral alliance with the socialist and republican parties. The PCE's participation in this alliance, which resulted in its winning sixteen seats in the February 1936 elections, was the first major breakthrough for bolshevik communism in Spain.[40]

Under the policy of the popular front the communist parties had two major political tasks. First, the forging of anti-fascist alliances to defend bourgeois democracy and working class liberties, including the political freedom of the left and the labour movement. Second, the building of popular coalitions for social progress, radical reform, and the extension of working-class power. Whether or not this dual strategy constituted a set of tactics applicable only in a pre-revolutionary period in which the threat of fascism loomed large or a distinct democratic and populist alternative to revolution and socialism Russian-style remained obscure in the 1930s. Only later, in the 1940s, did the international communist movement (with Moscow's blessing) move towards a more explicit embrace of national-popular alternatives to the Soviet model of revolution and socialism.[41] However, in their application of the Popular Front policy to Spain the

Comintern and the PCE came very close to such a radical innovation in the traditional politics of the communist movement.

Even before the outbreak of the Civil War the characteristic lines of communist policy in Spain were being formulated in Moscow. In a speech to the Comintern secretariat on 21 February 1936 Dimitrov emphasised the need to strengthen the democratic Republic in Spain and to support the Azaña government against reaction and counter-revolution.[42] This defensive stance was reaffirmed at a series of Comintern secretariat and presidium meetings between 20 and 26 May. Dimitrov, in particular, stressed the threat of fascism and counter-revolution and the task of completing the bourgeois-democratic revolution in Spain, rather than aiming at a rapid transition to a socialist revolution. Dimitrov's intervention, it seems, carried the authority of Stalin and was very much aimed at the over-optimistic reports of Spanish representatives in the Comintern about revolutionary prospects in Spain. The theme of consolidating what had been gained as a result of the Popular Front victory rather than pushing ahead with more radical measures was continued in Comintern secretariat resolutions on Spain in June 1936.[43]

On 24 July the Comintern secretariat issued its first post-mutiny directive to the PCE. The party was advised to concentrate all its efforts on defending the Republic and defeating the military revolt. On the question of PCE participation in government the Comintern's advice was to do so only if it would aid the Republican cause. This was in line with the Comintern's existing policy that the question of the participation of the communists in the Popular Front government would be 'decided in accordance with the interests of the popular front in the struggle against Fascism and counter-revolution.'[44]

The Comintern's next major consideration of events in Spain was at a series of secretariat and presidium meetings held between 17 and 19 September 1936. Perhaps the most important practical decision was that on 19 September to establish the International Brigades. In policy terms the most important development was Dimitrov's redefinition of the political aim of the Civil War as not just a defence of the democratic republic, but a fight for 'a special state with a genuine people's democracy. It will not yet be a Soviet state, but it will be an anti-fascist Left-wing state, participated in by genuine Left elements of the bourgeoisie.' This new, democratic state, said Dimitrov, would be one in which the popular front was of decisive importance and one in which production would be under the control (if not the ownership) of the working class and its allies. It would be 'a special form of the democratic dictatorship of the working class and peasantry'.[45]

A month later Togliatti, in a widely-published article on the 'Specific Features of the Spanish Revolution',[46] provided more policy detail and theoretical flesh for the Comintern's emerging conception of the events in Spain. The struggle in Spain, argued Togliatti, contained features of a national-revolutionary war – for national independence from German and Italian fascism and for the liberation of Catalonia, Galicia and the Basques. The Civil War was a national revolution, a people's revolution and an anti-fascist revolution which was anti-reaction, anti-feudal and aimed at completing the bourgeois-democratic revolution in Spain. Among the peculiar features of this bourgeois-democratic revolution was the cross-class character of the alliance that was carrying it through under conditions of Civil War – the working class, elements of the peasantry and the urban petty-bourgeoisie, sections of the liberal bourgeoisie, and oppressed national groups. Within this alliance the working class, because of its role in the Popular Front and its contribution to the military struggle, was, under the leadership of the PCE, striving for and achieving its hegemony. However, this latter process was complicated by the role of social democracy in the working-class movement and the mass influence of anarcho-syndicalism in Spain. In the struggle for a Popular Front military victory and for the completion of the bourgeois-democratic revolution a new type of democratic republic was being created in Spain. This new democratic republic would, concluded Togliatti, provide the basis for 'further economic and political conquests by the working people of Spain'.

What the Comintern's strategy for Spain meant in practice was summarised in the PCE's December 1936 manifesto on the Civil War, endorsed by the Comintern presidium on 28 December: popular anti-fascist unity in defence of the Republic; subordination of everything to the needs of the military struggle; military, political and economic discipline of the republican forces; nationalisation of industry and land reform only to the extent required by the war effort; and an active struggle against enemies and saboteurs of the Popular Front within the Republican camp.[47] Comintern-PCE strategy and policy in Spain developed and changed as the Civil War progressed,[48] but its basic thrust – mobilisation for military victory as both a precondition and a foundation for some kind of people's democratic republic – remained intact.

Some historians characterise Comintern-PCE policy as 'counter-revolutionary' and perceive a link between communist resistance to radical transformations in the Republican zones and Soviet state and political interests. Certainly, Moscow was fully behind the PCE's efforts to dampen and repulse the revolutionary ardour (some would say excesses and atrocities) of some sections of the Spanish working class and peasantry. Indeed, on one famous occasion Stalin himself intervened directly in Spanish internal affairs in order to urge a moderate political course on the Republican government. In his letter to Largo Caballero of 21 December 1936 Stalin advised the Spanish premier on a whole series of moderate measures designed to win over the peasantry, the petty and middle urban bourgeois and international public opinion to the side of the Republic.[49] Whatever the merits of such advice compared to a more militant socialist strategy, its inspiration, like that of the Comintern's strategy, was clear: to secure a Republican victory in the Civil War it was necessary to maintain broad-based popular unity, even if that meant compromises with pro-capitalist interests and political forces in Spain.

The ideological and political commitment to a Popular Front strategy in Spain was also at the root of the PCE's and the Comintern's most infamous 'counter-revolutionary' action: the anti-Trotskyist campaign and the repression of POUM. Typically, the crisis and conflict in the Republican camp which climaxed in the civil war within the Civil War in Barcelona in May 1937 has been seen as a tragic example of the export to Spain of the internal politics of Stalin's terroristic campaign in the USSR against Trotskyists and other supposed enemies of the people. What was exported to Spain, however, was not just an aspect of Soviet internal politics, but an ideological conviction that Trotskyism was a real, fascist-inspired counter-revolutionary threat to socialism in the USSR and to the socialist movement abroad.[50] Because of this conviction, which was widely-shared (or, at least, *spoken*) in the communist movement, the campaign against what was considered to be the disguised fascist threat of Trotskyism was an integral part of the Popular Front strategy, in Spain and elsewhere.

Most striking about the Comintern press in 1936-7 is its domination by two *intertwined* issues: the Spanish struggle and the campaign against counter-revolutionary Trotskyism. For example, here is Dimitrov's defence of the August 1936 show trial of Kamenev, Zinoviev and others:

> It was clearly proved that Trotsky, Zinoviev and their gang stood on the other side of the barricades, in the same camp as those who are fighting

against the Spanish people, sending airplanes, weapons and munitions to the rebel generals, and carrying on counter-revolutionary intervention in Spain. ... The trial of the terrorists, agents of fascism, is an integral part of the anti-fascist struggle of the international working class. True solidarity with the Spanish people is not compatible with the protection of the agents of fascism in other countries. One cannot sincerely support the Spanish people ... and at the same time play the part of the protector of the terrorist rabble in the Soviet Union which is helping fascism. Whoever supports counter-revolutionary terrorists in the USSR, directly or indirectly, is, at bottom, serving the ends of Spanish fascism, disrupting the fight of the Spanish people and facilitating the latter's defeat.[51]

In one of many such directives, on 27 December 1936 the Comintern instructed the PCE that 'the final destruction of the Trotskyists must be achieved, exposing them to the masses as a Fascist secret service carrying out provocations in the interests of Hitler and General Franco, attempting to split the Popular Front, conducting a slanderous campaign against the Soviet Union, a secret service aiding Fascism in Spain.'[52]

The virulence of this anti-Trotskyist invective was underpinned by another deeply felt communist ideological conviction of this period: the belief that nothing was more important – not Spain or any other struggle – than the defence of the USSR and its actions. Here is Dimitrov again, writing in November 1937:

In the present international situation there is not, nor can there be any other, *more certain criterion*, than one's *attitude* toward the Soviet Union, in determining who is the *friend* and who the *enemy* of the cause of the working class and socialism, of determining who is a *supporter* and who an *opponent* of democracy and peace. ... You cannot carry on a real struggle against fascism if you do not render all possible assistance in the strengthening the *most important buttress* of this struggle, the Soviet Union. ... You cannot be a *real friend* of the USSR, if you do not condemn its enemies – the Trotsky-Bukharinite agents of fascism.[53]

Moscow had no need to insist that the Comintern, the PCE and other communist parties subordinate their interests to the goals of the Soviet state. They did it for themselves, willingly and usually with enthusiasm, because they believed that anti-fascism, revolutionary struggle and defence of the socialist USSR constituted a unity. Spain, indeed, was from the Soviet-Communist perspective a graphic illustration of that unity. The defence of the Spanish Republic was a goal that united and served the interests and aspirations of the PCE, the Comintern and the Soviet state. There were tensions and differences when it came to the particularities and the practicalities of policy, but these were of a minor order compared to the strategic design, ideology and political conceptions that inspired and guided the communist component of the Civil War struggle.

Spain and Soviet Foreign Policy

What was the impact of the Spanish events on the course of Soviet foreign policy? A common suggestion in this regard is that the failure of the collective security approach in relation to Spain was an important contributor to the subsequent abandonment of that policy. Faced with a major policy failure in Spain, disillusioned by Anglo-French appeasement there and elsewhere, Moscow turned in 1939 to an isolationist pact with Nazi Germany. All this is true, but only partly so.

The Soviet commitment to the collective security strategy was, in fact, tenacious enough to overcome even the disappointments and frustrations of the Spanish affair (and, for that matter, Munich, too). This was because the collective security perspective was based on the idea that the objective interests of Britain, France and other states required (sooner or later) an alliance with the Soviet Union against Germany. Moscow took hope, too, from perceived divisions within British and French politics between appeasers and anti-appeasers. So, although Spain precipitated and reinforced a major deterioration in Soviet relations with the Western powers, the goal of an anti-Hitler international front remained central to Moscow's foreign policy outlook. Indeed, in the very days of the Spanish Republic's final collapse the Soviets were moving towards their most important collective security initiative of the whole decade. This was the attempted negotiation in April to August 1939 of a triple alliance with Great Britain and France.[54]

Despite the demise of the Republic, the Spanish background was far from being irrelevant to the outcome of the triple alliance negotiations. A major reason for the failure of the negotiations was Soviet suspicion that the British and French were not serious about standing up to Hitler. The experience of appeasement, in the Spanish case among others, dominated Soviet perceptions of Anglo-French proposals and actions during the course of the negotiations. Moscow feared that London and Paris were tempted by another non-intervention policy – this time in the form of standing by while the Soviet Union alone engaged Nazi Germany on the Eastern front.

As important for Soviet foreign policy were the long-term reverberations of the intervention in Spain. First, intervention established a new practice in Soviet foreign policy: direct interference in the internal affairs of another state. The habit of directing foreign affairs of states as well as those of the communist movement was formed – later to be reactivated when the Red Army liberated and occupied the countries of Eastern Europe at the end of the Second World War.

A second long-term consequence for Soviet foreign policy concerned the Popular Front strategy for Spain devised by the Comintern. The Spanish Civil War prompted the Comintern to develop the concept of transitional forms of state between capitalism and socialism. During the course of the Second World War the idea of 'people's democracy' – of non-socialist states where the communist party was strong and the working class hegemonic – was revived. It was an idea that meshed neatly with the then Soviet foreign policy priority of creating a zone of security in Eastern Europe. The establishment of people's democracies along the lines projected for the Spanish Republic would, on the one hand, guarantee the belt of friendly governments in Eastern Europe that Moscow was seeking and, on the other hand, bridge the gap in a gradual and long-term transition to socialism on a broad front. As in the case of the Spanish Republic, that project, too, was disrupted and perverted by a combination of Stalinist ideology and international developments.[55]

A third long-term consequence of Spain for the USSR was fainter and more distant, but by far the most radical and far-reaching. The period of the Popular Front and the Spanish Civil War marked the beginning of the break by some sections of the communist movement with the Soviet model of revolution and socialism. That long-drawn out process, which split the international communist movement, culminated in the Eurocommunist challenge to Soviet ideological hegemony in the 1970s and 1980s. That challenge was in turn an important intellectual influence on the process of liberalisation and democratisation in the USSR under Gorbachev. In the communist politics of the 1930s lay the distant roots of the political and ideological transformation and then disintegration of the USSR.

Conclusion

Moscow's intervention in the Spanish Civil War has been a subject of much controversy. This article has tried to show that in so far as the goals of Soviet policy are concerned that controversy has been misconceived. In outline, Soviet policy towards Spain followed a relatively simple and straightforward course. Given the constraints of real-world diplomacy and politics and perceptions of its own and republican interests, Moscow did what it could to aid the anti-fascist cause in Spain. In intention at least, the Soviet intervention in Spain was in many ways the most creditable episode in pre-war Soviet foreign policy.

Notes

* The author would like to acknowledge the financial assistance of the Arts Faculty, University College Cork.

1. S. O'Faolain, *The Irish*, London 1947. Cited by S. Aster, '"Guilty Men": The Case of Neville Chamberlain', in *Paths to War: New Essays on the Origins of the Second World War*, eds R. Boyce and E.M. Robertson, London 1989, 233.

2. There are various figures on Soviet military supplies to Republican Spain. According to M.T. Meshcheryakov, 'Sovetskii Souz i Antifashistskaya Voina Ispanskogo Naroda (1936-1939gg.)', *Istoriya SSSR*, January 1988: 31, between 1936 and 1938 the USSR supplied 648 aircraft, 347 tanks, 129 armoured cars, 1,186 artillery pieces, 20,486 machines guns, 497,813 rifles, 340 mortars, 826 million bullets and 3.4 million shells. A slightly different set of statistics is given in International Editorial Board, *International Solidarity with the Spanish Republic, 1936-1939*, Moscow, 1975, pp. 329-30. Further details of Stalin's involvement in Spanish affairs may be found in O. Klevnuk, 'Prichiny "Bolshogo Terrora": Vneshnepoliticheskii Aspekt', paper presented to the colloquium on *Russia in the Age of Wars (1914-1945): Towards a New Paradigm*, Cortona, October 1997, pp. 6-12.

3. For a case study of the Comintern campaign on Spain see J. Fyrth, *The Signal was Spain: The Aid Spain Movement in Britain, 1936-1939*, London, 1986. On the International Brigades: V. Brome, *The International Brigades, Spain 1936-1937*, London, 1965 and the articles published in *International Solidarity*.

4. See M.T. Meshcheryakov, 'SSSR i Grazhdanskaya Voina v Ispanii', *Otechestvennaya Istoriya* 3, 1993: 89-93.

5. For a representative sample in English see J.R. Campbell, *Soviet Policy and its Critics*, London, 1939, chap. 9; J. Sandoval and M. Azcarate, *Spain 1936-1939*, London, 1963; A.I. Sobolev et al., *Outline History of the Communist International*, Moscow, 1971, pp. 415-20 and 436-9; A. Landis, *Spain: The Unfinished Revolution*, New York, 1972, esp. pp. 231-44; M. Johnstone, 'Trotsky and World Revolution', *Cogito*, 1976; and *International Solidarity*.

6. See, for example, L. Trotsky, *The Spanish Revolution (1931-39)*, New York, 1973; F. Morrow, *Revolution and Counter-Revolution in Spain*, London, 1963; H. Thomas, *The Spanish Civil War*, rev. edn, London, 1965, 3rd edn, London, 1977; F. Claudin, *The Communist Movement*, London, 1975; B. Bolloten, *The Spanish Revolution: The Left and the Struggle for Power during the Civil War*, Chapel Hill, NC, 1979; P. Broué, *Staline et la révolution: le cas espagnol (1936-1939)*, Paris, 1993.

7. See J. Steele, 'Betrayed from Within', *Guardian*, 29 September 1995.

8. M. Blinkhorn, *Democracy and Civil War in Spain, 1931-1939*, London, 1988, pp. 48-9. More charitable interpretations of Soviet policy in standard works include G. Jackson, *The Spanish Republic and the Civil War, 1931-1939*, Princeton, 1965; S.G. Payne, *The Spanish Revolution*, London, 1970; R. Carr, *The Spanish Tragedy*, London, 1977. For an overview of the literature on the Spanish Civil War see P. Preston, 'The Historiography of the Spanish Civil War', in *People's History and Socialist Theory*, ed. R. Samuel, London, 1981.

9. D.T. Cattell, *Soviet Diplomacy and the Spanish Civil War*, Berkeley, 1957; E.H. Carr, *The Comintern and the Spanish Civil War*, London, 1984; J. Haslam, *The Soviet Union and the Struggle for Collective Security in Europe, 1933-1939*, London, 1984, chap. 7; M. Alpert, *A New International History of the Spanish Civil War*, London, 1994; S. Pons, *Stalin e la guerra inevitable, 1936-1941*, Turin, 1995, chap. 2; R.H. Whealey, 'Foreign Intervention in the Spanish Civil War', in *The Republic and the Civil War in Spain*, ed. R. Carr, London, 1971, pp. 213-38; D. Smyth, '"We are with you": Solidarity and Self-Interest in Soviet Policy towards Republican Spain, 1936-1939', in *Radicals, Rebels & Establishments*, ed. P.J. Corish, Belfast, 1985 (Revised and expanded version in *Republic Besieged*, eds Preston and Mackenzie, pp. 87-106); G. Stone, 'The European Great Powers and the Spanish Civil War, 1936-1939', in Boyce and Robertson, pp. 199-232; A. Viñas, 'Gold, the Soviet Union and the Spanish Civil War', *European Studies Review* 9, 1979: 105-28.

10. Cattell, *Soviet Diplomacy*, p. 120.

11. See reports in *Pravda* and *Izvestiya* under the heading 'Voenno-Fashistskii Myatezh v Ispanii' on 20, 21, 22, 23, 26, 27 and 29 July 1936; Haslam, *Struggle for Collective Security*, pp. 108-10; I. Maisky, *Spanish Notebooks*, London, 1966, pp. 11-17. Recently released decrypts by British Intelligence of messages between the PCE and the Comintern are interesting in this respect. On 20 July the PCE messaged Moscow that 'the military insurrection was crushed. ... It was all the workers' militia that decided the victory'; on 21 July 'we are convinced that we shall crush the enemy decisively, and that this will be the first step in the realisation of the revolutionary democratic programme'; and on 22 July 'the fascist insurrection is definitely crumbling.' Comintern HQ was less sanguine; its replies pointed out the danger of civil war and foreign intervention and requested more specific information on the military situation from the PCE. By mid-August the PCE was reporting on the deteriorating military position of the Republican government and asking for arms and munitions to counter Italo-German aid to Franco (message of 16 August). See PRO HW/17/27.

12. DVP vol. 19, doc. 242, Moscow, 1974; J. Degras (ed.), *Soviet Documents on Foreign Policy*, vol. 3 (1933-1941), Oxford, 1953, p. 203.

13. DVP 19, doc. 244.

14. For example E.H. Carr, *Comintern*, p. 17.

15. DVP 19, doc. 249; Degras, *Soviet Documents*, pp. 203-204.

16. DVP 19, doc. 260.

17. Ibid., doc. 292 (letter dated 4 Oct. 1936).

18. Ibid., doc. 296; Degras, *Soviet Documents*, pp. 211-12.

19. DVP 19, doc. 327; Degras, *Soviet Documents*, pp. 212-13.

20. Both Haslam, *Struggle for Collective Security*, and Cattell, *Soviet Diplomacy* contain good accounts of these developments.

21. DVP 19, doc. 258. Diplomatic relations between Spain and the USSR were established in 1933, but, for various reasons, there was no exchange of ambassadors; see ibid., doc. 129, and ibid., no. 72, pp. 737-738.

22. See Haslam, *Struggle for Collective Security*, and Cattell, *Soviet Diplomacy* for extensive quotations in this respect.
23. Cited by Meshcheryakov, 'SSSR i Grazhdanskaya', 85. Unfortunately, no date for this communication is given.
24. Ibid. The day after the decision on aid Kaganovich wrote to fellow-politburo member Ordzhonikidze: 'The Spanish affair is not going well. The Whites are approaching Madrid. ...We have aided them [the Republicans], and not only in the form of foodstuffs. Now there is a plan for greater aid, in the form of tanks and planes, but, in the first place, this is very difficult for us technically and, secondly, on their part they have little order and organisation – our party [the PCE] is still weak and the anarchists remain true to their ideals. ... If we had a common border with Spain, we would be able to expand our new aid now.' See *Stalinskoe Politburo v 30-e gody*, Moscow, 1995, p. 149. I am grateful to Klevnuk, 'Prichiny "Bolshogo Terrora"', for this reference.
25. Haslam, *Struggle for Collective Security*, p. 120.
26. The plan to aid Spain proposed that arms should be supplied on a commercial basis. It can be assumed that the endorsement of this plan coincided with signs that Madrid was planning to ship its gold reserves to Moscow.
27. Degras, *Soviet Documents*, p. 212.
28. On Soviet relations with Britain and France in the mid-1930s, see G. Roberts, *The Unholy Alliance: Stalin's Pact with Hitler*, London, 1989, pp. 59-81; and especially Michael Jabara Carley, 'End of the "Low, Dishonest Decade": Failure of the Anglo-Franco-Soviet Alliance in 1939', *Europe-Asia Studies* 45, 1993; idem, 'Down a Blind-Alley: Anglo-Franco-Soviet Relations, 1920-1939', *Canadian Journal of History* 29, no. 1, 1994: 147-72; idem, 'Prelude to Defeat: Franco-Soviet Relations, 1919-1939', *Historical Reflexions* 22, 1996; idem, '"A Fearful Concatenation of Circumstances": the Anglo-Soviet Rapprochement, 1934-1936', *Contemporary European History* 5, 1996.
29. See M. Litvinov, *Against Aggression*, London, 1939.
30. In relation to Italy see J. Calvitt Clarke III, *Russia and Italy Against Hitler: The Bolshevik-Fascist Rapprochement of the 1930s*, Westport, 1991, and I.A. Khormach, *SSSR-Italiya, 1924*-1939gg, Moscow, 1995; in relation to Germany, G. Roberts, *The Soviet Union and the Origins of the Second World War*, London, 1995, chap. 3.
31. See, for example, Molotov's speech on the anniversary of the Russian Revolution in IPC, no. 51, 1936.
32. On the Soviet role in the NIC, Cattell, *Soviet Diplomacy* remains unsurpassed. See also Alpert, *New International History*, pp. 48-52 and 72-82, and Maisky, *Spanish Notebooks*, pp. 45-63, 139-41, 159-73. A large number of documents relating to the NIC are published in DVP for the years 1936-38.
33. Cited in *Istoriya Vneshnei Politiki SSSR, 1917-1945*, Moscow, 1986, p. 321.
34. DVP 21, doc. 63, Moscow, 1977.
35. Meshcheryakov, 'SSSR i Grazhdanskaya', p. 87.
36. A number of examples in ibid., *passim*.
37. Cited by Smyth, '"We are with you"', 228.
38. In relation to this question Viñas, 'Gold', *passim*.
39. See *Report of the Seventh World Congress of the Communist International*, London, 1936.
40. E.H. Carr, *Comintern*, chap.1.

41. On the popular front strategy and subsequent developments K. McDermott and J. Agnew, *The Comintern*, London, 1996, chap. 4; G. Roberts, 'Collective Security and the Origins of the People's Front' in *Britain, Fascism and the Popular Front*, ed. J. Fyrth, London, 1985; J. Haslam, 'The Comintern and the Origins of the Popular Front, *Historical Journal* 26, no. 3, 1979: 673-91; E.J. Hobsbawm, 'The "Moscow Line" and International Communist Policy, 1933-1947' in *Warfare, Diplomacy and Politics*, ed. C.Wrigley, London, 1986; P. Spriano, *Stalin and the European Communists*, London, 1985; D. Sassoon, 'The Rise and Fall of West European Communism', *Contemporary European History* 1, no. 2, 1992; K.K. Shirinya, *Strategiya i Taktika Kominterna v Borbe Protiv Fashizma i Voiny (1934-1939)*, Moscow, 1979.

42. 'Novye Dokumenty G. Dimitrova', *Voprosy Istorii KPSS* 8, 1989, doc. 10. On 26 February 1936 the Comintern messaged the PCE that the Azaña government was not a Popular Front government but a 'bourgeois government of the Left'. Nevertheless, the government should be defended against attacks and possible coups, so that it could carry out the electoral programme of the Popular Front; PRO HW/17/26.

43. Ibid., doc. 15; Sobolev et al., *Outline History*, pp. 415-16; Shirinya, *Strategiya*, pp. 144-5; Meshcheryakov, 'SSSR i Grazhdanskaya', 88; E.H. Carr, *Comintern*, p. 7; M.T. Meshcheryakov, 'Kommunisticheskaya Partiya Ispanii i Komintern', *Novaya i Noveishaya Istoriya* 5, 1991: 19-20. See also Comintern message to PCE transmitted on 9 April 1936 which stated that 'in the situation as it stands the creation of Soviet power is not in the order of the day ... at the moment it is solely a question of establishing such a democratic rule that it will be possible to bar the progress of fascism and anti-revolution and to further in general the position of the proletariat and its allies.' (PRO HW/17/26)

44. Meshcheryakov, 'Kommunisticheskaya', 23; E.H. Carr, *Comintern*, p. 7.

45. Sobolev et al., *Outline History*, pp. 416-17 and 436. On the September Comintern meetings see also Pons, *Stalin* , pp. 87-95, Broué, *Staline*, pp. 89-90; E.H. Carr, *Comintern*, pp. 20-1.

46. IPC 16, no. 48, 24 October 1936: 1292-5.

47. J. Degras (ed.), *The Communist International 1919-1943*, London, 1971, vol. 3, pp. 396-400.

48. On subsequent developments in Comintern strategy, see E.H. Carr, *Comintern*, esp. chap. 6.

49. For the text of the Stalin letter (which was also signed by Molotov and Voroshilov) and Caballero's reply, see E.H. Carr, *Comintern*, pp. 86-8.

50. On the argument that the anti-Trotskyism campaign in the USSR was inspired, at least in part, by real, perceived fears of a fascist/counter-revolutionary threat, see, for example, R.W. Thurston, *Life and Terror in Stalin's Russia, 1934-1941*, Yale, 1996, esp. chap. 2.

51. G. Dimitroff, *The United Front*, London, 1938, p. 189.

52. Cited by Haslam, *Struggle for Collective Security*, p. 116. On 18 January 1937 the Comintern directed the PCE that the opening of the Radek-Piatakov trial in Moscow should be utilised for a massive press campaign against Trotskyists – who were characterised as terrorists, saboteurs and Gestapo agents. On 21 January there was a further message from Moscow: 'Utilise the trial of Piatakov and consorts to liquidate the POUM politically by attempting to obtain from the working-class elements of that organisation a declaration condemning Trotsky's terrorist gang.' (PRO HW/17/28)

53. Dimitroff, *United Front*, pp. 279-80.
54. See G. Roberts, 'The Alliance that Failed: Moscow and the Triple Alliance Negotiations, 1939', *European History Quarterly* 26, no. 3, 1996: 383-414.
55. See G. Roberts, *The Soviet Union in World Politics: Coexistence, Revolution and Cold War, 1945-1991*, London, 1998, chap. 2.

6

France, the Collapse of Republican Spain and the Approach of General War

National Security, War Economics and the Spanish Refugees, 1938-1940

Martin S. Alexander (University of Salford)

A RECENT general history of France in the first half of the twentieth century, Anthony Adamthwaite's *Grandeur and Misery* (1995), concludes by observing that 'France was the last large democratic country left in mid-1930s continental Europe'. It approvingly quotes a despatch from the British ambassador in Paris that 'France is not only peaceful and orderly ... but is really free. France is governed without recourse to concentration camps or islands for inconvenient critics. The press is not bridled ... and any political refugee can find a home here.'[1]

If such a sanguine view of France in the 1930s was ever accurate, it had certainly ceased to be so through her treatment of the problem of Spanish Republican refugees in 1939-40. For it was precisely by means of concentration camps,[2] press censorship and near-purblind ideological prejudice that the French public authorities approached the issues that were presented them by the sudden arrival on French soil in the spring of 1939 of more than half a million men, women and children. This influx of humanity was the direct product of a flight for their lives by the Spanish Republicans

– a flight from Franco's victorious Nationalist armies, his political police, prisons, torture chambers and firing squads.[3]

The long-delayed triumph of General Francisco Franco in the Civil War in February 1939 and the collapse of the Republican government of Juan Negrín the following month brought about the second major impact on France of the conflict that had raged to the south of the Pyrenees since July 1936. The first phase of Spain's fall-out upon French politics had stretched from the election victory of the *Frente Popular* in February 1936 to the decision of Léon Blum's government in early August to adopt the policy of non-intervention.[4] The second began early in 1939 and was concerned with the question of receiving Spanish people from the defeated Republic into France. As Marrus has graphically described:

> Early 1939 saw the Republican forces crumble, leading to a panic-stricken flight of refugees. Franco's troops entered Barcelona at the end of January and took Madrid in March. In the wake of these disasters, masses of refugees surged toward the French frontier. By the beginning of February, 300,000 had gathered at various border posts. The French admitted about 80,000, but sent back many of military age. Pressure mounted. Some of the refugees suffered severely from exposure, malnutrition, and typhoid fever. After hurried meetings with Republican officers, border guards allowed defeated soldiers and civilians to cross into France. Within days about 350,000 entered, over half of whom were once Republican soldiers. ... By the end of April, when the Nationalist forces had finally triumphed everywhere, over 450,000 Spanish refugees had reached France. Many were sick or wounded, and over a third were old people, women and children.[5]

Earlier in the inter-war period, France had been 'a country of immigration'.[6] It had also gloried in its post-1789 liberal tradition and reputation as a *pays d'asile*, rivalled only by the United States. The welcome for immigrants was especially warm after 1919. This owed much to necessity. The huge task of economic reconstruction in the regions of the north and north-east devastated by four years of trench warfare and German expropriations required quantities of strong, fit young labourers. It was beyond France to find these among an indigenous population bled white by four years of trench warfare. France's pre-war population of thirty-nine million had been grievously depleted. Aggregate war casualties ran at over three million. Much of the recovery and rebuilding thus fell upon new arrivals. During the 1920s France welcomed some three million immigrants, the principal inflows coming from Belgium, Poland, Italy and Russia, and significant but smaller numbers from Spain and Portugal.[7]

But even this accretion was insufficient to halt France's slide into a crisis of *dénatalité*.[8] At the same time, the influx of hundreds of thousands of Spanish refugees hence presented the administrative agencies of Edouard Daladier's government, which had taken office in April 1938, with both a challenge and an opportunity.

The latter came with the possibility of directing much of this influx into the French economy, which was creaking under the stresses of an attempt to force the pace of rearmament by 1939, and was in particular faced by a strangulation of production by the country's structural shortage of skilled labour. The attitudes of the French political class, leaders of big business and the press were, however, much more strongly influenced by contemporary fears for the social cohesion of France and for the preservation of industrial peace than by a sense of providential assistance which the Spaniards might offer as a way out of France's crippling economic/demographic conjuncture.

In April 1938 the success of the Nationalist armies at Vinaroz had brought about the physical division of the territory controlled by the Republicans. Thereafter the centre-south zone was separated from the Republican government and the national leaderships of the political parties and labour organisations, which were based in Barcelona until the fall of the city in January 1939. Particularly under the cautious, timorous, unsympathetic French governments of Camille Chautemps (June 1937 to March 1938) and Edouard Daladier (April 1938 to March 1940), French policy towards Spain aimed at isolating the conflagration south of the Pyrenees, avoiding action that might aggravate relations with Franco's German and Italian backers.[9] Thus, 'Planes for Spain' – the impassioned campaign of 1936 and 1937 to send military assistance to the Spanish Republic led by Pierre Cot, the Popular Front's Air Minister – was an all-but-forgotten battle-cry by 1938-39.[10] The French socialists no longer retained the leading place in a government which, during Blum's year as *président du conseil* (prime minister) from June 1936 to June 1937, had resulted in a porous Pyrenean frontier, the French authorities conniving at a criss-crossing of Spanish Republican personnel back and forth, along with an unstaunched flow of arms, medical supplies and international volunteers into Spain.[11] From late 1938, however, traffic across the Pyrenees became increasingly a one-way flow as Spaniards trekked north in growing numbers, in direct relation to the deterioration of the Republic's military position. The French position hardened. Under Blum's successor, the Radical Senator Chautemps (in June 1940 the first minister to suggest exploring armistice terms with Germany), the Pyrenees frontier was closed. In 1938, under Chautemps' successor, Daladier, France consciously turned away from its traditional 'open door' policy towards immigrants and fugitives from political repression.[12] Refugees 'were required to show identity papers or find themselves led back across the frontier'.[13]

Their columns included women as well as men, and indeed many entire families, with children. It has become commonplace for scholars to castigate French officialdom for heartless behaviour in the face of the vulnerability and human suffering of the frightened and defeated Spaniards.[14] However, Michael B. Miller, in his book *Shanghai on the Metro* (1994), offers a more benign evaluation of the Daladier administration. And Miller has found support from at least one other well-respected historian, William D. Irvine, whose approving comments have sufficient significance to warrant full citation:

> Miller makes a telling argument. One of the black marks of Edouard Daladier's government was the internment of refugees fleeing fascist Europe. Not only did these actions belie France's tradition of providing a refuge for the oppressed, but, some historians have argued, they suggest that the repressive and racist mind set of the Vichy regime was in place among French officialdom long before the collapse of 1940. Armed with a confident "feel" for the police culture of the period, Miller presents a sensitive and nuanced dissent. Never denying the very real human tragedy involved [he] argues nevertheless that the internment policy was not merely the consequence of xenophobia, anti-semitism and authoritarian reflexes. Some of that was there, of course, but so too was a good deal of concern for and sensitivity to the plight of the refugees. Their massive influx did present the French authorities with an enormous problem because it was inevitably the case that some small percentage of them were foreign agents, spies, or potential saboteurs. The internments of 1939-40 were not the [French] republic's finest hour and probably contributed little to national security. But they did not necessarily reflect some national 'decadence', nor prefigure Vichy either.[15]

The French official response did contain sufficient compassion, in any case, to permit a reaching of agreement between the administration of Juan Negrín, the last Republican Prime Minister, and the Quai d'Orsay whereby France granted asylum to 'the most compromised of the Republicans'.[16] Nor was it simply the rank-and-file to whom shelter was extended. Manuel Azaña, the president of the Republic, entered France on 7 February and moved to the Spanish embassy in Paris. Two days later Negrín and his Foreign Minister,

Julio Alvarez del Vayo crossed the frontier, setting up the government-in-exile in the Spanish consulate at Toulouse. The same month, with the Nationalists rapidly overrunning Catalonia, smashing organised Republican resistance into isolated pockets, the executive of the PSOE under Ramón Lamoneda, the secretary-general, crossed into France. It, too, was allowed to establish itself in Toulouse.

Negotiations with Franco also developed during February. With, so to speak, new mistresses in Spain, there had to be new suitors from Paris. It was 'out of the question' (in Pike's words) that Jules Henry, the French ambassador to the Spanish Republic, would be welcome at Burgos. Consequently he was side-lined. A conservative senator, Léon Bérard, later Vichy France's representative to the Vatican, was instead dispatched to Franco's capital on 4 February 1939. His mission was 'to insinuate himself as best he could into the good books of the Caudillo'.[17] For a fortnight the negotiations stalled, arousing heated polemics in the national French press, and in the newspapers of the Béarn and the Midi, over the propriety of granting recognition to Franco so long as France retained formal relations with Negrín's government. However, though he did not meet Franco, Bérard saw the Nationalist Foreign Minister, General Francisco Gómez Jordana y Souza on 18 to 19 and 23 to 25 February. By the end of the month the French political right, supported by a rising clamour for pragmatism among centrists and their newspapers, had prevailed. After a short debate in the Chamber, and a vote that produced a government majority of sixty-two, France (and Britain) formally recognised Franco's regime on 27 February.[18]

The Bérard-Jordana agreement quickly brought about a changing of the guard. A kind of grotesque, ritualistic, diplomatic minuet was danced on the grave of the Spanish Republic. France, Pike sardonically remarks, 'now tried to cosy up to Franco with an unseemly haste'.[19] José Félix de Lequerica was accredited to Paris with full ambassadorial rank as Franco's representative. Henry, French ambassador to the Republic, was removed. Believing that the *Caudillo* might accommodate himself most easily with a fellow soldier, Daladier and his Foreign Minister Georges Bonnet (in one of the most fateful appointments made in modern French history) announced on 2 March 1939 that France's new envoy to Spain was the 83 year-old 'Hero of Verdun', Marshal Henri Philippe Pétain.

French recognition of Nationalist Spain in the spring of 1939 seemed to be all give and no take. In Pike's view, 'France had obtained nothing.' She agreed to return gold reserves from the Bank of Spain, worth around eight million, that Negrín had transferred into France, along with all Republican war material (including war-ships, merchant vessels and vehicles), official documents and works of art.[20] Beyond sending a telegram to the British Prime Minister, Neville Chamberlain, on 22 February, stating that there would be 'an equitable peace for the vanquished' and that 'the notion of reprisals is totally alien to the Nationalist movement',[21] Franco offered no guarantee that defeated Republicans would escape persecution.[22]

Why did the French authorities not strike a harder bargain over recognition? This was, after all, a highly-prized status for Franco and an objective which, as revealed by the long-running furore over 'belligerent rights' during the war, was of great significance for him. Here, we need to understand that French policy was critically affected by the agitated mood and *mentalité* in France. Pike's care-ful study of the press demonstrates just how inflamed were the edi-torials and guest columnists of the papers, right and left, national and regional.[23] The passions aroused by the Spanish Republic's death agony revived a climate of fear in France, *la peur rouge du printemps '39* (the red scare of spring 1939), itself terrifyingly redo-lent of the fears of August–September 1936, that France herself might degenerate into civil war, or be sucked into a general war.[24]

The atmosphere provoked hard-nosed, narrow, selfish and defensive reflexes. For many French, every Spaniard was now regarded 'as an intruder'.[25] The male refugees, however, divided into two distinctive categories: the fleeing members of the Republi-can military units on the one hand, civilian workers and their fam-ilies on the other. Many of the latter came from the industrial towns and cities of the former Republican strongholds, particularly from Barcelona, and then from the smaller urban centres of Catalonia.

Throughout March and April 1939 the exodus turned into a flood. Tens of thousands fled Madrid. 'The PCE', as Helen Graham has written, 'had created of the republican capital a legendary sym-bol of antifascist struggle and a military stronghold. Yet, by 1939 Madrid had become "a trap which everyone sought to escape while there was still time".'[26] Republican soldiers fleeing before Franco's final offensives crossed into France bearing quantities of portable weapons, mostly machine-guns, rifles and small-arms, but also mobile field artillery, anti-aircraft guns, ammunition, vehicles and stores. About 200,000 Republicans soon agreed to return to Spain, but the soldiers and militiamen remained in France 'in holding cen-tres which became veritable concentration camps'.[27]

The plight of the Spanish fugitives became inextricably entangled in the wider question of French national security. Some of the better

Spanish war material, supplied by Soviet Russia and Czechoslovakia, was immediately commandeered by the French armed forces.[28] Even French conservatives who had earlier taken a benign view of Franco (if only because of their horror at the left-wing Republic of 1938-9) were now worried. Senator Henri de Kérillis wrote in *L'Epoque* on 19 January that he doubted France could preserve its security with enemy powers massed on three frontiers. Four days later he added that he viewed a Franco victory 'in the circumstances in which it is coming about, as a veritable catastrophe for France'.[29]

And indeed, once the Spanish Republic's final collapse became inevitable, General Maurice Gamelin, the French chief of staff for national defence and army commander-in-chief designate, focused on the implications for French security of the advent of a third 'military frontier' along the Pyrenees.[30] On 7 February 1939, Daladier (who, besides being *président du conseil*, remained in the office of Minister for National Defence and War to which Blum had appointed him in June 1936) approved the formation of battalions of French *chasseurs pyrénéens*, Pyrenees mountain infantry, raised among the inhabitants of Roussillon and the Béarn. These units were Gamelin's idea: 'battalions of reservists, with a few active cadres; but in view of the qualities of our people of the Pyrenees, worthwhile results were to be expected. If we turn out not to need them to face [Franco's] Spain, they'll be welcome in the Alps or the Jura.'[31]

On 24 April, Gamelin recorded, 'When the [Spanish] government troops fell back across the border into France we gathered up the material that they had with them, and we used the worthwhile items for ourselves, particularly the anti-aircraft guns.' Because of delays in output of French war material, these requisitioned munitions were sent to Tunisia and Djibouti where the French garrisons had particular shortages.[32] The French saw an opportunity for diplomatic leverage arising from this adventitious acquisition of Spanish arms. The Daladier government decided to offer a financial indemnity to the near-bankrupt Franco regime in exchange for retention of this war material and assurances from Madrid of a neutral stance towards France on the part of the Franco regime.[33]

Franco's regime nonetheless leaned towards Hitler's Germany in the succeeding months. But France played cards of its own in the poker game that developed over Spanish neutrality. This was especially so after September 1939. During the Phoney War Pétain 'strived to reach a military agreement with Franco, and a commercial accord, for Spain was on the verge of a famine and interest existed in exchanging wheat for strategic minerals (pyrites, mercury, wolfram, zinc). "The minds [of the Spaniards] are becoming more embittered with every passing day, wrote the Marshal on 3 January 1940, against a France accused of using delays to exercise a kind of blackmail-by-hunger over the Spanish people.'"[34]

In the immediate aftermath of Franco's victory, however, French security anxieties were exacerbated rather than eased. This applied not only to the defence of the Pyrenees frontier, but also in regard to the protection of French Morocco and the preservation of the international status of Tangier.[35] On 15 April 1939 Daladier approved precautionary measures along the Pyrenees.[36] It remains, however, striking that the minutes of the meetings of the CPDN on 5 December 1938 and on 24 February 1939 do not refer directly to the progress of the war in Spain. Neither meeting discussed the security implications of the rapid disintegration of the Spanish Republic.[37] The latter's military collapse in early 1939 caught France by surprise.

So, too, did the tide of refugees that then poured north. 'The French had expected a small fraction of this amount', notes Marrus, 'and were totally ill equipped to deal with the emergency.'[38] To be more precise, one should say that the crisis had not been the object of any contingency measures by officials of the French war and interior ministries. The hasty establishment of detention camps was *ad hoc* and improvised. 'For several reasons', argues Marrus, 'the French were desperately anxious to rid the country of the Spaniards … [so] the government of Edouard Daladier … strove to distance itself from the anti-fascist crusade associated with the defeated Republicans.'[39] All the same, during April Daladier and his Finance Minister, Paul Reynaud, dragged their heels over implementing the Bérard-Jordana agreements. They sought to link the return of the Spanish gold reserves to the repatriation of Spanish refugees. But the French government was divided on these tactics. They were reminded by Franco's officials that no linkage existed in the agreements and warned that procrastination might lead to Jordana's replacement by a figure such as Serrano Suñer, then Franco's Interior Minister, more hostile to France.[40] Bonnet and Pétain in the spring of 1939 were:

> eager to conclude an agreement with Franco, hoping to secure his neutrality in the event of the Franco-German conflict that was so widely feared. In addition, the government wanted to avoid the heavy economic burden of refugees. France, by this point, had the largest refugee concentration in the world, for which the government was paying about two hundred million francs a month. Firebrands on the right bitterly denounced this expenditure, fanning the xenophobic and anti-leftist hysteria.[41]

The potential pool of workers, female as well as male, represented by the arrivals from Spain was regarded with intense suspicion by French ministers charged with economic production and
by industrialists. Nor were French syndicalists any more receptive.
Taking into account the 'invisible' unemployed, including many
women, and those on short-time, as many as one million French
workers may have had no jobs, or very intermittent, temporary
ones, even as late as 1938.[42] Yet, organised labour was also suspicious towards the question of utilising the Spanish Republicans in
the sectors of the French economy where production was being
severely hampered by the acute labour shortage.

The French recovery from the economic depression, and especially from the crisis of under-production of armaments and munitions, depended on finding a solution to the labour shortfalls. The
SFIO and syndicalist leaders' belief of May to June 1936, that
France possessed a reservoir of labour among the unemployed, and
that all that was required was the application of a 'French New
Deal', had been revealed as illusory. It had not been enough to initiate proto-Keynesian policies of government stimulus to create an
upturn in consumer spending, a filling of industry's order-books.[43]

Of greater structural significance, however, was the exposure as
myth of the notion that France could meet the challenges of expanding armaments production by drawing on a deep pool or reservoir of
unemployed, including refugees. Reduction of unemployment – *la
lutte contre le chômage* – had been a central plank of the Popular Front's
platform during the winter of 1935-6. The Popular Front was much
more than another tactical and temporary alignment of parliamentary
parties for the purpose of fighting the elections to the Chamber of
Deputies in April to May 1936. It was, rather, a broad-based and
grass-roots movement. It was an organisation possessing both political breadth and social depth, motivated above all by passionate and
sincere opposition to fascism at home and abroad.[44] Anti-fascism and
the fight against the divisive social costs of the Depression united the
disparate strands of the Popular Front. Yet, it was perplexing and inad-
missible to the Popular Front that the French economy was not
rapidly lifted from the doldrums, and unemployment eradicated, by
hefty doses of economic interventionism.

In the spring of 1937, following revelations about structural
obstacles to more rapid French war preparation that emerged at a
meeting of the *Conseil Consultatif de l'Armement* in Paris on 3 May,
Gamelin had written to Robert Jacomet, the secretary-general of
the Ministry for National Defence and War. He warned that bottle-

necks were restricting output of essential military equipment. Expansion was 'limited at the present time by the productive capacities of our existing steel-works and the inadequate out-turn of some of our metallurgical factories. Production from the optical and explosives industries [Gamelin added] is also hitting its maximum, the production of the former being restricted by the question of labour [shortages].'[45]

French rearmament programmes expanded in this period much faster than did the productive capacity of French industry. This was partly a result of insufficient plant. Most seriously, nothing had been done to remedy the shortfalls in the labour supply. Relaxations of the forty-hour week in defence industries occurred in 1938. Yet defence orders were so large that, by the winter of 1938-9, the labour requirements surpassed anything that could be met by these derogations by Daladier of the forty-hour legislation by decree-law after August 1938.[46] Clearly, France's problem was a structural one.

Even so, it was with extreme reluctance that the French authorities and industrialists turned to the Spaniards to solve the labour crisis. What was the response, then, of the French authorities to the opportunity suddenly presented to make use of the Spanish Republican refugees as a labour resource to make good French shortfalls? When senior ministers and defence chiefs gathered for a further meeting of the CPDN at the War Ministry in Paris, on 9 April 1939, the seventh and last section of the meeting's protocol contained a section under the sub-heading, *'Réfugiés Etrangers'*. The minutes record that: 'It was decided to utilise a first echelon of 34 battalions of Spanish workers on road construction in the Alps and in French North Africa, and for the improvement of airbases.' Soon afterwards, noted Gamelin, 'I obtained an extension in the utilisation of the Spanish refugees to the north-eastern frontier, but in company strength.' The chief of staff of the French colonial forces, General Jules Bührer, stated that the Ministry for the Colonies required 15,000 workers to undertake the development of communications links between North Africa and French West Africa.[47]

In directly military terms, the French took steps to harness the resources represented by the arrival in France of men with military experience who had fled from fascist takeovers in their home countries. At the meeting on 9 April, Alexis Léger, secretary-general of the Quai d'Orsay, reported that the Czechoslovakian minister in Paris was offering France the services of 30,000 Czechs, 'either as workers, or as soldiers'. Gamelin then explained that a Bill was being prepared authorising the peacetime formation of a 'supplementary Foreign Legion' to utilise foreign combat veterans, and Daladier concluded the meeting by approving the preparation of a decree-law to this effect.[48] One of the holding centres, Barcarès, became a military training camp for re-enlisting Spanish veterans.[49] At the time of the French Armistice in June 1940, some 6,000 Spaniards were serving in the Foreign Legion.[50]

Daladier had, since Blum named him Minister for National Defence and War in June 1936, tightened the disciplinary ratchet on workers in military industries. He had always opposed the right to strike in factories working on defence contracts.[51] In the spring of 1939, syndicalists remained bent on forcing government and employers to recruit from the unemployed to meet industry's need for more workers. In 1936 to 1938, this had produced an impasse with 'both industry and labor uncooperative and intransigent'.[52] But, by the summer of 1939, Charles Pomaret, Minister of Labour from August 1938 to June 1940, was able to refute trade union claims that a pool of qualified jobless was awaiting work. France, reported Pomaret at a meeting of the Chamber's labour commission on 28 June, 'has no appreciable unemployment among her skilled workers'.[53]

The trade unions had mounted a stubborn and, in their own terms, successful resistance to the labour requirements of France's expanding industries. Some of these industries had toyed with hiring immigrants and refugees. However the obstructiveness of French syndicalism did nothing to meet the Spanish Republicans' desperate need of work, incomes, housing, even enough to eat – let alone begin their social integration and acceptance among the people of France. Notions of comradely solidarity with fellow trade unionists from the Spanish UGT and CNT labour confederations counted for little compared with the fear that the Spaniards might take jobs which might otherwise be filled by Frenchmen. And, to offer a gender perspective, the trade union leadership in France seems to have been unashamedly patriarchal and biased towards the promotion only of male workers' interests.

Revealing on these aspects, too, is the part taken by Raoul Dautry, appointed to the new post of Minister of Armaments by Daladier when the latter reorganised his government on 13 September 1939. Dautry was one of France's foremost businessmen who had built his reputation in the railway sector.[54] From the summer of 1937 Dautry took up a series of new appointments, as president of the aircraft manufacturer Hispano-Suiza, and simultaneously joining the board of the *Compagnie Générale de l'Electricité* (CGE). As he subsequently testified to the post-war French parliamentary inquiry into events between 1933 and 1945: 'I had many opportunities to note and to signal that France lacked ... not only machine-tools and raw materials ... but especially that, throughout the country and to a cruel degree, she lacked skilled workers.' He wrote in the name of Hispano-Suiza and the CGE to the Minister of Labour to propose the establishment of government-sponsored apprenticeship training centres. 'But my requests, repeated on several occasions, bore no fruit.'[55]

The greatest single cause of disruption to the French economy on the outbreak of hostilities with Germany was the lack of any regulatory framework prepared before the war in order to retain skilled workers in 'reserved occupations'. The mass call-up stripped scores of thousands of skilled men at random out of the civilian economy and put them into uniform as Series A or Series B (first or second class) reservists. This primacy of the fighting services over the requirements of the war economy was serious enough for agriculture. Daladier became aware of it only when he saw fields of unharvested crops beneath him as he flew over the Aisne and Somme *départements* on his way to the first meeting of the Anglo-French Supreme War Council in Abbeville on 12 September.[56] In a series of sharp written exchanges later that month, Gamelin refused point-blank to release reservists from farming backgrounds for harvesting work, on grounds that French intelligence had identified the reappearance of German units from Poland, indicating the imminence of a German offensive in the West. This stand-off provoked a change of policy over the Spanish internees, as an alternative means of meeting the agricultural crisis. On 2 October 1939, the Minister of the Interior, Albert Sarraut, notified the prefects that all Spaniards who had (by terms offered them in an earlier circular of 17 August) declared themselves to be refugees were to be put to work on the land unless they were already engaged in recognised work of national economic interest. Thus the rights of asylum granted by the French government were offset by labour-draft provisions.[57]

In industry, the call-up of Frenchmen of military age had brought factories to a near-standstill. A glaring example of the havoc wreaked by the call-up occurred at Renault in Boulogne-Billancourt, in south-western Paris. The firm had begun to convert productive capacity from civilian automobiles to military vehicles after Munich. But as a report from Armand Chouffet, Léon Courson and Pierre Taittinger on 12 December 1939 stated: 'At the moment when the war of '39 broke out, the situation at the Renault plants was as follows: of 32,000 employees, 20,000 were called-up to the armed forces; the 12,000 who remained faced with a far-from-full order book from the military.'[58]

The wholesale release of Spanish Republican detainees offered a significant resource to embattled French industrialists and war planners. The substitution of Spanish refugees for French workers in the factories, on the railways, and in the vast task of developing France's hinterland infrastructure offered a vital support to a war effort which Dautry himself predicted would be attritional and would mobilise all the assets of the nation. Gradually the lingering paranoia and climate of suspicion that had previously pervaded the milieux of French business, conservative politics and the police about the 'hidden peril' of extreme-left penetration, subversion and sabotage of French industry was dispelled.[59]

Discussing the Spanish refugees' situation in September 1939, Milza has written that 'At the declaration of war, many rejoined the armaments industries.'[60] The pattern was not in fact as uncomplicated as this bald statement suggests. Foreign workers were indeed taken on by French munitions firms during the Phoney War. But for some time, those preferred by French industrialists and by the officials of the ministries concerned (Labour, Commerce and Industry and Armaments) tended to be Polish refugees and workers from Belgium (still a neutral country, despite Franco-British pressure on Brussels to enter the war alongside the Allies in September 1939). This is not entirely explicable. One supposes that a residual goodwill existed for the Poles because they had been allied to France by a Treaty of Friendship of 1921. There may also have been an element of bad conscience in view of Poland's collapse without French military intervention in September 1939. In the case of the Belgians, perhaps their country's vexatious neutrality during the Phoney War (1939-40) did not entirely obliterate bonds of comradeship forged between French veterans and King Albert's troops in 1914-18.

Gradually, pragmatism came to characterise French policy towards the Spanish Republicans. On 17 October 1939 regional military commanders were instructed throughout France to constitute *Compagnies de Travail des Etrangers* (CTEs), in which Spanish refugees formed a large majority. All refugees still in camps were required to serve, excepting only those with wounds and those categorized as 'undesirable' or 'subversive'. In December 1939 women were no longer permitted to stay in the camps. Those whose husbands remained interned were required to find work. Mothers were instructed to find means of caring for their children, or to hand them over to the centres now being administered by the International Commission for Assistance to Spanish Refugee Children. Refusal of these instructions was now met by the serving of notice to return to Spain.[61]

All this represented a piecemeal, unplanned, improvised approach by France to the Spanish refugee question and its multiple problems and opportunities. Appearing before the labour commission of the Chamber of Deputies on 6 March 1940, Charles Pomaret, the Minister for Labour, admitted that France had been slow to make any constructive use of the Spaniards for industrial work, even though many among them were metallurgists. French employers – in both the state and private sectors – had been reluctant to tap this source of workers, he conceded, for they believed 'that the Spanish refugees were all wild communists [*des farouches communistes*]'.[62]

Gradually, however, the unrelenting hostility of 1939, which had blocked any employment for the Spaniards, gave way to a pragmatic appreciation of the multiple services which the Republicans could render France in its own hour of trial. Labour companies, each of about 250 men under a French commander, aided by a Spanish officer and interpreters, were formed. These were deployed on road-mending, railway-track maintenance, bridge repairs and so forth. Punishment units – *bataillons de marche* –were formed from those with Civil War combat experience. Others were deployed as working parties, strengthening and extending the Maginot Line after it was decided to extend the original fortifications with new pill-boxes and barbed-wire defences along the Franco-Belgian frontier.[63] Similarly, units of Spaniards were constituted to strengthen the defences facing Italy on the Alps and in eastern Provence, whilst Spaniards were also sent across the Mediterranean to reinforce French positions in North Africa, facing the Italian colony of Libya in the east and, ironically but appropriately, Spanish Morocco in the west.

Thus the pressures of war, combined with France's own chronic problem of *dénatalité*,[64] brought about this *volte-face* from the days when the French could not see their way beyond permanent incarceration for Spaniards who had struck fear into the French bourgeoisie and business community – a business community endemically suspicious of the left and the working class because of the great strike movement of May to June 1936 (and, it should not be forgotten, the subsequent 'winter of discontent' or 'second strike wave' in 1936-7, arguably even more damaging than the Popular Front's 'Red Spring' to French industry's profitability and the French rearmament effort).[65]

The efficacy of factories working for the defence effort was a matter of growing interest to the French parliament. In the autumn of 1939 the army commission of both the Senate and Chamber of Deputies increasingly sent missions of inspection to establishments all over France. At its meeting of 11 October 1939, the Chamber's army commission heard Etienne Baron report on an inspection of the state arsenals at Toulouse and Tarbes – both areas with large numbers of Spanish refugees quartered nearby. Housing for the workers at these much-expanded factories had caused the commissioners particular concern. Baron and another deputy, M. Beaugrand, has been to see Dautry himself that morning, prior to the meeting of the Commission. Edmond Miellet, the president of the Chamber army commission, 'observed that France, for a long time now, had lacked specialist workers. He expressed himself astonished, therefore, that no real effort had been agreed for the development of apprenticeship schools'. The Commission closed the meeting by a unanimous decision 'to press the government for action in this sense.'[66]

In a letter of exhortation to all directors of military enterprises under the direction of the Ministry of Armaments, on 29 December 1939, one finds a rare reference, Dautry writing to his top managers that:

> If you know how to utilise the skill, conscience and eagerness to work of French women, the competency of the Indo-Chinese, the energy of the Moroccans, the strength of the Kabyles; if, with patience and firmness, you restore to the unemployed the means and the pride of being workers; if the refugees rediscover in your establishment the atmosphere of well-regulated labour to which they are accustomed, then the current problem of basic production is close to being resolved.[67]

Originally, male Spanish Republicans, a potent and battle-hardened anti-fascist asset, were frequently treated as an even stronger industrial/employment liability. They were incarcerated. Detention camps and holding centres were swiftly constructed at Gurs, Le Vernet in the Ariège, Barcarès and Roovesaltes, Brens and Septfonds for the mass of humanity that poured northwards across the Pyrenees with the final disintegration of organised, formal republican military resistance and administration in February to April 1939. Gurs was one of the largest and most notoriously harsh. Situated some eighty kilometres from the Franco-Spanish frontier, it lay in the foothills of the Pyrenees, northwest of the small town of Oloron-Sainte-Marie, along the road to Navarrenx. Later, so-called 'hospital camps' were constructed, at Récédébou and Noé, outside Toulouse, in February 1941.

For all the ideological comradeliness between the men of the French left and the exiled Spaniards – with their hostility to Franco, Hitler, Mussolini and the French extreme-right – there was only competition, rivalry and fear in their relationships as workers. Hence neither on humanitarian grounds, nor on grounds of the needs of French national defence, did the French trade unions take a lead to save the refugees from ostracism, internment and, for many, a forcible return to the prisons, torture and death squads of Franco's Spain. According to Marrus, 'as the fighting began in Poland, therefore, [on 1 September 1939] the French were busily sending the Spaniards home. Although repatriation was voluntary, the French applied considerable pressure on the refugees to leave. Between 150,000 and 200,000 did so before the end of the year.'[68]

Later the Daladier government found these camps tailor-made for the internment of French Communists and those suspected of subversion (such as the names on the notorious Carnet B, the Sûreté Nationale's 'wanted list', at the time of mobilisation in early September 1939). On 26 August the PCF's newspaper, *L'Humanité*, was closed down. On 26 September Daladier used his decree powers to outlaw the Party altogether. Leading militants were subsequently arrested. Communist deputies had their parliamentary immunity revoked and were put on trial in January 1940 in the so-called *procès des 44*, for breaches of the censorship regulations and distribution of illegal tracts liable to incite disobedience in the armed forces. The purge of the PCF was pursued on the pretext that the party and its affiliated organisations were a menace to national security because of their rigid obedience to Moscow and the signature of the Nazi-Soviet Non-Aggression Pact on 23 August 1939.[69] This new 'Red Scare' (France's third since 1936), became a veritable witch-hunt. The paranoia and score-settling which characterised this unedifying phase of the Second World War served only to maintain, even aggravate, the suspicion in which the French authorities held the Spanish Republican refugees.

But with the decision of the French authorities to require as many as possible of the Spaniards to take up work in France (not least to alleviate the costs of housing so many unproductively in the camps) a series of decrees and circulars were issued by the Minister of the Interior, Albert Sarraut, between March and July 1939 so that almost 70,000 Spaniards were integrated into the French economy. A decree of 12 April authorised foreigners to join the French army. It is plain in all this that the treatment of immigrants was *ad hoc*, made up by Daladier and his ministers as they went along. On the outbreak of war, as Elisabeth du Réau notes, 'under pressure from a concerned public, the government preferred to incarcerate large numbers of foreigners rather than call upon their services'. And, she adds, the 'problem of the Spanish political refugees was one of the most sensitive points' in all this. 'France had never before had to take in such a mass of fugitives in such a short space of time'.[70] A more generous and even more pragmatic approach emerged only later. 'From the end of 1939', writes Rafaneau-Boj, 'the French government, through the Ministry of Labour, pressed employers to convert the status of draftees into that of salaried workers by giving them work contracts which would entitle them to an official *carte du travail*, a residence permit, and freedom of movement. In March 1940 the Spaniards had their position regularised as 'free workers' with the same rights as their French colleagues.'[71]

During the Phoney War, then, most Spanish workers found employment, whilst former Republican militiamen were dispersed the length and breadth of France (including 2,600 draftees dispatched in CTEs to French North Africa).[72] Draftees directly under orders of the French military had diminished to about 25,000 by May 1940 and the launch of Germany's offensive in the West. Most of these found themselves given weapons and thrown into the frontline in vain attempts to halt the *Wehrmacht*. Most became German captives. They were denied POW status, the Nazis categorising them as 'political prisoners'. Death awaited many: of 7,288 deported to Mauthausen, 4,676, or almost 65 percent, died. Other Spaniards at large in the French economy when France fell had the unenviable choice of submitting to the French police and returning to the overcrowded concentration camps (where conditions were rapidly deteriorating) or going underground, seeking to survive in a wartime France of police checks, censorship, curfews, rationing and black-out restrictions, where the invasive presence of the State was felt in heavy-handed guise even by French citizens. Yet, showing astonishing resourcefulness and courage, some of the Spaniards at large in 1940 did successfully 'disappear', submerging themselves in French civil society. Some were assisted by the pre-existing Spanish community in France, others lived by their wits or received shelter from the French Communist and anarcho-syndicalist underground. In due course, later in the war, these Spaniards would play a full part in the dangerous, self-sacrificing activities of sections of the Resistance, especially through the FFI-MOI (*Forces Françaises de l'Intérieur-Main d'Oeuvre Immigrée*).[73]

That tragic, courageous, postscript is not, however, the concern of this essay. In conclusion, one must puncture, or at least challenge, some of the growing quantity of rather heroic myth which has – partly as a result of the work of so many fine historians – gathered around the saga of the Spanish Republican refugees. This essay has, ultimately, concerned itself with French governmental and military decision-making. It has focused on the politics and prejudices of those in positions of power and influence, including the parliamentary labour and industry commissioners, trade union leaders and major business figures.

Dispiriting though it may be to recognize this, the fact is that the Spanish refugees did not dominate the agendas of French leaders between February 1939 and early 1940. Scouring the journals kept by Frenchmen in a position to influence national policy, such as Jules Jeanneney, president of the Senate, Senator Jacques Bardoux, Daladier, Gamelin, Colonel Paul de Villelume, what is remarkable is the dearth of references to Spain, Spanish refugees, the camps. The same absence of the Spanish refugee question characterises the diaries of even the celebrated left-wing citizen-soldiers, such as Georges Sadoul and Jean-Paul Sartre.[74] Absent are any encounters with the Spanish labour companies working among the French troops at the front.

Nor did chroniclers from the French Right pay the Spaniards much attention. Alfred Fabre-Luce mentions evacuees and refugees in his 1939-40 journal, even referring to the Spanish Republicans. But he did so only in the context of a diatribe against the French government's mishandling of mobilisation. 'There are no victims from [enemy] bombing', he noted, 'but there are victims of our own precautions ... above all, our evacuees who mope, far from their household gods, in overcrowded villages.' These 'wretches', he continued, had been sacrificed to the myth that war would commence instantaneously with bombing, invasion, massive devastation of civilian life and property:

> The government has placed our evacuees out of reach of invasion by a Germany that has turned east, and from reprisals against air raids which we forbear to launch. But it has not been able to protect them from an anarchy of its own making. Sound accommodation to shelter them has not been requisitioned. No blankets are to be found; people say they have been given to the Spanish Republicans. This vast migration by herds of human beings ... was the great drama of the war's outbreak. ... entire communities being ejected from home and hearth.[75]

The 1939 refugee scandal, for Fabre-Luce, lay in France's callous, chaotic southerly transportation of scores of thousands of its own people. The Spanish fugitives were, in this narrative, a drain on resources, fresh burdens not fellow victims. Their existence served only to magnify the sufferings of the French.

The contemporary French perspectives on the Spanish refugee question are suggested, too, by the records of the organs of government. Even during the flood-tide of the Spanish exodus, little was said in the meetings where French ministers, top civil servants and military authorities convened. The CPDN was convoked on four occasions between December 1938 and April 1939. The army council, the CSG (*Conseil Supérieur de la Guerre*), met in March and July 1939.[76] At four of these six gatherings of France's senior defence policy-makers, Spain got no mention. When the talk turned to the Iberian peninsula, it had to do chiefly with the advent of a 'third military frontier' for France, exposing the country's southern flank. Discussion also occurred, to a degree, over the military utility to France of Spanish refugees with civil war combat experience (*vide* the recruits who joined the Foreign Legion and the question of the formation of the CTEs). Later, in the autumn and winter of 1939-40, the refugees were gradually accepted as an economic resource – though, here again, this owed a lot to the condition of French national finances and to a desire to rid the State of the economic burden that prolonged mass incarceration would have created.

The Spanish Republic's collapse and the consequent flight of its supporters and former troops into France was just one among many problems crowding the agendas of the French public authorities in 1939. The issue of Spain's refugees was largely left to local officials – to the prefects, sub-prefects and police commissioners of the Pyrénées-Atlantiques, the Basses-Pyrénées, the Ariège, the Aude, the Haute-Garonne and their subordinates on the spot in the towns along the frontier. More than five months after the fall of Barcelona, Gamelin sent Daladier a nine-page summary of the conclusions of the army council's meetings of 13 March and 10 July 1939. This reported that the earlier of the two meetings approved five recommendations for changes in the army's organisation 'to take account of the evolution of the external situation, [and] the requirements brought to light by our pre-mobilisation of September 1938', with the reinforcement of North Africa in fifth and last place.[77] The report went on to say that:

Since March 1939 external events, notably the disappearance of Czechoslovakia, have brought out some new requirements for the French Army, whose urgency has been judged to prioritise them over some of the reinforcements envisaged before. These requirements concern on the one hand, *the organisation of our air defences* ... and on the other, *the constitution of a motorised manoeuvre corps for immediate intervention* ... if a part of the front becomes especially threatened – or, eventually, to seize terrain beyond our frontiers (the Scheldt area and the Jura in particular).[78]

The aftermath of Hitler's 'Prague coup', the rapid deterioration of German-Polish relations by July 1939 and the problem of the Soviet Union's likely posture had brought French strategists and political leaders sharply back to their habitual preoccupation with the threat from the Third Reich. In Paris *un regard vers le Sud* occurred only fleetingly (albeit for a short time, in February 1939, as a real source of alarm). But in its *regard vers l'Est*, a look fixed upon Germany, the gaze of Daladier, Gamelin and Dautry never wavered.

Notes

1. A.P. Adamthwaite, *Grandeur and Misery. France's bid for power in Europe, 1914-1940*, London, 1995, p. 231, quoting *British Documents on Foreign Affairs*, vol. 21, 204.
2. On the concentration camps used for the Spanish refugees and their subsequent role in the fate of the Jews in France see A. Grynberg, *Les camps de la honte: les internés juifs des camps français, 1939-1944*, Paris, 1991; R. Poznanski, *Etre juif en France pendant la seconde guerre mondiale*, Paris, 1994. Cf. A. Wieviorka, *Déportation et génocide: entre la mémoire et l'oubli*, Paris, 1992; A. Wieviorka and S. Barcellini, *Passant souviens-toi ! Les lieux de souvenir de la seconde guerre mondiale en France*, Paris, 1995. See also the ground-breaking analysis of Michael R. Marrus and Robert O. Paxton, *Vichy France and the Jews*, New York, 1981 (first published in French as *Vichy et les Juifs*, Paris, 1981).
3. The history of the Spanish refugees in France is multi faceted, full and extensive. It cannot be retold in detail in this essay. For more information see D.W. Pike, *Vae Victis! Los republicanos españoles refugiados en Francia, 1939-1944*, Paris, 1969; M.-C. Rafaneau-Boj, *Odyssée pour la liberté. Les camps des prisonniers espagnols, 1939-1945*, Paris, 1993, reviewed by D.W. Pike in *Guerres mondiales et Conflits contemporains*, no. 177, 1995: 195-6. Cf. G. Badia et al., *Les barbelés de l'exil*, Grenoble, 1979.
4. On French reactions to the Spanish Civil War as a whole see D.W. Pike, *Les Français et la Guerre d'Espagne, 1936-1939*, Paris, 1975; J. Sagnes and S. Caucanas (eds.), *Les Français et la Guerre d'Espagne. Actes du Colloque de Perpignan*, Perpignan, 1990; see also David W. Pike's contribution to this present volume.
5. M.R. Marrus, *The Unwanted: European Refugees in the Twentieth Century*, New York and Oxford, 1985, p. 191.
6. On the broader history of the impact of immigration and refugee movements on France in the mid-twentieth century see G.S. Cross, *Immigrant Workers in Industrial France. The making of a new laboring class*, Philadelphia, 1983; idem,

'Toward social peace and prosperity: the politics of immigration in France during the era of World War One', *French Historical Studies* XI, no. 4, 1980: 610-32; J.N. Horne, 'Immigrant workers in France during World War One', *French Historical Studies* XIV, no. 1, 1985: 57-88; R. Schor, *L'Opinion française et les étrangers, 1919-1939*, Paris, 1985; T.P. Maga, 'Closing the Door: the French Government and refugee policy, 1933-1939', *French Historical Studies* XII, no. 3, 1982: 424-42; O. Milza, *Les Français devant l'immigration*, Brussels, 1988; V. Caron, 'The Missed Opportunity: French Refugee Policy in Wartime, 1939-40', in *Historical Reflections/Réflexions Historiques* 22, no. 1, 1996: 117-57.

7. See esp. Cross's works cited above; also D.N. Reid, 'The Limits of Paternalism: immigrant coal miners' communities in France, 1919-1945', *European History Quarterly* 15, no. 1, 1985: 99-117.

8. See T. Judt, 'France without Glory', *New York Review of Books*, 23 May 1996.

9. On French strategic thinking during the Spanish Civil War see Peter Jackson's contribution to this present volume.

10. See 'Audition de M. Pierre Cot, Ancien Ministre de l'Air', 1 August 1947, in *République Française: Commission d'enquête parlementaire sur les événements survenus en France de 1933 à 1945. Témoignages et documents recueillis*, 9 vols, Paris, 1950-51, vol. I: 273-4.

11. See M. Livian, *Le Parti Socialiste et l'immigration. Le gouvernement Blum, la main d'oeuvre immigrée, et les réfugiés politiques, 1920-1940*, Paris, 1982.

12. See Maga, 'Closing the Door', *passim*. It was not just Spaniards who found entry into France more difficult from 1938 onwards. See V. Caron, 'Prelude to Vichy: France and the Jewish refugees in the era of appeasement', *Journal of Contemporary History* 20, 1985: 157-76; idem, 'The Politics of Frustration: French Jewry and the refugee crisis in the 1930s', *Journal of Modern History* 65, no. 2, 1993: 311-56; B. Stora, *Ils venaient d'Algérie. L'immigration algérienne en France (1912-1992)*, Paris, 1992.

13. Milza, *Les Français devant l'immigration*, p. 57.

14. See, for example, P. Webster, *Pétain's Crime. The full story of French collaboration in the Holocaust*, London, 1990, pp. 60-1.

15. W.D. Irvine, Review on H-France internet discussion group, 9 May 1996, of M.B. Miller, *Shanghai on the Metro: Spies, Intrigue and the French between the Wars*, Berkeley CA, 1994.

16. Milza, *Les Français devant l'immigration*, p. 57.

17. Pike, *Les Français et la Guerre d'Espagne*, pp. 350-1.

18. Ibid., pp. 351-6. Cf. G. Stone, 'Britain, France and Franco's Spain in the Aftermath of the Spanish Civil War', *Diplomacy and Statecraft* 6, no. 2, 1995: 373-407.

19. Pike, *Les Français et la Guerre d'Espagne*, p. 350.

20. Ibid., p. 357.

21. Quoted in ibid., p. 353.

22. Indeed, Jordana had orally assured Bérard that the Nationalist government would receive back all refugees without distinction and that the frontier would remain open without reserve. But he had added, in what could only be a warning of the inevitability of political reprisals, that those who had committed 'offences' would certainly be tried before Spanish tribunals (Stone, 'Britain, France and Franco's Spain', 378).

23. Pike, *Les Français et la Guerre d'Espagne*, pp. 337-57.

24. According to Pierre Taittinger, a millionaire hotel and champagne company owner, conservative deputy for Paris, founder of the authoritarian movement

Les Jeunesses Patriotes and prime mover of the extreme-right demonstrations in Paris against Daladier's earlier government on 6 February 1934, writing in the south-western paper *La Garonne* on 16 March 1939, Negrín had said to Jules Henry, as they crossed the frontier *en route* for Toulouse on 9 February 1939, that the Spanish Republic's sole remaining hope now lay in the outbreak of a general war. Cited in Pike, *Les Français et la Guerre d'Espagne*, p. 345.

25. Milza, *Les Français devant l'immigration*, p. 57.
26. H.E. Graham, *Socialism and War. The Spanish Socialist Party in power and crisis, 1936-1939*, Cambridge, 1991, p. 238.
27. Milza, *Les Français devant l'immigration*, p. 57.
28. See M.S. Alexander, *The Republic in Danger. General Maurice Gamelin and the politics of French defence, 1933-1940*, Cambridge, 1993, pp. 138-40, 356-9.
29. Quoted in Pike, *Les Français et la Guerre d'Espagne*, p. 340.
30. On French strategic thinking during the Civil War see Peter Jackson's contribution to this present volume.
31. M.-G. Gamelin, *Servir*, 3 vols, Paris, 1946-47, vol. II, *Le prologue du drame, 1930-août 1939*, p. 389.
32. Ibid., p. 408.
33. Ibid.
34. J.-B. Duroselle, *Politique étrangère de la France. L'Abîme, 1939-1945*, Paris, 1982, p. 129.
35. For the views of Pétain and the concerns of General Charles-Auguste Noguès, Resident-General in Rabat and commander-in-chief of French North Africa, over the threat to Tangier and French Morocco from the 'return to the Spanish zone of Morocco of several tens of thousands of Moroccan regulars' and the possibility of Franco conceding naval and air facilities to the Axis powers, see Stone, 'Britain, France and Franco's Spain', pp. 382-4. See also Martin Thomas's contribution to this present volume.
36. Gamelin, *Servir*, II, 408.
37. The minutes of these meetings are reproduced *verbatim* in Gamelin, *Servir*, II: 371-8, 391-401.
38. Marrus, *The Unwanted*, p. 191.
39. Ibid., p. 192.
40. See Stone, 'Britain, France and Franco's Spain', 379-80, 385-94.
41. Marrus, *The Unwanted*, p. 192.
42. See T. Kemp, 'The French economy under the Franc Poincaré', in *Contemporary France. Illusion, Conflict and Regeneration*, ed. J. C. Cairns, New York, 1978, pp. 66-91, and esp. p. 78.
43. See J. Colton, *Leon Blum: Humanist in Politics*, Durham NC, 1987, pp. 178-97; and the same author's 'Politics and Economics in the 1930s: The Balance Sheets of the "Blum New Deal"', in *From the Ancien Regime to the Popular Front. Essays in the History of Modern France in Honor of Shepard B. Clough*, ed. C.K. Warner, New York, 1969, pp. 181-208.
44. See J. Jackson, *The Popular Front in France, 1934-1938: Defending Democracy*, Cambridge, 1988; M.S. Alexander and H.E. Graham (eds), *The French and Spanish Popular Fronts: Comparative Perspectives*, Cambridge, 1989; G. Lefranc, *Histoire du Front Populaire*, Paris, 1970; J. Delperrié de Bayac, *Histoire du Front Populaire*, Paris, 1972.
45. SHAT, *Fonds Gamelin*, 1K 224 Carton 4, Dossier: 'Procès de Riom: Enquêtes et Notes', sub-dossier no. 4, annex 7 to report by Controller-General Valette, "La

mobilisation industrielle", Etat-Major de l'Armée: Section d'Armements et Etudes techniques, no. 1914 10/EMA, le général Gamelin, 'Note pour le Secré-taire-General (M. Jacomet). Objet: Fabrications d'Armement', 7 May 1937.

46. See E. du Réau, 'L'aménagement de la loi instituant la semaine de quarante heures', in *Edouard Daladier, chef de gouvernement*, eds R. Rémond and J. Bour-din, Paris, 1977, pp. 129-49.

47. 'Procès-verbal des décisions prises au cours de la conférence tenue au ministère de la guerre, le 9 avril 1939, Section VII – *Réfugiés Etrangers*', doc. reproduced in Gamelin, *Servir*, II: 407.

48. Ibid.

49. Milza, *Les Français devant l'immigration*, p. 57.

50. Rafaneau-Boj, *Odysée pour la liberté*, p. 177.

51. See Alexander, *The Republic in Danger*, p. 117.

52. Colton, *Léon Blum*, p. 171.

53. AAN, folder B102, dossier no. 2, Chambre des Députés: Commission du Tra-vail, 'Procès-verbal de la séance du 28 juin 1939: audience de M. Pomaret, ministre du travail', 5-6, 16e Législature (1936-1940).

54. See the excellent modern study by R. Baudoui, *Raoul Dautry, 1880-1951. Le technocrate de la République*, Paris, 1992. Dautry's importance and interest has belatedly attracted a number of scholarly studies. See E. du Réau, 'Un techni-cien parmi les politiques, Raoul Dautry, ministre de l'Armement, septembre 1939-juin 1940', Actes du Colloque Raoul Dautry, *Cahiers de l'IFA*, Paris, 1987; M. Avril, *Raoul Dautry, 1880-1951. La passion de servir*, Paris, 1993; V. Halperin, *Raoul Dautry, un batisseur de la SNCF au CEA*, Paris, 1996.

55. *Commission d'enquête parlementaire*, VII-VII, 'Séance du mardi 11 janvier 1949. Audition de M. Raoul Dautry, ancien ministre', 1945-1982 (quotation, 1947).

56. See Alexander, *The Republic in Danger*, pp. 354-5.

57. Rafaneau-Boj, *Odysée pour la Liberté*, pp. 172-3.

58. AAN, carton XV, République Française: Chambre des Députés, 'Mission d'in-spection effectuée le 1er décembre 1939 pour le compte de la Commission de l'Armée par MM. Chouffet, Courson et Taittinger, portant sur les Usines Renault et sur l'Arsenal de Puteaux', 2, 16e Législature (1936-40).

59. See Miller, *Shanghai on the Metro*, pp. 144-8.

60. Milza, *Les Français devant l'immigration*, p. 57.

61. Rafaneau-Boj, *Odysée pour la liberté*, p. 174.

62. AAN, folder B102, dr. no. 3, Chambre des Députés: Commission du Travail, 'Procès-verbal de la séance du 6 mars 1940: audience de M. Pomaret, ministre du travail', 19-20, 16e Législature.

63. Rafaneau-Boj, *Odyssée pour la liberté*, p. 175.

64. On this issue and its intersection with attitudes in France towards immigrants and refugees there is an extensive literature, including contemporary scholarly inquiries such as J.J. Spengler, *France Faces Depopulation*, Durham, NC, 1938, esp. pp. 127-33, 175-217, 242-300. For more recent analyses cf. D. Kirk, 'Popu-lation and Population Trends in Modern France', in *Modern France. Problems of the Third and Fourth Republics*, ed. E.M. Earle, Princeton, NJ, 1951, pp. 313-33; Schor, *L'Opinion française*; W.H. Schneider, *Quality and Quantity. The Quest for Biological Regeneration in Twentieth Century France*, Cambridge, 1991, pp. 230-55.

65. See Prost, 'Le climat social' and J.-P. Rioux, 'La conciliation et l'arbitrage oblig-atoire des conflits du travail', in *Edouard Daladier*, eds Rémond and Bourdin, pp. 99-111, 112-28.

66. AAN, Carton XVII, République Française: Chambre des Députés – Commission de l'Armée, 16e législature (1936-1940): 'Procès-verbal de la séance no. 66, du 11 octobre 1939', p. 3.

67. 'Aux directeurs des établissements militaires dépendant du Ministère de l'Armement', 29 December 1939, reproduced in R. Dautry, testimony, 11 January 1949, in *Commission d'enquête parlementaire*, VII-VIII, 1962-3 (emphasis added).

68. Marrus, *The Unwanted*, p. 192.

69. See G. Rossi-Landi, 'Le pacifisme en France (1939-1940)', in *Français et Britanniques dans la Drôle de Guerre*, Paris, 1979, pp. 123-52; J.K. Munholland, 'The Daladier government and the "Red Scare" of 1938-1940', in *Proceedings of the Tenth Annual Meeting of the Western Society for French History (14-16 October 1982)*, ed. J.F. Sweets, Lawrence, KA, 1984, pp. 495-506.

70. E. du Réau, *Edouard Daladier, 1884-1970*, Paris, 1993, pp. 324-5.

71. Rafaneau-Boj, *Odyssée pour la liberté*, p. 176.

72. About 148,000 Spanish civilian refugees were, according to Ralph Schor, accommodated in 'relatively acceptable' conditions. But the Spanish militiamen, some 209,000, plus a further 16,500 civilians, were confined in about fifteen insanitary and brutally-administered camps. Cf. Schor, *L'opinion française et les étrangers*, pp. 617-83; du Reau, *Edouard Daladier*, p. 325.

73. See J.C. Simmonds, 'Immigrant Fighters for the Liberation of France: a local profile of Carmagnole-Liberté in Lyon', in *The Liberation of France. Image and Event*, eds H.R. Kedward and N. Wood, Oxford and Washington, 1995, pp. 29-41; G. Laroche, *On les nommait des étrangers; les immigrés dans la Résistance*, Paris, 1965; K. Bartosek *et al.* (eds), *De l'exil à la Résistance. Réfugiés et immigrés d'Europe centrale en France, 1933-1945*, Vincennes, 1989; S. Courtois, D. Peschanski and A. Rayski, *Le sang de l'étranger. Les immigrés de la MOI dans la Résistance*, Paris, 1989.

74. G. Sadoul, *Journal de guerre, 2 septembre 1939-20 juillet 1940*, Paris, 1977; *The War Diaries of Jean-Paul Sartre. November 1939-March 1940*, trans. Q. Hoare, New York, 1984.

75. A. Fabre-Luce, *Journal de la France. Mars 1939 – Juillet 1940*, Paris, 1940, pp. 120-1.

76. The minutes of these CSG meetings of 13 March and 10 July 1939, along with a summary of their conclusions by Gamelin ('Rapport fait au ministre de la Défense nationale et de la Guerre par le général Gamelin, le 18 juillet 1939') are in SHAT, carton 1N 22.

77. SHAT, CSG, carton 1N 22, 'Rapport fait au ministre de la Défense nationale et de la Guerre par le général Gamelin' (18 July 1939), pp. 1, 3.

78. Ibid., pp. 3-4.

7

Germany's Conception of Spain's Strategic Importance, 1940-1941

Norman J.W. Goda (University of Ohio, Athens)

I

IN JUNE 1940, the Spanish Government of Francisco Franco offered to enter the Second World War on the side of Adolf Hitler's Germany. When the German reply arrived six days later, it was lukewarm at best; Berlin did little more than acknowledge the Spanish offer. Yet seven months later, in January 1941, the German Government demanded that Spain enter the war. Berlin presented Franco with a two-day deadline to acquiesce, and threatened the end of Nationalist Spain should he refuse. Now it was Franco's turn to maintain silence, and in the end, Spain did not enter the conflict. This turnabout in German-Spanish relations during the early stages of World War II is one of the most interesting yet least understood episodes of the Second World War. It is best explained through an examination of Germany's strategic ideas concerning Spain during the conflict.

Previous scholarship on German interest in Spanish belligerence has defined Spain's importance in terms of a peripheral Mediterranean strategy against Britain. The argument runs as follows. The defeat of France in June 1940 left Germany unable to compel Britain's surrender through the direct measures of blockade, bombardment, and the threat of invasion. Hitler thus seized upon the suggestion of his advisers that the Axis could end the war with attacks on

Britain's Mediterranean targets of Gibraltar and the Suez Canal. By the autumn of 1940, Hitler hoped that this strategy could end British resistance so that Germany's flank would be clear by spring 1941 for the primary aim – the annihilation of the Soviet Union and the acquisition of *Lebensraum* in the East. Spain's entrance into the war, then, was to have been part of an interim strategy to permit the isolated war in the East that France's defeat alone had failed to create. The deterioration of Italy's position in the Mediterranean in the winter of 1940-1, meanwhile, made Spain's participation in the war and the conquest of Gibraltar all the more urgent. Confronted with Italian disasters in Greece, Taranto, and North Africa, the Germans now had to seal the western Mediterranean or allow the Axis to suffer serious setbacks. Thus the furious demands in early 1941 for Spanish cooperation.[1]

The present analysis will examine German interest in Spanish belligerence in a different context, and will argue the following: Hitler's interest in Spanish support perhaps had less to do with a Mediterranean strategy on Germany's part than has previously been assumed. It is true that the OKM began to advocate a peripheral strategy against the British in the autumn of 1940. Yet Hitler himself never fully subscribed to this idea, despite continued British intransigence and Italian misfortunes. Hitler's interest in Spain might have had more to do with the fate of the French empire in north-west Africa and with the Spanish and Portuguese islands off the coast. The Germans hoped to obtain base sites in this general region for development and eventual use in a future war against the United States. The question of strategic bases on and off the coast of north-west Africa preoccupied Hitler throughout the autumn and winter of 1940. His original interest in the Gibraltar Strait – and thus in Spain's entry into the war – lay in the Iberian peninsula's position as the gateway to north-west Africa. The level of his interest at any given time thereafter was directly related to the possibility that French North Africa could defect from the Vichy French Government to Free France, Britain, or the United States. Shifting German policies toward Spain together with Germany's ultimate failure to bring the Spaniards into the war are better understood within this context.

II

Since the 1920s, Hitler had argued that the Nordic struggle for racial dominance would one day assume global dimensions. Indeed, racial struggle was a dialectical historical process; it could not end until one race had made itself supreme. Thus following the conquest of Europe, Germany would have to confront the United States, which in Nazi lore was a racially mongrelised yet industrially powerful society.[2] In the famous 'Hoßbach Conference' of November 1937, Hitler announced to his military aides that Germany would complete the conquest of Europe between 1943 and 1945.[3] German weapons contracts, however, were already looking further ahead. Already in the mid-1930s, the German Navy had begun to place orders for a mammoth battle fleet which was to be complete in its essentials by 1946 – when Europe would supposedly lie conquered. The 48,000 ton battleship *Bismarck* was ordered in 1935; its sister ship *Tirpitz*, in 1936; and in 1939 six more battleships, each to have a displacement of 56,000 tons, were ordered and begun. Since the time needed to complete a battleship of this size was at least six years, we can assume that the Germans believed that they would need such a navy not during, but rather after the European war which then loomed on the horizon. We can assume the same about the Messerschmitt 264 – the so-called *Amerika-Bomber*. Design work on this four-engined aircraft, which was to have a range of over 12,000 kilometers, began in 1935.[4] These projects slowed following the outbreak of war in 1939 but resumed their prewar pace following the defeat of France in 1940.[5] Hitler on more than one occasion gave voice to his expectation that the bomber at least would be ready for use against the United States by the end of 1941.[6]

Yet where would the Germans station their new weapons? Germany itself enjoyed no easy access to the ocean. With Hitler's approval the German Navy in 1940 began planning a massive new complex at the Norwegian site of Trondheim, complete with shipyards and an authentic German town which was to be linked to Germany by *Autobahn*.[7] Still, more forward Atlantic sites remained desirable. The most favourable area was north-west Africa, including French Morocco and Senegal, Spain's Canary Islands, and Portugal's Azores and Cape Verde Islands. Borrowed or shared bases, as will be seen, were insufficient. Germany needed to *own* the sites in order to develop them, especially for the aircraft and warships which it would deploy following its European victories. During the 1930s, the German Navy had wistfully mentioned the possibilities that such sites would offer.[8] Yet the defeat of France in June 1940 for the first time made the acquisition of such sites a real possibility.

The German Armistice Treaty with France made no territorial demands in the French empire. By such apparent reticence, Hitler simply hoped to prevent French Africa's defection from the new government of Marshal Henri Philippe Pétain, soon to be located at Vichy. He also hoped that the imperial-minded British, who seemed near defeat themselves, would make peace as well.[9] Yet Berlin fully intended to change this seemingly generous stance concerning Africa at a later peace conference. On 20 June 1940, the day before cease-fire talks with France *had even begun*, Hitler and Grand Admiral Erich Raeder spoke of future German installations in Morocco, Senegal, and the Spanish and Portuguese Islands. Such bases, the two agreed, would grant a strategic advantage against future enemies in the Atlantic. With France defeated and Britain seemingly close behind, 'future enemies' could only have meant the United States.[10]

Except in its capacity as the donor of one of the Canary Islands to Germany, Spain did not fit into these calculations. Franco, however, was hoping for a much greater role in the emerging new world order. France's military catastrophe on the continent opened up a list of long-standing Spanish territorial claims in French Africa. Already on 14 June the Spaniards had taken advantage of France's misfortunes to occupy the French-administered international zone of Tangier.[11] Yet Madrid was expecting more, namely a generous extension of the Spanish protectorate of Morocco. Having failed in late June to wring from the French Government an adjustment of the protectorate borders, and having decided at the last moment not to invade French Morocco due to insufficient air strength, Madrid decided to become a German ally.[12] On 19 June, Franco's Government offered to enter the war against Britain in return for economic aid, support in defending the Canary Islands, and a list of prizes in North Africa which included all of French Morocco and the Oran district of Algeria.[13] Berlin all but ignored Madrid's overtures. With France defeated and Britain seemingly close behind, a high-priced alliance with a destitute country in a war that seemed over found little enthusiasm. Three days after Franco's offer to enter the war, Berlin had still yet to reply, and the German embassy in Madrid had to ask its own foreign ministry what Germany's policy was![14]

In the meantime, Hitler tried to gain a foothold in French Morocco without consulting Madrid at all. On 15 July he demanded from France eight airbases near Casablanca to be chosen by a special German Commission, along with the use of the railways from Tunis to Rabat to outfit the bases properly. Historians have tied the German demand to Britain's attack of 3 July on the French fleet at the Algerian port of Mers-el-Kébir, arguing that Berlin aimed to protect French naval units in Casablanca from a similar strike while disrupting British communications with the Egyptian theater. This explanation is problematic. Aside from the unfinished battleship *Jean Bart*, France had few warships in Casablanca worth attacking, and nearly two weeks had elapsed between Mers-el-Kébir and the Casablanca demand with no hint of an impending British raid there. Hitler, meanwhile, was convinced of an imminent triumph over Britain, which would have rendered bases in Casablanca extraneous if he had truly intended their use against the Royal Navy. The same week as the Casablanca demand he crafted a verbal peace offer to London and predicted that even should the British refuse an arrangement, German bombardment would force surrender within four weeks. Hitler during that week had in fact turned to post-war Atlantic projects like naval and strategic base development. On 11 July, he and Raeder discussed at length future battleship design and the possibility of a new German base in one of the lesser Canary Islands, which, like Trondheim, would need substantial development. It is likely that the prospective bases in Casablanca fitted into these post-war schemes rather than the current conflict. The planned use of the Tunis-Rabat railroad alone meant that their development would have demanded more time than the four weeks Hitler allowed for continued British resistance. In any event, the *Luftwaffe* in the summer of 1940 was massing its strength on the English Channel, not in Africa. In truth then, Hitler attempted to use the Mers-el-Kébir raid to bypass the Armistice Convention with France and to justify what would doubtless have become a permanent German presence in French Morocco. As matters emerged, Pétain rejected the Casablanca demand as beyond the Armistice Convention.[15] Yet the episode revealed Hitler's interest in the northwest African region for the post-war period. It also revealed that in mid-July 1940 Spain was so far removed from German strategic thinking that bases across the Gibraltar Strait would apparently not even necessitate its participation in the war.

An understanding with Spain and the conquest of Gibraltar became urgent in the late summer of 1940 due to several factors. The first was Hitler's staff announcement of 31 July that Germany would annihilate the Soviet Union the following spring. This step would provide Germany with its *Lebensraum* in the East while also depriving the British, if they chose to continue their vain resistance, of their last continental hope. Spain's participation in the war now became more pressing, but not due to Gibraltar's value in the war with Britain. Hitler argued in the 31 July meeting that Germany would still defeat Britain by direct means; that the invasion of England, Operation Seelöwe, could still occur in 1940; and that Gibraltar's worth against Britain was only diversionary.[16] Yet Gibraltar was important in another context. In the spring, the *Wehrmacht* would turn eastward, and north-west Africa would lie vulnerable to British or perhaps U.S. attack. If Germany were to guarantee itself a presence in north-west Africa after the conquest of Europe, it would need to gain at least a foothold there before the Eastern Campaign. Vichy's rejection of Hitler's Casablanca demand meant that Germany needed another junior partner in north-west Africa – Spain, and another route to north-west Africa – the Gibraltar Strait. The second factor which added to the strategic importance of Spain would be Charles de Gaulle's coup of late August in French Equatorial Africa. The coup, which began in Chad and spread all the way to Gabon, triggered the concern in Berlin that strategically more important areas in French North and West Africa could also defect to the Free French movement. Hitler had even begun, incorrectly, to suspect secret ties between de Gaulle and Vichy.[17] The third factor would be the German concern that Washington would use de Gaulle and/or the British to secure strategic regions in north-west Africa for itself. The Destroyer-Base Deal between London and Washington on 2 September 1940, which gave the United States eight bases in the West Atlantic, prompted the following statement from the German Naval Command, to which Hitler agreed:

> One can hardly reckon with decisive [U.S.] aid to [Britain]. ..Yet the possibility of ... American action looms in the occupation of the Spanish and Portuguese islands ... and ... of the French colonies of West Africa. ... [An] American landing would doubtless lead to ... permanent establishment ... in [this] area. Thus ... after the British defeat [!], the Anglo-Saxon world would maintain strategically important positions while making the desired German establishment there difficult if not impossible!![18]

Thus in August and September 1940 Berlin embarked on a grandiose scheme to gain full strategic control of north-west Africa before the commencement of the Eastern Campaign. The gateway to the entire region was Spain and the Gibraltar Strait.

After six weeks of silence, Berlin began to move on the Spanish offer of 19 June. On 2 August 1940 Foreign Minister Joachim von Ribbentrop informed the German embassy in Madrid that, 'we want to achieve ... Spain's early entrance into the war.' Ribbentrop even planned to visit Madrid himself to make final arrangements with the Spaniards. By the end of the month, the OKW had completed the planning for the conquest of Gibraltar, codenamed

Operation Felix.[19] Spain's economic and material needs were staggering – much more than Hitler would have underwritten for a diversion, and much more than the OKW wished to underwrite for any reason. The objections of Four-year Plan director Hermann Göring and Army Chief of Staff Franz Halder are both particularly noteworthy in this regard. Yet Hitler was determined that Spain's material needs not stymie the Gibraltar operation, and by mid-September, Berlin, at Hitler's insistence, had agreed in principle to Madrid's economic demands.[20]

A look at the Gibraltar operation's further development further opens to reinvestigation the traditional argument that an understanding with Spain was part of a peripheral Mediterranean strategy aimed at Britain. It is true that by the autumn of 1940 the German Navy had arrived at the hope that a strategy which focused on Gibraltar and Suez would convince London to surrender. Operation Seelöwe had always been problematic to the OKM, and it had repeatedly objected to an invasion of the Soviet Union before Britain's defeat. The Mediterranean theatre offered the sole hope of defeating the British before the Eastern Campaign or the entry of the United States into the war made the task more difficult.[21] The evidence shows, however, that Hitler remained convinced that the British were already beaten, and that it was time to take preliminary steps for a war against the United States. In the first place, he would insist in November – over the objections of the German Army Operations Staff – that once Gibraltar fell, two divisions, including the Third Panzer Division, would move into Spanish Morocco. The Army argued that if Germany needed to help seal the entrance to the Mediterranean by protecting its southern shore from a British landing, then no more than a few artillery pieces and a battalion to guard them would be needed. The Spaniards already had their best seven divisions in Spanish Morocco and neither Tangier nor Ceuta were ports fit for major naval operations anyway. Still, Hitler insisted that the two divisions be moved.[22] Their function, as Hitler's later comments would show, was not to guard Tangier and Ceuta, but rather to occupy French Morocco should it show any sign of joining de Gaulle. For the interim, Berlin in the third week of September sent an espionage mission composed mainly of *Luftwaffe* officers to Casablanca specifically to examine the political situation and reconnoitre base sites. As Hitler wrote to Benito Mussolini on 17 September,

> There is still the danger of a [French] secession movement in [the North African] colonies. There is no assurance that [it] might not even

occur in secret agreement with the French Government. ... But as soon
as there is a reliable bridge to North Africa via Spain I would no longer
consider this danger to be very great.[23]

Moreover, the decision to send the two divisions to Morocco was
made after Hitler's decision not to send the same armoured units to
Egypt, where the Italians needed a push in their drive for the Suez
canal.[24] Hitler's decision to send two divisions to well-defended
Spanish Morocco, where there was no war in progress, instead of to
Egypt, where there was indeed a war, shows that his intentions had
less to do with the Mediterranean as such. In addition, the Gibraltar campaign was soon expanded to include related objectives. On
5 September, three days after the Destroyer-Base Deal was
announced, Hitler ordered a very reluctant OKW to plan the capture of the Portuguese Azores and Cape Verde Islands. The occupation was to be executed concurrently with the Gibraltar
operation, and German troops would occupy Portugal if the government in Lisbon made any objections.[25] Finally, the diplomatic
preparations for the Gibraltar campaign were substantially geared
toward securing African bases for Germany. In return for Spanish
cooperation, Hitler agreed in principle to Spain's economic needs,
and he was willing to honour Madrid's claim to French Morocco,
thus rejecting an equally-vocal Italian claim to that protectorate.[26]
Yet in return, he would insist that Franco cede to Germany one of
the Canary Islands as well as bases on the French Moroccan coast
should the French zone go to Spain.[27] This insistence, as will be
seen, would go a long way toward wrecking any strategic arrangement with Madrid. Thus Berlin would prioritise the supposed need
for post-war bases in Africa for a future war against the United
States over the conquest of Gibraltar as a means to cripple the
British in the present conflict. As Ribbentrop explained to Italian
Foreign Minister Galeazzo Ciano on 4 November, 'this huge programme must not be regarded as ... directed against England. As
far as England is concerned, the war is already won. ... The programme has more of an anti-American character.'[28]

III

The implementation of German plans would ultimately wreck on the
shoals of inadequate diplomacy. Hitler would insist on outright German ownership of the new bases, he would hide the full truth of his
aims from his prospective junior partners in north-west Africa, and

he would refuse to negotiate with them as equals. Problems immediately emerged with Madrid on the issue of German bases in Spanish territory. On 16 September 1940 Ramón Serrano Suñer, Franco's Interior Minister and brother-in-law, arrived in Berlin for two scheduled discussions; one with Ribbentrop and one with Hitler. The Germans pressed him for bases in Morocco and the Canaries, arguing that within the decade aircraft technology would shrink the distance from North America to Africa, that the United States was interested in the regions in question, and that there was no time to lose. Shared bases were unsatisfactory, for as Ribbentrop counselled,

> present wars are won by those who have the best technical equipment, and who ... have prepared materially for the struggle for decades ... construction of ports, buildings, airfield installations, and similar material preparations ... would have to be completed long in advance, during peacetime.[29]

Ribbentrop tried to rattle Serrano, a novice at high-level diplomacy by prohibiting the Spanish ambassador from attending the discussions and by refusing to drop the issue of bases. He also detained Serrano Suñer for additional meetings.[30] Yet with Franco's hearty approval Serrano firmly rejected the notion of German-owned enclaves in Spanish territory. Franco was willing to share bases in a long-term alliance with the Germans, but as he had written to Serrano in Berlin, Spain would suffer no more Gibraltars.

> Our presence in the Axis offers ... the security and the domination of the western Mediterranean and the possibility of defence of our continent including North Africa, making it invulnerable to Anglo-American attacks. ... In this it is necessary to open a channel to the idea of what an alliance is; in the order of war, the bases of one become the bases of another. If we are to defend the European front, we will prepare our bases.[31]

A frustrated Hitler could only make the following complaint to Benito Mussolini on 4 October, when the two met at the Brenner Pass. 'Germany,' he said, 'was not interested in Spanish harbors ... she needed bases of her own, already equipped by herself during peacetime.'[32]

The African picture would grow muddier thanks to Vichy's spirited defence against the Anglo-Gaullist attack on Dakar on 23 September. As Vichy's statesmen made clear after the episode, Berlin would now have to give the French the hope of keeping their empire, lest they not repel future attacks. Berlin took the threat seriously, especially since it was convinced that Washington had somehow or another ordered the attack on Dakar.[33] The need to square German, Spanish, and now French aims in Africa led to Hitler's famous October rail journey to Montoire and Hendaye to meet with Pétain and Franco respectively. The trip was to be, as Hitler privately described it, a 'Grand Deception'.[34] France, despite defending its empire, would still surrender key parts of it to Germany and Italy. Perhaps France could be compensated with Nigeria once the British surrendered. Spain would allow the German conquest of Gibraltar, but now its reward would be no more than a slight extension of Spanish Morocco. Neither France nor Spain would learn the truth until after the peace and would receive vague assurances in the meantime.

The rail journey was thus smoke and mirrors from the German standpoint. Marshal Pétain and Vice-Premier Pierre Laval promised at Montoire to defend France's empire against its former allies for Hitler's murky promise that the empire could thus avoid 'considerable diminishment'.[35] At Hendaye, Franco and Serrano Suñer were more difficult to swindle. Though still willing to enter the war – Spain had ignored a French offer of 30 September to extend the border of Spanish Morocco[36] – the Spaniards demanded a firm German guarantee for all of French Morocco. Hitler refused, arguing that such a promise would trigger a north-west African defection from France and possibly to America. 'The greatest threat existing at the moment,' said Hitler,

> was that a part of the colonial empire would … desert France and go over to de Gaulle, England, or the United States. … The greatest problem to be solved at the moment consisted in hindering the de Gaulle movement … from … extending itself and thereby establishing … bases for England and America on the African coast.[37]

The Spaniards were fully alive to the Gaullist danger. Since the Armistice they had been pressing Rome and Berlin to disarm French forces in Morocco with greater alacrity. Still, Franco and Serrano insisted on a written promise for French Morocco, which they planned to defend themselves against Allied encroachments.[38] Despite the visible irritation of the Spanish delegation, and despite the absence of a firm written agreement which guaranteed Spain's entry into the war, Hitler left Hendaye believing that his arguments had carried the day, and that the German scheme would carry forward. North-west Africa, in fact, was his main topic of discussion when he met with Mussolini in Florence on 28 October, despite the commencement of Italy's potentially disastrous campaign in Greece on the same day.[39] The Führer was still aglow with the apparent success of the trip on 12 and 13 November when he described its supposed results to Soviet Foreign Minister V.M. Molotov. 'The United States,' Hitler said,

> was now pursuing an imperialistic policy. It was not fighting for England, but only trying to get the British empire into its grasp. They were helping England, at best, in order to further their own rearmament and to reinforce their military power by acquiring bases. In the distant future it will be a question of establishing a greater solidarity among those countries which might be involved in case of an extension of the sphere of influence of this Anglo-Saxon power, which had by far a more solid foundation than England. In this case, it was not a question of the immediate future; not in 1945, but in 1970 or 1980, at the earliest, would the freedom of other nations be seriously endangered by this Anglo-Saxon power. At any rate, the continent of Europe had to adjust itself now to this development and had to act jointly against the Anglo-Saxons and against any of their attempts to acquire dangerous bases. Therefore, he has undertaken an exchange of ideas with France, Italy, and Spain, in order with these countries to set up in the whole of Europe and Africa some kind of Monroe Doctrine and to adopt a new joint colonial policy by which each of the powers concerned would claim for itself only as much colonial territory as it could really use.
>
> In the West, between Spain, France, Italy, and Germany, he believed he had found a formula which satisfied everyone alike. It had not been easy to reconcile the views of Spain and France, for example, in regard to North Africa; however, recognizing the greater future possibilities, both countries had finally given in.[40]

If the troops to be employed against the USSR were to be available by the spring then Gibraltar had to fall by February 1941.[41] In November, the Germans hoped to tie up the loose diplomatic ends with Spain, and thus implement the capture of the Rock. Yet Berlin vastly overestimated the degree to which it had brought the Spaniards along with German aims. Though still willing to enter the war, Franco remained far more uneasy about Berlin's refusal to promise French Morocco to Spain than the Germans understood.[42] In mid-November 1940, Hitler summoned Serrano Suñer to Berchtesgaden in order to reach final agreement on Spain's entrance into the war. Irritated by Serrano's continued insistence on a written promise for French Morocco, Hitler made what were for Madrid startling new disclosures. A pledge for French Morocco would cause its defection from Vichy: 'Morocco would immediately break away and the conquest of Gibraltar would have no sense anymore. [A written agreement over Morocco] would lead to the loss of the object of that agreement. ... He [Hitler] would then prefer that Gibraltar remain in English hands and Africa with Pétain.'

Once Gibraltar had fallen, Hitler continued, German forces stationed in Morocco would prevent the defection of the French zone. After the peace, Spain would receive its just rewards in Morocco, and Germany would have a base there.[43] These statements, in my opinion, ended the possibility of Spanish participation. Hitler gave no promises regarding Madrid's aims in north-west Africa. Worse, he revealed for the first time to a Spanish official that he aimed to use the Gibraltar Strait to place German troops in Morocco – the centrepiece of what Franco saw as Spain's imperial future.

On 7 December, Franco refused the official German request that Spain enter the war by 10 January, and when asked, he refused to say when Spain would be ready.[44] Franco cited his country's economic difficulties, and these were certainly a factor. But Spain's economy had been wretched throughout the autumn of 1940, and the Spaniards remained willing to enter the war throughout that time.[45] Madrid's reticence seems to have stemmed more from conflicts over Africa, and especially Hitler's aims there, which Spain would have had to swallow should it have entered the war and permitted German passage through the Iberian peninsula. The bulk of available evidence tends toward this contention. In the first place, Franco and Serrano Suñer continued to complain loudly and often after the Berchtesgaden talks that the Germans had not been forthcoming enough concerning territorial rewards.[46] Meanwhile, in Spain's territories overseas, German agents suddenly confronted roadblocks to their activities. In the second half of November 1940, distrustful Spanish authorities refused to cooperate with the German naval officials in augmenting the defences in the Canaries, even though German help in defending the islands had been part of Franco's original price for belligerence in June and the weak defences there were among his stated reasons for remaining at peace in December. In late November, the Spanish ambassador to Berlin addressed a blistering note to Ribbentrop which condemned German propaganda and other illicit activities in Morocco.[47] In Morocco, German nationals were confronting difficulties in entering Tangier, and at year's end the German consul in Tetuán would complain that:

The Spanish effort to exclude us systematically from Morocco has been evident ... on unimportant occasions as well as in matters of principle. In the French zone, too, which certainly does not belong to the Spaniards, they do not want any German influence. A shipment from the Madrid embassy to the consulate containing Arabic propaganda material, which by reason of its text and sense could only be used in the French zone, was confiscated by the High Commissariat in a way that I consider to be contrary to international law [!]. ... Spanish policy here ... is a bad sign for the future, if Spain should really succeed in gaining possession of the French zone entirely or even in part. Spain would have only one aim. It would never rest until the last German had left the country.[48]

Though the AA was furious and the Armed Forces disappointed with Franco's refusal, Hitler accepted it with the utmost calm. The absence of Madrid's annoying demands, he believed, would allow greater and more profitable cooperation with Vichy over Africa. It seemed as though he was correct. On 10 December in Paris, three days after Franco's refusal, the French Government unveiled to a high-level German delegation elaborate plans to reconquer French Equatorial Africa from de Gaulle – plans which almost certainly would have caused a Franco-British war while forcing the French to accept a large German presence in the African colonies.[49] On the same day, Hitler cancelled Operation Felix; all preparations save reconnaissance were to cease.[50] If Germany could work with France, then Spain's participation would not be needed after all. On the 12th, the OKW happily announced that 'there [can] be no doubt about the sincerity of the political and military intentions of the French Government.' Germany would thus contribute 15,000 mts of fuel to the French plan, and also began taking steps to release from captivity the French officers, NCOs, and soldiers needed for service in Africa.[51]

Yet the prospects of working closely with Vichy over Africa soon vanished as well. Pétain's 13 December dismissal and arrest of Vice Premier Pierre Laval, one of the architects of German-French collaboration in Africa, convinced Hitler that France was as treacherous as ever. Worse, Hitler persuaded himself that the Germanophobe French Delegate-General in Algiers, Maxime Weygand, had engineered Laval's ouster, and that Weygand could defect with French North Africa at any time. On the final day of 1940, Hitler commented to Mussolini that

the reasons officially communicated to me [for the dismissal and arrest of Laval] are untrue. I no longer doubt for a second that General Weygand is sending extortionist demands to the Vichy Government and that the latter does not feel able to proceed against General Weygand without assuming the risk of losing North Africa. I consider it possible that in Vichy itself, quite a number of persons are [secretly] covering the Weygand policy. I do not believe that General Pétain personally is acting disloyally. However one cannot be sure of that either.[52]

Voices from the OKW, the AA, and from Vichy itself insisted that the French Government dismissed Laval for internal reasons and still wished to work with Berlin toward positive results in Africa. Still, Hitler remained unconvinced. On 19 January 1941 he lamented to Mussolini that even declarations of loyalty from Pétain and Weygand would not induce him to trust the French again. He wanted Laval back in the French Government, but feared to force the issue since overt steps by Germany might cause the exodus of French Africa. 'If Gibraltar were in the hands of the Axis,' he noted wistfully,

> this would ease the situation extrordinarily relative to North Africa and would put an end to the whole de Gaulle magic, especially if two German divisions could be transferred to Spanish Morocco and a few air bases could be set up there. Unfortunately, Franco [has] failed to recognize this situation. He [is] only an average officer who because of an accident ... [has] been pushed into the position of Chief of State. He [is] not a sovereign but a subaltern in temperament.[53]

Thus in January 1941, Berlin returned to the Gibraltar operation, and the High Command was told to resume preparations.[54] In a series of blistering notes to Madrid which began on 21 January, Ribbentrop demanded that Franco agree to enter the war within forty-eight hours, and insisted that without Hitler and Mussolini, there would be no Franco. The Foreign Minister added the following transparent threat: 'Unless the Caudillo decides immediately to join the war of the Axis powers, the Reich Government cannot but foresee the end of Nationalist Spain.'[55] It has been argued that Germany's renewed interest in Spain was due to Italy's latest disasters in the eastern Mediterranean.[56] Yet Operation Felix was first cancelled on 10 December 1940, the day after the commencement of General Archibald Wavell's North African offensive, and since the Directive number used for Felix, nineteen, was given to another operation on the same day, one can assume that Hitler did not plan to return to Felix anytime soon. On 19 and 20 December, with the Italian position collapsing in both Greece and Libya, Hitler and Ribbentrop still spent most of their time cursing French sedition in Africa when they met with Mussolini and Ciano in Munich. Hitler's exhortation to the Italians to hold Tobruk was made mainly for fear that Tobruk's fall would encourage the French to even bolder steps, and the Germans now even insisted that Mussolini try his luck in convincing Franco to enter the war so that Germany could end France's perfidy.[57] In any event, Ribbentrop's ultimatums accomplished nothing; it was now Franco's turn to delay. Madrid resisted Berlin's pressure well into February, by which time Felix could not run without risk to the timing of the Eastern Campaign. Germany's best chance to enter north-west Africa was over. Hitler himself had only the following comment for the Spanish Chief of State: 'two months have been lost which otherwise might have helped to decide world history.'[58]

Important opportunities had indeed been lost. Germany would not only fail to gain bases on and off the coast of north-west Africa; it would also fail to take Gibraltar and rob the Royal Navy of one of its most important bases. The Germans intended to return to the Gibraltar operation after the successful conclusion of Operation Barbarossa – the attack on the Soviet Union – but events in the East never allowed the Germans to focus their energies on Spain again.[59] Yet it had been the German, not the Spanish Government, that had frittered the opportunities of late 1940 away. How did the Germans manage to turn a willing ally into a suspicious bystander? The answer lies in Hitler's territorial aims, which despite a great deal of prodding, finally became clear to the Spanish Government in November 1940. Hitler was never interested in an alliance of equal sovereign states whereby Spain would receive its own place and responsibilities in the New Order. He was never even interested in sharing bases in the future. Rather Spain was to allow German troops to pass through its territory so that they could occupy one of Spain's few remaining imperial possessions. Spain was also to cede to Germany present and future Spanish territories so that the blood spilt in yet another war would result in dubious gains for the new Franco Government. As an irritated Franco had said in September 1940, 'the world is big enough so that Spain should not have to suffer any mortgage on its territory or its economy.'[60] Spain remained outside of the conflict, ultimately, because Hitler did not agree.

Notes

1. Donald S. Detwiler, *Hitler, Franco und Gibraltar: Die Frage des spanischen Eintritts in den zweiten Weltkrieg*, Wiesbaden, 1962, pp. 27-36; Charles B. Burdick, *Germany's Military Strategy and Spain in World War II*, Syracuse, NY, 1968, pp. 16-130; MacGregor Knox, *Mussolini Unleashed: Politics and Strategy in Fascist Italy's Last War*, New York, 1982, chap. 6; Militärgeschichtliches Forschungsamt

(gen. eds), *Das deutsche Reich und der zweite Weltkrieg, vol. III: Der Mittelmeerraum und Südosteuropa*, Stuttgart 1983, pp. 162-222; Gerhard Schreiber, 'The Mediterranean in Hitler's Strategy in 1940: Programme and Military Planning,' in *The German Military in the Age of Total War*, ed. Wilhelm Deist, Dover, N.H., 1987, pp. 252-3.

2. Jochen Thies, *Architekt der Weltherrschaft: Die 'Endziele' Hitlers*, Düsseldorf, 1980, pp. 9-31; Gerhard L. Weinberg, *World in the Balance: Behind the Scenes in World War II*, Hanover and London, 1981, pp. 53-95.

3. DGFP, series D, Washington, 1956, vol. I, doc. 19.

4. On the naval contracts, see Jost Dülffer, *Hitler, Weimar und die Marine: Reichspolitik und Flottenbau, 1920-1939*, Düsseldorf, 1973, pp. 455-6 and pp. 570-1. On the Messerschmitt 264, see Thies, *Architekt*, pp. 136-47.

5. Gerhard Wagner (ed.), *Lagevorträge des Oberbefehlshabers der Kriegsmarine vor Hitler 1939-1945*, Munich, 1972 (hereafter *Lagevorträge*), pp. 113-18; Michael Salewski (ed.), *Die deutsche Seekriegsleitung 1935-1945*, vol. III: *Denkschriften und Lagebetrachtungen 1938-1944*, Frankfurt/Main, 1973, pp. 122-30.

6. See Hitler's comments to Raeder and Mussolini of 14 November 1940, 22 May 1941, and 3 June 1941 in *Lagevorträge*, pp. 151-65, 227-39; Percy Ernst Schramm (gen.ed.), *Kriegstagebuch des Oberkommandos der Wehrmacht (Wehrmachtführungsstab)*, 4 vols, Frankfurt/Main, 1961-65, vol. I: *1 August 1940 – 31 December 1941*, ed Hans-Adolf Jacobsen (hereafter KTB/OKW), I, entry of 15 November 1940; DGFP, D, XII, doc. 584.

7. *Lagevorträge*, pp. 108 and 263; BA/MA RM 6/74, OKM/AMA/C II d B. Nr. 435 gKdos., June 1941.

8. See, for example, Dülffer, *Marine*, pp. 183-7, 370-6 and 476-8; Robert H. Whealey, *Hitler and Spain: The Nazi Role in the Spanish Civil War*. Lexington, Ky, 1989, pp. 117 and 126-7.

9. For a full account and the text of the Armistice Convention see Hermann Böhme, *Der deutsch-französische Waffenstillstand im zweiten Weltkrieg*, vol. I: *Entstehung und Grundlagen des Waffenstillstandes von 1940*, Stuttgart, 1966.

10. For the 20 June 1940 meeting see *Lagevorträge*, pp. 106-108. Supporting documents are in Salewski, *Seekriegsleitung*, III, pp. 115-16.

11. See Martin Thomas's contribution to this present volume.

12. See also my 'Germany and Northwest Africa in the Second World War: The Politics and Strategy of Global Hegemony' (Ph D diss., University of North Carolina, 1991), pp. 275-93.

13. PA/AA, Büro des Staatssekretärs (hereafter StS), Marokko, I, Stohrer to AA, 19 June 1940; DGFP, D, IX, doc. 488. For the official justification of Spain's demands, see José María de Areilza and Fernando María Castiella, *Reivindicaciones de España*, 2nd edn, Madrid, 1941, pp. 267-501.

14. PA/AA, StS, Marokko, I, Stohrer to AA, 22 June 1940. Berlin's eventual reply of 25 June was a simple acknowledgement. See DGFP, D, X, doc. 16. For a full account of Franco's unsuccessful overtures to Berlin in the summer of 1940, see my 'Germany and Northwest Africa', pp. 264-336.

15. For a full explanation of the Casablanca demand and its background, see my 'Hitler's Demand for Casablanca in 1940: Incident or Policy?', *International History Review* XVI, no. 3, 1994: 491-510.

16. For the 31 July meeting see *Lagevorträge*, pp. 126-9; Hans-Adolf Jacobsen (ed.), *Generaloberst Halder: Kriegstagebuch*, vol II: *Von den geplanten Landung in England bis zum Beginn des Ostfeldzuges*, Stuttgart, 1963 (hereafter *Halder Diary*),

entry of 31 July 1940; KTB/OKW, I, entry of 1 August 1940. On 1 August Hitler issued a directive calling for intensified air and sea war against England to create the preconditions for its 'final defeat'; see Walter Hubatsch (ed.), *Hitlers Weisungen für die Kriegführung 1939-1945: Dokumente des Oberkommandos der Wehrmacht*, 2nd edn, Frankfurt am Main, 1983, pp. 65-6.

17. DGFP, D, XI, doc. 69, Hitler to Mussolini, 17 September 1940. For a full account of German reactions to the Gaullist Coup of 26-30 August 1940 see my 'Germany and Northwest Africa', pp. 218-63.

18. Werner Rahn and Gerhard Schreiber (eds.), *Kriegstagebuch der Seekriegsleitung 1939-1945: Teil A*, Bonn, 1988-, vol. XIII (hereafter KTB/Skl.), entries of 3 and 10 September 1940. For previous statements in the same vein see ibid., XII, entries of 12, 21 and 30 August 1940. Raeder passed these views to Hitler in their meeting of 6 September 1940. See *Lagevorträge*, pp. 134-41. For concurring views from the German embassy in Washington see DGFP, D, X, doc. 342, Friedrich von Bötticher (German Military and Air Attaché) and Hans Thomsen (German Chargé d'Affaires) to OKW/Ausland, 14 August 1940; ibid., XI, 10, Thomsen to AA, 3 September 1940; see also *Halder Diary*, II, 23 August 1940.

19. For Ribbentrop's comments see DGFP, D, X, doc. 274, and note 1. Ribbentrop in fact never went to Madrid. For the military planning see KTB/OKW, I, entries of 20 and 24 August 1940; Burdick, *Germany's Military Strategy*, pp. 38-9.

20. According to Spanish government estimates, Spain would need a minimum of 300,000 mts of grain, 400,000 mts of gasoline, 200,000 mts of coal, 200,000 mts of fuel oil, and a further shopping list that included diesel fuel, manganese, hemp, cotton, and much more. For economic discussion in Germany regarding Spain see DGFP, D, X, docs. 313, 329, 355, 404 and note 2, and 407; ibid., XI, docs. 16 and 62; *Halder Diary*, II, 21 July, 9 and 27 August 1940; KTB/OKW, I, 2 September 1940.

21. *Lagevorträge*, 134-41; BA/MA, RM 8/1257, Kurt Aßman, 'Die Seekriegsleitung und die Mittelmeerkriegführung'.

22. For the Army argument see BA/MA, RH 2/444, 444 K-2, (OKH/GenStdH) Op. Abt. (IIb) Vortragsnotiz (gKdos.): Sperrung der Meerenge von Gibraltar, 13 November 1940. On Hitler see KTB/OKW, I, 25 November 1940; Walther Hubatsch (ed.), *Hitlers Weisungen für die Kriegführung 1939-1945: Dokumente des Oberkommandos der Wehrmacht*, 2nd edn, Frankfurt/Main, 1983, pp. 67-78. On planning for the movement of the divisions to Morocco see *Halder Diary*, II, 4, 7, 8, 13, 16 and 20 November 1940.

23. DGFP, D, XI, 69. On the *Luftwaffe* mission see my 'Germany and Northwest Africa', pp. 246-49, 259-62 and 378-81. The espionage mission was also to visit Dakar but did not go thanks to the British-Gaullist raid there later in the month.

24. KTB/OKW, I, 4, November 1940.

25. Ibid., 5 September 1940; Hubatsch, *Weisungen*, pp. 67-71. For planning in general concerning Portugal and its islands, see my 'Germany and Northwest Africa', pp. 467-98.

26. For Italy's claim to Morocco and Germany's reaction, see Böhme, *Waffenstillstand*, pp. 25-7; McGregor Knox, *Mussolini*, pp. 126-7; Goda, 'Germany and Northwest Africa', pp. 54-60.

27. See the German protocol of 27 August 1940 in DGFP, D, X, doc. 405. The Protocol does not specify which bases Hitler wanted in French Morocco, but Ribbentrop would mention Agadir and Mogador to Franco's envoy, Ramón Serrano

Suñer on 16 September The protocol also does not refer to the Canary Islands, but Hitler had already expressed his interest in them to Raeder on 11 July, and Ribbentrop would mention this interest to Serrano Suñer in the same meeting of 16 September; See ibid., XI, doc. 63. The German *Luftwaffe* commission, mentioned above, was also sent to Casablanca in September to reconnoitre base sites.

28. Malcolm Muggeridge (ed.), *Ciano's Diplomatic Papers*, trans. Stuart Hood, London, 1948 (hereafter *Ciano Papers*), pp. 405-6.

29. DGFP, D, XI, doc. 97, Ribbentrop meeting with Serrano Suñer, 24 September 1940. Hitler repeated the exact concerns to Mussolini on 4 October at the Brenner; see ibid., doc. 149; *Ciano Papers*, pp. 395-8.

30. For Serrano's other meetings in Berlin from 16-25 September, see DGFP, D, XI, docs. 63, 66, 67 and 117. For the troubles of Spain's new Ambassador, General Eugenio Espinosa de los Monteros, together with the detention of Serrano Suñer for additional meetings, see Espinosa's report to Spanish Foreign Minister Colonel Juan Beigbeder, AMAE R1188/3, no. 292, 3 October 1940; see also the original itinerary of Serrano Suñer's trip in ibid.

31. Franco to Serrano Suñer, 21 September 1940, in Ramón Serrano Suñer, *Memorias: Entre el silencio y la propaganda, la historia como fue*, Barcelona, 1987, pp. 331-40, author's emphasis. Franco repeated these sentiments in a personal note to Hitler of 22 September; see DGFP, D, XI, doc. 88.

32. DGFP, D, XI, doc. 149.

33. See Hitler's comments to Serrano Suñer of 25 September 1940, in DGFP, D, XI, doc. 117. See also von Bötticher's report of the previous day in ibid., doc. 99. The German Navy and members of the High Command advocated full military cooperation with France in north-west Africa; see ibid., doc. 92, Wolfgang Welck (AA representative to German-French Armistice Commission, Wiesbaden) to AA, 23 September 1940; KTB/OKW, I, entries of 24, 25, 30 September and 1 October 1940; BA/MA, RW 34/9, DWStK/Der Chef des Stabes/Nr. 8/40 gKdos. Chefs., 4 October 1940; KTB/Skl., XIII, entries of 24, 25 and 30 September 1940. On 26 September, Raeder himself pressed Hitler for an arrangement which would include both the conquest of Gibraltar and full German-French cooperation in north-west Africa; see *Lagevorträge*, pp. 143-6.

34. *Halder Diary*, II, entry of 3 October 1940. Hitler spelled out his ideas at the time to Mussolini and Ciano at the Brenner Pass on 4 October; see DGFP, D, XI, doc. 149; *Ciano Papers*, pp. 395-8. A full consideration of the rail journey is provided in my 'Germany and Northwest Africa', pp. 406-64.

35. For the protocols of the Montoire discussions of 22 and 24 October 1940, see DGFP, D, XI, docs. 212 and 227.

36. See Martin Thomas's contribution to this present volume.

37. My italics. What remains of Hitler's discussion with Franco is printed in ibid., doc. 220. For Ribbentrop's discussion of the same day with Serrano Suñer and the famous 'Hendaye Protocol' see ibid., docs. 221 and 235, and pp. 466-7. See also Serrano Suñer, *Memorias*, p. 294. On the French offer to adjust the Spanish-French border in Morocco, see AMAE R2295/5, José Felix de Lequerica (Spanish Ambassador to France) to Beigbeder, 30 September 1940; Francois Charles-Roux, *Cinq mois tragiques aux affaires etrangeres*, Paris, 1949, pp. 243-8.

38. For Franco's confidence regarding Spain's ability to defend north-west Africa from Allied encroachments, see Serrano Suñer, *Memorias*, p. 299 and 301-5. For Spanish complaints about the slowness of French disarmament in Morocco, see my 'Germany and Northwest Africa', *passim*.

39. DGFP, D, XI, doc. 246; *Ciano Papers*, pp. 399-404.
40. DGFP, D, XI, docs. 326 and 328.
41. *Halder Diary*, II, entry of 5 December 1940; KTB/OKW, I, entry of 5 December 1940; Burdick, *Germany's Military Strategy*, pp. 71-2.
42. See especially Franco's letter to Hitler of 30 October 1940, in Serrano Suñer, *Memorias*, pp. 301-5.
43. For the protocol of the 18 November meeting see DGFP, D, XI, doc. 352. Author's emphasis.
44. KTB/OKW, I, entry of 8 December 1940; DGFP, D, XI, doc. 500.
45. In this regard it should be mentioned that Serrano Suñer, Spain's Foreign Minister in November 1940, was given ample opportunity to reject Ribbentrop's invitation to Berchtesgaden should he have wished to do so. See my 'Germany and Northwest Africa', pp. 505-6.
46. DGFP, D, XI, doc. 398, Stohrer to Ribbentrop, 25 November 1940; ibid., doc. 414, Stohrer to AA, 28 November 1940; ibid., doc. 420, Stohrer to Ribbentrop, 29 November 1940. See also Franco's statements to Mussolini at their February 1941 meeting in Bordighera in ibid., XII, doc. 49, memo by Weizsäcker, 14 February 1941; *Ciano Papers*, pp. 422-6.
47. For the German Navy's problems with the Canary Islands in late November and early December 1940 see my 'Germany and Northwest Africa', pp. 530-42. For Spanish complaints on German activity in Morocco, see PA/AA, StS, Marokko, I, no. 620, Espinosa de los Monteros to Ribbentrop, 30 November 1940.
48. PA/AA, StS, Marokko, I, no. 273, Herbert Georg Richter to AA, 26 December 1940. On the problems of German activity in Morocco see my 'Germany and Northwest Africa', pp. 517-30.
49. KTB/OKW, I, pp. 984-94.
50. *Halder Diary*, II, entry of 9 December 1940.
51. DGFP, D, XI, doc. 506; KTB/OKW, I, entry of 12 December 1940.
52. DGFP, D, XI, doc. 586. On Hitler's suspicions see also ibid., docs. 564-6, 586 and 672; *Ciano Papers*, pp. 419-20; KTB/OKW, I, entry of 9 January 1941.
53. DGFP, D, XI, doc. 672; *Ciano Papers*, pp. 419-20.
54. KTB/OKW, I, entries of 20 and 21 January 1941; *Halder Diary*, II, entries of 20 and 23 January 1941; Hubatsch, *Weisungen*, pp. 96-7; KTB/Skl., XVII, entries of 22-23 January 1941; BA/MA, RM 7/1002, B. Nr. 1.Skl. I op 73/41 gKdos. Chefs. 23 January 1941.
55. Stohrer tried to convince Ribbentrop to reword the final phrase for fear of antagonizing Franco, but failed to convince the Foreign Minister. See Ribbentrop to Stohrer, DGFP, D, XI, doc. 682 and n. 2. On this series of exchanges in general, see also ibid., docs. 677, 692, 695; PA/AA, StS., Spanien II, no. 197, Stohrer to Ribbentrop, 20 January 1941; ibid., no. 225, Stohrer to Ribbentrop, 22 January 1941.
56. Detwiler, *Gibraltar*, p. 89; Burdick, *Germany's Military Strategy*, pp. 113-22; Knox, *Mussolini*, chap. 6.
57. DGFP, D, XI, docs. 672 and 679; *Ciano Papers*, pp. 417-20.
58. DGFP, D, XII, doc. 17, letter of 6 February 1941.
59. For an account of German planning for the period after the Eastern Campaign, see my 'Germany and Northwest Africa', chap. 9.
60. Letter to Serrano Suñer, 21 September 1940, in Serrano Suñer, *Memorias*, pp. 331-40.

8

French Morocco–
Spanish Morocco
Vichy French Strategic Planning against the 'Threat from the North', 1940-1942

Martin Thomas

(*University of the West of England, Bristol*)

O N 27 June 1940, reflecting upon the French armistice agreements completed three days earlier with Germany and Italy, Comte Renom de la Baume, French Ambassador to Madrid, warned that the Spanish government was much divided in its attitude to Marshal Philippe Pétain's new administration. Foreign Minister Juan Beigbeder Atienza was said to fear the wider consequences of France's defeat and was known to respect Pétain's effort to salvage French dignity. But the Interior Minister, Ramón Serrano Suñer, led those who insisted that the fall of France offered unprecedented opportunities for Spanish territorial acquisitions, in Morocco above all. To make matters worse, the French Foreign Ministry was uncertain where General Franco stood after the abortive attempt to secure the *Caudillo's* services as armistice intermediary in the previous week.[1] Relocated to Vichy in July, the mouthpiece of a defeated and partially occupied nation, Pétain's government lacked strength and genuine independence. This was surely a propitious moment for Spain to press its claims in North

Africa, based upon an extension of Spanish colonial control into French territory beyond the narrow coastal enclave of Spanish Morocco. But the Madrid government was itself constrained by the likely implications of any such action upon its neutral status, upon its relations with both Britain and the Axis powers, and upon Spain's longer-term relationship with France in the North African Maghreb.

This paper investigates one focal point of Spanish-French relations between 1940-1942: their mutual interests in Morocco. After their joint defeat in 1926 of Abd el-Krim's uprising in the Rif mountain range straddling Spanish and French Morocco, the French judged that there were five major causes of tension between France and Spain in North West Africa. First and foremost was the Spanish desire to acquire more territory at the expense of the French Moroccan Protectorate to the south. This paramount Spanish claim dated to a series of abortive Franco-Spanish negotiations in 1902. At this point Spanish negotiators had sought possession of the entire Sebou basin – the agricultural heartland of Morocco – including the neighbouring cities of Rabat, Meknès and Fez. A second cause of friction was the attendant Spanish claim to possession of the Oranie sector of western Algeria. By 1936 Oranie contained some 100,000 Spanish settlers – a figure broadly equivalent to French settlement in the region.[2] The third focus of Spanish interest was the international port of Tangier – a scandalously vibrant, cosmopolitan centre nestling in the comparatively poorer hinterland of the Spanish Moroccan zone. These three territorial claims were complicated by a fourth issue: Spanish dissatisfaction with the terms under which the northern zone had been conferred upon Spain in 1912 in the form of a sublease from France. Finally, in order to strengthen its credentials as a more efficient ruling power, the Franco government had occasionally encouraged dissension, if not outright sedition, among nationalist groups in French Morocco.[3] In spite of these obstacles, until General Dwight Eisenhower's invasion force descended upon French North Africa in November 1942, the Spanish and Vichy French authorities in Morocco coexisted in an unstable equilibrium. It is the purpose of this paper to indicate how this curious peace was preserved between June 1940 and 1943. The ebbs and flows of the Franco-Spanish relationship in Morocco and, in particular, the course of French strategic planning to meet the perceived Spanish threat, indicate that neither side held the freedom of manoeuvre in North Africa which they professed to enjoy.

I

The extent of French and Spanish influence in Morocco and Ifni had been codified by treaty in November 1912. Far from clarifying the position, this agreement caused lasting confusion. It took little account of local geographical features and the ethnic distribution of indigenous tribes. While making common cause in the Rif war, during 1925 and 1926 the French and Spanish authorities pursued three further attempts to fix their respective zones of influence along their common Moroccan land frontier – itself the frontline during the Rif operations.[4] The Rif region contained eleven principal tribal groups, Abd el-Krim's B'ni Uriaghal being the most numerous. After the failure of their rebellion, many of the Rif Berbers had migrated to the coastal ports, especially Tangier. But the Rif interior was not entirely pacified.[5] As a result, the French refused to cede control of those key points formerly in Spanish hands which had proved strategically vital to Abd el-Krim's forces. Hence, neither Primo de Rivera's government, nor those which followed it, were entirely satisfied with the outcome.

By contrast with later wartime tensions, the early years of the Second Republic were a golden age of Spanish-French cooperation in Morocco. In February 1933 Premier Manuel Azãna had delighted a French delegation to Madrid, led by Moroccan Resident General, Lucien Saint, with promises of the fullest Spanish assistance in maintaining ordered European colonial control across the Sultanate. President Niceto Alcalá Zamora added that the Tetuán High Commission would avoid giving undue preference to Spanish settler interests in the Spanish zone the better to maintain harmonious relations with the local Arab elite. This was music to the ears of French colonial officials schooled in Marshal Louis-Hubert Lyautey's ideas of indirect rule in Morocco.[6] This effort to marry Spanish and French colonial policies in Morocco was still evident in late 1935, as evinced by French satisfaction at the appointment of Lieutenant-Colonel Agustín Muñoz Grandes as delegate for native affairs in Tetuán.[7] But the outbreak of the Civil War, launched from the *Africanista* heartland in Spanish Morocco, quickly undermined the previous colonial collaboration with France. By 1937 the regular use of the Spanish zone as a marshalling point for Italian forces *en route* to Spain gave added impetus to French strategic planning for Morocco.[8] Furthermore, the fact that the Spanish zone was, in a sense, the heartland of Franco's nationalist militarism compounded long-standing French fears that any determined High Commissioner in Tetuán would be able to rouse support within a Spanish administration for renewed territorial claims against French Morocco.[9]

II

In October 1926, in the immediate aftermath of the Rif war, French War Minister, Paul Painlevé, approved revised terms of command which passed the initiative for defensive planning to the French Moroccan Resident General and his local force commander in Rabat. The French Residency was to prepare all schema for the protection of the territory against external attack and internal uprising. The division of French Morocco into areas covered by civil or military administration further entrenched the powers of the local colonial commanders. By 1939 the Resident General appointed by Léon Blum's Popular Front government in 1936, General Charles-Auguste Noguès, enjoyed wide powers of strategic responsibility. In addition to his powers within Morocco, Noguès' appointment as Commander-in-Chief for French North Africa had been confirmed in late November 1938. Any French action against the neighbouring coastal strip of Spanish Morocco would rest with him.[10] Noguès was always outspoken in his opposition to any surrenders of French Moroccan territory. He reminded his superiors at the Vichy Foreign and War Ministries that the population of the disputed Beni Zeroual region preferred French to Spanish administration. The French had, after all, won the right to administer these people at a cost of over 3,000 French military casualties in Beni Zeroual during the Rif war. By August 1940 it was clear that Noguès was the principal impediment to the fulfilment of Spanish ambitions in the Maghreb.[11]

In 1938 the French High Command incorporated a scheme for a pre-emptive strike against Spanish Morocco into their strategic war plan E1. This proposal remained in place until the fall of France, though in practice utmost priority was always attached to the uninterrupted reinforcement of France with colonial troops, rather than to preparations for the eviction of Spanish forces from their Moroccan defences.[12] While the Czech crisis reached a climax in September 1938, Franco's Nationalist government had resolved to correct the imbalance between Spanish and French forces within Morocco. As the Civil War neared its close in early 1939, the garrison in Spanish Morocco was strengthened. Although Foreign Minister Francisco Gómez Jordana y Souza insisted that this was a purely defensive measure, on 27 April French Prime Minister Edouard Daladier formally warned the Madrid authorities that France would crush any hostile action in Morocco. Noguès was instructed to maintain an extra vigilance.[13]

Before the 1940 armistice agreements, all French military plans regarding Spanish Morocco were built upon a simple assumption. Having to defend over 500 kilometres of common land frontier between Namours in the east and Port Lyautey in the west, and aware that Spanish forces might also strike northwards from the Rio de Oro, General Noguès had convinced the Paris War Ministry that the most economical means to safeguard Morocco against any Spanish threat was to seize the initiative and evict the *Africanistas* by a bold strike. Noguès had devised an attack plan based upon a three-pronged assault by four divisions and a cavalry brigade against Tetuán in the west and Melilla in the east, with a roving central force advancing northward to cut Spanish communications between its two principal Moroccan ports. In the event that Spain entered the war alongside Italy, simultaneous French offensives were planned against Spanish Morocco and Italian Libya. The thinking was the same. Far better to kick the enemy out quickly than allow them to mass their forces at leisure.[14]

On the eve of war in August 1939, Noguès's schemes to expel the Spanish from Morocco provoked dissension between Daladier's War Ministry and the Foreign Ministry under Georges Bonnet. In his role as military commander, Noguès reported to the former, while in his role as imperial governor, he was responsible to the latter. This inter-ministerial dispute had also surfaced earlier in the year. The possibility of a Franco-British military occupation of Tangier had been discussed in joint staff conversations over Mediterranean strategic planning, held in Rabat between 3 and 6 May 1939. Although the British War Office made plain that French land forces would have to act alone against the Spanish, both Daladier and Chief of General Chief, Maurice Gamelin, offered tentative support to Noguès's plan to occupy Tangier. If Spain remained neutral upon the outbreak of war, Franco would be invited to participate in this pre-emptive occupation, intended to secure the southern entrance to the Gibraltar straits. If Spain joined the Axis, a quick strike against Tangier – thus impeding any future reinforcement of Spanish Morocco – made equally good sense.[15] Bonnet was deeply alarmed at this proposal. The action suggested would be in violation of the 1923 Tangier statute governing the international status of the port. It was bound to alienate Franco, totally undermining the work of Marshal Pétain, who had just started his high-profile ambassadorial mission to Spain.[16] In the event, Madrid's announcement of neutrality, the reconstruction of Daladier's government in September, and the speed of Poland's fall effectively precluded any decision over Tangier.

In the last fortnight of the battle for France in June 1940, the positions were reversed. Having formally pledged to uphold the international statute in Tangier, Beigbeder informed Paul Reynaud's government on 11 June that, as a neutral power, Spain was best qualified to maintain the peace in the city. Of itself, this claim was hardly new. Throughout the Civil War, Spanish Morocco had been a vital base for nationalist activity. In French eyes, the frequency of troop movements and the occasional presence of Italian and German forces within the Spanish zone had long since called into question the neutral status of nearby Tangier.[17] Three days after Beigbeder's assertion, on 14 June 1940 a unilateral Spanish military occupation of the port began. Eager to emphasise their greater sensitivity to traditional Moroccan institutions, the Spanish placed troops loyal to the Khalifa of Tetuán in the vanguard of the occupying force.[18] Though the French government had, perforce, consented to this in advance, the manner of Colonel Yuste's takeover – a full military parade, Falangist salutes and anti-French demonstrations in the evening – caused outrage in Rabat.[19] Faced with France's imminent defeat, and soon to be confronted with the need to decide whether to defy Pétain and continue the war from French North Africa, Noguès was all but powerless to react.

In the months following the armistice accords, the French government worked hard to conciliate Spain. In August, General Maxime Weygand, the former French supreme commander soon to be appointed Vichy's Delegate-General in French Africa, suggested that the Tetuán High Command in Spanish Morocco be invited to inspect the forces in the neighbouring French territories. Intended to encourage mutual trust, Weygand's proposal was rejected by Beigbeder for fear of an adverse Italian reaction liable, in turn, to provoke British annoyance with Spain. Of greater moment was Foreign Minister Paul Baudouin's suggestion to his Spanish colleague that France would be prepared to revise the frontier settlement in Morocco to restore the territory that had been under Spanish control at the outset of the Rif war. In practice, this meant the eventual transfer of Beni Zeroual – prized Rif land along the Ouergha river to the north of Fez.[20] This concession was conditional upon an unequivocal Spanish renunciation of any further territorial claims in North Africa. Spurred on by dire warnings from Marshal Louis-Hubert Lyautey, the elder statesman of French imperialism in Morocco, Pétain – himself a distinguished veteran of the Rif campaign – stipulated that the proposed concessions could only take effect at the end of the war.[21]

In September, the French drew encouragement from the evident demotion of two of Serrano Suñer's closest supporters, General Juan Yagüe Blanco (sacked in late June) and Rafael Sánchez Mazas. Still, even the more pragmatic Beigbeder was expected to lay claim to French Moroccan territory if opportunity arose. The Foreign Minister had, after all, built his reputation in Morocco. His term as High Commissioner in Tetuán during the Civil War had been hailed a triumph and his belief in Spain's mission in Africa was easily discernible. Britain's Ambassador to Madrid, Sir Samuel Hoare, recollected that discussions with Beigbeder always came round to Morocco. Rather colourfully, Hoare noted of the Foreign Minister's office, 'From time to time the winds of Africa would break into the stifling heat of Madrid and, in the middle of a discussion of high politics, he would start an Arabic chant from the illuminated Koran that always lay on his table.'[22]

On 24 September, de la Baume delivered a formal Vichy protest over Serrano Suñer's highly publicized tour of northeastern France to inspect the sites of Germany's most recent victories. Beigbeder did not sympathize with his colleague's crude show of pro-Germanism. But he warned the French Ambassador that if the Madrid government judged that Vichy no longer represented the independent will of France, the Spanish would feel at liberty to march into French Morocco.[23] When Serrano Suñer took over as Foreign Minister in October 1940, the Vichy government recognized that Spanish policy would become more aggressive in tone, but hoped there would be little change in substance.[24] By then, Vichy had received a formal Spanish rejection of the proposed frontier alterations along the Ouergha river. On 30 October Serrano Suñer informed de la Baume that the development of Spanish-Vichy relations would be governed by two concerns. On the positive side, Franco was reportedly delighted at Pétain's efforts to re-build a 'real', conservative, and Catholic France, purged of the last remnants of Popular Frontism. By contrast, Serrano Suñer insisted that, until legitimate Spanish claims in North Africa were met, the cultural, racial and ideological affinities between Spain and Vichy could not be developed. On 16 November Vichy Deputy-Premier, Pierre Laval, held conversations with Serrano Suñer in Paris. Ignoring Laval's readiness to make concessions, Serrano Suñer attacked French obstructionism over Morocco and Tangier. Though he made no specific demands, the Spaniard left Laval in no doubt that Madrid would press substantial claims in the near future.[25]

By January 1941, de la Baume's replacement as Ambassador, the former French Minister of Marine, François Piétri, was convinced that Serrano Suñer was exploiting alleged Italian pressure for Spain to enter the war in order to strengthen his claim for a re-drawing of frontiers in northern Morocco and Oranie.[26] Pétain had supported Piétri's appointment to Spain as a means to flatter Franco. The Marshal was ideally placed to assess the importance of this. It was still only months since Premier Paul Reynaud had recalled him from his diplomatic posting as Madrid Ambassador, a difficult mission facilitated by Pétain's near-legendary military standing in Franco's eyes. In fact, the Marshal's awesome reputation had sometimes been a barrier to frank discussion. Neither Franco nor Beigbeder had put the Spanish case for frontier revision in Morocco directly to Pétain. Their coyness was not entirely explicable as a delaying tactic. Franco, it seems, was sometimes reluctant to antagonize the hero of Verdun. Whatever the case, by the time Piétri arrived, the Madrid government was less backward in coming forward.[27] Apart from his career in the Third Republic, Piétri had served as Minister of Communications in Pétain's first Vichy administration. He had pedigree as a man of the right; a supporter of the military and religious values both Spain and Vichy were supposed to embody.[28]

The early days of Piétri's Ambassadorship were none the less inauspicious. It appeared that Serrano Suñer was guided by the irredentist claims of Colonel Tomás García Figueras, the Secretary-General at the Tetuán High Commission. Figueras had long been demonised by the French Residency in Rabat as the personification of the worst excesses of Falangist imperialism. Violently Francophobic, Figueras had published a book reiterating Spain's historic right to mastery in Morocco. During 1941 and 1942, first as Secretary-General and then in the newly created post of Delegate for Educational Culture, Figueras lectured in cities across Spain regarding the country's historic claims in North Africa. Though the French found little echo of this imperialist thinking among public opinion in metropolitan Spain, it was impossible to overlook Figueras's influence.[29] In September 1940 he assisted Serrano Suñer during the Pact of Three talks in Berlin, exchanges which Beigbeder had insisted did not involve discussion of Morocco. On five separate occasions between 13 and 21 September 1940, de la Baume had questioned Beigbeder about Serrano Suñer's discussions in Germany. Eventually Beigbeder conceded that his own views had been persistently countermanded by Serrano Suñer's Ministry of Interior, while in Spanish Morocco Figueras played a similarly disruptive role.[30] Echoing Figueras, during the early months of 1941, Serrano Suñer warned Piétri that Spain was honour-bound to reverse the erosion of its influence in Morocco that the French had conspired in between 1904 and 1925. As Piétri recalled in his memoirs, though he always doubted Franco's willingness to abandon Spanish non-belligerence in pursuit of aggrandizement in North Africa, with so many imperial enthusiasts surrounding the *Caudillo*, it was hard to remain sanguine.[31]

III

In parallel clauses, the disarmament provisions of the Franco-German and Franco-Italian armistices limited the French North African army – the *Armée d'Afrique* – to an internal security force of 120,000 men. More important, this force was deprived of almost all its mechanized weaponry and transport equipment. Though Moroccan cavalry brigades and artillery batteries remained intact, French forces in Morocco were fundamentally weakened. Within three months of the Spanish occupation of Tangier in June, the forces deployed in Spanish Morocco matched the numerical strength of the entire *Armée d'Afrique* stretched across French North Africa as a whole.[32] To the French Moroccan Residency and Vichy's Secretariat of War it seemed that offensive planning was now impractical. In spite of Noguès's nostalgia for a surprise attack upon Spanish Morocco – intended as a means to overcome the numerical superiority of the defending Spanish forces – such a risky venture aroused alarm in Vichy. Ironically, François Charles-Roux, Secretary-General to Foreign Minister Baudouin, warned Noguès in July 1940 that the Spanish might be tempted into a pre-emptive strike in Morocco in order to forestall any British scheme to undermine the Spanish foothold in North Africa.[33]

Between 1940 and 1942, what artillery the French still possessed in North Africa was almost all concentrated along the Spanish Moroccan frontier.[34] In March 1941, Noguès warned General Weygand that the effectives for the armistice army in French Morocco were perilously small. Where Noguès possessed forty batallions, the

Spanish had deployed 104 along their Moroccan frontier. The ratios
for cavalry and field artillery were much the same. French forces
were outnumbered almost three to one by their Spanish neighbours.
Spanish Morocco was a compact territory easily reinforced from
Spain. Unlike the position in the far larger French territory to the
south, Spanish forces were, in effect, permanently concentrated in
an easily defensible colony. Though by 1941, many Spanish troops
had been reassigned to defend the Spanish Moroccan coast, it would
take less than three days to move the entire garrison southwards to
their well-fortified land frontier. According to Noguès, the British
naval blockade of French North Africa threatened to undermine the
relative passivity of the Arab and Berber population in the principal
cities of Morocco. The one consolation was that tribal unrest in the
Spanish Rif appeared more severe. As Weygand noted, the Spanish
were 'genuinely hated' by their Moroccan subjects.[35]

Regardless of these difficulties, Noguès remained convinced that
the Spanish could still be defeated, provided that the French
retained the advantage of surprise, and that the Rif tribes could be
incited to turn on their Spanish masters. Though he had limited
intelligence about Spanish plans, in essence, the outlook of the
Rabat Residency was as bullish as it had been prior to the fall of
France. More surprising was the fact that Weygand was equally
unequivocal about the Moroccan position. On 11 November 1940,
he advised Pétain that, while he appreciated the need to conciliate
Franco, Spanish behaviour in the northern zone was clearly
intended to undermine French imperial prestige. At worst, Serrano
Suñer might convince Franco to risk a military adventure across the
Rif mountains. At best, Spain's deliberate humiliation of France as
a colonial power, if left unchallenged, was bound to provoke nationalist unrest throughout Morocco.[36]

The belligerence of Noguès's command had not gone unnoticed
in London. In January 1941, Sir Samuel Hoare warned Churchill
that Noguès was a loose cannon unlikely to appreciate the nuances
of Franco's attitude to Morocco. Furthermore, the French railway
network in Morocco was largely concentrated on the arterial east-
west route between Oran and Fez. Most of the main lines ran
within a short distance of the Spanish Moroccan frontier. This
would remain a temptation for the hot-heads on both sides to suggest a military adventure: the French to secure their railway, the
Spanish to seize it.[37] But by 1941 the British government had severed the diplomatic channels to Noguès that had been used in an
effort to persuade him to fight on in June 1940.

In an effort to overcome their lack of reliable intelligence information from within Spanish Morocco, in May 1941 the French army's
colonial planning staff submitted a detailed evaluation of the Spanish
threat in the colony. The planning staff's conclusions were measured:

> For reasons as much political as economic, the Spanish Government
> would like to avoid involvement in the war, at least until this year's har-
> vest is in. But if a German order has already been formulated by which
> Spain should either participate or allow an [Axis] operation against
> Gibraltar in order to close the Strait, it is estimated that Spain, out of
> self-respect, will not stand back but will participate.[38]

To Vichy's military planners, a pre-emptive strike still made sense.

Once the Anglo-Free French campaign opened in Syria in mid-
June 1941, the French commanders across North Africa were
forced to turn their attention to the possibility of an Allied descent
on their shores. For Noguès, this meant the dispersal of his troops
from the frontier with Spanish Morocco in order to garrison the
Atlantic coast of French Morocco more effectively.[39] Fortunately,
this redeployment coincided with a slight reduction in cross-border
tension. Two factors contributed to this above all. First, the Vichy
authorities were growing more used to Spain's unilateral control of
Tangier, now effectively governed as an integral part of Spanish
Morocco. Secondly, the Spanish High Commission in Tetuán, having encouraged Moroccan sedition against the French since June
1940, had at last realized that this was counter-productive. Both of
these issues merit closer analysis.

On 14 November 1940 the Franco government officially took
sole charge of the administration of Tangier. The international
agencies – the Committee of Control, the Legislative Assembly and
the International Information Bureau – were all moth-balled. This
peaceful coup elicited French and British protests but little more.
In February 1941, Churchill formally delegated the matter to
Hoare, claiming that he had far more pressing matters to worry
about.[40] By contrast, the Vichy authorities, inherently prone to see
the hand of Germany in all matters affecting North Africa, had
much more time for navel-gazing. In a curious attempt to reassure
Vichy, Serrano Suñer insisted that Spain's action had been driven
by Mussolini's refusal to cooperate over the Tangier administration.
By taking matters into their own hands, the Spanish government
would also keep German involvement to a minimum. This was
surely to French advantage.[41]

159

In fact, as early as August 1940, the Vichy government had contemplated the unilateral abandonment of France's treaty privileges in Tangier as a goodwill gesture to Franco. By contrast, the Moroccan Khalifa in Tetuán refused to acknowledge this extension of Spanish authority. The equally uncompromising Si Mohammed Tazi, the Mendoub of Tangier, was forced by the Spanish High Commission to retire in March 1941. With Mohammed Tazi out of the way, there was little effective opposition to the authority of General Carlos Asensio Cabanillas, the Tetuán High Commissioner now in overall charge of Tangier.[42] Spain's actions had been facilitated by the system of rotating administration established under the original Tangier Statute. Under the terms of this, Dr Manuel Amevia y Escandon had been duly appointed port administrator in June 1940. Once the new administrator took office, the Moroccan nationalist leaders, Abdel Khalek Torrès and Brahim El Ouazzani, received active Spanish encouragement in their campaigns against French rule to the south.[43] On 13 December 1940, the day after Asensio arrived in Morocco, the Spanish began to assume control of all branches of government in Tangier. This process began with the removal of the French commissioner of police, Palazat. By February 1941, Tangier was officially designated in Madrid as a 'region' of Spanish Morocco; Asensio's associate, Commandant Grigori, was referred to as the regional administrator for the port. Plans were also in hand to end Tangier's separate monetary status.

The Vichy Secretariat of War intelligence section began to view these developments with greater alarm in March 1941. Later that month the Spanish started the redeployment of a modern tank regiment to Spanish Morocco, greatly adding to the offensive potential of their existing forces. A convoy from Barcelona brought in a mixture – in quality as well as type – of over sixty Soviet and Italian light and medium tanks. This was soon followed by other, lesser deliveries. Within days of the arrival of the Barcelona convoy, to the delight of the local Falange a German consulate was opened with Franco's blessing.[44] The German Consul, Nöhring, quickly became a vocal force in Tangier politics. This compounded Vichy fears that the German Armistice Commissioners in Morocco, apart from evaluating the merits of an Axis takeover, were encouraging nationalist sedition.[45]

Yet by September 1941 French fears had subsided. In mid-May, High Commissioner Asensio and his regional commander, General Miguel Ponte y Manso de Zúñiga, were replaced by General Luis Orgaz y Yoldi, previously the Captain-General of Catalonia. A Rif veteran with long experience in Morocco, in 1926 Orgaz had been appointed *Secretario de la Dirección General de Marruecos y Colonias* in Madrid. Orgaz's credentials as solid colonial administrator were reassuring to Vichy. Piétri immediately assured Foreign Minister and Deputy-Premier, Admiral Jean-François Darlan, that Orgaz was a pragmatist who did not share Asensio's sympathy for Serrano Suñer.[46] Over the summer months Orgaz showed no inclination to challenge his French neighbours with the considerable forces – now estimated at over seven divisions – at his disposal. Furthermore, one of Orgaz's first actions as High Commissioner was to shunt Figueras into the oddly named Tetuán Delegation of Education and Culture. This enabled Orgaz to recall his Civil War comrade, General Salvador Múgica Buhigas, to take over as Secretary-General. On 9 July Noguès travelled to Arbaoua on the Franco-Spanish Moroccan frontier to confer with his new Spanish clients. He returned confident that Orgaz would curb Figueras's influence, allowing tension to diminish. Orgaz was said to respect French imperial achievements, and he recognized the shared Franco-Spanish interest in containing Moroccan nationalism.[47]

Henceforth, the Vichy Foreign Ministry emphasized the duality of Spanish policy-making in regard to Morocco. It seemed that Franco was content to see a mirror image of his Cabinet's divisions over relations with Vichy in the tensions between Orgaz and Figueras within the Tetuán High Commission. Vichy pundits in Rabat would have agreed with Hoare's wry comment about the Spanish leadership: the 'military market' was variable, as was the will to make war.[48] As Noguès confided to Weygand, though Figueras and his coterie of Falangists in the Tetuán staff were loyal to Serrano Suñer rather than Orgaz, the outcome of this power struggle lay entirely in Franco's hands. The French Resident General drew comfort from the assumption that, in permitting Orgaz a freer rein in Spanish Morocco, the *Caudillo* indicated the limits to his support for Serrano Suñer's more aggressive policies.[49]

In August 1941 it was announced that over 2,000 troops were to leave Spanish Morocco to join the *División Azul* for service on the Russian front. Significantly, the Spanish High Commission had allowed the French Consul at Larache, M.J. Dumarçay, who had noted these developments, to remain in post. This allowed him to provide his masters in Rabat with better intelligence on military deployments in the Spanish zone. During 1941 and 1942, Dumarçay consistently advised that the principal concern at the Tetuán command was to protect the Spanish Moroccan coast, not to prepare for an assault upon French territory.[50] As Consul, Dumarçay drew information from his Spanish counterpart in Larache, Propper y Callejon, who had previously served as First Secretary in the Spanish Embassy in Paris. The fact that a senior ranking Spanish diplomat had been posted to an insignificant Consulate near the French Moroccan frontier was itself powerful evidence that Propper's primary function was to act as a diplomatic barometer, assessing the prospects for Spain's claims to the nearby Sebou basin. Though clearly from the Figueras school of Spanish imperial history, the Rabat authorities found Propper a reasonably cautious individual.[51]

Perhaps more reassuring were the obvious divisions among the Moroccan nationalist leadership in the Spanish zone. Always hostile to the French, Abdel Khalek Torrès was now bitterly critical of Spain's treatment of its Moroccan subjects, a stance which alienated him from Mekki Naziri, whose rival nationalist faction was still prepared to cooperate with Tetuán. During his tenure at the Tetuán High Commission, Beigbeder had worked hard to perpetuate this factionalism. But by 1941, Moroccan nationalists were less malleable.[52] In August 1941, Mohammed Moktar Tensamani, the Pacha of Tangier appointed by the Spanish to replace the deposed Mendoub in March, defected to Gibraltar. From there he began broadcasting anti-Spanish propaganda via the BBC, much to the annoyance of Hoare. The Ambassador dreaded the implications of possible British approval for SOE proposals to support a nationalist uprising in the Spanish zone. The hitherto impressive results yielded by Hoare's patient diplomacy in Madrid were sure to be undermined by any discovery of blatant British subterfuge in Spanish territory. Hoare took little interest in the beneficial effect of Moroccan nationalist unrest upon Vichy-Spanish relations.[53] Within days of Tensamani's arrival in Gibraltar, even the Falangist newspaper *Arriba* acknowledged the value of the French presence in Morocco to curb the power of Arab nationalism. Tangier, it seemed, was becoming more of a headache for the Spanish authorities. In September both Piétri in Madrid and Weygand in Algiers advised Darlan to abandon the previous year's proposals for frontier concessions over Spanish Morocco at war's end. The interim benefits to Vichy-Spanish relations would be outweighed by the resultant loss of French prestige in the eyes of the Moroccan Sultanate and Maghreb nationalists.[54]

IV

By December 1941, Vichy's military planners were convinced that the likelihood of Spanish action against French Morocco would turn upon Germany's fortunes in the war. On 5 February 1942, Noguès returned from discussions with Orgaz at Larache fearful that the German High Command was pressing the Spanish to make fresh claims to the northwest pocket of French Morocco which included Port Lyautey and a small oilfield based around the town of Petit Jean. He did not, however, expect any attack in the short term. Only if the British exerted a more powerful stranglehold on Spanish maritime trade, or if German forces threatened to sweep through the Iberian Peninsula, was Franco expected to come off the fence.[55] In the interim, though Spain's expansionist ambitions subsisted, a unilateral Spanish attack on French Morocco was judged improbable.

It was, however, impossible for the Vichy government to remain entirely calm. As the prospect of Allied landings in French North Africa increased in the months leading up to the launch of Operation Torch in November 1942, so the perceived Spanish threat re-emerged. Furthermore, Weygand's replacement as land forces commander in French North Africa, General Alphonse Juin, also tended to exaggerate Spanish military strength, partly in an effort to secure himself additional resources.[56] If French North Africa became a major theatre of war, sucking in more Axis forces to contain the Allies, the Madrid government was expected to seize what might be a singular opportunity to grab territory. As in late 1940, the Vichy Foreign Ministry reverted to an obvious truth. With his Cabinet still divided between cautious neutralists and more hawkish nationalists, all hinged upon Franco maintaining his balancing act between the two.[57]

Hence, during 1942, the Vichy authorities continued planning for a pre-emptive strike on the Spanish zone, still drawing upon the original programmes refined by Noguès before June 1940. The Rabat command still pinned its hopes upon a multi-pronged assault, the major forces being deployed to cross the Atlantic coastal plain from Souk el Arba towards Tangier in the west, and to traverse the El-Garet plain towards Melilla in the east. These lines of approach were rather obvious, dictated largely by the intervening presence of the Rif highlands. Yet, by January 1942, Spanish fortifications were deemed virtually impregnable. While the Spanish Moroccan frontier was still defended in strength, it was now also protected in depth. The Spaniards were close to completing a tiered fortification system which culminated in a series of emplacements, bunkers and stores on the landward side of the major coastal towns.[58] No surprise French attack was likely to make it to the Mediterranean coast before Spanish reinforcements arrived.

Vichy strategic planning was thorough, well balanced and creative. But in one sense it always lacked realism. For any French action against Spanish Morocco, even if purely defensive, was bound to fall foul of the German government. Only if one accepts the proposition that Vichy was prepared to risk German anger in defence of its North African possessions can one attach much credence to Vichy's military preparations. Vichy France was clearly not a viable independent state. Once German and Italian Armistice Commissioners descended on French North Africa in late 1940 the cornerstone of the French Empire was no longer outside Axis influence. This was particularly noticeable in respect of the remaining French air force units deployed across French North Africa. Armistice provisions had decimated the *Armée de l'Air*. To use aircraft in support of his forces in any clash with the Spanish, Noguès would have to call upon squadrons from as far afield as southern Algeria and Tunisia. More important, the German Armistice Commissioners in Morocco had insisted that French military airbases near the Franco-Spanish Moroccan frontier be abandoned. By 1941 it was apparent that the German Commissioners had earmarked these bases for possible use by the *Luftwaffe* alone.[59] With monitoring stations of the German *Abwehr* installed further north along either side of the Gibraltar Strait, there was an obvious logic to *Luftwaffe* usage of French Moroccan airfields for any operations against Allied shipping entering the Mediterranean.[60]

In spite of these constraints, in one crucial respect both Spanish and Vichy planning regarding Morocco could proceed independent of German or Italian wishes. In Tetuán and Rabat it was generally agreed that the most probable circumstance in which conflict would arise would be that in which the Axis powers were confronted with a crisis in their North African position. Germany might be forced to enter Morocco to impede Allied landings. Conversely, the Allies might try to beat the German High Command to the punch. Whichever scenario unfolded, there was likely to be a brief moment of flux during which the fate of Vichy France or Franco Spain in Morocco might be decided. In an unguarded moment at a reception on 27 May, Captain Luis Carrero Blanco, Under-Secretary of the Presidency, confirmed to the Vichy Naval Attaché, Rear-Admiral J.R. Delaye, that the Spanish army was inclined to intervene in French Morocco, ostensibly to protect the country from Axis or Allied domination, but in fact to secure rich pickings for Spain from whichever Powers ended up in control of North Africa.[61] It was on this premise that Vichy planning had come to rest by mid-1942.

Until Franco's replacement of Foreign Minister Serrano Suñer by the more conservative and Anglophile Jordana in August 1942, the Vichy Secretariat of War reckoned that the prospect of a Spanish thrust into French Morocco had impeded Anglo-American planning for an invasion of North West Africa.[62] Though the Vichy government drew comfort from the promotion of Jordana, it was now feared that Franco might coax the Allies into offering African concessions at French expense in return for fresh assurances of Spanish nonbelligerence. This was to figure, if only in passing, in Admiral Darlan's thinking prior to his abrupt change of sides on 10 November 1942. In late October the Rabat Residency and the Consulates in Tangier were awash with rumour. Few of the suggestions of either a Spanish or French pre-emptive military strike had any foundation. Rather, the tension was built upon the tendency of both sides – acutely conscious of their actual military shortcomings – to 'talk big' in order to conceal their real weakness.[63]

Once the 'Torch' landings began, the Spanish government recalled several thousand reservists to the flag. But no major reinforcement of Spanish Morocco took place. Instead, Franco was careful to emphasize the importance of the personal assurances received from President Roosevelt and Prime Minister Churchill regarding Allied respect for the integrity of all Spanish territory. In its replies, Madrid chose to emphasize the volatility of Moroccan nationalism, warning that any incitement of unrest would prove counter-productive.[64] As Piétri noted with glee, the Spanish now had time to reflect upon what it was really like to be powerless in the face of a much stronger presence in North Africa.[65] As expected, the Spanish press gave a high profile to the conversations in Tetuán on 5 January between Generals Orgaz and Patton, in which the American relayed Eisenhower's promise of noninterference in Spanish Morocco.[66] Though welcomed by Franco, the Allies were not compelled to issue such assurances. Spain's freedom of action in Morocco was thoroughly undermined by Anglo-American control of the sea-lanes between Iberia and North Africa, and by the local aerial supremacy enjoyed by the R.A.F. Without renewed German intervention in the Mediterranean, the supposed Spanish threat either to French Morocco or to the progress of the 'Torch' operations was a paper tiger. This was soon transparently clear. In early February 1943, the British Chiefs of Staff duly stood down the preparations for Operation Backbone – a possible military strike against any Spanish force massing in southern Spain or Spanish Morocco to join in the conflict alongside the Axis.[67] On the other side of the Moroccan frontier, under Generals Henri Giraud and Alphonse Juin, the French *Armée d'Afrique* was preoccupied with its adjustment to the role of junior partner in an Allied coalition. Preparations against a Spanish threat were consigned to the preceding Vichy era of General Noguès.

V

For those interested in the wider history of the Second World War, this brief survey of what was, for the early part of the conflict at least, a relative backwater is perhaps of interest for four main reasons. First, from the French side, the strategic planning of Vichy commanders reveals a marked commitment to defend French territory against any invader. The caricature of Vichy's military leaders as wanton, collaborationist creatures is as inappropriate with regard to French Morocco as it is for the Spanish military leadership in the neighbouring northern zone. Secondly, though a Franco-Spanish clash never actually occurred, it seems clear that both sides thought it a genuine threat, and that neither would give ground easily. This raises a third point. Since French strategic planning between 1940 and 1942 still rested on the assumption that attack constituted the best form of defence, it appears that both the Axis and Britain missed an obvious opportunity to foment tension. For Hitler this might have helped bring Spain into the war. For Britain, exploitation of the Spanish challenge to French Morocco might have driven a wedge between Vichy and Berlin, or between Vichy and its North African commanders. Given the opportunity to play peacemaker between two client governments in Morocco, Hitler might have found a means to press additional demands upon Madrid or Vichy. Fanciful speculation, perhaps, but surely not outside the realms of possibility. Finally, the uneasy wartime coexistence of French and Spanish rule in Morocco provides something of a mirror image of the tensions between Spain and Vichy France in Europe. Superficially linked by the similarities of their situation as neutrals with a foot in the Axis camp, the fall of France had only sharpened the colonial rivalry between them. The war had laid bare the limitations of French and, to a lesser degree, Spanish power. In so doing, it had also added to the importance attached to possession of Empire by both states. Increasingly marginalised as continental players, the need to conserve imperial prestige had become a possible cause of conflict between the two neighbours.

Notes

1. ANMAE, Guerre 1939-1945, série M, Vichy-Maroc, vol. 27, tel. 773, de la Baume to Paris, 27 June 1940.
2. Francis Koerner, 'Les répercussions de la guerre d'Espagne en Oranie (1936-1939)', *Revue d'histoire moderne et contemporaine* 22, no. 3, 1975: 476; William A. Hoisington, *The Casablanca Connection. French Colonial Policy, 1936-1943*, Chapel Hill, NC, 1984, pp. 153-4.
3. PRO, SOE French North Africa files, HS 3/47, FO Research Department memo, 10 March 1944.
4. ANMAE, série M/vol. 30, Rabat Residency memo, 'Note sur la délimitation des zones française et espagnole du Maroc', 15 March 1939.
5. PRO, SOE Morocco files, HS 3/204, Tangier station memo, 'Notes on the Riff', 4 June 1941.
6. ANMAE, série Z/vol. 243, no. 108, Jean Herbette to Joseph Paul-Boncour, 13 February 1933.
7. ANMAE, série Z/vol. 243, no. 1642, Herbette to Pierre Laval, 9 November 1935.
8. For details, see J.F. Coverdale, *Italian Intervention in the Spanish Civil War*, Princeton, 1975. Regarding the effects of the war on Spanish Moroccans, see Gervase Clarence-Smith, 'The Impact of the Spanish Civil War and the Second World War on Portuguese and Spanish Africa', *Journal of African History* 26, 1985: 312-15 and 324-5.
9. Archives Nationales Centre d'Outre-Mer, (hereafter ANCOM), *Affaires politiques*, carton 518, dossier 26, Possessions espagnoles, no. 1, p. 137, Jean Herbette to Louis Barthou, 1 September 1934.
10. SHAT, Carton 1P141/Dossier 5, Décret, commandement au Maroc, 3 October 1936.
11. ANMAE, Fonds 1940, Papiers Paul Baudouin, vol. 8, no. 447, Noguès to Baudouin, 13 July 1940; no. 292, Ambassadeur de Lequerica conversation with Baudouin, 25 August 1940.
12. SHAT, 1P33/D2, EMA, deuxième bureau, 'Etude sur l'importance militaire des colonies', n.d. February 1941.
13. ANMAE, série Z, vol. 243, no. 49, Pétain, San Sebastian, to Bonnet, 15 April 1939; no. 137, Bonnet to Pétain, 27 April 1939.
14. SHAT, 1P33/D2, EMA-2, 'Etude sur l'importance militaire des colonies', n.d. February 1941.
15. ANMAE, série M/vol. 121, no. 1720/DN3, Gamelin to Noguès, 23 August 1939; regarding the Rabat conversations, see the author's 'Plans and Problems of the Armée de l'Air in the Defence of French North Africa before the fall of France', *French History* 7, no. 4, 1993: 486-7.
16. ANMAE, série M/vol. 121, no. 422, Bonnet to Daladier, 12 August 1939.
17. ANCOM, Aff. pol. C901/D4, Résidence Générale, Maroc, direction des affaires indigènes rapport, 16-31 July 1936.
18. For full details, see, C. Halstead, 'Aborted imperialism, Spain's occupation of Tangier, 1940-1945', *Iberian Studies* 7, no. 2, 1978: 53-71.
19. ANMAE, série M/vol. 121, no. 686, de la Baume to affaires politiques, 11 June 1940; no. 112, Avonde to Paul Reynaud, 15 June 1940.
20. ANMAE, série M/vol. 28, no. 450, Baudouin to de la Baume, 8 September 1940; vol. 30, direction Afrique-Levant, note for Baudouin, 5 July 1940.
21. ANMAE, série M/vol. 28, Lyautey letter to Pétain, 27 September 1940.

22. Samuel Hoare, *Ambassador on Special Mission*, London, 1946, pp. 37 and 50. Regarding French views of Beigbeder's High Commission, see Hoisington, *The Casablanca Connection*, pp. 146-9.

23. ANMAE, Papiers Baudouin, vol. 8, no. 1312, de la Baume to Baudouin, 24 September 1940.

24. ANMAE, série M/vol. 27, direction politique, 'Note – attitude de l'Espagne', 11 September 1940; no. 1564, de la Baume to Vichy, 30 October 1940.

25. ANMAE, série M/vol. 27, no. 1564, de la Baume to Vichy, 30 October 1940; vol. 28, Afrique-Levant, note for Weygand, 25 October 1940; vol. 28, Laval to Noguès, 17 November 1940.

26. ANMAE, série M/vol. 27, no. 144, Piétri to direction des affaires politiques, 26 January 1941.

27. ANMAE, série M/vol. 121, no. 450, Noguès to direction des affaires politiques, 13 July 1940; Matthiéu Séguéla, *Pétain-Franco. Les secréts d'une alliance*, Paris, 1992, pp. 37-45 and 81-93.

28. ANMAE, série M/vol. 28, M1H, Pierre-Etienne Flandin to Weygand, 21 Dec. 1940.

29. PRO FO 371/31277, C10096/3453/41, Hoare to Eden, 10 October 1942; ANMAE, série Z/vol. 243, no. 61, Madrid Chargé report to Paul Reynaud, 24 January 1940.

30. ANMAE, série M/vol. 28, no. 779, Noguès to direction des affaires politiques, 14 September 1940; no. 614, Baudouin to Madrid, 29 September 1940; Papiers Baudouin vol. 8, texts of de la Baume tels. to Baudouin, 13-21 September 1940.

31. ANMAE, série M/vol. 28, no. 365, Piétri to direction des affaires politiques, 1 March 1941; François Piétri, *Mes années d'Espagne 1940-1948*, Paris, 1954, p. 98.

32. SHAT, 3P51/AFN, no. 936, EMA-1, 'Organisation de l'Armée de l'Armistice en AFN', 17 January 1941; ANMAE, série M/vol. 122, no. 120/SGP, Weygand to Pétain, 11 November 1940.

33. ANMAE, série M/vol. 28, no. 93, Charles-Roux to Noguès, 13 July 1940.

34. SHAT, 1P141/D1, EMA-2, 'Ordre de Bataille – AFN-fin Octobre 1942'; 1P33/D2, EMA-2, 'Etude sur l'importance militaire des colonies', n.d. February 1941.

35. SHAT, 1P141/D1, no. 396, Noguès to Weygand, 8 March 1941; no. 53/FS-3, EMA-3, 'Etude d'ensemble sur les opérations Maroc', 16 May 1941; 1P89/D3, Weygand report to Pétain, 10 November 1940.

36. ANMAE, série M/vol. 122, no. 120/SGP, Weygand to Pétain, 11 November 1940.

37. PRO, PM's Office files, PREM 3/317/1, Hoare to Churchill, 11 January 1941.

38. SHAT, 1P33/D1, E-M Colonies, note 131, 3 May 1941.

39. SHAT, 1P141/D2, no. 984, Noguès to Weygand, 6 June 1941.

40. PRO PREM 3/317/3, Churchill to Eden, 6 February 1941.

41. ANMAE, série M/vol. 122, no. 132, Castellane, Tangier, to direction des affaires politiques, 3 November 1940; no. 663, de la Baume to Vichy, 5 November 1940.

42. ANMAE, série M/vol. 28, Baudouin to Noguès, 31 August 1940; SHAT, 1P136/D2, no. 3920/EMA-2, bulletin de renseignements, Pays Musulmans, 30 April 1941.

43. SHAT, 1P136/Affaires Musulmanes, no. 6335/EMA-2, Questions Musulmanes, 26 October 1940.

44. SHAT 3P104/D3, EMA-2 bulletin, 'Préparatifs Hispano-Portugais', n.d., April 1941; 1P136/D2, no. 1042, EMA-2, Pays Musulmans, 15 May 1941.

45. SHAT, 2P12/D2, no. 9382, DSA rapport 22, 7 October 1941.
46. ANMAE, série M/vol. 27, no. 241, Piétri to Darlan, 14 May 1941.
47. ANMAE, série M/vol. 145, no. 958, Noguès to section Afrique-Levant, 7 October 1940; vol. 28, no. 745, Noguès to section Afrique/Levant, 9 July 1941.
48. PRO PREM 3/317/3, Hoare to Churchill, 30 July 1941.
49. ANMAE, série M/vol. 28, Noguès to Weygand, 21 September 1941.
50. ANMAE, série M/vol. 145, nos. 21 and 34, Dumarçay to section Afrique-Levant, 25 March and 29 May 1942.
51. PRO FO 371/31277, C6346/3453/41, Gascoigne to Eden, 25 June 1942. Propper y Callejon had pressed Spanish claims in numerous meetings with Noguès, but had acknowledged the General's determination to preserve French Morocco intact.
52. PRO HS 3/204, no. 77, Central Department memo, 'Spanish Morocco: the Moroccan Nationalists', 17 February 1942.
53. PRO HS 3/204, SOE, A/DB to H, 30 May 1941; A/D to CEO, 16 April 1942; as for Hoare's achievements, see Denis Smyth's assessment in 'Screening "Torch": Allied Counter-Intelligence and the Spanish Threat to the Secrecy of the Allied Invasion of French North Africa in November, 1942', *Intelligence and National Security* 4, no. 2, 1989: 338-9 and 342-3.
54. SHAT, 1P136/D2, no. 7542, EMA-2, Pays Musulmans, 15 September 1941; ANMAE, série M/vol. 27, no. 476, Piétri to Darlan, 15 September 1941; ANMAE, série M/vol. 28, no. 33, Weygand to Darlan, 5 September 1941.
55. PRO FO 371/31277, C3453/3453/41, Gascoigne to Eden, 11 March 1942.
56. PRO FO 371/31277, C4744/3453/41, Gascoigne to FO, 6 May 1942.
57. SHAT, 3P104/D3, no. 31, EMA-2, note de renseignements, 24 September 1942; ANMAE, série M/vol. 27, no. 492, Piétri to direction des affaires politiques, 9 October 1942.
58. SHAT, 1P136/D2, EMA-19e région, 'Renseignements sur la fortification espagnole', n.d. January 1942.
59. SHAT, 1P138/D4, no. 550, Odic to Weygand, 25 February 1941, no. 3571/EMAA-3, 'Défense du Maroc – terrains d'opérations', 14 October 1941; ANMAE, série M/vol. 138, no. 4015, EMA-2, note d'information, 17 February 1941.
60. Smyth, 'Screening "Torch"', pp. 337-9.
61. Service Historique de la Marine Archive, carton TTA40/FMF-deuxième bureau, no. 955, Delaye to Secrétariat d'Etat, Marine, 9 June 1942.
62. SHAT, 3P104/D3, no. 31, EMA-2, note de renseignements, 24 September 1942.
63. PRO FO 371/31277, C10190/3453/41, Gascoigne to FO, 23 November 1942.
64. Smyth, 'Screening "Torch"', 351-2.
65. ANMAE, série M/vol. 29, no. 569, Piétri to Laval, 14 November 1942.
66. SHAT, 3P104/D3, EMA-2, 'Situation militaire espagnole', 31 January 1943; ANMAE, série M/vol. 27, no. 9, Piétri to Laval, 7 January 1943.
67. PRO CAB 122/41, COS to Joint Staff Mission, Washington, 1 February 1943.

9

Programm Bär

The Supply of German War Material to Spain, 1943-1944

Christian Leitz (University of Auckland)

D URING the Second World War German-Spanish relations
experienced several transformations which, as this paper will
show, can be illustrated through an examination of the role of German exports of war material to Spain, and in this context, the most
ambitious supply programme, *Programm Bär.*

The question of war material deliveries was brought up by both
Spanish representatives and German armaments producers soon
after the end of the Spanish Civil War. For Franco and many of his
officers it made more sense to continue with the use of weapon systems on which their soldiers had been trained than to change over
to completely different types. In addition, the Civil War had left the
Nationalist army in particular need of German spare parts for the
repair and upkeep of their own equipment and the material left
behind by the Condor Legion. Finally, despite its preference for
German equipment, the Spanish military nevertheless also
approached other producers of war material. Yet, the generally hesitant, and often hostile response it received from Britain and the
United States during subsequent years, only further enhanced Germany's role as a supplier.[1]

In October 1939 General Juan Yagüe Blanco, newly appointed
Spanish Air Force Minister, proposed an ambitious plan of expansion to Franco. As an undefined proportion of the proposed 5,000

aircraft were to be produced in Spain, the plan emphasised the need for a huge construction programme which would require a total expenditure of 6,000 million pta. over a ten-year period.[2] As most of the arms negotiations with Germany during the first half of 1940 concentrated on the supply of aircraft, it may be concluded that Franco did not reject Yagüe's 'master plan' out of hand.[3] As a first step, in December 1939, the German Government agreed to a minor general agreement (*Rahmenvertrag*) covering a meagre RM3.5 million worth of spare parts, engines and other material. The Spanish Air Force Ministry was clearly not satisfied and continued to press for a more satisfying response from the German authorities. In January 1940, Lieutnant-Colonel Francisco Arranz, director for material acquisitions in the Ministry, demanded not only German planes and spare parts of a total value of RM40 million, but also the investment of RM45 million in the projected expansion of the Spanish aircraft industry. However, he encountered a discouraging response, in particular from Hermann Göring.

At this point in the war, the Nazi regime clearly put Spain low on its priority list of arms supplies as the country did not fulfil any of the factors which might have enticed the regime to be more forthcoming. Spain's declared neutrality precluded the possibility of strengthening a potential ally. In any case, such supplies would have been obstructed by the geographical detachment of Spain which, prior to the defeat of France, created a very problematic transport situation. Even if the Nazi regime had ignored these factors and judged Spain purely by considerations of economic usefulness, it would not have been inclined to be any more generous as the Spanish authorities showed some reluctance to release sufficient quantities of such vital goods as lead, wool and oil.

Prior to Germany's defeat of France, which confirmed the conviction of many Spanish officers of the superiority of German armaments, little progress was thus made by the Spanish Government in its quest to secure large quantities of German war material, let alone in its ambitious plans for military expansion.[4] The dramatic change in the military situation forced a new sense of urgency upon the Spanish authorities. With the declaration of non-belligerency, followed by Franco's offer to enter the war on 19 June 1940, Spanish rearmament plans had turned from domestic planning 'games' about possible military requirements into the stark reality of having to prepare Spain for war *now*.

Yet, obstacles certainly abounded. For a start Hitler showed little interest in Franco's original offer, though, as we know, he changed his mind soon after.[5] Spain's dire economic situation certainly hampered its readiness for war. Over the coming months Spain's growing requests for such essential goods as wheat, oil, cotton, fertilizers and coal, and German claims on British and French companies in Spain and mining companies in French Morocco, were to provide the material for increasingly heated exchanges between German and Spanish negotiators. In view of Spanish demands, including Franco's not very welcome quest for territorial expansion in North Africa, Göring even expressed scepticism about the usefulness of a Spanish entry into the war.[6] Considering the differences over economic and territorial demands, the need to supply Spain with German war material appeared to have been one of the least contentious issues during the crucial period of discussions between German and Spanish officials in September and October 1940.

Spanish military requirements were certainly not low. In October, the Spanish authorities set their needs at 2,000 lorries, 200 tanks, 40 Junkers Ju 88, 100 artillery pieces (15.5 cm) with 1,000 shells each, and 100 howitzers (21 cm) with 1,000 shells each.[7] Despite the sheer volume of demands, German observers had to admit that the Spanish army was in no fit state to function effectively and that it needed substantial improvements to its equipment level. As a result, and at a time when the meeting of the two dictators at Hendaye on 23 October 1940 brought no real progress towards a Spanish entry into the war, discussions on trading German war material against Spanish raw materials appeared to reach a more successful outcome.

Yet, ultimately the negotiations did not live up to their initial promise. A comprehensive separate agreement on a direct barter of war material and raw materials was never concluded. In early 1941, it was finally decided to incorporate arms and Spanish raw materials into the general trade between the two countries.[8] Around the same time, the Nazi regime reached the conclusion that Spain's excessive economic and military demands had to be interpreted 'as an expression of the endeavour ... to avoid an entry into the war'.[9] Yet, the Nazi regime continued vainly with its efforts to convince Spain to join the war on its side. Such efforts received a temporary boost when, after Germany's invasion of the Soviet Union in June, Franco permitted the formation of the Blue Division. The unexpected continuation of the Eastern campaign into autumn and then winter of 1941, and the entry of the United States into the war caused, however, quite the opposite effect on German-Spanish relations to that which the Nazi regime had anticipated just a few months earlier. Instead of Spain willingly slipping into the role of Germany's obedient military partner, a role reversal was looming. Germany was to experience a growing dependence on certain Spanish goods, in particular wolfram.[10] Owing to the urgent need to equip German troops in the Soviet Union with winter clothing wool, woollen products and hides also had to be imported in larger quantities. In fact, during 1942, 35 percent of the *Wehrmacht*'s requirements of clothing hides depended on supplies from the Iberian Peninsula.[11]

The change in the economic relationship found its expression in Germany's growing deficit in the clearing with Spain. As the Nazi regime was not in a position to fulfil urgent Spanish demands for wheat, oil, and not even manufactured products, it moved the focus of bilateral negotiations more and more towards offering war material. Although subsequent supplies never achieved an equilibrium in the trading relationship with Spain, and Germany continued to experience disruptions to her import of vital Spanish raw materials, they certainly moderated the annoyance of Franco's regime and helped to prevent an even more damaging situation. After all, this was an area where the Nazi regime was certain to kick at an open door. Franco's government was dominated by military men and, during the Second World War, all three armed forces ministries together were usually responsible for more than 50 percent of the State's consumption.[12]

Official negotiations and informal talks between German and Spanish officials during the period 1942 to 1944 were therefore increasingly dominated by the issue of German war material. Officially, both governments continued to refer to military reasons to explain requests for and supplies of arms. In reality, however, Germany's requirements of certain Spanish raw materials came to form the background to her willingness to supply war material. Considering the needs of Germany and her allies, the Nazi regime was not really in a position to release war material. Yet, this consideration had to be weighed against the knowledge that without sufficient imports of important raw materials Germany's war effort would also be hampered. The rationale, as expressed by one officer, was simple: 'The central idea behind the decision to supply war material to Spain was to create – as far as militarily possible – counter-supplies for important Spanish supplies and services.'[13] In practice, the condition 'militarily possible' meant that Germany regularly supplied far fewer arms than Spain's often heavily exaggerated requests demanded.

The German Government also proved to be reluctant to accommodate Spanish appeals for the transfer of German war material production to Spain. Even Franco himself received a negative reply from Germany after he had approached Stohrer about the matter during the celebrations of the third anniversary of the victory in the civil war.[14] In practice, this would have meant either the use of Spanish facilities to produce war material for Germany or the construction of new production sites with the help of German expertise. Occasionally, it quite simply implied the handing over of German weaponry plans and designs to Spanish officials.[15] Several reservations influenced the lack of interest of the Nazi regime. First, it was certain that Spain would not produce and export war material without charging for it. An added burden to Germany's already severe financial problems was therefore to be expected. In addition, Spain would have to be supplied with some raw materials and machinery to increase production. Secondly, even if these problems were solved, worries would remain about the quality of Spanish production. Finally, considering the corruption and rivalries amongst Francoist officials, it could not be guaranteed that German construction plans would not be passed on to the Allies, or that the Allies would not start buying up Spanish war material produced with German help.[16]

It is therefore not surprising that comparatively little evidence exists about such transfer deals. By late July 1942, the German Government had sold arms licences and patents worth a meagre RM1 million to Spain, though further contracts on licences and patents valued at RM16,475,000 were apparently near conclusion.[17] A small quantity of ships were constructed in Spain for the OKM, though the whole scheme proved to be laborious and costly.[18]

From a German point of view the export of war material was preferred. This stance found its reflection in round after round of talks commencing with major economic negotiations in July 1942. Once started, the negotiations suffered from frequent interruptions. Franco's dismissal of Serrano Suñer and his reappointment of the more anglophile General Francisco Gómez, Conde de Jordana y Souza as Foreign Minister in September 1942 resulted in some delay. Seemingly excessive Spanish demands caused the German delegation to procrastinate while the Spanish Government pointed at Germany's trade deficit. Finally, the successful Allied landings in North Africa in November proved to be a further distraction.

Hitler finally decided to order his delegation to be more accommodating towards the Spanish Government and, as a result, a new interim trade agreement was signed on 16 December 1942.[19] The agreement made direct references to the export of German war material, including a list of specific German requirements of Spanish non-ferrous metals to be used in the production of German arms for Spain. Germany also promised to finalise all details of an earlier deal between the Brünner Waffenwerke and the Franco regime. In early 1942, Brünner Waffenwerke had offered to supply 500 anti-aircraft machine guns, 5,000 light machine guns and 1,000 heavy machine guns with ammunition at a total value of about RM80 million. A first contract for 250 anti-aircraft machine guns with ammunition worth RM30 million was eventually signed on 31 March even though Brünn had not consulted German Government officials about the availability of adequate amounts of raw materials.[20] Despite some initial reluctance, the German Government had eventually come to favour the transaction owing to its potential usefulness in the economic negotiations with Spain, an apparent Spanish willingness to supply required raw materials, and, above all, the pressure of the clearing deficit with Spain. During the first half of 1943, such considerations also forced the German Government to support Brünn's original offer of 5,000 light and 1,000 heavy machine guns. Of the entirety of these contracts 1,000 heavy, 250 extra heavy and 100 light machine guns arrived in Spain by the end of 1944 – unfortunately for the Spanish army without target-sights.[21]

In addition to the Brünn deal, the OKM and the RLM had also agreed upon new supply contracts with their Spanish counterparts during the summer of 1942. The navy contracts included barrage artillery, ammunition, and speedboat engines (RM22.6 million) and licensing rights (RM2 million). It also gave the Spanish navy the option to place an additional order worth RM3-4 million for further equipment. In addition to the contract, a badly damaged German submarine, which had been brought into a Spanish port, was sold for RM1.5 million. For both air ministries, Field Marshal Milch and General Roca signed a special compensation agreement in Berlin on 21 July 1942. It committed the German air force industry to supply about RM9.5 million of air force material, including one Heinkel 111 H6, aircraft engines and 500 mts of aluminium. In compensation for German supplies, about RM7.3 million worth of vital Spanish ores were to be exported to Germany with decisions on the remaining RM2.2 million to be taken at a later stage. While, by early February 1943, no supplies had reached either side, the whole transaction was completed in summer 1943 though not apparently to the satisfaction of the RLM.[22]

Neither the German nor the Spanish government was wholly satisfied about the navy and air force deals of summer 1942. Officials in the Nazi regime were unhappy about the prices which had been agreed. From a Spanish point of view the deals could only very partially satisfy the hunger for German war material. Much more comprehensive demands by the Spanish army, navy and air force were eventually put to the German delegation in December. It was therefore decided to commence more detailed negotiations soon after.[23]

In January 1943, a Spanish military commission led by Captain Santiago Antón Rosas arrived in Berlin for preliminary negotiations on Spanish war material requests. Under the direction of Ernst von Weizsäcker and Ginés Vidal y Saura, the new Spanish ambassador, a new round of official talks commenced on 15 January. Jordana had instructed Vidal y Saura that his principal mission was to ensure supplies of armaments and, subordinated to this, of machinery and arms production licences. To begin with the Spanish ambassador therefore made a concrete demand for 100 Me 109 and twenty-five Ju 88. In reaction, exactly one month later General Krahmer, German air attaché in Madrid, informed Jordana about Hitler's personal offer of fifteen Me 109, twelve Ju 88 and anti-aircraft and artillery material while, in Berlin, General Georg Thomas made similar proposals to the Spanish military delegation.[24] Although the initial reaction of the MAE was negative, these developments nonetheless led to major new negotiations which started in earnest on 15 March, three days after a Spanish delegation led by General Carlos Martínez Campos had arrived in Berlin.

The March negotiations took place with both sides all too aware that just three months after the economic agreement the Nazi regime had already palpably failed to live up to the promises made in December. No substantial alteration to the imbalance in the economic relationship between the two countries had been achieved. While Spain fulfilled its part of the December agreement for the period to 28 February 1943, Germany supplied less than a third of the promised RM60 million of exports.[25] Threatened with delays in the exportation of vital Spanish goods to Germany, the Nazi regime had to ensure a dramatic improvement in the supply of German goods to Spain. Consequently, it was to be expected that Martínez Campos would not return to Spain empty-handed.

During its two-week stay, which included visits to arms factories and testing grounds, the Spanish delegation was received by General Thomas, to whom Martínez Campos presented the Spanish list of requests. It included demands for 250 fighter aircraft, 2,421 anti-aircraft guns, 4 reconnaissance seaplanes, 6 speedboats, 8 diesel engines, 120 torpedoes, 2,000 depth charges and various communication equipment. Although the OKW was apparently shocked by the list, some members of the German delegation regarded the demands as militarily justified.[26] On 18 March Hitler pointed out to Martínez Campos that he would have to know whether Spain's requests for war material were to be treated as purely commercial, or whether they would be of a political-military nature. If the latter was the case, then Germany would expect renewed Spanish commitment to defend itself against any Allied military intervention – as agreed upon in a secret protocol signed in February.[27] Otherwise, Hitler argued, he could not justify transferring arms away from his own, and other Axis, troops. While in November 1942 – in reaction to Operation Torch – and even more recently, the Spanish Government had emphasised the need to defend itself against a possible Allied invasion,[28] Martínez Campos now proved to be more evasive as he put the Spanish position somewhere between 'commercial' and 'political-military'. Despite this somewhat vague reply, Hitler expressed his willingness to help Spain.[29]

On 29 March, Martínez Campos returned to Spain to report on the German list of war material which, as was to be expected, did not correspond to the highly ambitious Spanish demands. Anticipated supplies for the Spanish navy included diesel engines, optical equipment, radio stations, anti-aircraft and other guns, six speedboats and torpedoes while the Spanish air force was to receive fifteen Me 109 F4, ten Ju 88 A4 (or alternatively He 111 H6), anti-aircraft guns, radio equipment, search equipment and ammunition. The Spanish army, finally, received promises for substantial quantities of automatic weapons, 450 anti-tank guns, anti-tank mines, 120 Russian howitzers, various types of grenades, 30 mark IV tanks, motocycles and communication equipment. Delivery periods varied between immediate and the beginning of 1945.[30]

Heading a delegation of fifteen Spanish military officials, Martínez Campos eventually returned to Germany on 28 April for further discussions and arms inspections. A week later, negotiations on the economic side of the arms deal commenced in Madrid. When the German delegation led by Joachim von Ribbentrop's envoy Ernst Eisenlohr entered into official talks with the Spanish Government on 5 May, it was already in possession of a draft arms agreement. On 30 April the *Ausfuhrgemeinschaft für Kriegsgerät* (AGK) had held a meeting with the four companies (Friedrich Krupp, Rheinmetall-Borsig, Carl Zeiss, Brown-Boveri) at the centre of the planned war material supply programme. During the meeting a draft of the arms agreement with Spain was put together, which was then passed on to the OKW for comments. Several changes were subsequently made to the agreement, codenamed *Programm Bär*. The OKW, for instance, decided to leave quantity control and transport of arms to Schenker & Co., a private company with major experience in the transport of goods between Germany and Spain. Some changes were also included on the basis of suggestions made by the arms producers involved.[31] On 24 May the *Bären* (bears), as the Spanish Government was often referred to in the communications of German Government and company officials,[32] were presented with the – amended – draft agreement. Further changes were made over the following weeks until the final version of the agreement was accepted by the Spanish Government at the beginning of July.

To be precise, the 'agreement' was really a sample contract as it was set out in such a way that each of the three Spanish armed forces ministries had to complete a copy of it together with each company from which it purchased war material. This arrangement was made very clear in the first few lines of the contract: 'Between the Spanish .... Ministry – subsequently shortened to "Ministry" – represented by .... *on one side*, and the company "X" – subsequently shortened to "X" – represented by .... *on the other side* the following contract is concluded for the supply of the material listed below.' In the first of the subsequent sixteen articles the exact details of the war material to be delivered were listed, while the second article dealt with any 'additional supplies', namely documentation (blueprints, drawings, etc.) concerning the material. Delivery periods were covered by the third article followed by an article which contained permissible reasons for any delay in delivery, particularly 'military, political or other such events which are outside of "X"'s or its subsupplier's power'. Article V provided information on the organisations responsible for the quality control of the material. In the case of arms from *Wehrmacht* stocks and captured material separate controls were not undertaken and instead replaced by certificates from German military sections confirming the readiness for use of the equipment. War material taken from company production or especially manufactured for the Spanish ministry was checked and certified by the relevant inspection unit of the *Wehrmacht* though a Spanish representative was permitted to attend the final inspection. Article VI committed the arms producer "X" to replace faulty equipment or parts during a period of six months after the final inspection. Quantity control was regulated under Article VII and was to be undertaken by a German transport company as the representative of the Spanish ministry. Once quantities had been ascertained, confirmatory protocols were signed and the transport company (presumably Schenker & Co.) would then transport the arms to Spain. After the completion of the confirmatory protocols, the risk for accidental loss and damage transferred to the Spanish ministry (Article VIII).

A crucial area of concern for both sides was covered in Articles IX, X and XII which dealt with the question of prices, date for and conditions of payment and supplies of Spanish raw materials. Payment conditions were regulated according to the expected delivery date. In the case of material ready for supply, 25 percent of the total price had to be paid within thirty days of the contract coming into effect, while the remainder had to be paid for each item thirty days after its arrival at the Spanish border or within eight weeks of the confirmatory protocols. In the case of longer delivery periods, again 25 percent of the total sum was due within thirty days of the contract, a further 25 percent after half of the delivery period had passed while the remainder was again payable as above. Finally, in the case of equipment already supplied at the time of the signing of the contract the totality of the payment had to be made within thirty days of the exchange of signatures. All payments were to be made into the German-Spanish clearing. The German authorities treated them as fulfilled only when they reached ROWAK, the German end of the clearing, in Berlin. Via ROWAK payments finally reached the relevant German arms producer.[33]

In the first official copy of the sample contract the question of war material prices and Spanish raw material supplies was expressly left out to be decided by the ongoing German-Spanish negotiations in Madrid. In fact, this proved to be the most troublesome aspect of the whole arms deal, not only at a government-government level, but even initially among company and government officials in Germany. At a meeting at the OKW on 17 May it was decided to use factory gate prices of 1939 as the basis for Germany's demands.[34] Yet, the German Government clearly intended to go substantially beyond these prices. Indications that massive price increases were to be expected had emerged as early as March 1943. Then, the AA had demanded an increase of at least 300 percent by arguing that Turkey had accepted such price increases, while the RWM insisted on an even higher surcharge of 400 percent.[35]

On 25 and 26 May, the question resurfaced in a meeting between Hans Eltze of the AGK, Carl Clodius, Permanent Secretary in the

AA, and Lieutnant-Colonel Radtke of the OKW. After lengthy discussions, Clodius insisted on a 200 percent surcharge. This horrified Eltze, particularly as Clodius demanded that 'die Industrie' was to run the negotiations over prices. Eltze rejected this idea very forcefully and complained that neither from a technical nor from a production cost angle could the industry stand up for such demands. After all, he added, the *Bären* were in possession of numerous past offers for some of the types of material included in the programme and were therefore able to compare prices. As the price increase was of a purely politico-economic nature, it was the task of the AA and the RWM, and not within the remit of the AGK, to negotiate it. Clodius, however, continued to insist on both the surcharge and that negotiations were to be undertaken by the arms producers. In a subsequent meeting, on 26 May, it was therefore decided to supply the complete list of war material with an overall average surcharge of 200 percent included. Yet, all company representatives agreed strongly that they would not want to be involved in the actual price negotiations and they referred again to the politico-economic motivation behind the surcharge.[36] On the following day, it was therefore left to Clodius to hand over the list of prices for the *Sofortprogramm* (immediate programme) to Martínez Campos who, 'without looking at it', embarked on his return trip to Spain.[37]

Even though negotiations had not yet come to a conclusion, the *Sofortprogramm*, the first stage of *Programm Bär*, was immediately put into motion. From 27 May until the departure of the last train on 25 June 1943, sixty-five wagons with air force material and 293 wagons with other war material left Germany for Spain. In addition, fifteen fighter planes were sent to Spain with a further ten fighters to follow later. Yet, just when the sample contract had been agreed by both sides, and the transition between *Sofortprogramm* and *Restprogramm* (remaining programme) of *Bär* was to take place, the German authorities told the arms producers to put supplies on halt. The reason given was simple, namely the persistent differences over the question of prices.[38]

To everybody involved in these discussions, whether in the German Government or in the AGK, it was clear that the former pursued one clear objective: to compensate the inflated prices it had to pay for Spanish goods, most notably wolfram, by demanding increased prices for its supplies of war material. In the end, the AGK succeeded with its flat refusal to get involved in the pricing negotiations. While individual arms contracts were negotiated in Germany directly between German arms producers and the relevant Spanish attaché, discussions over prices were undertaken by Eisenlohr's delegation. It was instructed to put the total value of arms supplies at RM625 million, more than three times their 1939 value. This was the figure which the delegation announced to its Spanish counterpart though it had permission to allow price rebates of not more than an average of 25 percent, or *in toto* down to roughly RM470 million. The Spanish reaction proved to be predictable. Franco made it absolutely clear to Hans Heinrich Dieckhoff, the new German ambassador, 'that the prices were far too high and that such high price demands had left a very unfavourable impression with the Spanish Government and the Spanish generals'. Dieckhoff's attempts to explain the rationale behind these prices, that is, to compensate for the vast price increases of Spanish exports of raw materials, fell on deaf ears. Franco and his government would not budge.[39]

By the end of July, discussions had therefore reached an impasse. At the beginning of August, Eltze reported to Krupp managers Karl Pfirsch and Hermann Vaillant that the most the Spanish Government would apparently accept was an increase 'of about 10 percent over normal export prices'. As on previous occasions, Eltze expressed indignation over Clodius's approach to the negotiations which the latter attended as a member of Eisenlohr's delegation. It appears that Clodius together with Friedrich Bethke, director of ROWAK and *Referent z. b. V.* in the RWM, and Roggenbrodt of the Ministry of Armaments, made Eisenlohr's position even more difficult than it already was. Owing to 'the development that had, in the meantime, taken place in Sicily and Italy', namely the Allied landings and advances, the Spanish Government was, in fact, taking an even more guarded attitude.[40]

The German delegation undoubtedly found itself in an increasingly precarious position. Franco's rejection of inflated prices meant that the commencement of the *Restprogramm* continued to be delayed. Without sufficient arms supplies, however, Germany's trade deficit could not be combatted and would undoubtedly threaten vital supplies of Spanish raw materials. In the end, the German Government backed down when a German-Spanish sub-commission on prices came up with recommendations favouring the position of the Spanish Government. When both sides eventually arrived at a general economic agreement, signed on 18 August 1943, the Spanish Government had reduced Germany's attempt at a surcharge for war material to about 20 percent. The new agreement was an extension to the economic agreement of 16 December

1942 and ran until 30 November 1944. In total, the value of expected German exports amounted to RM516.5 million of which RM216.5 million were allocated to *Programm Bär*.[41]

The whole of the *Restprogramm* (RM177.2 million) was supposed to comprise a total of about 670 wagons of war material for Spain.[42] The *Sofortprogramm* stipulated that the Spanish army was to receive RM112 million worth of arms, the navy RM65.75 million, and the air force RM28.75 million. Major supplies included 298 anti-aircraft batteries and guns (RM31.11 million), 645 other types of artillery guns (RM52.9 million), bombs, grenades, mines and other ammunition (RM52.1 million) and radio and communication equipment (RM21.1 million).[43] By the end of 1943, all transports were still running according to plan, and, in value terms, about half of the agreed supplies had reached Spain. Yet, in early 1944, the pace of transports slowed down.

At the same time, however, and despite the increasing needs of the German war machine, the Nazis were prepared to offer Spain a further war material supply programme alongside the on-going *Programm Bär*. In a lengthy letter to the AA in October 1943, Dieckhoff had underscored the necessity of new arms supplies to Spain, particularly as the Spanish service ministries had again expressed their desire to increase purchases of German war material. Dieckhoff argued that Spain might otherwise purchase weaponry from the Allies who were already supplying Portugal with war material, including German booty weapons. Moreover, he pointed to Germany's continued trade and clearing problems which could only be alleviated by exporting arms to Spain. In fact, Dieckhoff was convinced that the capacity of Germany's war material production would allow for such exports without endangering the German supply situation.[44]

Dieckhoff's intervention was immediately followed up by the Spanish ambassador. As with Dieckhoff's report, Vidal y Saura pointed to the Portuguese case and supplied the AA with a secret list of British arms supplies to Portugal.[45] Hitler reacted in a matter-of-fact way to the information. According to his aide Hewel:

> he first wants to know, what the Spaniards could and would supply to us. The whole matter is purely business. We cannot and do not want to prevent the Spaniards from buying arms from our enemies. At present, we cannot supply everything. This does not mean that the Spaniards would use these weapons [of the Allies] against us, just as little as we expect the Spaniards to fight with our weapons against the *Angelsachsen*. Before he continues to occupy himself more with the matter, he would like to know what Spain was going to supply.

Hitler's attitude towards the question of arms supplies to Spain was clearly conditioned by their potential economic benefits and not by apparent Allied attempts to sell war material to Portugal. Hitler was not really impressed by the secret list of Portuguese receipts of arms.[46] Yet, although it appears that Hitler reacted somewhat casually to Spanish requests, a comment soon after demonstrated that Hitler was only too aware that his regime was in no position to abandon war material supplies to Spain. On 22 January 1944, he made it absolutely clear that 'the greatest amounts of Spanish raw materials, above all wolfram, had to be secured'. To achieve this he was prepared 'to accommodate Spanish demands for aircraft as much as possible. He stated that the supply of 100 Me 109 and 25 Ju 88 had to be made possible. In comparison to the numbers [of aircraft] which were being destroyed on [German] airfields, this number appeared to be bearable.' Field Marshal Keitel was instructed to approach the RLM about Hitler's decision.[47]

Although Spain was never to receive the aircraft which Hitler had mentioned, the Nazi regime nonetheless attempted to respond to Spanish demands for war material. This was intended to prevent a further detachment of Spain which, since late 1943, had come under increasing pressure from the U.S. Government to discontinue all friendly acts towards Germany, particularly the export of wolfram. Allied pressure and the negative development of the war thus impacted badly upon Germany's position *vis-à-vis* Spain. In addition, Franco's dissatisfaction about inadequate quantities of German imports – with the deficit reaching RM240 million in late September – continued to worsen Germany's position just when, in late 1943, the German Government had worked out a new purchasing programme of Spanish goods which partly depended on further war material deliveries.[48]

After the major negotiations in summer 1943, January 1944 thus saw renewed armaments discussions. Eltze's official visit to the Iberian Peninsula in December 1943 to January 1944 brought a flood of requests from all three Spanish armed forces ministries. In addition, much interest was again expressed in the purchase of licences and patents, and the production of German war material in Spain.[49] After a further request by General Jordana, the German Government therefore commenced preparations on *Programm Ankara*.[50] This new programme was finally offered to the Spanish Government in early June 1944 'as continuation of the present programme of purchases', namely *Programm Bär*. Germany's continued interest in Spanish raw materials, particularly wolfram, demanded that the Franco regime, which had only just signed an agreement with the Allies,[51] was wooed with further supplies of war material. Among the sixteen groups of material proposed under *Ankara*, the German Government had included thirty-three tanks with ammunition and command tanks mark IV, twenty-five 88 mm anti-aircraft guns, twenty-five complete Oerlikon 20 mm anti-aircraft batteries, ammunition, 200 motocycles, and various types of radio and communication equipment. At the same time, and separate to the government offer, the AGK, represented by Eltze, offered Spain even more arms in the form of sixty-seven tanks mark IV with ammunition and command tanks, sixty-three Rheinmetall 75 mm guns, one Rheinmetall 150 mm gun and one Skoda 210 mm canon. In addition to supplies of arms, the German Government also reacted positively to Spanish requests for machinery to expand Spain's armaments industry.[52] On 14 July 1944, the Spanish ambassador officially accepted Germany's new offers, and negotiations commenced immediately. Yet, the rapid deterioration of the transport situation after the Allied landings in France not only slowed down *Bär* supplies, but also prevented the implementation of other war material agreements.

In summer 1944, negotiations commenced on how to continue *Programm Bär* and plans were drawn up to transport goods via Switzerland or by air. In fact, the latter method was used until Germany's capitulation in May 1945! At irregular intervals the German authorities managed to use Lufthansa flights to Barcelona in their attempt to fulfil arms contracts beyond the RM158.4 million of *Bär* supplies which had arrived in Spain by December 1944.[53] Between 3 February and 5 May 1945, a number of German planes arrived in Spain with additional equipment for both the Me 109 and the Ju 88 which had been supplied as part of *Bär*. The last recorded arrival on 8 May 1945 contained Rheinmetall plans destined for the Spanish navy.[54] Just as the Spanish authorities used the same Lufthansa service to export small quantities of material requested by Germany, the German Government felt equally obliged to respond to Spanish demands.

Conclusion

From the outbreak of the Second World War until June 1940, German-Spanish relations were detached and, from the point of view of the Nazi regime, only of minor importance. During subsequent months, however, Germany's attitude was to change dramatically with Hitler eventually making an all-out effort to convince Franco to enter the war. This period of wooing and pressurising Spain continued into 1941 when preparations for Operation Barbarossa diverted the *Führer*'s attention. Yet, hopes for a Spanish entry into the war did not subside and were given a temporary boost by the dispatch of the Blue Division to the Eastern Front. Surprisingly little was, however, done to prepare Spain's armed forces for a participation in the war. Despite constant Spanish pleas, German war material supplies remained disappointingly low. While Franco regarded arms as a necessary precondition for a Spanish entry into the war, the Nazi regime insisted that Spain's commitment to an entry should precede any substantial release of arms. It seems therefore surprising that armaments supplies came to occupy a central role in relations between the two countries when a Spanish entry into the war had become a near-impossibility. In fact, in 1943 the value of German war material contracts with Spain peaked. At RM258 million (of a total of RM1,304 million), Spain had become Germany's biggest customer, just ahead of Italy.[55]

The expansion of arms contracts with Spain in 1942 (from RM5.4 million in 1941 to 76 million), followed by the dramatic increase in 1943 undoubtedly signify the changing nature of the role of war material towards becoming a tool of pure economic necessity. The crucial transitional period, during which military motives for supplying Spain increasingly lost their significance, can be identified as between Operation Torch in November 1942 and the Allied landings in Italy in summer 1943. Initially, with the likely prospect of an Allied invasion of the Iberian Peninsula, military considerations influenced both sides. By March 1943, however, after the *Wehrmacht*'s catastrophic defeat at Stalingrad and successive Allied successes in North Africa, the Spanish Government had distanced itself from its initial commitment to a defence of Spain against the Allies. Hitler, on the other hand, continued to anticipate Spain's use of German arms against the Allies, though he also acknowledged the economic importance of exporting war material to Spain.

With the Allied landings in Italy, the military factor lost its importance for the *Führer* as an attack on German-occupied Europe via Spain became very unlikely. Thereafter, the motivation behind German supplies of arms concentrated exclusively on the economic factor which, in practice, had already been the central one for more than a year. With other German exports totally insufficient to cover the growing quantity (and price) of vital imports of Spanish materials, supplies of arms constituted the only way to combat the clearing deficit with Spain and appease the Spanish Government. Appease, not satisfy, as from a Spanish point of view actual supplies never matched demands. The Nazi regime usually managed to negotiate Spanish demands downwards, indeed, Spain did not even receive all of the contractually promised supplies. The most obvious reason for this gap between contractual obligations and actual supplies stemmed from the effects of the Allied invasion of France which, initially, slowed down transports by rail to Spain and then very rapidly led to their cessation. Subsequent attempts to shift more material, including plans, patents and blueprints, to Spain yielded only pitiful results. In fact, attempts throughout the Second World War to secure German expertise to build up a major indigenous Spanish arms industry proved to be a disaster, particularly compared with Spain's hugely ambitious military expansion plans of 1939.

Yet, despite such obvious reasons for the Spanish military to complain about the inadequacies of Germany's supply policy, 'positive' aspects should not be ignored. Above all, Nazi Germany constituted the only major source of arms for the Spanish armed forces. And, although Spanish troops never had to use German arms in an international conflict – with the exception of the Blue Division – they probably proved to be of some value to the Franco regime. It can be assumed that German tanks, machine guns and aircraft found their use in Franco's ruthless suppression of Republican guerrilla activities during the Second World War and directly after.[56] A detailed examination of the correlation between German arms exports (and technical advisers) and Franco's anti-guerrilla campaigns remains, however, a desideratum.

Notes

1. In 1945, Anthony Eden claimed that 'no war material ha[d] been supplied to Spain since the outbreak of the Civil War', PRO PREM4 21/2A, War Cabinet memo 'Supply of Equipment to Spain', 10 April 1945. On the attitude of the U.S. government, see C. Leitz, *Economic Relations between Nazi Germany and Franco's Spain*, Oxford, 1996, pp. 128-9. During 1943 and 1944, the value of military equipment of non-German origin amounted to only £57,058 and £24,468; BE DE-IEME Estadística, libro 22865.
2. Fundación Nacional Francisco Franco, *Documentos inéditos para la historia del Generalísimo Franco* (hereafter *Documentos*), Madrid, 1992, vol. I, pp. 610-12, 'Yagüe project to create a great Air Force', October 1939.
3. See, for instance, FCO AA3868/045919, Sabath to German embassy in Madrid, 7 December 1939.

4. The Spanish navy had also presented Franco with grand expansion and modernization plans; *Documentos* I, pp. 616-36, memo by Luis Carrero Blanco, 30 October 1939, and pp. 640-50, memo by Admiral Salvador Moreno, 16 November 1939.

5. For the most detailed examination of Hitler's growing interest in a Spanish entry into the war during the second half of 1940, see Mathias Ruiz Holst, *Neutralität oder Kriegsbeteiligung? Die deutsch-spanischen Verhandlungen im Jahre 1940*, Pfaffenweiler, 1986. See also Donald S. Detwiler, *Hitler, Franco und Gibraltar: Die Frage des spanischen Kriegseintritts in den zweiten Weltkrieg*, Wiesbaden, 1962; Paul Preston, 'Franco and the Axis Temptation', in Paul Preston, *The Politics of Revenge; Fascism and the military in twentieth-century Spain*, London, 1995, pp. 60-71; Paul Preston, 'Franco and Hitler: The Myth of Hendaye 1940', *Contemporary European History* 1, 1992: 1-16; Walther L. Bernecker, 'Neutralität wider Willen: Spaniens verhinderter Kriegseintritt', in *Kriegsausbruch 1939: Beteiligte, Betroffene, Neutrale*, eds H. Altrichter and J. Becker, Munich, 1989, pp. 153-77.

6. ADAP, series D, X, doc. 404, 463, note 2 to a memo by Woermann, 27 August 1940.

7. *Documentos* II-1, pp. 373-4, report on Spain's military resources, October 1940.

8. DGFP, D, XII, doc. 562, 904-5, AA to RWM and OKW, 27 May 1941.

9. FCO AA2174/471436-41, report by Wiehl on a memo of the Spanish General Staff, 12 February 1941; DGFP, D, XII, doc. 28, 51-3, Stohrer to AA, 7 February 1941.

10. See C. Leitz, 'Nazi Germany's Struggle for Spanish Wolfram during the Second World War', *European History Quarterly* 25, 1995: 71-92.

11. BA/MA RW19/435, Appendix 25 of War Diary No. 4 of OKW WiAmt, WiAusl IVa to OKM/M Rüs IIb, 30 January 1943.

12. A. Carreras, 'Depresión económica y cambio estructural durante el decenio bélico (1936-1945)', in *El primer franquismo: España durante la segunda guerra mundial*, ed. J.L. Garcia Delgado, Madrid, 1989, p. 20.

13. BA/MA RW19/442, report of official in charge of VIIb, in War Diary No. 2 of OKW WiAmt WiAusl VII, 1 July-30 September 1942.

14. FCO AA1308/844-51, memo by Stohrer, 17 June 1942.

15. BA/MA RW19/246, note on Spanish requests for war material orders, 14 March 1942.

16. BA/Pots 09.01/68454, Wiehl to German embassy in Spain, 16 May 1942; BA/MA RW19/436, weekly report 5-10 July 1943, 16 July 1943. See FCO AA1308/347023, Enge to AA, 25 September 1942 for a scathing report on the expected inability of both patent offices and potential arms producers to keep German patents secret.

17. BA/MA RW19/443, AA to Detzner (OKW), 6 August 1942.

18. The German army only entered into three contracts with Spain, two for pistols and one for batteries; BA/MA Wi/IB 2.13, Report by Major Ludwig, January 1944.

19. BA/MA RW19/434, War Diary No. 3 of OKW WiAmt WiAusl III/IV, 1 October-31 December 1942 contains the trade agreement with enclosures. See also K.-J. Ruhl, *Spanien im Zweiten Weltkrieg: Franco, die Falange und das "Dritte Reich"*, Hamburg, 1975, pp. 164-5 and A. Viñas, J. Viñuela, F. Eguidazu, C. Pulgar-Fernández, S. Forensa, *Política comercial exterior en España, 1931-1975*, 2 vols, Madrid, 1979, vol. I, pp. 396ff.

20. FCO AA5386/361764-8, memo by Schüller, 17 February 1943; BA/Pots 09.01/68454, M. Prince Hohenlohe to Wiehl, 10 October 1942.
21. BA/MA RW19/381, weekly report by OKW Wstb (Ausl) 3/IIIc, 18 December 1944.
22. BA/Pots 09.01/68454, memo by Wiehl, 26 September 1942; BA/MA RW19/442, War Diary No. 2 of OKW WiAmt WiAusl/VII, 1 July-30 September 1942; BA/Pots 80Re1/5791, Wigru Luftfahrt-Industrie to Nagel, 1 February 1943; BA/Pots 09.01/68455, Dieckhoff to AA, 31 October 1943; BA/Pots 09.01/68455, memo by Sabath, 17 November 1943.
23. BA/MA RW19/443, War Diary No. 3 of OKW WiAmt WiAusl/VII, 1 October-31 December 1942.
24. R. García Pérez, *Franquismo y Tercer Reich*, Madrid, 1994, pp. 376, 380 note 145, and 383-4.
25. Viñas et al, *Política comercial*, p. 406.
26. On the list and German reactions, see Ruhl, *Spanien im Zweiten Weltkrieg*, pp. 225-6.
27. U.S. Department of State, *The Spanish Government and the Axis*, Washington, 1946, doc. 14, 35, secret protocol, 10 February 1943.
28. See Ruhl, *Spanien im Zweiten Weltkrieg*, pp. 162-3.
29. ADAP, E, V, doc. 226, pp. 431-5, memo on conversation between Hitler and Martínez Campos on 18 March, 20 March 1943.
30. BA/MA RW19/444, enclosure 8, 27 March 1943 in War Diary No. 4 of OKW WStb (Ausl) 3. Abt., 1 January-30 June 1943.
31. IWM Krupp files 65a, AGK to Krupp, 8 May 1943, copy of draft agreement attached; ibid., AGK to Krupp, 13 May 1943; ibid., Krupp, Rheinmetall, Zeiss, Brown-Boveri to AGK, 17 May 1943; ibid., memos by Vaillant (Krupp), 21 and 24 May 1943.
32. See, for example, Krupp 65a, Vaillant to AGK, 21 May 1943.
33. Krupp 65a, Vaillant to Brombacher, 17 June 1943; ibid., memo by Vaillant, 22 June 1943; ibid., AGK to Krupp with final version of sample contract enclosed, 7 July 1943.
34. Krupp 65a, Vaillant to Mecking, 17 May 1943.
35. BA/Pots 09.01/68454, memo by Schüller, 8 March 1943.
36. Krupp 65a, memo by Vaillant, 26 May 1943.
37. Ibid., memo by Vaillant about AGK meeting of 28 May, 29 May 1943.
38. Ibid., memo by Grunewaldt, 30 July 1943. It appears that the *Restprogramm* commenced on 28 June 1943 when Brünner Waffenwerke and the Spanish Government agreed on about 75 million pta. of arms supplies; BE DE-IEME. Secretaría Caja 167, memo, 5 August 1943.
39. FCO AA88/639993-9, memo by Clodius, 22 June 1943. See ADAP, E, VI, doc. 119, pp. 207-208, Ribbentrop to embassy in Madrid, 28 June 1943, on Ribbentrop's anger about Franco's attempt to lower prices, and Viñas et al, *Política comercial exterior*, pp. 406ff note 254, for a defence of the Spanish rejection of Germany's attempted price increases.
40. Krupp 65a, memo by Vaillant, 5 August 1943.
41. FCO AA3205/D697664-5, Additional Agreement to the German-Spanish Economic Agreement of 16 December 1942, 8 August 1943.
42. BA/MA RW5/v.429, report on *Programm Bär*, 25 June 1943.
43. For a detailed breakdown of *Programm Bär* as agreed in August 1943, see García Pérez, *Franquismo y Tercer Reich*, p. 401, table V-2.

44. BA/Pots 09.01/68455, Dieckhoff to AA, 31 October 1943.

45. Ibid., memo by von Steengracht, 5 November 1943.

46. Ibid., report by Hewel for Ribbentrop, 18 December 1943.

47. FCO AA89/102244-5, report by Hewel for Ribbentrop, 22 January 1944. On German-Spanish relations and the wolfram question, see Leitz, 'Nazi Germany's Struggle for Spanish Wolfram', *passim*.

48. BA/Pots 09.01/68455, memo by Wiehl, December 1943; ibid., undated memo by Sabath on further war material supplies to Spain.

49. FCO AA6503H/E487181-3, report by German embassy on Eltze visit, 22 January 1944.

50. BA/MA RW5/v.429, report on *Programm Bär*, 26 January 1944.

51. See Leitz, *Economic Relations*, pp. 190-1; see also Paul Preston's contribution to this present volume.

52. AMAE R2149/7, three letters by Carlos Asensio to Jordana, 9 June 1944; BA/MA RW19/448, War Diary No. 8 of OKW WStb (Ausl) 3. Abt., 1 April-30 June 1944.

53. BA/MA RW19/381, weekly report by OKW WStb (Ausl) 3/IIIc, 14 December 1944.

54. AHN, Presidencia de Gobierno, Dirección General de Adquisiciones (DGA), legajo 150, various letters by Air Ministry to DGA, 15 January-7 May 1945.

55. O. Dankelmann, 'Die imperialistischen Großmächte und Spanien während des zweiten Weltkrieges' (PhD Diss., University of Halle, 1966), p. 148, cited in Ruhl, *Spanien im Zweiten Weltkrieg*, p. 396.

56. Asensio indicated as much when he expressed the need for German war material to 'search and find the location of clandestine stations within the nation'; AMAE R2149/7 Asensio to MAE, 10 July 1944.

10

The Degree of British Commitment to the Restoration of Democracy in Spain, 1939-1946

Glyn Stone
(University of the West of England, Bristol)

FROM the outset of the Spanish Civil War in July 1936 the British Government maintained a strict policy of political and military non-intervention, refusing to recognise the belligerent rights of either party in the struggle and dominating the proceedings of the International Committee for Non-Intervention in Spain which was located in London. In pursuing non-intervention the government sought to be impartial between the Republican and Nationalist administrations despite the fact that the former represented the continuation of the democratic second Spanish Republic while the latter had no such legitimacy, based as it was on an unsuccessful attempt to militarily overthrow Spanish democracy in the time-honoured tradition of a military *pronunciamento*. In fact, and despite the appearance of impartiality, the Conservative-dominated National Governments of Stanley Baldwin and Neville Chamberlain tended to sympathise with General Francisco Franco and his Nationalist cause.[1] This was particularly true of the Admiralty who continued to condemn unreservedly the killing of Spanish naval officers by Republican sailors during the early weeks of the civil war, regardless of the fact that these officers were in open revolt and committing treason against the democratically elected government of Spain. The FO in August 1936 was equally dismissive of Spanish democracy denying the legitimacy of the Republican Government because of its failure to restore law and order prior to the civil war and condemning its arming of the civilian militias, even though the alternative was surrender in the face of the military rebellion.[2]

In November 1937 a special agent, Sir Robert Hodgson, was sent to Nationalist Spain to represent British interests there in exchange for the Duke of Alba who performed a similar task for Franco in London. The Government's denial to the contrary, this was tantamount to *de facto* recognition of the Franco régime and thereby an undermining of the legitimate authority of the Republican Government.[3] When Barcelona fell in January 1939 Chamberlain's government rushed to grant *de jure* recognition and the Prime Minister found it necessary to warn his Cabinet colleagues to 'avoid showing any satisfaction at the prospect of a Franco victory'.[4] In short, support for Spanish democracy, itself tainted by the need to maintain Soviet support in the absence of British and French assistance, had been relegated to the level of insignificance as the British authorities, already prejudiced against the Left in Spain, sought to appease Fascist Italy and Nazi Germany and their Spanish Nationalist allies. In March 1939 Republican Spain joined democratic Czechoslovakia as sacrifices on the altar of British appeasement.[5]

The abandonment of Spanish democracy did not rest heavily on the consciousness or consciences of the British Government during the period preceding the outbreak of the Second World War. The haste to recognise Franco's régime in February 1939 had been determined by the need to restore favourable Anglo-Spanish relations and to counter Italian and German influence in Spain, with the ultimate objective of securing Spanish neutrality in the event of a European war.[6] Between March and August 1939 the British endeavoured to wean Franco's régime from the Rome-Berlin Axis but with little or no success. They sought to persuade the *Caudillo* of their good intentions, for example, through economic assistance, and to dispel any doubts or suspicions he might have concerning British attitudes towards developments within Spain, in particular the question of a restoration of the monarchy; it was stressed that the future form of government in Spain was a matter for Spaniards alone to decide.[7] Unfortunately, following the outbreak of the Second World War, Franco's Spain did not remain strictly neutral. Instead, it pursued a policy of neutrality which was benevolent towards Germany, notably in the provision of refuelling bases for German submarines engaged in attacking British Atlantic shipping, and after June 1940 towards Italy.[8] Indeed, when Italy joined the war and the threat of a French invasion had been removed, Spain became a non-belligerent fulfilling Franco's promise to the Italian Foreign Minister, Galeazzo Ciano, of 19 July 1939, that Spain intended, in the event of a short war, to maintain 'a very favourable – even more than very favourable – neutrality towards Italy'. The Spanish leader had intimated that should there be a long war it would not be possible to maintain neutrality, for events would lead Spain 'to take up a more definite position'.[9] As Paul Preston has recently shown, Franco did not take up a more definite position because the German *Führer*, Adolf Hitler, preferring to retain good relations with Vichy France, refused to pay his price for belligerence, namely the dismemberment of the French North African Empire.[10] Despite his increasing dependency on British and U.S. economic assistance, Franco maintained Spanish nonbelligerency in favour of Germany until 1944 when, confronted with the impressive military successes of the Western Allies and the Soviet Union, he resumed a policy of neutrality.[11]

The British Government went to war in 1939 to challenge Nazi Germany's intention to dominate the European continent rather than to create a new and democratic order in Europe. Accordingly, as long as Spain maintained its neutrality Franco's régime had nothing to fear from the British. Despite the considerable reservations of their own labour movement, incensed by Franco's repression of hundreds of thousands of Republicans, the British authorities signed a trade treaty with Spain in April 1940.[12] Apart from the promotion of Anglo-Spanish trade, the treaty was intended to assist in stabilising conditions in Spain, thereby 'averting disorders and uncertainties which play into the hands of those powers which seek to profit from the internal weaknesses of other States'. The last thing the FO and its Ambassador in Spain, Sir Maurice Peterson, wanted was an anti-Franco debate in Parliament because it could benefit no-one but Germany.[13] Until at least 1944 anti-Franco articles appearing in the British press and hostile questions in the House of Commons continued to incense the FO and the embassy in Madrid because they threatened to undermine the carefully prepared strategy of maintaining Spanish non-belligerency by means of controlled economic assistance to the Iberian peninsula while secretly planning contingencies for seizing the Spanish and Portuguese Atlantic islands including the Canaries and the

Azores.[14] Spain's massive economic problems arising from the devastation caused by the civil war and her dependence on British and U.S. supplies of foodstuffs and raw materials, notably oil, were increasingly exploited by London and Washington as the war continued. The economic weapon was used to extract concessions from the Franco régime, not least its assurances that Spain would maintain her non-belligerency and preferably neutrality. At the same time, before 1944 there was no question of either Britain or the United States threatening to intervene or conspire to overthrow the Franco régime which, despite its Falangist tendencies and overt support for Nazi Germany, retained the Allies' tacit support; tacit because although they grew to despise the régime, they could not and would not contemplate an alternative in case this resulted in either Spain's intervention on Germany's side or a German invasion of the Iberian peninsula which would destroy not only Spain but Portugal as well and result in the loss of Gibraltar.

Thus, while the outcome of the war remained in the balance, the British Government preferred to avoid a leap in the dark as far as Franco's Spain was concerned. That they had no intention of intervening in the internal affairs of Spain was made abundantly clear by Sir Samuel Hoare, sent to Spain as Ambassador 'on special mission', in May 1940. Following Franco's declaration of non-belligerency Hoare saw the Spanish Foreign Minister, Colonel Juan Beigbeder, on 22 June to deny the rumours spread about Madrid that the British Government was plotting to overthrow the Franco régime. The exact opposite was the truth because the British Government was convinced that a change of Government in Spain 'would only lead to greater confusion and danger' and Hoare had been appointed to do what he could 'to help the present Government in the much needed work of reconstruction and in its efforts to keep out of the war'.[15] Denial of any intention to intervene in Spain's internal politics accompanied by reassurances to that effect became a constant theme of Hoare's tenure as Ambassador at Madrid. So too was the embassy's criticism of anti-Franco articles in the British press and their wish that they be curbed. The Prime Minister, Winston Churchill, and the Foreign Secretary, Lord Halifax, intervened often in press circles in 1940 to prevent or, at least, moderate press attacks on Franco but with indifferent success and the latter was compelled to warn Hoare that the Government could not legally prevent the publication of anti-Franco material.[16] Accordingly, anti-Franco attacks continued to appear in the British press to the continued chagrin of the FO and the Madrid embassy.[17]

Apart from the anti-Franco sentiments of part of the British press, the FO and, in particular, the Madrid embassy lost no opportunity in expressing their anxiety lest the continued presence of Spanish Republican exiles in the United Kingdom, notably Juan Negrín, the last Prime Minister of Republican Spain, undermine their assurances of British disinterest in the internal politics of Spain and confirm German propaganda that the British Government wished to overthrow the Franco régime. The presence of Negrín in the United Kingdom from late June onwards was particularly galling. The FO attempted to persuade Negrín to go to the United States. The former Republican Prime Minister was not averse to this but the U.S. Government refused to grant him a visa, much to Hoare's dismay who was 'terribly disappointed that you could not push him [Negrín] off to the U.S.A. I very much hope, however, that you will get him to Mexico or South America.'[18] Although Negrín had been given permission to come to the United Kingdom for only three weeks he was still there four months later when his position was discussed by the British Cabinet. At a meeting on 1 November 1940 Halifax argued that Negrín's continued presence in the country lent support to the view that the British Government was intriguing in Spanish politics and plotting the overthrow of the Franco régime and that this provided admirable material for German propaganda. The Foreign Secretary continued that if the Germans marched into Spain the real hope of Spanish resistance turned on the attitude of the army, but the army leaders were unlikely to resist if they believed that the British were intriguing with Spanish revolutionaries. He concluded:

> Our object in this matter had nothing to do with internal Spanish affairs but turned on the best way to win the war. For this purpose we wanted to keep Spain out of the war and to keep the leaders of the Spanish Government friendly to us. The Left-Wing in Spain were in any case likely to be more friendly to us than to the Germans.

The Lord Privy Seal and Deputy Prime Minister, Clement Attlee, leader of the Labour Party, emphasised that the question of Spain's entry into the war would be decided by Spanish interests and Spanish xenophobia. While he believed that Negrín's departure would have little effect on 'those of the present leaders in Spain who professed to be our friends', it would have a 'most discouraging effect on those people, the world over, who believed that we were fighting for democracy and on those who might otherwise carry on disruptive activities in the occupied territories'. The Secretary of State for Air, Sir Archibald Sinclair, leader of the Liberal party, warned his colleagues that many Liberals would take it amiss if Negrín was asked to leave the country. Churchill stressed that by keeping Negrín in the United Kingdom a further strain was imposed on the country. However, in view of Cabinet differences and because it was not clearly established that Negrín's continued residence threatened mortal hurt to British interests, he was prepared to consider what he believed was a compromise solution, namely that Halifax and the First Lord of the Admiralty, A.V. Alexander, should see Negrín and persuade him to leave the United Kingdom for the time being at least and offer him support in making suitable arrangements such as an extended visit to universities in South America or some other overseas territories. It was admitted that if Negrín refused to leave the country there was 'no present intention of compelling him to go'.[19]

In the event, Negrín was only prepared to go to the United States or Canada and since neither of these countries was prepared to grant him a visa he was allowed to remain in the United Kingdom.[20] Before this decison was taken, however, the Government was confronted with the prospect of public discussion of Negrín's residence in the form of a parliamentary question in the House of Commons and a debate in the House of Lords. Churchill was adamant that it was undesirable that the matter should be discussed openly in parliament and that if a question was put in the House of Commons he proposed to reply in very general terms, for example, by remarking 'that this country had always maintained its right to offer asylum to political refugees from abroad'. He was equally adamant that if a debate on the issue took place in the House of Lords it should take place in secret session.[21] The Government's attitude was hardly calculated to serve the wider democratic interests referred to by Attlee on 1 November but these clearly had a very low priority when measured against the compelling strategic considerations – in relation to the western Mediterranean and the eastern Atlantic – which required the maintenance of Spanish neutrality. None the less, Churchill's and Halifax's insistence in pressing Negrín to leave appears perverse when it is considered that the Spanish press failed even to mention the Prime Minister's friendly references to Spain in his speech before the House of Commons of 8 October 1940. He could hardly have been more categorical in his support for the Franco régime:

> As to the political affairs of Spain, His Majesty's Government have made it equally clear that they wish neither to interfere with them themselves

nor to see interference by any other power. They have already stated the form of government that Spain desires is a question exclusively for Spaniards to settle for themselves. The statement circulated by enemy propaganda that His Majesty's Government desire to bring about a change of régime in Spain is totally untrue. His Majesty's Government in the United Kingdom have not the least intention of meddling in the internal affairs of any country, and certainly not of Spain, where the sentiment of national independence is so firmly rooted in the national character.[22]

This apparent perversity is explained by reference to Hoare's insistence that it was the continued presence of Negrín and other Republican leaders in the United Kingdom which prevented more favourable propaganda for their cause in Spain.[23]

The whole tenor of the Negrín case was symptomatic of the weak position of the British Government during the second half of 1940 when the United Kingdom faced its greatest ever crisis. It is hardly surprising that Churchill and his colleagues would wish to avoid alienating Franco's Spain and/or provoking a German invasion of the Iberian peninsula or that the extension of democracy was not highly placed on their agenda, if at all. By the end of 1941, however, there had been a considerable improvement in the fortunes of war with the inauguration of Lend-Lease in March, the German invasion of the Soviet Union in June, the Anglo-American declaration of the Atlantic Charter in August, and the entry of the United States into the war in December.

These improvements notwithstanding, the British Government continued throughout 1941 to appease the Franco régime, maintaining and strengthening the policy of controlled economic assistance to the Iberian peninsula despite the lack of gratitude shown by Franco and his ministers, notably the pro-Axis Falangist Foreign Minister, Ramón Serrano Suñer, who had succeeded Beigbeder in October 1940. Indeed, no time was lost in instructing Hoare in February 1941 to give Franco a personal assurance from both Churchill and Eden that the last thing they wanted to do was 'to interfere in Spanish internal affairs nor would we countenance such action for a moment'.[24] The German invasion of the Soviet Union in June and the despatch of the Spanish Blue Division of 18,000 troops to the Eastern front[25] made no difference as far as the British authorities were concerned except to endorse Hoare's stricture that from the point of view of the peninsula it was most important to avoid any actions or statements that seemed to identify the British empire with the communists.[26] Indeed, so successful were they in distancing themselves from their Soviet ally that Hoare was able to report in late July that the effect of Britain's alliance with Soviet Russia had been much less hostile than expected in Spanish military circles in which there was an appreciation that 'our alliance with the U.S.S.R. was dictated for purely military reasons and was not a step towards communism, in spite of German propaganda to the contrary'.[27]

If the invasion of the Soviet Union had no impact on Britain's Spanish policy it might have been expected that a hostile speech by Franco on 17 July, on the occasion of the fifth anniversary of the military *pronunciamento* which provoked the Spanish Civil War, would have forced a change. In his speech the *Caudillo* declared publicly that Britain had lost the war. The speech provoked Sir Auckland Geddes, chairman of the Rio Tinto company, which had the largest foreign holdings in Spain, to approach the FO and recommend that the time had now come for the Government to encourage a wide resistance movement to the Falangist-dominated Franco régime. He suggested that Negrín and other Republican leaders in Britain and France should be approached to organise such resistance against what he considered to be the weakest of the fascist governments in Europe. The time was ripe because the German army was fully engaged in Soviet Russia and there was probably no German armoured division in France.[28] In the circumstances, the Government's response was surprisingly mild but reflected their policy of measured caution in Spanish matters; certainly, there would be no *volte face* involving encouragement and support for an anti-Francoist movement.[29] The response, approved by Cabinet, was to question whether the Franco régime really desired economic assistance, as Eden informed the House of Commons on 24 July:

> His Majesty's Government have now noted that General Franco, in his speech to the Falange National Council on the 17th of July, displayed complete misunderstanding not only of the general war situation but also of British economic policy towards Spain. If economic arrangements are to succeed there must be goodwill on both sides, and General Franco's speech shows little evidence of such goodwill. His statements make it appear that he does not desire further economic assistance for his country. If that is so, His Majesty's Government will be unable to proceed with their plans, and their future policy will depend on the actions and attitude of the Spanish Government.[30]

The outcome was a continuation of the policy of controlled economic assistance and by mid-August Churchill had convinced himself that Franco's speech was not so hostile after all. In this respect, he agreed with Hoare that far from giving himself over to the Axis, Franco was trying to put himself at the head of his own movement and to reconcile Germany in advance to some arrangement by which Serrano Suñer would be restrained or excluded.[31]

It was certainly true that Serrano Suñer's position in Franco's Government was by no means secure. During the autumn of 1941 the embassy in Madrid received accumulating information which suggested that the leading Spanish generals, discontented with Falangist maladministration, had completed their plans for an early *coup d'état* designed to get rid of Serrano Suñer and of the *Falange* and possibly also Franco himself. The FO remained sceptical that a new junta of generals would be any less influenced by Germany than Franco's régime. Eden advised his Cabinet colleagues that the German preoccupation with the Russian campaign did not alter the strategic fact that Germany was in a position at relatively short notice to dispose of any Spanish resistance and that, therefore, 'the substitution of a less unpopular régime, which would still find itself compelled to bow to German pressure, might not benefit us to any important extent'. The Foreign Secretary remained sceptical of the likelihood of a *coup d'état* by the Spanish generals in the near future and reiterated his doubts as to whether a change of régime in Spain would be to their advantage until German influence lessened and the new régime was therefore able to carry out a truly independent policy.[32] Although Eden remained sceptical about the prospects of a coup he changed his mind about wishing to see Franco's régime continue in Spain. On 1 December 1941 he minuted: 'The Generals may be broken reeds but I would dearly love to see Suñer go and maybe Franco too, and I am certainly not prepared to pretend otherwise'.[33] But pretend he did because on 3 December Hoare was informed that Eden agreed that they 'should stand aside and not appear as taking any steps to secure [the] removal of [the] present Minister for Foreign Affairs much though I should like to see him go'. The Ambassador was advised that a change of régime might not be an unmixed advantage until German influence lessened and Britain's capacity for supporting a more friendly régime in Spain was increased. Eden emphasised that an attitude of non-intervention in the Spanish domestic political scene would be best.[34]

While the discontent within Spain failed to produce an anti-Francoist coup it was clear by early 1942 that it had fuelled a revival of the Monarchist movement. According to Hoare the incompetence of the *Falange* had united town and country in favour of a royal restoration in the person of the Spanish Pretender, Don Juan de Borbón, and that this was supported not only by the parties of the Right but also by the professional classes, formerly Republicans, and by the thousands of so-called 'Reds', still left in prison, who believed that only by the return of the King would they obtain a political amnesty.[35] While there were those, including the Duke of Alba, Ambassador at London, who believed that Franco might wish to play the role of General Monk, the *Caudillo* was not one of them and there seemed no prospect of a monarchist restoration any more than the return of the Republic. British policy remained one that eschewed interference in Spanish internal politics. The BBC Spanish programmes continued during 1942 to reproduce Churchill's statement to the House of Commons of 8 October 1940.[36]

The removal of Serrano Suñer as Foreign Minister and his replacement by the less offensive General Francisco Gómez Jordana in September 1942 was naturally welcomed by the British Cabinet[37] which remained committed to the existing policy of non-intervention. Indeed, this was underlined by the need to keep Spain completely neutral during the projected Allied invasion of North Africa under Operation Torch. Hoare insisted that the previous assurances of non-intervention should be emphatically repeated to the Franco authorities. Under instructions from the FO he told both Franco and Jordana on 20 October that the policy of the British Government towards Spain remained unchanged in its two fundamental principles, namely, no British intervention in the internal affairs of Spain both during and after the war and no British invasion of Spanish territory on the mainland or overseas. Moreover, all the rumours that Britain was plotting to put the Reds back were untrue as were the rumours that it was encouraging separatism in Spain.[38]

In early November the British Government reinforced its earlier assurances and sent a verbal message to the Spanish authorities associating itself with assurances given previously by the U.S. President, Franklin Delano Roosevelt:

> the Spanish Government need have no fears regarding the course of these operations, which are solely directed to removing the Axis threat to French North African territory. His Majesty's Government are in full sympathy with what they understand to be the desire of the Spanish Government to save the Iberian Peninsula from the evils of war. They wish Spain to have every opportunity to recover from the devastation of the Civil War and to take her due place in the reconstructed Europe of the future.[39]

On 10 November in a speech at the Mansion House Churchill publicly expressed similar sentiments. However, this did not satisfy the

Spanish Government who, having received both verbal and written assurances from the United States, wished the British Government to do the same and provide written assurances. Eden told Alba on 4 December that he could see no difficulty in meeting his Government's wishes and repeated that the British Government had 'no intention to interfere in the internal affairs of Spain and we only wished to see that country prosper'.[40] The Foreign Secretary kept his promise and wrote to Alba on 16 December requesting that he inform his Government that the assurances communicated on 8 November represented the policy of the British Government towards Spain, not only for the period of operations then in progress in North Africa but for the duration of the war.[41]

During 1943 German reverses in Soviet Russia and North Africa and the demise of fascist Italy increasingly drove the Franco régime towards a policy of stricter neutrality although the Blue Division continued to operate on the Eastern front and the Spanish Government continued to supply the Third Reich with vital raw materials, notably wolfram ore. When Allied pressure finally caused the Blue Division to be withdrawn in late 1943 it was immediately replaced by the (much smaller) Blue Legion. Spanish efforts to float the idea of a negotiated peace between the Allies and Germany to forestall, as they saw it, the triumph of communism, were immediately punctured by the British insistence that the statement made by Churchill and Roosevelt at the Casablanca Conference of January 1943 represented 'the unalterable decision of the allies to fight the war to a decisive finish and to maintain a solid front in which no ally would act separately or divergently from the other'. Accordingly, there could be no premature peace or separate peace between one section of the Allies and the Axis.[42] Similarly, when Jordana enquired of Hoare as to what the position of neutral states was to be in the future Europe the Spanish Foreign Minister was provided with a firm and unwelcome warning to the effect that when the time came to integrate the few remaining neutrals into the post-war international community based upon the United Nations, the latter would 'inevitably be influenced by the policy and attitude shown during the war, and in particular between now and the end of the war, by individual neutrals, such as Spain'.[43]

Although it was prepared to take a tougher stance on international issues, the British Government throughout 1943 maintained its previous assurances and studiously avoided any interference in the internal affairs of Franco's Spain. However, at the end of the year the FO, prompted by Hoare, engaged in a thorough review of their Spanish policy and for the first time seriously discussed the question of intervention in Spain. It was admitted that there had been a number of favourable developments in the policy of the Franco régime during the last six months including the satisfactory Spanish reaction to the Azores agreement reached between Britain and Portugal in October 1943, the withdrawal of the Blue Division from the Eastern front, the continued Spanish recognition of the pro-Allied Badoglio Government in Italy coupled with the improved relations between Madrid and Algiers, the maintenance of only low levels of wolfram exports to Germany despite the resumption of German exports to Spain, and the improved passage of escaped prisoners of war and Allied refugees through Spain. At the same time, there remained a number of outstanding grievances, in particular, the continued presence of the Blue Legion on the Eastern front, German sabotage and espionage activities in Spain, the delay in the departure of Italian warships from the Balearics, and Allied representations concerning the removal of the German consulate-general from Tangier. Rather than change policy the FO preferred to continue pressurising the Spanish Government to settle these grievances. It was agreed that, even if Franco was somewhat complacent about his own position within Spain and was prepared to go on making concessions to Germany, there could be no question of the Allies intervening in Spain's internal affairs.

Provided that Spanish neutrality was maintained and Britain's own interests were not unduly affected the British Government had no wish to make difficulties for Franco's régime. Eden accordingly informed Hoare that no major modification of the Government's policy was called for unless and until it was decided that they should work for a change in the internal Spanish régime. There seemed less demand in Spain than in the recent past for such a change and the Government had no interest in encouraging a change at a time when there appeared 'to be no alternative régime in prospect, which could be relied upon to establish and to maintain a stable government and a neutral, still less an Allied policy'. At the same time, the Foreign Secretary sounded a warning:

> With the favourable development of the war, however, public opinion in the United Kingdom and throughout the United Nations is likely to take a more lively interest in the affairs of neutral countries, and of Spain in particular, and there can be little doubt that, if the Spanish Government persists in giving unneutral assistance to the enemy long after it is possible for them to plead *force majeure*, His Majesty's Government would not, even if they so desired, be able to maintain their present policy towards Spain.[44]

On one point at least the Government was right, there certainly appeared to be no alternative régime in prospect in Spain. In March 1944 Hoare stressed that Franco, confronted with a demand from the Pretender Don Juan that as the monarchy was the only juridical government of Spain he should immediately retire, had recently asserted his own credentials as head of the Spanish State, credentials which were rooted, he claimed, in the reality of his leadership during the civil war and after. Apart from asserting his own sovereign credentials, Franco was alienated from Don Juan believing him to be both a liberal and a freemason. The ambassador believed that the monarchists had missed a golden opportunity in late 1941 to mobilise the country against the Franco régime at a time when it was extremely unpopular owing to the machinations of Serrano Suñer and the Falangists. It was, however, probable that this was not their last chance because if they showed themselves definitely united upon a programme and equally resolute in carrying it out the chances of a restoration could not be written off, particularly if they formed a centre *bloc* with sections of the Left both in and out of Spain. Hoare was convinced that there was 'a want of leadership in the various oppositions'. The Left outside Spain was bitterly divided against itself; the communists were fighting the socialists and the individual leaders were bitterly jealous of each other. Within Spain the Left could not show its head but there did appear to be a definite tendency towards accepting a moderate constitutional régime, whether it be Monarchical or Republican, as a means of obtaining a platform from which to launch a programme of reform. The substantial number of political prisoners who had been released recently tended to strengthen the movement in favour of caution and moderation. Hoare was unwilling to speculate about the future. Four years in Spain had taught him that it was unwise to make a prophecy and it was even more unwise for the Allies 'to meddle in the chaos, confusion and bitterness of Spanish internal politics'.[45] The Central Department of the FO was inclined to agree and endorsed Frank Roberts' view that Franco was clearly the shrewdest leader in Spain and that there was no particular reason why he should not go on trimming his sails for quite a long time in the future.[46]

In international affairs Franco was certainly prepared to trim his sails and to acknowledge the growing reality of the war even before the D Day landings in June 1944 removed any lingering prospect of a German invasion of the Iberian peninsula. The Blue Legion was withdrawn, the German Consulate in Tangier was closed down and the export of Spanish wolfram to Germany brought officially to a virtual standstill. As a result Churchill was prompted to praise Spain's role in keeping out of the war when Britain was at her most vunerable in 1940 and at the time of the North Africa landings in 1942. He told the House of Commons on 24 May 1944 that he would always consider that 'a service was rendered at this time by Spain, not only to the British Empire and Commonwealth, but to the cause of the United Nations'.[47] These remarks aroused much criticism in the U.S. press and Churchill justified them to Roosevelt on the grounds that while he did not care about Franco he did not wish 'to have the Iberian peninsula hostile to the British after the war'. He went on to say that he did not know whether there was more freedom in Stalin's Russia than in Franco's Spain but he 'had no intention to seek a quarrel with either'.[48]

Unfortunately for Franco, concessions in the international sphere failed to deflect criticism of his régime as the influence of the United States and Soviet Russia increased with the seemingly endless victories over the German armed forces. Moreover, during the summer and autumn of 1944 the *Caudillo*, oblivious to the effect of his actions abroad, increased internal repression in Spain, including the acceleration of political executions and the intensification of a violently anti-communist campaign with the Falange as his chosen instrument.[49] At his last meeting before departing for London, Hoare, now Viscount Templewood, was moved to personally warn Jordana's successor as Spanish Foreign Minister, José Félix de Lequerica, that the Franco régime had been so deeply compromised with Hitler's Germany and Mussolini's Italy that it was impossible for the British Government to forget the past. Moreover, the form that this régime maintained was not distinguishable in the minds of the ordinary Englishman from nazism and fascism. Spain was now, by refusing to abolish or reform this régime, running the risk of finding itself isolated from the other countries of Western Europe. Lequerica, in response, was adamant that Spain was anxious 'not only to break away from Nazi and fascist influences but to follow the direction of Great Britain in the field of future politics in Western Europe', and he wished this assurance to be communicated to both Eden and Churchill.[50]

By this time, however, some members at least of the British Government were anxious to explore the possibility of bringing about a more democratic government in Spain. Attlee wrote a paper for the Cabinet in which he argued that there was not one of Britain's Allies who would not wish to see the Franco regime destroyed and he warned that the Government was 'running into the danger of being considered to be Franco's sole external support'. He was aware that it was unlikely that a democratic government could be established with general support owing to the deep divisions among the Spanish people but there was still much that could be done. The Government should aim at getting in Spain a government which would be inclined towards toleration and which would prepare the way for developments towards a democracy:

> To this end we should stiffen our attitude towards the present régime and make it very clear that its disappearance would be welcome to the United Nations and would bring definite advantages to the Spanish people. We should use whatever methods are available to assist in bringing about its downfall. We should, especially in the economic field, work with the United States and France to deny facilities to the present régime.[51]

Eden also advocated tougher measures believing that the survival of Franco's régime was a 'serious anomaly in post-war Europe'. He feared that the continuance of a moderate policy would only convince Franco that he could always rely on Great Britain and the United States for support to ensure his survival without needing to carry out democratic reforms such as the abolition of the Falange. The Minister of Economic Warfare, Lord Selbourne, remained unconvinced. In another Cabinet paper Selbourne considered that there was no reason to believe that Franco was more authoritarian or more severe to his political opponents than their allies, the Soviet dictator, Joseph Stalin, and Oliveira Salazar, dictator of Portugal, and he attacked Attlee for proposing economic sanctions arguing that they would be counter-productive because 'the people who would primarily suffer would be British traders and the people of Spain, whose resentment they should arouse and deserve'. What the world, not least Spain, most needed was peace and a revival of trade: 'I think we should be well advised to abstain from doing anything that would hinder the cause of either'.[52]

At a meeting on 27 November 1944 the Cabinet discussed Attlee's and Selbourne's papers and also a personal letter from Franco himself which had been communicated via Alba.[53] Eden judged that if the Franco régime persisted there was bound to be an explosion before very long and he preferred to see an evolution of the Spanish Government as an insurance against the revolution, which was inevitable if Franco continued on the lines he had so far followed. Given this what should the Government's policy be? Churchill was adamant that there was great danger in interfering in the internal affairs of other countries. Britain's traditional policy had been to refrain from doing so. It seemed likely that Franco had been encouraged to write his letter, in which he had called for the clarification of Anglo-Spanish relations with regard to 'the future concert of Western Europe', by the Prime Minister's speech in the House of Commons of 24 May 1944. Churchill excused the speech on the grounds that it had been intended to pay tribute to Spain and not the Franco régime of whose evil features he was fully aware. He now intended to reply to Franco's letter in terms designed to disabuse him of any illusions that the British Government needed his help or was anxious to cooperate with Spain under his government and to make it clear that Spain would not be represented at the peace conference when the war ended. However, the Prime Minister was determined that there would be no active intervention in the internal affairs of Spain. He was content to provide Franco with a tough reply and 'leave him and his government "to stew in their own juice" while refraining from any active steps to encourage the overthrow of that government'. The rest of the Cabinet, including the Labour leaders Attlee and Ernest Bevin, concurred in Churchill's summation.[54]

Almost two months elapsed before Churchill's reply was delivered to Franco and the Prime Minister was very frank; he criticised the Falangist character of the Spanish State, confirmed that his government would not support Spanish claims to participate in the eventual peace settlement, and stated that it was unlikely that an invitation would be forthcoming for the admission of Spain to the future world organisation. However, consistent with the discussion of 27 November no threats of British interference in Spain's internal affairs were made.[55] Spain would be isolated but left to develop as it chose without external intervention. Moreover, association with opponents of the Franco régime was to be treated with extreme caution. This was confirmed in mid-January 1945 when Cabinet discussed the visits to the United Kingdom of three exiled Spanish political leaders: Indalecio Prieto, Belarmino Tomás Alvarez and José María Gil Robles. The first two were exiled Republican Socialists in Mexico who had been invited to attend a forthcoming conference of the Trades' Union Congress while Gil Robles, the Spanish Monarchist leader, wished to stop off in London on his way to Switzerland. Churchill did not oppose the visits but he was adamant that while in the United Kingdom these individuals should be on their best behaviour: 'in the interests of good relations with countries with whom we were in diplomatic relations it should be clearly understood that there would be no question of any transgression on the part of any of these visitors of the normal limits of decorum or any attempt to raise a violent quarrel with another country, during the visit here of the exiled leaders from Mexico'.[56]

Keeping Spain isolated but abstaining from interference in its internal affairs was also the policy of the United States Government who in April 1945 informed their British counterparts that while public sentiment in the United States was profoundly opposed to the present Spanish Government, because of its record of unfriendly acts and its reliance on undemocratic principles, the official policy was not 'in normal circumstances to interfere in the internal affairs of other countries'. Moreover, it was neither in the interest of the Spanish people nor in the general interest of 're-establishing peace and order in Europe and of rehabilitating deves-tated areas' that there should be a recurrence of civil strife in Spain. At the same time, the Roosevelt Administration shared the British hopes that 'any successor régime in Spain will be based on democratic principles, moderate in tendency, stable and not indebted for its existence to any outside influences'.[57] Previously, in March, Roosevelt had instructed his new Ambassador to Spain, Norman Armour, to inform Franco that the President would be lacking in candour if he did not tell him that 'I could see no place in the community of nations for governments founded on fascist principles'.[58]

Clearly, in wishing to avoid taking action to compel changes in Spain the British Government could count on U.S. inaction and in particular their disinclination to impose economic sanctions. Indeed, it was partly from concern at U.S. competition that the Cabinet in April 1945 discussed supplying semi-military equipment to Spain, including dockyard equipment, meteorological equipment, ordinary transport vehicles, training aircraft and engines for training aircraft. Eden in a memorandum recommended that in the interests of British export trade and post-war commercial competition Cabinet should permit the export to Spain of articles which were not purely military and, in particular, the semi-miltary articles referred to above. In discussion the Foreign Secretary's proposals were supported in the interest of the country's post-war trade, the disposal of surplus military equipment and the restoration of a favourable trade balance between Spain and the United Kingdom. However, it was also strongly urged that action on these lines would expose the British Government to grave risk of misinterpretation and that the political dangers involved more than outweighed the commercial arguments. It was agreed, at Churchill's urging, that the FO should ask the U.S. Government what view they took of this matter and propose that both countries should pursue a common policy. It was suggested, quite cynically, that if the United States had no objection to supplying Spain the British Government would be in a stronger position to meet any criticism for having supplied such material. If, on the other hand, the United States had any doubts both countries might agree to refrain from supplying Spain.[59]

When the U.S. Government replied in July it was to the effect that while actual weapons of war should not be supplied to Spain exports of a semi-military kind could be made provided they were destined for civilian purposes and calculated not to increase the strength of the Spanish armed forces. In other words, except in obvious cases of weapons and weapons system, Washington chose to adopt a pragmatic position reserving their right to determine what should and should not be embargoed. When the issue was raised again by the Cabinet in October 1945 the Labour Foreign Secretary, Ernest Bevin, advised his colleagues that the Government should accept, as a general principle, the U.S. distinction between goods destined for civilian use and goods destined for the strengthening of the armed forces. The question was how was this principle to be applied in practice? Bevin suggested that goods of a military and semi-military nature, which were included together in Group 17 under the export of Goods (Control) Order of 1945, should be subject to licence and that in current circumstances licences should be refused except in cases where goods were manifestly intended for civilian use, including civil aircraft and training aircraft not destined for the Spanish armed forces, and engines for such aircraft.[60] The Foreign Secretary emphasised that he was averse to doing anything which would strengthen the Franco régime but it seemed clear that if the Government adopted too strict a policy in controlling exports to Spain the result would be to divert valuable export orders from the United Kingdom to the United States. The Cabinet concurred in Bevin's suggestion concerning the use of licences to control exports to Spain but also insisted that the President of the Board of Trade would consult with the First Lord of the Admiralty and the Secretary of State for Air with regard to the export of aircraft and of items not covered by Group 17 which might be used to strengthen the Spanish armed forces.[61]

The Labour Government's decision to retain a selective approach with regard to exports to Spain was clearly based on the earlier considerations of Churchill's administration and represented an essential continuity in approach to the Spanish problem. Prior to

Labour's electoral triumph in July 1945 the Franco régime had endeavoured to improve its image. Apart from continuing international criticism, Franco was concerned about the activities of the Spanish Republicans and Spanish Monarchists. In October 1944 a Republican Government-in-exile was established in Mexico while at the same time military operations commenced against Spain conducted from French territory by large groups of communists and Republican guerrillas, many of whom had fought in both the civil war and in the French Resistance. In the long run these activities had little real effect except to consolidate the Spanish generals' support for Franco's régime.[62] Following the Yalta Conference, the Spanish Pretender, Don Juan, issued his Lausanne Manifesto on 19 March 1945 which called on all monarchists to mobilise for the replacement of Franco and the establishment of a moderate democratic constitutional monarchy in the hope that monarchist sympathisers, such as General Alfredo Kindelán, would take up this call. Franco responded by summoning a meeting of the *Consejo Superior del Ejército* on 20 March and over the next three days succeeded in misleading the generals that Spain was so orderly and contented as to ensure the approval and even emulation of foreign countries, including the United States.[63] Afterwards, in order to consolidate his internal position and to broaden the base of his support while attempting to meet external criticism, Franco introduced a number of political changes. The most fundamental of these was the *Fuero de los Españoles* which the Cortes passed on 13 July 1945. This was similar to a bill of rights and recognised Catholicism as the official religion of the State, guaranteed political participation through the family, the municipality and the syndicate and allowed freedom of expression as long as this 'did not attack the fundamental principles of the State'. Franco also reduced the constitutional representation of the *Falange* by abolishing the *Secretaría General del Movimento* as a ministry of the government and by reducing the number of Falangist ministers in his Cabinet. One victim of this purge was Lequerica who was succeeded as Foreign Minister by the 'clever but pliable' Alberto Martín Artajo who quickly became the acceptable face of the Franco régime.[64]

Although it was claimed that the *Fueros* constituted a form of 'organic democracy' it was a sham because members of the representative organs created were chosen invariably by the Government from politically reliable groups. Certainly, Spain's 'organic democracy' could not be compared with a system of representative democracy based on universal suffrage and competing political parties and, unsurprisingly, it was rejected as utterly inadequate.[65] When the new British Ambassador at Madrid, Sir Victor Mallet, saw Martín Artajo on 26 July he informed him that there had been practical unanimity among all parties during the General Election that really cordial relations between any British Government and the present Spanish régime were not possible. On the following day Mallet repeated to Franco personally that it was quite clear that there was a universal feeling of distrust towards the existing régime in Spain.[66] This distrust was emphatically underlined in the declarations of the Potsdam Conference which were issued on 2 August. In the section dealing with admission to the UN Spain was singled out as the only 'neutral state' not to be admitted as a member of the organisation on the grounds of its origins, nature and record which did not justify its membership. This represented the total isolation of the Franco régime but it could have been worse because, thanks partly to Churchill's efforts, more serious measures advocated by the Soviet Union, such as breaking off diplomatic relations or great power intervention in Spain were not taken.[67]

Indeed, as the Cabinet decision to continue supplying semi-military goods to Spain demonstrated, there was no strong will or even inclination on the part of the new Labour Government to force changes in Spain by economic sanctions or otherwise. This, despite impassioned appeals made by opponents of the Franco régime such as that made by Fernando de los Ríos, Foreign Minister of the Republican Government-in-exile in September 1945. In his appeal, de los Ríos emphasised that the objective of his government was to achieve a democratic Spain through peaceful transition. He regretted that the Potsdam declaration on Spain had not been reinforced by other practical measures, in particular, breaking off diplomatic and other relations with Franco Spain:

> I therefore take the liberty of calling your attention to the incongruency between the decision of Potsdam to deny admittance of the Franco régime as being unworthy to the international community, and the fact of maintaining diplomatic and other relations with that same régime. If the two are considered compatible then the international principle involved in the Potsdam declaration is an empty sentence which has no historical consequence whatsoever. If this were so, would it not merely be a new variation of Non-Intervention? Would not this mean preserving the most illigitimate régime of all those existing today, having been created by the joint action of international fascism and nazism, which intervened in the Spanish war? Please bear in mind, on the other hand, the constitutional procedure which has been followed by us in the task

of reconstructing the Spanish Republican Government, the legitimacy of its régime, the hopes which we have placed today in your comprehension of our policy.[68]

De los Ríos failed to impress the Labour Government who preferred to put their faith in the application of strong diplomatic pressure without the threat of rupture of relations. Accordingly, in November 1945 they rejected the call of the Republican Government-in-exile for all countries to break with Franco and recognise the Republic as the only legitimate régime for Spain.[69] Moreover, in December they rejected a call from the French Government to break off relations with Spain on the grounds of the disclosure of Franco's secret correspondence with Hitler and Mussolini which had led to a sharp reaction of public opinion in France; this was reflected in strong pressure on Premier Charles de Gaulle and his Foreign Minister, Georges Bidault, both of whom were previously opposed to taking action against Franco.[70]

The constrained policy appeared to be working at the beginning of 1946 when Bevin reported to the Cabinet that monarchist and Republican leaders had arrived in Portugal for discussions with Franco or his representatives. He stressed that although they had made it abundantly clear that they wished to see the end of the Franco régime, it was imperative that the British Government should not appear to favour either of the alternatives which confronted the Spanish people. There was no clear indication whether majority opinion in Spain would favour a monarchist or a Republican solution, but there was some reason to think that many people in Spain would now prefer a Republican régime if they were satisfied that it could be secured without civil war.[71]

This air of complacency was shattered, however, when the Government learned that far from accommodating the Republican exiles Franco was busy executing those in Spain, including some who had fought in the French Resistance, while imprisoning others. It was reported that following a trial at Alcalá de Henares thirty-seven members of the General Union of Workers had received sentences ranging from twelve to thirty years for trying to reorganise the Spanish Socialist Party. Attlee was sure that this action by the Franco régime would give great offence to public opinion in the United Kingdom and France. Other members of the Cabinet did not dispute this but were divided as to what action to take. There was no support for any action that might precipitate a civil war in Spain and economic sanctions were not considered. At the same time, Aneurin Bevan, the Minister of Health, stressed that it was essential to give some overt sign to Republican forces in Spain that the British Labour Government were sympathetic towards them. Attlee agreed, in Bevin's absence, to review the Government's policy towards Spain in the light of recent events and to consider whether further steps might be taken to expedite a change in the present political régime in Spain.[72]

Events in Spain and increasing demands by the French Government for action, including a referral of the Spanish question to the Security Council of the UN on 27 February 1946, persuaded the British and U.S. Governments to take further action in the form of a declaration expressing the hope that 'the Spanish people might soon find the means to bring about the peaceful withdrawal of Franco, the abolition of the *Falange,* and the establishment of an interim Government which would give the Spanish people the opportunity to determine freely the type of government they wished to have and to choose their leaders'. Despite the risks of precipitating another civil war or the replacement of Franco by somebody worse, the declaration was endorsed by the Labour Cabinet on 4 March, three days after the French closed their Pyrenees frontier with Spain.[73]

The declaration by itself proved ineffective without positive measures to bring it about. Although neither the United States nor Britain wished to proceed and France was prepared to go slow on the issue, the Soviet Union was determined that the Spanish question should be discussed by the Security Council and in April encouraged the Polish Government to request that it be placed on its agenda.[74] For the next six months there was considerable diplomatic wrangling, essentially over the question as to whether the Security Council had the power to take action under the various articles of the United Nations Charter. Eventually, it was decided that because the Franco régime was not a present threat to peace and security under article 39 the Security Council could not take action but, because the régime constituted a potential threat under article 34, it could be referred to UNGA for action. The issue was referred to the Assembly in November 1946 and in December a resolution was passed urging the withdrawal of all members' ambassadors from Spain. The British and U.S. Governments complied with this resolution.[75]

The withdrawal of the ambassadors was hardly calculated to persuade Franco to surrender, especially as the resolution did not include other diplomats in the embassies which remained open for business. The only really effective means of challenging his régime remained armed intervention or economic sanctions. No-one seriously suggested the former, not even the exiled Republicans, and while the latter were considered in both London and Washington they were never implemented although the Labour Cabinet discussed the imposition of sanctions in January 1947.

In a memorandum prepared for the Cabinet Bevin argued that the effect of economic sanctions could not be rapid unless they were universally applied, and there seemed little prospect that all countries would cooperate in imposing them. They would probably impair Britain's long-term commercial relations with Spain; and the burden of imposing them would fall largely on the British Government. Bevin emphasised that in addition to Royal Air Force assistance twenty-six naval craft would be required to patrol the 1,800 miles of Spanish coast. In discussion there was general agreement about the importance to the British economy of Spanish exports, particularly fertilisers and iron ore. From the long-term point of view, there was a potentially large market for British exports to assist Spain's economic development including her need for machinery. No-one in Cabinet doubted that from the angle of British economic interests the Government could ill afford to impose economic sanctions on Spain. It was also recognised that the most effective sanction would be to deny oil to Spain but this could not be made effective without the full cooperation of the U.S. Government and there was no assurance that this would be forthcoming. It was admitted that if the Franco regime constituted a danger to world peace, all members of the UN would be obliged to impose sanctions under the Charter. In fact, it could not be argued that the political situation in Spain constituted a danger to world peace and, accordingly, the Government would be well advised to make that its main ground for resisting the application of sanctions to Spain. Cabinet agreed that they should not take any initiative in raising in the UN the question of applying economic sanctions to Spain.[76]

It is doubtful that even if sanctions had been applied, they would have persuaded Franco to abdicate his power. By the end of 1946 it was already clear that the *Caudillo* had succeeded in turning external pressure to his own advantage to consolidate his régime by playing the national card. On 9 December a huge crowd, variously estimated but at least 300,000 strong, demonstrated in the Plaza de Oriente in Madrid against UN interference in the affairs of the Spanish sovereign state, crying the slogan 'ni rojos ni azules, solo espanoles' (neither red nor blue, only Spaniards).[77] Unbeknown to the Spanish dictator the following year would be the turning point in his fortunes. 1947 was the year of the inauguration of the Truman Doctrine, of the global containment of communism. As the Cold War increased its momentum the Franco régime would come into its full political inheritance for no-one, with possibly the exception of Salazar of Portugal, had better anti-communist credentials than Generalísimo Francisco Franco and the strategic significance of Spain to the Western world was undeniable.[78] Spanish democracy was one more victim of the Cold War. Its renaissance only followed the death of the *Caudillo* in 1975 and was the inevitable response to a dictatorship whose time was clearly up, having become, even for conservatives in Spain, a profound obstacle to economic and social progress.

Notes

1. See Enrique Moradiellos's contribution to this present volume.
2. G. Stone, 'The European Great Powers and the Spanish Civil War', in *Paths to War: New Essays on the Origins of the Second World War*, eds R. Boyce and E.M. Robertson, London, 1989, pp. 213-14.
3. Ibid., p. 212.
4. G. Stone, 'Britain, Non-Intervention and the Spanish Civil War', *European Studies Review* 9, no.1, 1979: 131-2.
5. E. Moradiellos, 'Appeasement and Non-Intervention: British Policy during the Spanish Civil War', in *Britain and the Threat to Stability in Europe, 1918-1945*, eds P. Catterall and C.J. Morris, London, 1993, pp. 94-104.
6. See G. Stone, 'Britain, France and Franco's Spain in the Aftermath of the Spanish Civil War', *Diplomacy and Statecraft* 6, no. 2, 1995: 375.
7. Ibid., pp. 381-2.
8. For details of the submarine bases see C. Burdick, '"Moro": the Resupply of German Submarines in Spain, 1939-1942', *Central European History* 3, no.3 1970: 256-83. See also P. Preston, *Franco: A Biography*, London, 1993, pp. 336-7 and H. Höhne, *Canaris*, London, pp. 426-7.
9. M. Muggeridge (ed.), *Ciano's Diplomatic Papers*, London, 1948, p. 291.
10. P. Preston, 'Franco and Hitler: the Myth of Hendaye 1940', *Contemporary European History* 1, no. 1, 1992: 1-16. See also Paul Preston's contribution to this present volume.
11. Franco's policy of nonbelligerency included economic cooperation on a large scale with the Third Reich. See C. Leitz, *Economic Relations between Nazi Germany and Franco's Spain 1936-1945*, Oxford, 1996.
12. PRO FO 425/417 C5983/30/41, Lord Halifax to Sir Maurice Peterson, Madrid, 19 April 1940.
13. PRO FO 425/417 C6032/75/41, Peterson to Halifax, 20 April 1940.
14. For details of this strategy see D. Smyth, *Diplomacy and Strategy of Survival: British Policy and Franco's Spain, 1940-41*, Cambridge, 1986 and G. Stone, *The Oldest Ally: Britain and the Portuguese Connection, 1936-1941*, Woodbridge, 1994.
15. PRO FO371/24515 C7281/113/41, Hoare to Halifax, 22 June 1940.

16. Smyth, *Diplomacy and Strategy of Survival*, p. 53.
17. As an indication of the continuing anxiety concerning anti-Franco press opinion, when Franco made a number of ministerial changes in May 1941, which appeared to be to Britain's advantage, Anthony Eden, Halifax's successor as Foreign Secretary, felt compelled to warn his colleagues that 'it was still most necessary that the Press should not comment on these changes'; PRO CAB 65 WM 49 (41), 12 May 1941.
18. PRO FO 371/24510 C6473/75/41, Hoare to Halifax, 30 July 1940.
19. PRO CAB 65 WM 281 (40), 1 November 1940.
20. PRO CAB 65 WM 285 (40), 8 November 1940. PRO CAB 65 WM 298 (40), 28 November 1940. For a full discussion of the Negrín case see PRO FO 371/24510-13 File 75 and D. Smyth, 'The Politics of Asylum, Juan Negrín and the British Government in 1940', in *Diplomacy and Intelligence during the Second World War: Essays in Honour of F.S. Hinsley*, ed. R. Langhorne, Cambridge, 1984, pp. 126-46.
21. PRO CAB 65 WM 295 (40), 25 November 1940. In this connection, it is worth noting that the FO had endeavoured to dissuade a Labour MP, William Dobbie, from asking a parliamentary question about the Negrín case. When this failed and Dobbie asked his question R.A. Butler, the Parliamentary Under Secretary of State for Foreign Affairs, had replied on 20 November that: 'His Majesty's Government have no intention of departing from the established practice of this country in the general treatment extended to those who seek refuge here, and no steps have been taken to oblige Dr. Negrín to leave ... it is of course understood that Dr. Negrín should continue to refrain from all political activities'. PRO FO 371/24512 C11725/75/41, minute by R.A. Butler, 20 November 1940. *Hansard Parliamentary Debates*, HC, 5th ser., vol. 365, col. 1954.
22. *Hansard Parliamentary Debates*, HC, 5th ser. vol. 365, col. 302.
23. PRO FO 371/24511 C9159/75/41, Hoare to Halifax, 10 October 1940.
24. PRO FO 371/26904 C986/46/41, Halifax to Hoare, 2 February 1941.
25. For the most recent examination of the despatch of the Blue Division see D. Smyth, 'The Despatch of the Spanish Blue Division to the Russian Front: Reasons and Repercussions', *European History Quarterly* 24, no. 4, 1994: 537-53.
26. PRO FO 371/26939 C6810/222/41, Hoare to FO, 22 June 1941.
27. PRO FO 371/26940 C8416/222/41, Hoare to Eden, 23 July 1941.
28. PRO FO 371/26906 C8104/46/41, minute by Cadogan, 18 July 1941.
29. PRO CAB 66/17 WP (41) 174, 'Our Policy in Spain: Memorandum by the Secretary of State for Foreign Affairs', 20 July 1941.
30. PRO CAB 65 WM 72 (41), 21 July 1941. *Hansard Parliamentary Debates*, HC, 5th ser., vol. 373, cols. 1074-5.
31. PRO FO 371/26907 C9813/47/41, Churchill to Eden, 16 August 1941.
32. PRO CAB 66/19 WP (41) 266, 'Situation in Spain', memo by Eden, 10 November 1941.
33. PRO FO 371/26899 C13225/836/41, minute by Eden, 1 December 1941.
34. PRO FO 371/26899 C13225/33/41, Eden to Hoare, 3 December 1941.
35. PRO FO 425/419 C514/220/41, Hoare to Eden, 5 January 1942.
36. PRO FO 371/31230 C704/175/41, Eden to Hoare, 31 January 1942.
37. PRO CAB 65 WM 124 (42), 14 September 1942.
38. PRO FO 371/31230 C10035/175/41, Hoare to FO, 20 October 1942.
39. PRO FO 425/420 C10871/10738/41, 'Text of Message from His Majesty's Government to the Spanish Government' enclosed in Eden to Hoare, 8 November 1942.

40. PRO FO 371/31230 C12161/175/41, Eden to Hoare, 4 December 1942.
41. PRO FO 371/31230 C12161/175/41, Eden to Alba, 16 December 1942. Eden minuted in this connection: 'If we are giving so much should we not soon begin to ask for better behaviour?'
42. PRO FO 371/34810 C2507/75/41, Hoare to Eden, 1 March 1943.
43. PRO FO 371/34811 C3399/75/36, Eden to Hoare, 16 April 1943.
44. PRO FO 425/421 C14756/C14887/623/41, Hoare to Eden, 11 December 1943; Eden to Hoare, 20 December 1943.
45. PRO FO 371/39675 C4145/26/41, Hoare to Eden, 25 March 1944.
46. Ibid.
47. *Hansard Parliamentary Debates*, HC, 5th ser., vol. 400, col. 771. Hugh Dalton, Labour MP and President of the Board of Trade, noted in his diary that, according to Gladwyn Jebb of the FO, Churchill had 'made up his praise of Franco and his Government' at 2.30 a.m. on the morning of his speech. The FO did not see a draft of the Prime Minister's speech until an hour before it had to be delivered and although they had done their best to tone it down they had met with hardly any success. *The Second World War Diaries of Hugh Dalton 1940-1945*, ed. B. Pimlott, London, 1986, diary entry, 9 June 1944, pp. 755-6.
48. W.S. Churchill, *The Second World War: Closing the Ring*, London, 1954, vol. 5, p. 554.
49. PRO FO 371/39677 C12532/26/41, Viscount Templewood (Hoare) to Eden, 3 September 1944.
50. PRO FO 425/422 C13318/23/41, Templewood to Eden, 3 October 1944.
51. PRO CAB 66/57 WP (44) 622, 'Policy towards Spain', note by Attlee, 4 November 1944.
52. PRO CAB 66/58 WP (44) 651, 'Policy towards Spain', memo by Selbourne, 15 November 1944.
53. See n. 2 to the contribution of Qasim Ahmad to this present volume.
54. PRO CAB 65 WM (44) 157, 27 November 1944.
55. PRO FO 425/423 C17827/23/41, Churchill to Franco, 15 January 1945.
56. PRO CAB 65 WM (45) 6, 15 January 1945.
57. FRUS 1945, vol. V, 672-3, *Aide Mémoire*, State Department to British embassy, 6 April 1945. See also PRO PREM 8/106.
58. FRUS, 1945, vol. V, pp. 673-6, memo of conversation by the ambassador in Spain, 12 April 1945.
59. PRO CAB 66/64 WP (45) 230; PRO CAB 65 WM (45) 49, 23 April 1945, 'Supply of Equipment to Spain', memo by Eden, 10 April 1945. See also note 1 to the contribution of Christian Leitz to this present volume.
60. PRO CAB 129/3 CP (45) 220, 'Supply of Equipment to Spain', memo by Bevin, 10 October 1945.
61. PRO CAB 128/1 CM 45 (45), 23 October 1945.
62. R.W. Kern and M.D. Dodge (eds), *Historical Dictionary of Modern Spain, 1700-1988*, Connecticut, 1990, p. 48.
63. Preston, *Franco*, pp. 528-9.
64. Ibid., pp. 537-9. On Martín Artajo see also José Luis Neila's contribution to this present volume.
65. Preston, *Franco*, pp. 537-9.
66. PRO FO 425/423 Z9172/Z9229/537/41, Mallet to Churchill, 26 July 1945; ibid., Mallet to Bevin, 27 July 1945.
67. DBPO, *The Conference at Potsdam, 1945*, London, 1984, ser. I, vol. I, pp. 424-7.

68. PRO FO 800/504, Fernando de los Ríos to Herbert Morrison, 12 September 1945.
69. PRO FO 425/423 Z13280/18/41, Charles Bateman (Ambassador at Mexico City) to Bevin, 13 November 1945. The second session of the Republican Cortes (in-exile) had taken place between 7-9 November 1945 in Mexico City. A vote of confidence in the Republican government-in-exile, led by José Giral, formerly Prime Minister and then Republican Spain's Ambassador to the United States during the civil war, was passed in addition to the call to all countries to break off relations with the Franco régime.
70. FRUS, 1945, vol. V, Caffery to the Secretary of State, 12 December 1945, p. 698. Preston, *Franco*, p. 543.
71. PRO CAB 128/5 CM 11 (46), 4 February 1946.
72. PRO CAB 128/5 CM 18 (46), 25 February 1946.
73. PRO CAB 128/5 CM 20 (46), 4 March 1946.
74. See Geoffrey Swain's contribution to this present volume.
75. See Q. Ahmad, *Britain, Franco Spain and the Cold War 1945-1950*, Kuala Lumpur, 1995, pp. 47-58, and his contribution to this present volume. In fact, the United States had refused to appoint an ambassador to replace Armour when he retired in December 1945.
76. PRO CAB 129/16 CP (47) 2, memo by Bevin, 'Economic Sanctions against Spain', 3 January 1947; PRO CAB 128/9 CM 2 (47), 6 January 1947.
77. F. Portero, *Franco aislado: La cuestion española 1945-1950*, Madrid, 1989, p. 216. According to Paul Preston, Francoist sources claim there were 700,000 attending in the Plaza. Whatever the veracity of this claim, as he says, it was a very impressive demonstration; *Franco*, p. 561.
78. See P. Preston and D. Smyth, *Spain and the EEC and NATO*, London, 1984.

11

Britain and the Isolation of Franco, 1945-1950

Qasim Ahmad (Universiti Malaysia Sabah)

DURING the Second World War the involvement of the Franco regime in support of the Axis was not in doubt. One of the outstanding examples was the dispatch of the Blue Division to fight with the *Wehrmacht* on the Eastern Front. Franco Spain also supplied the Axis with materials and facilitated other belligerent activities. It was certainly a measure of the realisation of his government's entanglement with the Axis powers that even before their defeat was certain, Franco was already taking stock of his own position and that of his regime. He confided to Italy's Foreign Minister, Galeazzo Ciano, that 'after the defeat of the other and older totalitarian regimes' the survival of his, Franco's, own government 'is out of the question'.[1] Therefore, in 1944, with the fortunes of his mentors rapidly waning, Franco turned to Britain for possible succour. In a letter to Winston Churchill in October, Franco cleverly distanced Madrid from both Berlin and Rome. At the same time he proposed a new partnership between Britain and Spain, the only two 'virile' nations, he said, that had not been completely mauled by the war. The new agenda was to save and protect Europe from the 'insidious might of Bolshevism'.[2]

Franco's attempt to drive a wedge between London and Moscow at this early juncture did not succeed. Churchill did not fall for it – or was not ready to. He recalled that 'throughout the war German influence in Spain has been consistently allowed to hinder the war

219

effort of Great Britain and her allies and it is a fact that a Spanish division was sent to fight our Russian allies.'[3] Churchill emphasised to Franco that His Majesty's Government would stand by the 1942 Anglo-Soviet Treaty.[4] In the same year, Franco received a similar diplomatic rebuff from Washington. U.S. President Franklin D. Roosevelt declared that 'our victory over Germany will carry with it the extermination of Nazi and similar ideologies.'[5] The statement was made on the occasion of the appointment of the new U.S. Ambassador to Spain, Norman Armour. The President took great care to explain that the sending of the ambassador did not imply approval of the Franco regime. This juxtaposition of a hostile statement with what seemed a friendly diplomatic gesture must be seen as a deliberate and pragmatic attempt to be politically correct. The United States obviously preferred this course of action to breaking off relations with Spain, the drastic step that had been taken by Guatemala two months earlier.[6]

That being politically correct was not synonymous with being politically supportive was again demonstrated by the United States in 1946. The United States gave its 'complete accord' to a proposal made by Mexico at the UN Founding Conference in San Francisco disqualifying Spain from membership of the world body. Madrid was penalised on the grounds that the Franco government had been established 'with the help of military forces which have waged war against the United Nations [*sic*]'.[7] Clement Attlee, the future Prime Minister of Britain, also threw his weight against Franco, though in private. Concerned that the Mexican resolution might be defeated, he assured the representative of the *Junta Española de Liberación* of his unremitting dislike of Franco. Banking on the Labour Party's victory at the ensuing July elections, Attlee promised that his government, when formed, would 'break relations with Franco'. He added, 'we shall give you great support with other nations.'[8] Attlee's concern and support were not out of place. The resolution was adopted.[9]

Spain's ineligibility for UN membership was further endorsed by the United States, Britain and France at the end of the Potsdam Conference on 2 August 1945. By then Attlee had replaced Churchill as Britain's Prime Minister. Soon after Potsdam, the Spanish government-in-exile was established under the premiership of José Giral y Pereira. In the course of the year a number of countries followed in the footsteps of Guatemala and severed diplomatic relations with Franco Spain.[10]

Threatened though Franco's position seemed in 1945 and 1946, seeds for the derailment of the subsequent anti-Franco campaign had in fact already been sown at Potsdam. Ironically, they were planted by Churchill who had earlier, in the closing months of the Second World War, rebuffed Franco's diplomatic overture seeking better rapport with Britain. Decisions made at Potsdam cast a long shadow on the subsequent debate on Franco Spain at the UN. The understanding reached at the tripartite conference, latent or manifest, helped determine the kind of actions that the UN was later disposed to take against *Generalísimo* Franco.

At Potsdam, Churchill, Roosevelt and Stalin had to decide on how precisely the Spanish question was to be framed. Two options were open to them. On the one hand, they could take Franco Spain to task for being an accomplice of the defeated Axis powers. This line of action was certainly possible. Alternatively, they could view the thorny issue primarily or exclusively as Spain's domestic concern. After a protracted debate the latter line prevailed. Initially, Churchill tried to prevent the Spanish question from being discussed at all. In contrast to both Stalin and Truman, he refused to permit the matter to be deliberated at the meeting of their respective foreign ministers, arguing that 'we should not interefere in the domestic affairs of a country which had not been involved in a war against us, and which we had not liberated.'[11] Strangely, he conceded that Franco Spain had dispatched the Blue Division against Russia. However, if in the previous year Churchill had told Franco that this misdemeanour, and others, could not be mitigated by whatever sporadic and indirect favour Madrid had shown towards the Allied powers, in Potsdam in 1945 Churchill countered Stalin by inverting this very argument. Churchill contrasted the Spanish regime's aggression in the Blue Division episode with the restraint it had shown during Operation Torch mounted by Anglo-American forces in North Africa in 1942.

Stalin stood his ground, at least for a while. He reminded Churchill that Franco had provided bases for German submarines, and that Britain as well as other powers had suffered the consequences of this and other actions of Franco. Stalin also knew that Churchill had previously dismissed as worthless Franco's charitable posture during the Allied North African campaign, for a copy of Churchill's letter to the Spanish Caudillo had also been sent to him. On its part, the United States had issued a White Paper detailing Franco's hostile actions and pronouncements against the Allies during the war.[12] It was certainly not too difficult to build a case against an accomplice of the defeated powers, but Stalin decided against such a course of action. The Russian side, Stalin said, did not want to press home this point.[13]

It became plain to Stalin that Churchill was not going to concur with moves aimed at harassing Franco Spain or any other action that could be deemed in any way interventionist. Non-interventionism being the objective, Britain would naturally have preferred that the Spanish question, if possible, not be raised at all. Whitehall had known for months that Moscow intended to raise the subject 'as soon as the war was over'.[14] However, Britain gave no indication that it had prepared itself for such an eventuality at the Peace Conference.

After being summoned to Potsdam, the FO expert on Spain, Counsellor Frederick Hoyer-Millar, on 19 July suggested to Sir Alexander Cadogan, the Permanent Under-Secretary of State for Foreign Affairs, that the British should aim for 'some fairly anodyne form of anti-Franco resolution'. The idea was to placate the Russians and thus dissuade them from being intractable in matters considered more significant by Britain. In trying to firm up this strategy Acting Counsellor William Hayter, a member of the British delegation at the Conference, proposed a package deal: a statement on Spain would be made together with one congratulating Yugoslavia on its liberation from the Axis. This, Hayter believed, would facilitate Churchill's consent and would resolve the worrying Anglo-Soviet diplomatic tiff. By 21 July the Russians had taken the cue. They had already been 'persuaded' to settle for a 'watered down' version of their original proposal.[15] Certainly more than persuasion was used to bring about this Russian acceptance.

An important underlying theme surfaced later on 24 July, at the eighth plenary meeting. During this session Churchill and Truman confronted Stalin with an issue that could have had tremendous bearing on Russia's position and standing at the United Nations. The two Western leaders threatened not to recognise Bulgaria, Finland, Hungary and Rumania, unless their governments were first democratised. If the threat were to materialise, their UN membership could be in jeopardy. This obviously incensed Stalin who countered that these governments were not fascist. Their political records, Stalin argued, were better than that of Argentina, which had already gained admission to the world organisation. That Russia was being pressured and that the Spanish question was part of this bigger political web was confirmed by Hoyer-Millar, who observed on the following day that 'peace treaties with the Balkans' have become 'curiously entangled' with 'utterly irrelevant subjects' including 'a kick in the pants for Franco'.[16]

Twenty-four hours later, on 26 July, Churchill lost the British General Election to Attlee. By this time the Conservative leader had apparently already wrapped up the debate on Franco at Potsdam. A State Department source indicated that the Spanish question did not appear again for discussion after Attlee took Churchill's place at Potsdam.[17] Churchill said the same thing to the House of Commons. Of what happened to the decision on the Franco regime when Labour took office, Churchill said, 'no alteration was made, as far as I am aware, by the new Foreign Secretary in the terms of that most wounding, and deliberately wounding, declaration against that regime.'[18] Admiral Luis Carrero Blanco also testified to this fact in 1945, minus, of course, the kind of exaggerated claim made by Churchill regarding the debilitating impact the decision had on the Franco regime. Writing to Franco in September, he said, 'it is necessary to recognise that at Potsdam we were defended energetically by Truman and Churchill ... in the presence of Attlee who, as Prime Minister himself, did not try to go back on what had been agreed.'[19] That being the case, the reason why Stalin 'finally accepted without much discussion'[20] the public declaration barring Spain's UN membership must be sought in the fact that the issue had been 'curiously entangled' in a host of other issues. Ostensibly, the Soviet leader had backed off from more severe measures like the breaking off of relations with Franco Spain lest his wartime allies pushed him hard on the sensitive and difficult issue of the democratisation of the East European states. This was the *quid pro quo*.

If there was a trade-off, it fitted in well with the then or subsequently revealed political calculations and pronouncements on the matter. Churchill's thoughts on leaving Eastern Europe in the Russian sphere of influence are well known.[21] Stalin had reciprocated on this. In private, if not in public, it had been made known to the Spanish Republicans-in-exile that Spain was in the Western sphere and that this imposed constraints on the actions of Stalin's government. In 1946, Vyacheslav Molotov, Stalin's Foreign Minister, told Alvarez del Vayo that 'Spain was mainly the affair of the Western democracies and that it was for them to decide their policy in the first place.'[22]

Given that the Big Three had reached a compromise on the Spanish question at Potsdam, the positions they later took at the UN must be viewed with greater circumspection. They did not always adhere religiously to the understanding formulated in the relative seclusion of Potsdam. This, however, did not mean that they were entertaining any serious hope of departing from it. In the more open but also more crowded UN forum, the verbal encounters between the Russian and the Western camps understandably assumed a more threatening note. They were, after all, in this second bout, directly appealing to a wider constituency. The numbers game, with regard to the occasional votes on the Spanish question at the UN, seemed earnest enough. Even though Russia, the emerging socialist superpower, could rely on its known political allies, and its Western adversaries on theirs, the floating vote was by no means insignificant.

Nevertheless, the element of uncertainty attending the Spanish issue could not have been too disturbing to the nations that had taken part in the post-war conference in Germany. That the Potsdam understanding on noninterventionism might be breached at the UN was possible, but, all things considered, highly improbable. The compromise was, after all, a crucial basis for a more complex international balance of power. In addition, the Soviet Union faced no easy task in mustering the sheer number needed to see through a UN resolution advocating radical anti-Franco measures; more extreme than the one already conceded at Potsdam or, previous to that, at San Francisco. Of what value then, one might ask, was the political exercise at the UN? To the British, absolutely none: hence they would have preferred that the matter not be raised at all; or if raised, that it be quickly and tamely settled. Foreign Secretary Ernest Bevin had announced to the House of Commons in August 1945 that 'I cannot go further than the declaration issued at the Berlin Conference.'[23] It was a statement for which MAE was 'profoundly thankful'.[24]

As far as the Russians were concerned, they could certainly expect some diplomatic and political mileage, even if the line already drawn at Potsdam was unlikely to be crossed. The British suspected as much. After the Potsdam Conference, Britain only sanctioned a Polish move to have the matter discussed at the Security Council after presumably being persuaded by the United States that exclusion of the issue from the agenda would be tantamount to absolving Franco by default.[25] Should the matter be dropped from the Security Council agenda, the East Europeans, one could surmise, would still be presented with an opportunity to mount a propaganda campaign against the Western powers. The Russians therefore had nothing to lose by raising the matter. If the Kremlin could not, or did not want to, inflict upon Spain a severe penalty, then, at the very least, it could hope to embarrass the Western democratic powers.[26]

The British strategy in handling the Spanish question at the UN thus differed little from the one employed at Potsdam. Attlee did not come out in full support of the Spanish Republicans-in-exile. As it turned out, the conduct of foreign affairs was largely left to Bevin who, as noted, had already made clear his stand *vis-à-vis* the Spanish question.

That the parameters of the debate at Potsdam did not change significantly at New York was underlined by Poland's rationale for advocating the international action against Spain. Franco's wartime record was not postulated as the basis for the onslaught. Instead, Poland claimed that Spain was a threat to international peace, and hence that the UN ought to take concrete measures to contain or resolve the problem. Inadvertently, this line of reasoning worked, in the end, against Poland's own position. It was obviously a lot harder to prove that Spain, after the war, was a threat to universal peace than to arrive at a decision regarding Franco's complicity with the Axis powers during the war. It came as no surprise to many, therefore, that the five-member Security Council sub-committee set up to look into the Spanish question could not establish the dangerous nature of the Franco regime. In its report submitted to the Security Council on 1 June, the sub-committee testified that there existed 'incontrovertible documentary evidence' regarding Franco's guilt, alongside Hitler's and Mussolini's, in waging war against nations that eventually banded together to form the United Nations. It did not, however, consider Spain a threat to peace and merely conceded that the country could be 'a potential menace to international peace and security.'[27] A possible diplomatic catastrophe for Madrid was averted and the threat of economic embargo or military intervention greatly lessened.

The Spanish question was subsequently debated at both the Security Council and UNGA. The long-drawn-out debates culminated in the passage of the resolution of 12 December 1946, 'Relations of the Members of The United Nations With Spain'. It departed little from the points already covered by the sub-committee. Two specific actions against the Franco regime were recommended. One was the withdrawal by all member states of their respective ambassadors and ministers plenipotentiary from Madrid, and the other the barring of Spain from membership of all UN agencies.[28] On the surface, the withdrawal of ambassadors and ministers plenipotentiary was damaging to Madrid's international standing. But with regard to the practical day-to-day interests of the government, the damage could not be said to be at all severe. Many of the subsequently withdrawn ambassadors were in due course replaced with chargés d'affaires. It was a downgrading exercise rather than the complete severance of diplomatic relations. As an added consolation to Franco, not all of the UN member states acted upon the Resolution's recommendation that ambassadors be recalled from Madrid; notable amongst them was Perón's Argentina.

The 1946 UN Resolution on Spain dictated the fate of the Franco regime for the next four years. From 1946 to 1950, Franco Spain had to endure moral disapproval but was spared economic embargo. Ostracised and marginalised, the Franco regime did what it could to regain international acceptance. MAE was particularly active in pursuing this objective. The energies of Spanish diplomatic representatives overseas were fully harnessed. A Spanish lobby was nurtured and operated untiringly in the United States. The immediate target was to swing the majority opinion at the United Nations to Franco's side.[29]

Later, the Francoist camp was to praise itself when the climate of opinion began to shift in Franco's favour. In reality, this shift was a direct consequence of the determined stand of the Western democracies against any possible interventionist move against Spain. The Cold War fever steadily engulfing Europe after the end of the Second World War also worked to the advantage of Madrid. Britain relentlessly and meticulously defended the non-interventionist strategy from the start, while the United States, riding high on the crest of the Cold War tide, became instrumental in catapulting Franco Spain out of international backwaters.

The 1946 UN Resolution on Spain was crucial in further accentuating the apparent rift between the Western democracies and the Soviet bloc with regard to the Spanish question. Bevin had emphatically declared that in dealing with the Franco government, Britain could not be expected to go beyond the terms agreed upon at Postdam. The Russians knew this.[30] But as has been said, the Russians had nothing to lose by stirring up this issue again at another forum, the UN. The reason why the 1946 UN Resolution drove a wedge between the West and the East European bloc was rather obvious. The former was anxious to ensure that whatever was recommended by the Resolution would not later be made any more severe. The utmost limit of the condemnatory stance, it felt, had been reached. The latter, on the other hand, had no qualms about posturing as advocates of more radical sanctions and moves against Madrid.

Indicative of the unwillingness of the Western powers to give countenance to any interventionist action was the position articulated by Britain. The British Delegation at the UN specifically opposed a provision in the Resolution calling upon the Security

Council to consider taking adequate measures should the political situation in Spain fail to improve. Britain did not foresee the probability or the possibility of such action against Franco Spain and hence it was not going to be a 'party to what might turn out to be empty threats'.[31] Later, the FO was to explain that Britain had voted for the 1946 Resolution merely out of respect for the 'spirit of the Assembly and not with any conviction that such a proposal would promote a solution of the Spanish question or that it was justifiable within the Terms of the Charter'.[32]

The Polish delegation was gunning for sterner anti-Franco measures – well beyond the stipulations of the 1946 Resolution. Had the charge that Franco Spain was a threat to universal peace been proven, then it would have had to brace itself against a possible UN-backed total embargo or even a military campaign.[33] The Polish delegation had advocated complete severance of relations between UN member states and Spain.[34] However, no serious contemporary observer believed that Franco Spain posed a threat to world peace. Failure to uphold the allegation naturally undermined the Polish strategy.

On the other hand, even though proving Spain's wartime complicity with Germany and Italy was not at all difficult, it was never made the basis for haranguing Franco. This omission had its precedent in the Potsdam Declaration. Similarly, the Polish delegation did not anchor its campaign to Franco's wartime record, just as Stalin did not want to at Potsdam.

This recurring omission, observable in the decision at Potsdam and the deliberation at New York, and Bevin's emphatic declaration that Britain could not be expected to go beyond Potsdam, could only enhance further the suspicion that the big powers had in fact reached a *quid pro quo* over Spain.[35] They had compromised over the Spanish issue not only because they had different views on what to do with the Franco regime but also because a compromise served their respective interests well. At the very least, it was in their interest to have a clearer international demarcation with regard to their respective spheres of influence in Europe.

This difference between the Western camp and the communist bloc on the Spanish question, as well as Stalin's simultaneous need to strike an understanding with his Western counterparts, unavoidably complicated matters. To unravel the complication, a closer look at the leading protaganists' statements or posturings and their respective readings of the contemporary situation is essential.

In the early Cold War period the preoccupation of the Western powers was how to prevent Franco Spain from being replaced by a leftist government. This preference for a non-leftist government in Madrid went back to the days of the Spanish Civil War. Then, when both Germany and Italy flouted the NIA, the Western powers still refused to aid the legitimate Republican Government under siege. When the Russians stepped in where the Western powers refused to tread, the Republican cause inevitably became tainted with Soviet Communism.[36] A similar pattern could be observed later in the post Second World War period, though in the diplomatic rather than the military field.

After the Second World War, the Western powers refused to recognise the Republican government-in-exile formed in Mexico in late 1945. By the early months of 1946 many of the countries that had terminated relations with Franco Spain and/or recognised the Spanish Republican Government, headed by José Giral y Pereira, were those from the East European bloc. This decidedly coloured the perception of the Western powers towards the Republican Government. It mattered little to the West that communists were excluded from the cabinet line-up or that the Russians adopted an 'ambiguous attitude' towards the Giral government (out of their realisation that Spain belonged to 'the Western sphere of influence').[37]

It was unavoidable that in the Cold War climate the *quid pro quo* regarding spheres of influence was put to the severest of tests. Bevin, for instance, could not suppress his suspicions about Russia's designs on Western Europe. Not long before the passage of the 1946 Resolution on Spain, Bevin wrote thus to Attlee: 'in Spain their [the Soviet] objective is the civil war which would follow active intervention.' In fact, Bevin believed that the Russians were casting their net even wider: the 'Soviet game in Europe is the establishment of Communist Governments not only in Italy but also in France.'[38] Bevin's point of view was shared by many in the FO. In the United States it was widespread, which explains why the Spanish lobby there thrived much better than elsewhere. In the course of his years of isolation, Franco developed an unmistakable penchant for capitalising on this anti-communist zeal. Real or imagined, the communist bogey served to justify further the refusal of the West to take or endorse precipitate actions against the *Generalísimo*. It also underlined in no uncertain terms the diverging stands of the major powers, once partners in war, *vis-à-vis* Franco Spain.

It was upon this East-West split that the Francoist camp was banking to save the day for its leader. As early as September 1945, Carrero Blanco had told the Spanish dictator that the West and the Russians would not see eye to eye over the issue of the Spanish

Republican government-in-exile: 'England and the United States will not recognise this bastard creation of an exiled government in Mexico because it is filocommunist; and even less so if Stalin recognised it right away. Would to God that he would do so.'[39] On the other hand, and quite naturally the East-West discord was what the Republican side feared most. In the same month that saw the passage of the 1946 Resolution, Dolores Ibarruri (*la Pasionaria*) warned her colleagues of the dire consequences of such a divide. She said: 'If the unity among the great powers should be broken it would be a true catastrophe for Republican Spain.'[40]

The 1946 UN Resolution was the first and last occasion when the major Western powers and the Soviet bloc voted in unison on the Spanish question. It was achieved after a great deal of deliberation and even then it remained a fragile compromise. The fact that the voting was carried out only on the resolution as a whole, and not on its various parts, further facilitated the achievement. The compromise lasted less than a year, as the Western powers and the East European countries had conflicting aspirations regarding it. The former made no secret of their unwillingness to condone any measure exceeding the terms of the 1946 Resolution. They feared that such a breach would lead to more radical actions amounting to, or bordering on, actual intervention. The latter, on the other hand, were pushing, seriously or otherwise, for interventionism.

The build-up of Cold War tension in the months following the 1946 Resolution ensured that the compromise was shortlived. The Greek Civil War was undeniably a major cause of the heightened tension, and formed an immediate background to the Truman Doctrine of March 1947, which promised to 'assist free peoples to work out their own destinies in their own way.'[41] The worsening of East-West relations and the principle underlying the Truman Doctrine eventually worked to Franco's advantage. Truman wanted to save not only Greece but also Spain from communism. To do that, the State Department spawned a conspiracy, in April, to oust Franco and help install a liberal government in Madrid. It was believed that a democratic administration in Spain would prevent any possible civil strife and hence forestall communist infiltration. However, Bevin, ever distrustful of any action having the slightest smack of interventionism, dismissed the idea as 'ill-considered.'[42] Out of respect for its longstanding European ally, the United States aborted its plan. The idea of keeping communism at bay in Spain, however, persisted.

The Truman Doctrine was followed in June by the launching of the Marshall Plan. After some initial wranglings, the Soviet Union and its satellites were excluded from this economic recovery venture. By this time, the key political elements in the United States were, as LaFeber puts it, 'increasingly convinced by Truman that Communists had to be fought, not fed.'[43]

Later, in November 1948, Franco told a U.S. correspondent that 'Spain really does not need Marshall Plan assistance as much as other European countries.'[44] This was patently false. In 1947, labouring under the hardship of post-war economic problems and a bad harvest,[45] Spain would have more than welcomed any help it could get from the United States. In fact, in 1947 Franco assiduously courted the United States. On 31 March, nineteen days after the proclamation of the Truman Doctrine, Franco announced his so-called Law of Succession, claiming to transform Spain into a monarchy eventually. The Spanish *Cortes* duly approved the Law on 7 June, two days after the launching of the Marshall Plan. On 6 July, a referendum on the Law was held. The timings could not have been better, but none of the political manoeuvres impressed the Western powers.[46] Franco Spain was left out of the Marshall Plan and received no immediate or direct benefit from the Truman Doctrine.

Bevin's unwillingness to exert pressure on *Generalísimo* Franco was again demonstrated in his handling of the visits of Indalecio Prieto and José María Gil Robles in September. The meeting with Prieto of the PSOE and Gil Robles, who represented the monarchist groups, angered the Francoist camp. Formal protests were made to the British Government, street demonstrations organised, press condemnations unleashed, and the Spaniards even tried to prevail upon a number of foreign governments to inject, as they put it, a certain sense into the British mind.[47] In the face of the Spanish wrath, described by the British Chargé d'Affaires in Madrid as 'the fiercest onslaught on us since the episode of the Ambassador's departure',[48] Bevin held fast to his noncommittal position. On 11 November he despatched an official reply to the Spanish Government stating that Britain stood by the non-interventionist principle of the 1946 Tripartite Declaration. Moreover, he reminded Madrid that His Majesty's Government had 'consistently resisted' what it perceived as 'unjustifiable attempts at the UN to intervene in the internal affairs of Spain'.[49] The counterbalance to this, however, was also made clear by Bevin in the same note: 'I am not prepared', he said, 'to do anything which would hinder a union of his [Franco's] opponents.'[50] This balancing act was the hallmark of the position adopted by the FO throughout this period of Franco's diplomatic ostracism.

One might not want to question the genuineness of Bevin's non-interventionist stance, but given the Labour Party's known sympathy for the Republican cause, a sympathy that went back to the Civil War days, the stance was most disappointing to both the Spanish Republican government-in-exile and the Labour Party's rank-and-file.[51] Bevin was well aware of the criticism and the dissatisfaction of the rank-and-file. Hence, when later there was a move to include Spain in the Marshall Plan, Bevin relayed his stern opposition to the U.S. Government, arguing that 'it would cause a complete revolt in the Labour Party here, as well as among many Conservatives who have bitter memories.'[52] Other Western governments were also very conscious of the sensitiveness of the issue and acted most circumspectly. Thus, while they disagreed with the exclusion of Franco Spain from the UN specialised agencies, they were not prepared in 1947 openly to support, let alone sponsor, a resolution to allow Spain's participation in them. Such action, it was feared, would engender 'violent debate' at the UN, and nations sponsoring or supporting the resolution would be dubbed as friendly to Franco.[53]

Aware though the United States Government was of the anti-Franco feelings and 'bitter memories' in Europe, it was keen, all the same, to bring Spain into the Western camp. Initially, it thought this could be accomplished by ousting Franco from power, but when, as already seen, the idea was jettisoned, a new strategy was formulated. Spain, it was then decided, would be recruited despite Franco. This shift in the U.S. position was first mooted in October 1947. It was the result of a State Department review of its Spanish policy. On 24 October, George Kennan, in charge of the study, advised George Marshall, the Secretary of State, that '*instead of openly opposing the Franco regime, we should work from now on towards a normalisation of U.S.-Spanish relations, both political and economic.*'[54]

A manifestation of the above policy change first became evident when the 1946 Resolution on Spain was tabled for reaffirmation in November 1947. When the 1946 Resolution was voted on as a whole, the voting pattern was similar to that of 1946. When the 1947 Resolution was voted upon part by part, however, the part calling for the reaffirmation of the 1946 Resolution failed to secure a two-thirds majority. The United States with fifteen other nations voted against the reaffirmation at both the Committee stage and the Plenary Session. Britain, on the other hand, voted for the reaffirmation clause and landed herself on the side of the Soviet camp. It created a gross embarrassment, and the FO was acutely aware of the undesirable impression it had created amongst Spaniards.[55]

Taking stock of this, the British representative at the UN argued that except for the manner of approach, there was no fundamental difference between the policy of Britain and that of the United States *vis-à-vis* Franco Spain.[56] It was a brave attempt at explanation but it did not reflect the changing reality.

Despite the attempted explanation, the rift in the Western ranks was not missed by Madrid. The Spaniards had always hoped that the worsening of East-West relations would directly benefit them. An indication that this gamble could pay off was already visible in 1947, at least as far as relations with the United States were concerned. Britain, on the other hand, refused to be drawn.[57] In fact, a few months earlier, Sir Orme Sargent, the British Permanent Under-Secretary of State for Foreign Affairs, had dismissed as 'nonsense' the Spanish hope for an improvement in Anglo-Spanish relations in proportion to the deterioration of Anglo-Soviet relations.[58]

Anglo–Soviet relations certainly continued to worsen in 1948, reflecting the overall trend of East–West relations. In his New Year's Address, Attlee condemned what he termed Russia's persistent aggressive conduct in international affairs. On this score, the Prime Minister justified his country's growing cooperation with the United States. In the same month, on 22 January, Bevin delivered a strong condemnation of Russia's political behaviour and called for the consolidation of Western Europe. Less than two months after this House of Commons speech, the Brussels Treaty was signed. Russia was fenced out. By mid–1948 the Berlin blockade had caused East–West relations to plummet to a new low.

Orme Sargent had been right when he said that the worsening of Anglo–Soviet relations would not necessarily propel Britain to seek the outstretched hand of Franco. Despite all the anti-Soviet rhetoric, war with the Soviet Union was not considered imminent. Spain's help, therefore, was not high on Britain's priority list.[59] Even if war was imminent, Britain knew that economically stricken Spain lacked the war material that could make it a worthwhile ally.[60] Britain did not have the means to bail Spain out militarily. Then there was the ever-present domestic political consideration, which would rule out any possibility of Britain selling arms to Franco Spain. The internal political factor was deemed so sensitive that the FO overruled a Defence Ministry proposal to sell to Spain demilitarised corvettes for use as fishing vessels and demilitarised landing craft for coastal trade. In September 1948, Bevin warned his colleague, A.V. Alexander, the Secretary of State for Defence, that 'we would lose the support of all good Democrats in Western Europe if we touch Franco.'[61]

Obviously, the Berlin blockade had not changed the Labour Government's attitude and position *vis-à-vis* Franco Spain.

If the worsening East-West conflict could not move Britain in the direction of Madrid, the same could not be said of the United States. Unlike Britain, the U.S. was not burdened with a war-ravaged economy and, at home, it had no anti-Franco opposition to speak of. In other words, there was no economic or political obstacle to hamper Washington's effort at *rapprochement* with Madrid. Indeed, 1948 saw a further softening of U.S. policy towards Franco Spain. The Kennan recommendation was steadily being put into effect. The protests of European governments, that of Britain for instance, were heeded less and less. In January 1948 Theodore Achilles, Chief of Western European Affairs in the State Department, relayed the new policy to Paul Culbertson, the U.S. Chargé d'Affaires in Madrid. Culbertson was told that 'the "kick-Franco-out-now" policy is over as far as we are concerned.'[62]

In the following month, the U.S. Secretary of State jolted the FO with his statement that there was nothing to prevent Spain from joining the Marshall Plan. The British were only mollified when told that Spain's entry was contingent upon the agreement of the already participating nations. It seemed, therefore, that Britain could still hold its ground. However, unknown to it, Culbertson, had forwarded to Marshall an ingenious strategy to overcome British opposition. Culbertson suggested that Spain be brought into the Marshall Plan by means of a majority decision of the ERP countries. This, Culbertson reasoned, 'would give Bevin an out because he certainly has no veto power and could so explain in Parliament'.[63] On 31 March, two days after Culbertson wrote to Marshall, the House of Representatives passed an amendment making it possible for Spain to participate in the Marshall Plan. This amendment, carrying the same qualification embodied in the earlier Marshall proposal, was later rejected by the Senate. It had, nevertheless, caused some anxieties in Britain.

The developments in the U.S. inevitably resulted in the widening of the gap between the position of the U.S. and that of Britain on Spain. If the Berlin blockade in June did not push Britain any nearer to Spain, it certainly did the United States. For a start, the morale and the aspirations of the Francoist lobby in the U.S. definitely received a boost. To complete the picture, the U.S. administration's softening attitude towards Franco Spain was complemented by a similar change in U.S. public opinion which, it was observed, 'was more positively in favour of forgetting General Franco's past'.[64]

Franco was not averse to capitalising on the increasingly pro-Franco mood in the United States. In the last quarter of 1948 he gladly played host to a number of notable U.S. visitors. In the months of September, October and November Franco received, amongst others, Senator Chan Gurney, Chairman of the Senate Armed Services, Rear-Admiral Hillinkoetter, Director of the CIA, and seven U.S. Congressmen, six of whom were members of the House of Representatives Armed Services Committee. All of the visitors called for the inclusion of Spain in the Western Alliance. Franco was more than happy to reciprocate. To U.S. journalists with whom he had interview sessions in November, the *Generalísimo* publicly declared Spain's willingness to establish an alliance with Western powers, in particular with the United States. Hinting that he was privy to the inner recesses of Anglo-U.S. diplomatic communication, the Caudillo accused the British Government of undermining the *rapprochement* process jointly undertaken by Washington and Madrid, saying 'whenever the United States attempts to make a sympathetic gesture towards Spain, the British immediately step in and say their public opinion would not stand for it.'[65]

Given the worsening Cold War situation, Britain was understandably keen to ensure that the subject of Franco Spain would not be raised for discussion in any public forum. It was not that it feared being pushed into embracing Franco Spain – unless of course UN policy on Spain changed. Britain simply did not want to be taunted for refusing to endorse or take more radical action against Franco Spain. The Labour administration could certainly do without being embarrassed at the UN by the Soviet Union and at home by its own party members. In order to avoid such embarrassment, Bevin suggested to both Schuman and Marshall that they should conspire to relegate the Spanish item, due for discussion at the UN November session in Paris, to last place.[66] Bevin was much relieved when debate on the Spanish item was postponed to 1949.

The postponement was a respite for Britain and a setback for Spain. However, the power that held the trump card was the United States. Rich, powerful and assuming the leadership of the free world against communism in the immediate post-war years, the U.S. was expected to have little difficulty in influencing the way many nations would vote at the UN. Hence, policy pronouncements by U.S. leaders on U.S. policy towards Franco Spain were keenly followed, not only by Spain but by other nations. In 1949 such statements were aplenty.

Britain, having played an active and effective role in ensuring that the 1946 Resolution on Spain was of a moderate nature, had always maintained subsequently that its policy towards Franco Spain was dictated by the UN Resolution. Unsparing at times in verbal condemnations of Franco,[67] Britain was always anxious simultaneously to uphold the principle of noninterventionism. Britain had confidence neither in the Spanish Republican government-in-exile, nor in any other opponent of Franco, and was both unwilling and unable to help any party wrest power from the dictator. Hence, Britain maintained that any untoward action against Franco could create a political crisis that would be exploited by the communists. The only problem with this claim was that the British also knew that the communist threat within Spain was negligible,[68] and that the Russians, due ostensibly to the sphere of influence consideration and others, could not be expected to repeat their Civil War foray into Spain.[69] However, in the Cold War years, the fear of communism seemed a sound enough basis for policy formulation. It certainly appealed to the broad political audience, and in this particular case helped to justify the other aspects of Britain's Spanish policy as well. As already explained, Britain was not keen to have the Spanish question debated openly, as the government leaders did not want to raise the political temperature unnecessarily amongst its strongly anti-Franco rank-and-file. This explained why Bevin and the FO had to persuade Marshall and the State Department, time and again, to soft-pedal the Spanish issue.

In early 1949, however, there occurred some brisk diplomatic communications between Britain and the United States when the latter declared its intention to vote for the annulment of the operative parts of the UN 1946 Resolution on Spain. For its part, Britain explained that it would not vote for the return of ambassadors to Madrid nor for the participation of Spain in UN specialised agencies. It would not, however, oppose such proposals. Admittedly, this was a shift from its position in 1947 when it voted for the reaffirmation of the various parts of the 1946 Resolution on Spain. But then, the shift in the U.S. position was even more radical. The U.S. seemed bent on moving closer and faster to Franco Spain. Hence the stage was set for the divergent stands between these two traditional allies. In the circumstances, Franco would be delivered a diplomatic stick, in the form of a pro-Spain U.S. vote, with which to beat Britain. As it turned out, Franco was to be much disappointed. He was denied the expected joy when the State Department, after an intense internal debate, backtracked at the last moment and did not vote for the modification of the 1946 UN Resolution on Spain. Instead, along with Britain and France, the United States abstained. The backtracking was obviously meant to be a temporary measure, for after this May 1949 UNGA, the U.S. Secretary of State, Dean Acheson, reaffirmed his country's desire to bring Spain into the European family of nations. The stumbling-block, Acheson said, was the unfavourable 'fundamental facts' still existing in the Spanish administration. The undemocratic political system and the politicised judiciary were among the disturbing facts enumerated. The United States, continued Acheson, could not simply ignore the views of its European allies on these matters nor behave as if it could not care less about them.[70]

After May, the Spanish question was not raised again at the UN in 1949. Public interest in the issue, however, continued unabated. In July, the Senate Appropriation Committee approved a $50 million (U.S.) loan to Spain. It was rejected by the full Senate in August and also vetoed by Truman, who argued that the U.S. was 'not on friendly relations with Spain at the present time'.[71] Patrick McCarran, the Nevada Democratic Senator who initiated the loan proposal, was unrepentant and declared his intention to continue pursuing his objective. McCarran was castigated by the President at the latter's press conference in mid-September.[72] Britain could not have been more pleased and Bevin, who was then in the United States, had in fact told Acheson the day before to 'let sleeping dogs lie'.[73]

Bevin's wish was not to be fulfilled. As for Truman, his opposi-tional stand was subject to increasing scrutiny. The Cold War had everything to do with this. In the same month, September, the Pres-ident himself made the sensational announcement that the Rus-sians had successfully exploded their own atomic bomb. This prompted Robert Taft, a leading Republican Senator, to urge the U.S. Government to 'adjust our relations with Spain'.[74] The event, coupled with the communist advances in China, put further politi-cal pressure on the State Department, already held responsible by the powerful Chinese lobby for the 'loss' of China. The State Department was goaded by its critics into conducting its affairs in the most patriotic manner possible.[75] The State Department, pre-sumably, would not cherish adding the 'loss' of Spain to its record.

In the last quarter of 1949, leading U.S. politicians continued to voice support for the renewal of full diplomatic relations with Spain. In response to all this, Dean Acheson made a far-reaching statement in January 1950. He declared his country's desire to return to 'normal practice in exchanging diplomatic representation'. He said that the withdrawal of ambassadors and ministers plenipotentiary from Madrid on account of the Spanish regime's disagreeable politics was an 'anomaly' in international relations, which had to be corrected. This was a clever twist to the whole argument against Franco: the ideological argument as it had hitherto been perceived by many nations. Acheson had taken the bait, so it seemed, put out by the pro-Franco politicians who had argued, like Churchill in Britain, that it was ridiculous to have an ambassador in Moscow but not in Madrid. Policy-makers on both sides of the Atlantic had of course known all along that this comparison was spurious. It did not give due justice to the anti-Franco argument as a whole. Acheson failed to spell out the earlier and proper context of the whole Spanish issue, and this further facilitated the undoing of the case against Franco Spain at the UN.

To recapitulate, it is pertinent to recall the political considerations within which the issue of Franco Spain was encased. The primary concern, when the Spanish issue was first raised at the UN, was what action ought to be taken against Franco Spain. The regime, after all, was the last remnant of the defeated Axis line-up during the Second World War, and action against it would have been accepted by many as an integral part of the mopping-up exercise. As already pointed out, when Roosevelt dispatched Armour to Spain in March 1945, he had told the ambassador that 'maintenance of normal relations with Spain did not imply approval of the Franco regime'.[76] Hence, the principle underlying the exchanges of diplomatic representatives was adhered to right from the start. Consequently, the eventual withdrawal of ambassadors from Spain, was not a violation of this principle: it was simply a way of punishing Franco Spain. The passage of time, presumably, had erased the memory of this from the minds of many an administrator.

Taken in the above context, the inappropriateness of not branding the regime of Franco as an accomplice to those of Hitler and Mussolini becomes obvious. However, this letting Franco off the hook is not wholly inexplicable, not when one considers the possible collective and compromised stand of the major powers discussed earlier. Taken in this context too, Britain's adamant refusal right from the initial stage to support, let alone advocate, any anti-Franco measures makes a great deal of sense. It was certainly futile to withdraw ambassadors from Madrid and bar Spain from participation in UN's specialised agencies if that was all that the world body was prepared to do. True, the December 1946 Resolution on Spain did say that the Security Council would be directed to take further measures against Franco Spain should the political situation in the country fail to improve. How real was this projection? To Britain it was nothing more than diplomatic sabre-rattling, and ineffective at that. It refused to lend its support to this 'empty threat'. Britain believed that even this mild diplomatic rebuke (mild if contrasted with Franco's wartime record) was interventionist in nature and hence went against the grain of UN's principle of respecting the sovereignty of nations. In the international onslaught against Spain, Britain, along with many other Western democracies, successfully insisted throughout that the anti-Franco measures encompassed in the 1946 UN Resolution went as far as they were prepared to sanction. The Soviet camp, at least on the surface of things, wanted to carry the campaign further. But at the UN it could not muster the numbers to carry through such a proposal; with the Cold War escalating, the task became proportionately more difficult day by day.

In the 1940s, Whitehall was not alone in realizing the futility of the whole anti-Franco exercise if the action or threat alluded to in the 1946 UN Resolution on Spain was not going to be followed through. Without more drastic action being contemplated, a contemporary U.S. political commentator pointed out, the 'bluff ... will be quickly called'.[77] The FO too was under no delusion that Franco would bow down merely as a result of diplomatic pinpricks. The dictator, having 'a skin like a rhinoceros',[78] would weather out such irritants. It was, in the end, this stand-off that worked out in Franco's favour.

Britain's unwillingness to subscribe to any forcible action against Spain helped to derail the United States' attempt to oust Franco. However, when the United States later wanted to move closer to Madrid, Britain, fearing serious objections from Labour politicians and others, baulked at the U.S. plan. As has been pointed out, the United States was quite deferential towards Britain. However, this deference, as it turned out, lasted for only as long as the international climate permitted.

In 1950, the Cold War tension reached a new peak when the Korean War broke out in June. The reverberations were felt across Europe and the United States. The Madrid correspondent of the *New York Times* reported that as a result of the war, pro-Franco Spaniards believed that the 'United States will be more willing to help us, financially and politically'.[79] From Madrid too the U.S. Embassy informed Washington that MAE was 'extremely favourable' to Truman's 'energetic action' in Korea.[80] In July, speaking at the anniversary of Franco's uprising, José Antonio Girón, the

Spanish Minister of Labour, claimed that the whole world had come round to Spain's way of thinking and 'yet we have not swerved from the line that we took 14 years ago'.[81]

On 1 August, the U.S. Senate approved a $100 million (U.S.) loan to Spain, and on the very same day the Spanish embassy in Washington announced Spain's willingness to fight the communists in Korea.[82] In Britain, Franco Spain found support in Churchill, who repeated his earlier call for the inclusion of Spain in NATO. Spain's membership of the Western defence alliance, Churchill contended, would 'close the hideous gap on the European front'.[83] Churchill's call was not heeded by the Attlee administration, which still had a very low opinion of Spain's combat readiness.[84] The United States too was not unaware of the poor state of Spain's military arsenal but, unlike Britain, was willing and able to refurbish it. Earlier in the year Acheson had already announced the resolve of the United States to normalise relations with Franco Spain, and the conflict in the Far East could only further enhance the climate for the impending *rapprochement*.

The United States had underlined its determination to mend fences with Spain by not forewarning or consulting Britain prior to the 1950 policy shift. This departure from previous conventions also signalled the declining importance of Britain in international affairs and the unmistakable increase in that of the U.S. When the State Department formally notified the FO of the U.S. decision to support any move at the UN to revoke the 1946 Resolution on Spain, the information was no longer news. It was left to the British to make light of the matter and this they did.[85] When the United States announced its commitment to end Spain's diplomatic isolation, the revocation of the 1946 UN Resolution on Spain was widely expected. There was no need for the United States to sponsor a resolution advocating it: it had merely to lend its support. Hence, Bevin initially flirted with the idea of voting for the rescinding of the 1946 Resolution as well. It was thought that a pro-Spain vote at the UN would place the next British ambassador in Madrid, once appointed, on an advantageous footing. However, Bevin submitted an open-ended paper for his colleagues to consider. The Cabinet stuck to the old policy.[86] Thus at the ensuing debates and votes at the UN, the British Delegation took refuge in neutrality, a position condemned by a leading Labour backbencher, Michael Foot, as amounting to 'an abdication of duty'.[87]

The resolution to rehabilitate Franco Spain was submitted by Bolivia, Costa Rica, the Dominican Republic, El Salvador, Honduras, Nicaragua, the Philippines and Peru. First debated in the Ad Hoc Political Committee, the resolution confined itself to the issues of ambassadorial representation in Madrid and Spain's participation in UN specialised agencies. It was silent on the history and character of the Franco regime. On 1 November 1950 the Ad Hoc Political Committee approved the resolution by 37 votes in favour to 10 against with 12 abstentions. The United States voted for the resolution while Britain along with Australia, Burma, Cuba, Denmark, Ethiopia, France, India, Indonesia, New Zealand, Norway and Sweden abstained. The Soviet bloc together with Guatemala, Mexico, Uruguay, Israel and Yugoslavia voted against. On 4 November, UNGA duly endorsed the decision. With it the diplomatic *cordon sanitaire* thrown around Franco Spain was lifted.

In the ending of Spain's diplomatic isolation, the Cold War presented Franco Spain with a tremendous advantage. The influence of the United States was crucial and that of Britain immaterial. Britain's intermittent opposition to earlier attempts by the U.S. to adopt a pro-Franco stance was not so much due to being against the move *per se*, but to its fear of a possible revolt amongst the Labour Party rank-and-file. Bevin, after all, had always insisted that the anti-Franco UN measures were interventionist in nature. Britain did what it could to moderate the UN actions in 1946. Hence, when the 1946 Resolution on Spain was targeted for annulment in 1950, it was not surprising that Bevin even contemplated supporting it openly. He was stopped in his tracks by his Cabinet colleagues. Bevin and Britain, in the end, did not lose much by sticking to safe diplomacy.

Notes

1. Malcolm Muggeridge (ed.), *Ciano's Diplomatic Papers*, London, 1948, p. 291; see also Julio Alvarez del Vayo, *The Last Optimist*, London, 1950, p. 380.
2. The full text of Franco's letter and that of Churchill's reply can be found in Samuel Hoare, *Ambassador on Special Mission*, London, 1946, Appendix A, pp. 300-6.
3. Ibid.
4. Ibid.
5. FRUS 1945, vol. V, p. 66, Roosevelt to Armour, 10 March 1945.
6. On the attitude of the United States towards Spain during the last year of the war see also the contribution of Glyn Stone to this present volume.
7. FRUS 1945, vol. I, p. 302, footnote I, memo by the Acting Secretary of State Joseph Grew (extracts), 9 July 1945.
8. Louis Stein, *Beyond Death and Exile: The Spanish Republican in France, 1939-1955*, Cambridge, MA, 1975, p. 187.

9. FRUS 1945, vol. I, p. 302, footnote I, memo by Grew (extracts), 9 July 1945.

10. The countries were Panama and Cuba. In December 1945 the Foreign Affairs Committee of the French Constituent Assembly voted for the same course of action.

11. FRUS 1945, vol. II, p. 123; see also PRO F0371/49612, Z9049/537/G/41.

12. See U.S. Department of State, *The Spanish Government and The Axis: Official German Documents*, Washington, 1946; see also *Manchester Guardian*, 5 March 1946.

13. PRO FO371/49612, Z9049/537/G/41.

14. PRO F0371/49610, Z 2003//537/G/41, Barker (British Embassy, Madrid) to FO, 10 February 1945.

15. DBPO, London, 1984, ser. I, vol. I, doc. 359, p. 821, Hoyer-Millar to Harvey, 21 July 1949.

16. Ibid., doc. 409, p. 902, Hayter to Howard 25 July 1945.

17. FRUS 1945, vol. II, p. 1175, memo by Yost, 8 August 1949.

18. Hansard, *House of Commons Debates*, 413, 16 August 1949.

19. Laureano López Rodó, *La larga marcha hacia la monarquía*, Barcelona, 1977, p. 60.

20. FRUS 1945, vol. II, p. 1175, memo by Yost, 8 Aug, 1949.

21. See Martin Gilbert, *Road To Victory: Winston S. Churchill 1941-1945*, London, 1989, pp. 992-3; B.R. Kuniholm, *The Origins of the Cold War in the Near East: Great Power Conflict and Diplomacy in Iran, Turkey, and Greece*, Princeton, 1980, pp. 100-29.

22. PRO F0371/603441A, Z7178, British Embassy (Moscow) to FO, 6 August 1946. See also Alvarez del Vayo, *Last Optimist*, p. 354; and Qasim Ahmad, *Britain, Franco Spain and The Cold War 1945-1950*, Kuala Lumpur, 1995, pp. 132-3.

23. Hansard, 413, 20 August 1945.

24. PRO F037/49613, Z9844/41, Mallet to FO, 22 August 1945. See also The Monitoring Service of the British Broadcasting Service, Monitoring Report 2, p. 227, 21-22 August 1945; and Noel-Baker's Papers NBKR 4/663, correspondence on Spain 1939-46, Noel Baker to Mildred Bamford, 30 August 1945.

25. FRUS 1946, vol. V, 1067, Halifax to FO, 10 April 1946; ibid., Byrnes to Stettinius, 12 April 1946; PRO FO371/60355, Z3516/36/41, Garran's minute, 12 April 1946.

26. See Florentino Portero, *Franco aislado: La cuestión española (1945-1950)*, Madrid, 1989, pp. 334-5.

27. UN Security Council, Official Records 1st Year (1946), 2nd ser., spec. supp., *Report of the Sub-Committee on the Spanish Question*, p. 2.

28. Ibid.

29. See Boris Liedtke's contribution to this present volume.

30. PRO F0371/49613, Z9949/537/41, Bevin to Sir A. Clarke Kerr, 24 August 1945.

31. *The Times*, 10 December 1946.

32. AuA A1838/2, 852/10/10 Pt. 1, secretary of state for Dominion affairs to minister of external affairs, 5 June 1947.

33. Ahmad, *Britain*, p. 48.

34. Ibid., p. 49.

35. See above.

36. See Geoffrey Swain's contribution to this present volume.

37. Hartmut Heine, 'Political Opposition to the Franco Regime between 1939-1952' (PhD Diss., University of London, 1981), p. 421.

38. PRO F0800/492/PER/46/64 (Bevin's Papers), Bevin to Attlee and McNeal, 15 November 1946.
39. López Rodó, *Larga marcha*, p. 58.
40. Stein, *Beyond Death*, p. 191.
41. DSB, 23 March 1950, p. 536.
42. PRO FO371/67868, 24093/3/41, Bevin to Sargent, 25 April 1947.
43. W.L. LaFeber, *American, Russia and the Cold War, 1945-1984*, New York, 1980, p. 60.
44. Franco-Weinthal interview, *Newsweek*, 22 November 1948.
45. See Ahmad, *Britain*, pp. 171-3.
46. *The Times*, 24 June 1947; *New York Times*, 10 June and 10 July 1947.
47. PRO F0371/67870, Z9291/3/41, Howard to FO, 23 October 1947; PRO F0371/67870, Z9304/3/41, 23 October 1947; PRO F0371/67870, Z9314/3/41, 24 October 1947; PRO F0371/67870, Z9333/3/41, 25 October 1947; PRO F0371/67870, Z9426/3/41, 28 October 1947. *Ya*, 22 October 1947; *A.B.C.*, 22 October 1947; *The Times*, 23 and 24 October 1947; *The Daily Telegraph and Morning Post*, 25 October 1947; PRO F0371/67871/ Z9493/3/41, Sir Nigel Ronald (British Embassy, Lisbon) to F0, 1 November 1947; PRO F0371/67871, Z9841/3/41, Crosthwaite's minute, 8 November 1947; PRO F0371/67871, Z10684/3/41, Miguel Espinos (Consul General for Spain, South Africa) to D.D.Forsyth (Secretary for External Affairs, Pretoria), 14 November 1947.
48. PRO FO371/67871, Z10061/3/41, Howard to FO, 12 November 1947.
49. PRO F0371/67871, Z9841/3/41, F0 to Madrid, 12 November 1947.
50. Ibid.
51. For Bevin's persistent encounters with critics from the Labour Party rank-and-file see Ahmad, *Britain*, chap. VII.
52. PRO F0371/73335, Z2791/84/41, Bevin to Lord Inverchapel, 1 April 1948.
53. This was revealed when the Australian representative at the United Nations consulted representatives from all the British Commonwealth countries, the USA, Belgium, France and some Latin American countries on this very issue; see AuA A1838/2, 852/10, PT.1, Australian Delegation, UN Assembly, New York, to External Affairs, Canberra, 12 November 1947.
54. FRUS 1947, vol. III, p. 1094, George F. Kennan to Marshall and under secretary of state, 24 October 1947, Annex: U.S. Policy Towards Spain (emphasis as in the original). See also Boris Liedtke's contribution to this present volume.
55. PRO FO371/67871, Z9836/3/41, minute, 18 November 1947, (signature not identifiable).
56. UNGA, 2nd session, vol. II, 1947, p. 1097, 118th. Plenary Meeting, 17 November 1947.
57. See above.
58. PRO FO371/67869, Z7449/3/41, Crosthwaite to Howard, 26 August 1947.
59. Ibid.
60. For various assessments of Spain's military capability in these years see UN, *Report of the Sub-Committee on the Spanish Question, 1946*, 22–6; Americans For Democratic Action, *What Does (Stalin) Want Us To Do About (Franco)? Questions And Answers On Franco Spain*, Washington, 1949?, p. 9; Walter Lipmann, 'Common Sense and the Problem of Spain', *Daily Mail*, 18 May 1949; *The World Today* VI, no. 9, 1950: 368. Without exception, all these reports gave a very negative picture of Spain's military capability.

61. PRO FO371/7356, Z6639/84/G, Bevin to Alexander, 28 September 1948; see also ibid., Alexander to Bevin 11 August 1948.
62. FRUS 1948, vol. III, p. 1017, Achilles to Culbertson, 5 January 1948.
63. FRUS 1948, vol. III, p. 1017, Culbertson to secretary of state, 29 March 1948.
64. Peter Calvocoressi, *Survey of International Affairs 1947-48*, London, 1952, p. 129.
65. *Newsweek,* 22 November 1948.
66. FRUS 1948, vol. III, p. 1054, memo of conversation by secretary of state, 4 October 1948.
67. See, for instance, Hansard, p. 496, 20 September 1948, statement by Christopher Mayhew, Parliamentary Under-Secretary of State for Foreign Affairs.
68. PRO FO371/79686, Z3685/10156/41, W. Horsfall Carter's minute, 18 May 1949; PRO F0371/73334, Z1804/84/41, memo by Crosthwaite, 6 March 1948.
69. See Geoffrey Swain's contribution to this present volume for a detailed analysis of Stalin's plans toward Spain.
70. *The Times,* 12 May 1944; DSB, 22 May 1949, pp. 660–1.
71. PPUS (Harry S. Truman 1949), Washington, 1964, p. 381; *New York Times,* 15 July 1949; *The Times,* 15 July 1949.
72. PPUS (Harry S. Truman 1949), p. 474.
73. FRUS 1949, vol. IV, pp. 758–9, memo of conversation by secretary of state, 14 September 1949.
74. See FRUS 1949, vol. IV, p. 761, Culbertson to secretary of state, 3 October 1949.
75. Ibid.
76. FRUS 1945, vol. V, p. 66, Roosevelt to Armour, 10 March 1945.
77. Lipmann, 'Common Sense'.
78. PRO F0371/49613, Z1010S/537/81, Hoyer-Millar's minute, 3 September 1945. See also Paul Preston, *Franco*, London, 1993, p. 543.
79. *New York Times,* 1 July 1950.
80. See FRUS 1950, vol. VIII, pp. 321-2, Acheson to all diplomatic missions and certain consular officers, 29 June 1950.
81. *The Times,* 5 August 1950.
82. *The Daily Telegraph and Morning Post,* 2 August 1950.
83. *Manchester Guardian,* 28 August 1950.
84. See *The World Today* VI, no. 9, 1950: 368. Even after Korea, the Defence Ministry's poor opinion of Spain's military standing persisted, see DEFE 5/34, C.O.S. (51) 646, *Relationship of Spain to the Defence of Western Europe,* 8 November 1951.
85. See *The Times,* 21 January 1950.
86. See Cab. 128, vol. 18, 56(8), Cabinet Conclusions.
87. Hansard, 480, 1 November 1950.

12

Stalin and Spain, 1944-1948[1]

Geoffrey Swain
(University of the West of England, Bristol)

I

AFTER the dissolution of the Comintern in May 1943, Stalin relied on 'messages from Moscow' to guide the actions of foreign communist parties according to his vision of where the countries of Europe fitted into the post-war world.[2] Stalin's message to the PCE was delivered in mid-October 1944 when Enrique Lister was summoned to a meeting with Dimitrov:

1. Stalin wanted to thwart the plans of the imperialists, and above all the British, who wanted to keep Franco in power despite the defeat of fascism on the battle field;
2. it was necessary to force the socialist, anarchist and Republican leaders to abandon their policy of passivity and the hope that the Spanish problem could be resolved through the authority of the imperialists;
3. it would be necessary to form a government, or similar institution, which could talk in the name of the Spanish people; and this government, liberation committee or whatever it was called would be best headed by Negrín;
4. and finally, this representational form for Spanish democracy must develop a popular movement, one of whose manifestations, in the Spanish context, would be guerrilla struggle.[3]

Implementing these guidelines did not prove to be easy, for Stalin was himself uncertain if the 'plans of the imperialists' could best be thwarted through confrontation or cooperation. As so often during the Spanish Civil War, Stalin's contradictory position as both instigator of world revolution and world statesman was to upset the plans of the Spanish communists. No sooner had these guidelines been issued, than tension developed between Stalin and the Spanish communists on how to implement them. In October 1944, Stalin seemed to favour confrontation and the development of guerrilla war. Between spring 1945 and spring 1946 Stalin came to believe that the future of Spain could serve as a 'test' of the Allies' commitment to cooperation in a new world order for diplomatic affairs; as a consequence the Spanish communists were pushed unwillingly into compromise with former opponents and participation in a government-in-exile. When the Allies failed the 'test' in spring 1946, Moscow's unleashing of the Spanish communists represented one of the first signs that Zhdanov was in charge of a new Soviet policy of confrontation.

II

Stalin's guidelines of October 1944 were issued to regularise the activity of guerrillas committed to the forcible overthrow of Franco. The success of the D-Day landings in June 1944 and the subsequent liberation of France had opened up a whole new theatre of war and meant that the large number of Spaniards involved in the French resistance, most of whom were loyal to the Communist Party, could begin to consider how best to extend their struggle to Spain itself. The PCE was agreed on the need to start a national uprising against Franco; but the correct tactics to pursue were soon a matter of dispute. Against the opposition of many of the military commanders among the Spanish guerrillas within the French resistance, the PCE leadership opted for an invasion of Spain, one big dramatic action to shatter the image of Franco's security. The French Communist leader and close associate of the PCE, André Marty, had severe doubts about this enterprise, informed Moscow of the plan in September 1944, and Santiago Carrillo was instructed to take charge. Carrillo arrived in Toulouse just after the 'invasion of the Valle de Arán' had started on 18 October, with communist military commanders holding a crisis meeting on how to respond to what seemed imminent disaster; Carrillo threw his weight behind those calling for retreat.[4]

Carrillo was not opposed to guerrilla warfare – and as the guidelines made clear, neither was Stalin – but Carrillo was aware of the diplomatic ramifications of the invasion plan. The PCE's war-time leadership was convinced that an invasion, once started, would draw the Allies into the reconquest of Spain: it was this notion that offended Carrillo most and that was the true concern of Marty and Moscow. In published reminiscences Carrillo noted: 'in order [for the invasion plan to succeed] it would have been necessary to have had the agreement of the French authorities, and even that of the Allied forces', while in a secret report for Moscow these concerns were even more clearly expressed. He pointed not only to the express opposition of the 'French comrades' to the invasion but stressed that the 'order' for the invasion had assumed that 'during the course of this action, we can and must bring into it guerrillas from MOI – the French Communist Party's organisation for immigrant workers – and many volunteer French guerrillas.' The mistaken attempt to internationalise the struggle, Carrillo went on, had had disastrous international consequences: 'this operation had meant that the months of September, October and part of November 1944 had, to all intents and purposes, been lost, when they could have been used to move into Spain, in true guerrilla formation, the majority of the men and material.' It gave Franco the chance to bring huge pressure to bear on France and force the French to take action which nearly ended in the dissolution of the guerrilla units, and forced the PCE to put them under French control; all units were subsequently withdrawn to 40 km from the border and Radio Toulouse suspended.[5] One of the main purposes of Stalin's guidelines, therefore, was not to stop cross-border activity but to clarify that the future lay not in an invasion of Spain, but in the extension of guerrilla warfare.

The other clear message of the guidelines was that talks should begin with Negrín. Precisely what Stalin was calling for in October 1944 was left rather vague, and the PCE saw no necessity at first to abandon its favoured policy of the 'popular front from below',[6] expressed in the call for a *Unión Nacional* resistance front; although notionally this included all opponents of Franco, it was actually dominated by the communists like the war-time fronts formed throughout Mediterranean Europe. Until February 1945, the Party insisted that its task was to convert the *Unión Nacional* into an authentic directorate for the whole resistance movement.[7] Before Stalin's 'message' the policy had been to make the *Unión Nacional* the 'only government of Spain',[8] but its modification in November 1944 to recognise the legitimacy of Negrín's government was purely notional.[9] When the PCE leader Dolores Ibarruri first contacted Negrín about talks in December 1944, her proposal was still in the context of the *Unión Nacional*. She made clear that if special circumstances made it essential in the future for an 'organ of power' to operate outside Spain, then it would be wrong to create one artificially which had no links with the country, thereby throwing to one side a government which already existed and was 'still more than ever remembered with affection in contemporary Spain, i.e. the last legal government of Negrín'. But she made clear that the main task of this government-in-exile would be to stimulate and direct the efforts and activities of the emigration in support of those struggling inside Spain; at no point did this letter suggest that the *Unión Nacional* should be dissolved as the organising body for action in Spain, and the point was made repeatedly that a government-in-exile should busy itself exclusively with events abroad, while supporting a struggle at home over which its authority was unclear.[10] The same hybrid between the *Unión Nacional* and a government-in-exile was described by Carrillo in January 1945 in *España Popular*.[11]

The line began to change from confrontation to cooperation early in 1945. When Stalin issued his guidelines on Spain, he was aware of Churchill's public defence of the 'services rendered by Spain' in parliament in May 1944, and no doubt also aware, through other channels, of Churchill's comment to Roosevelt in June 1944 that he would not 'seek to quarrel' with Franco, and his rejection in October 1944 of the idea of British economic sanctions on Spain; Churchill feared communism would spread to France and Italy if the Spanish domino fell, and Stalin knew it. However, no sooner had Stalin issued his guidelines in October, than the situation began to change. Churchill pointedly rejected Franco's letter, handed to him on 21 November 1944, which suggested joint Anglo-Spanish action against communism to secure democracy in France and Italy, and, to allay Stalin's suspicions, copied the whole correspondence to the Soviet leader.[12] Stalin reciprocated in December 1944 when the Greek communists were left without support during their ill-starred insurrection, and after de Gaulle's visit to Moscow any revolutionary plans of the French communists were quickly vetoed. Give and take seemed to bring Stalin results, as the Yalta Conference confirmed in February 1945. By then *Pravda* noted that public opinion in Britain was increasingly hostile to Spanish fascism, and Stalin felt that his relations with Churchill and Roosevelt were such that the future of Spain could be resolved through cooperation and negotiation with his Allies.[13]

Solving the Spanish problem through agreement between the Allies required a change of tactics from the communists. Wherever Stalin wanted the communists to assume power at the end of the Second World War, he favoured a policy of the 'popular front from below'; where he did not intend them to seize power, they were instructed to abandon that policy and join a coalition government. From February 1945 the PCE was instructed to behave like the French and Italian communists, end the 'popular front from below' and come to an understanding with their rivals. As Carrillo noted bitterly, Stalin's plans 'would pull the socialists' and anarchists' nuts out of the fire' and enable them 'to look to the English and Americans for protection'.[14] In February 1945, the hybrid *Unión Nacional* government-in-exile proposal was dropped and members of the *Unión Nacional* offered to cooperate with the rival anti-Franco parties grouped in the *Junta Española de Liberación* (JEL); in March the Party began to dissolve *Unión Nacional* regional organisations.[15]

III

The change in line, necessitated by the imminent Allied victory and the likelihood that the UN would take up the issue of Spain, lasted until spring 1946 when, for Stalin, the Cold War became a reality. Negrín attended the San Francisco meeting to establish the UN which opened in April 1945 and lasted until June; on 22 June 1945 *Pravda* published a favourable report on these events and supported wholeheartedly the proposal from Mexico that Spain should not be allowed to join the UN. To facilitate any such diplomatic moves, on 25 June 1945 the Spanish communists announced the dissolution of the *Unión Nacional*.[16] But the path of cooperation rather than confrontation was far from being a smooth one, for Stalin was constantly probing to see how genuine was the West's commitment to a new diplomacy.

By summer 1945 the tenor of the Soviet diplomatic offensive on Spain had become clear. On 6 July 1945 *Pravda* published a keynote article which set the pattern for many subsequent ones: first came the veiled threat, the 'thousands' of partisans active in Spain who might establish a communist regime; then came the attempt to play on divisions among the Allies and prevent the consolidation of an anti-Soviet bloc – for this was the key to whether Stalin would pursue a policy of cooperation rather than confrontation. Thus readers were reminded that 'it was not only Hitler and

Mussolini who brought Franco to power, it was international reaction and all sorts of "conciliators"' – in other words, by implication, those involved in the NIC established by Britain and France during the Spanish Civil War. But, having attacked both France and Great Britain by implication, *Pravda* then sung the praises of the post-war French, welcoming the decision of the French Consultative Assembly to recommend a break in diplomatic relations with Spain, and agreeing: 'it is time to put an end to this regime!' And so the Russians put Spain on the agenda for Potsdam and proposed joint action to remove the Franco regime.[17]

Using the UN as a forum for joint international action against Spain was, in Stalin's eyes, a test for the validity of the notion that the Second World War had ushered in a new era in international relations when a grand alliance of democratic powers had learnt to act in concert. Spain had been a symbol of 'the Munich spirit', of all that was wrong, from the Soviet perspective, with the diplomacy of the 1930s; therefore intervention rather than nonintervention in post-war Spain was an easy touchstone against which Stalin could judge whether or not things had really changed. In Soviet terms, the Potsdam communiqué on Spain was a success and was welcomed by *Pravda*.[18] It was sufficient to persuade Spanish republicans that a government-in-exile had to be formed. Mindful of Stalin's 'message', the communists announced that they would only join a government-in-exile led by Negrín; determined to prevent this, the Prieto socialists announced they would never support a Negrín ministry; the net result was a government formed on 27 August 1945 by Giral which both Negrín and the PCE undertook not to oppose.[19]

This lukewarm attitude to Giral's administration reflected the first hiccough in the policy of cooperation. Bevin's first parliamentary speech on foreign policy angered the Russians most because of his forthright comments about Hungary, Romania and Bulgaria, but *Pravda* also noted what Bevin had to say about Spain, in particular his remark that, since the future of Spain was for the Spanish people to decide, the British Government 'could go no further' than Potsdam.[20] Picking up the theme of nonintervention first advanced in July and always referred to at times of Anglo-Soviet tension, *Pravda* noted on 24 August Negrín's comment that none of General Casado's supporters deserved to be included in any government since 'Casado had acted as an agent of British and French intelligence which both worked for the fall of the Republic in 1939'; two days later *Pravda* commented that this was not the first time that British policy on Spain had been one of nonintervention: 'in the past

Franco used the policy of "nonintervention" in order to seize power in Spain; now he hopes to use "nonintervention" in order to keep power in his hands, and, thereby, preserve a fascist base in Spain.'[21] In a further move against Giral, *Pravda* reported on 31 August 1945 that 'an agreement had been reached in Spain' insisting that Negrín's government was still the only legitimate government.

The failure of the London Conference of Foreign Ministers, 11 September to 2 October 1945, to make any progress in ushering in a new era of international diplomacy prompted *Pravda* to go further and link the issue of Spain to Stalin's growing concern that Britain, France and the United States were forming a Western bloc against him. On 23 September 1945, the *Pravda* commentator 'Observer' seized on the publication in the British press (on 18 September 1945) of the Franco-Churchill exchange of November 1944. The paper noted how Franco had then made no bones about how – when faced with imminent communist insurrection in Italy and France – he envisaged the two ancient sea-faring powers of Europe making common cause against the Soviet Union. Franco's ideas were similar, 'Observer' concluded, to current talk of a 'Western bloc'. This theme was developed further in *Pravda* on 18 November 1945 when readers were again reminded that the idea of a 'Western Bloc' had first surfaced in Madrid during the war, as an attempt to divide the war-time coalition.

During autumn 1945 Soviet criticism of the British was mirrored by continuing communist hostility to Giral. When on 7 to 9 November 1945 the Cortes met in Mexico, the leading communist Vincente Uribe attacked Giral and called for a 'firm' Negrín government.[22] Later in the month Negrín wrote publicly about the poor performance of Giral's government: its attitude was described as 'ambiguous' and it had drifted from opposition to defeatism, or a recognition that the republic had been destroyed. By the end of November leading republicans in Mexico had also condemned Giral, accusing him of passivity, of trying to save Spain by 'dubious negotiations'; in particular it appeared he was 'rejecting the role played by partisans'.[23] And yet, when the PCE held its Plenum on 5 to 8 December 1945, all criticism of Giral was forgotten and the communists rushed headlong into joining the government-in-exile.

This dramatic *volte face* was occasioned by the sudden improvement in inter-Allied relations brought about by the U.S. proposal of 23 November 1945 to hold a further Conference of Foreign Ministers in Moscow. Suddenly it looked to Stalin as if differences between Britain and the United States could be successfully exploited; and some of these differences related to Spain. In contrast to Bevin's attitude, towards the end of 1945 the U.S. stance towards Franco was increasingly hostile. On the eve of the Moscow Conference the State Department not only warned the Spanish ambassador in Washington that a rupture in diplomatic relations was inevitable, but let Giral's Foreign Minister understand that such a break was imminent. Whether the question of Spain was to be discussed at the Moscow Conference, held from 16 to 27 December 1945, was uncertain right up until the last moment. The Spanish ambassador in Washington was told on the eve of the conference that it could well be on the agenda, and the Soviets carefully staged a series of rallies throughout the proceedings by international organisations, such as the World Federation of Trade Unions and the International Federation of Women, calling for action on Spain.[24] But Spain was kept off the agenda. Britain decided against a diplomatic break on 21 December 1945 and by the end of the month it was clear that this was not an issue on which Britain and the United States intended to disagree.

The immediate Soviet verdict on the Moscow Conference was that it had been a success: with all sides showing give and take; it was a model of how the new post-war diplomacy could operate on a genuine tripartite basis. On 28 December *Pravda*'s editorial stated: 'the conference just concluded is a new step forward in implementing the war-time cooperation among the three powers.'[25] But what had been achieved after all? The Soviet Union had made concessions in Eastern Europe, but Spain, the outstanding issue in Western Europe, had not even reached the agenda. Stalin summoned a meeting of the Politburo on 29 December 1945, the first he had attended since the winding up of the State Defence Committee in September 1945; his clear purpose was to restore his authority in both domestic and foreign-policy matters. He was clearly worried about the weakness of the Soviet Union in the area of foreign affairs and proposed creating within the Politburo a special group of some fifty people, to be drawn from activists throughout the country which would specialise in foreign affairs, plus a Politburo Commission on Foreign Affairs comprising himself, Molotov, Beria, Mikoyan, Malenkov and Zhdanov.[26]

Pravda at once dropped the optimistic tone of its 28 December editorial. When on 13 January 1946 the authoritative 'International Observer' column took up the theme of Spain and the UN, it noted concern at the opening session of the UN and continuing Western pressure to weaken the powers of the Security Council. 'The Rules of the UN,' readers were reminded, 'were the fruit of discussions of freedom loving states brought together in a common cause in the days of wartime' and could not be changed at whim. As to the decision of the French, British and the United States to hold talks on Spain to the exclusion of the Russians, the paper went on:

> it is clear that serious discussion of this question is unthinkable without the participation of all great powers ... any other discussion of the Spanish problem could only give rise to unfounded hopes in the Franco camp. ... It is time, it has long been time, to move from words to action on the Spanish question. Liquidating the last remnants of fascism – that is the most urgent task which must be resolved by creating a post-war system of peace and security.

When Gromyko addressed UNGA on 18 January 1946 he made precisely the same point. The military victory over fascism had not resulted in its complete eradication – and that task therefore had to be a task for the UN since 'it would be a mistake to consider that military victory removes the necessity for the further persistent struggle for the complete liquidation of the nests of fascism which remain.'[27]

As the first UN session started its work, the omens for it resolving the question of Spain did not look promising. The British attitude was clear, and any differences the U.S. administration might have had with Britain about the correct attitude to Spain were put right by the detailed telegram received from ambassador George Kennan on 3 February 1946; this argued that the Russians were determined to regain the influence they had once had in Spain during the Civil War. 'As far as Spain is concerned Russians have learned nothing and forgotten nothing since the civil war. Their only programme is to return to that struggle unabashed by chaos which might ensue,' Kennan concluded.[28]

Stalin's own position was still ambivalent. His Supreme Soviet election speech on 9 February 1946 showed how domestic matters still weighed most heavily on his mind; on foreign affairs he still accepted the duality of the Second World War, a war which had begun as an 'imperialist struggle' but had been transformed into an anti-fascist struggle of freedom loving peoples.[29] Zhdanov on the other hand used his election speech on 8 February 1946 to denounce and challenge the West.[30] Two months later any doubts which Stalin might have had were resolved. The UN resolution on Spain of 9 February 1946 fell far short of Soviet desires, since it simply recalled the previous decisions taken at San Francisco and Potsdam and called on members to 'act in accordance with the letter and spirit of these statements in the conduct of their future relations with Spain';[31] the 4 March 1946 tripartite statement on Spain signed by Britain, France and the United States was bland in the extreme. When condemning it, *Pravda* readers were reminded that at Potsdam only the Soviet Union had called for a break in diplomatic relations; ominously there then followed another history lesson on the subject of nonintervention during the Spanish Civil War.[32]

On 13 April 1946, when the Politburo next discussed foreign affairs in detail, the meeting endorsed a number of crucial changes in the working of the Secretariat and Orgburo. In particular it clearly differentiated the spheres of activity of Malenkov and Zhdanov: Malenkov was to concentrate on organising the Party and all the republican Party organisations within the USSR; Zhdanov was to be responsible for all aspects of propaganda and to have overall charge of the new Foreign Policy Department in the Bolshevik Party Central Committee. Not only was he to be in charge, but he was to shake things up and improve agitational work at all levels. As part of this shake up, *Pravda*'s editorial team for foreign affairs was strengthened and Suslov appointed to direct the day-to-day running of the Foreign Policy Department.[33] Gromyko's tone when the Spanish question was next raised in the UN Security Council on 19 April 1946 reflected these changes. He told delegates that Stalin had, long before the war, warned people and politicians of the dangers contained within fascism, but his call for determined measures to be taken against the growing fascist aggression had been ignored. It was for this reason, because the Soviet Union was opposed to fascism *per se*, that it was impossible for it simply to abandon the Spanish question.[34] The question of Spain had helped prepare the ground for Zhdanov's ascendancy.

Throughout the Moscow Conference and the UN session, when it looked as if the post-war coalition might at last jointly take up the issue of Spain, it was essential for the PCE to be involved in the work of the government-in-exile. After the Plenum of 5 to 8 December 1945 the Party's first move was to join the Alliance of Democratic Forces (AFD), an organisation established by the JEL within Spain and seen until then as a forum for the Party's opponents. Then, shortly after the Plenum, Ibarruri wrote to Giral seeking to open talks about the communists joining the government-in-exile.[35] Giral played for time, using the threat of the communists joining the government-in-exile to pressurise the U.S. Government into more active support of the anti-Franco cause.[36] When this failed, he forced the communists to abandon all their preconditions before agreeing to appoint just one communist minister. As Ibarruri explained to the next Party Plenum in April 1946, developments at the UN meant that the Party felt obliged to accept Giral's terms.[37] She must have felt some humiliation, however, as she reassured her audience that the Party would try to increase its number of ministers,[38] and stressed the one big gain for the communists – that henceforth resistance inside the country would be under the control of the government-in-exile, for Giral had promised that the AFD would become more active in organising resistance within the country.[39] In this way, under the new authoritative leadership of a government-in-exile which included the communists, resisters within Spain would soon find themselves being supported by 'all democratic peoples and countries,' she concluded.[40] It was ironic in the extreme, therefore, that at the very moment the PCE was being forced to eat humble pie at the April Plenum, Stalin had resolved that there was no future in the idea that the post-war coalition could resolve the Spanish question.

IV

Stalin was gradually moving from a policy of acquiescence towards his former war-time allies to one of confrontation, and the Spanish Communist Party was the first to appreciate this change. Events in Greece clearly showed the evolution of Stalin's views: at the time of the March 1946 elections he had advised the Greek communists against an election boycott and had ignored their request for help in launching a civil war; when this request was repeated in September 1946, the Soviet Communist Party welcomed it, although the final dispatch of war materials was delayed.[41] It was inevitable that the Spanish communists should detect this change of line over the summer of 1946 since both the Spanish and Greek Communist Parties dealt with the same officials in Moscow, the most important being L.S. Baranov, and both had guerrilla training bases in Yugoslavia – for Tito had committed himself to supporting guerrilla warfare in Spain even before the Second World War was over, and, unlike Stalin, had welcomed the Greek communists' approach of April 1946.

Many of those Spaniards with military service in the NKVD Special Battalion or among the Soviet partisans became the core of those returned to Spain for guerrilla action. Most followed the same route: thus Pelegrín Pérez, a veteran of the 1936 siege of Madrid as well as the NKVD Special Battalion, arrived in Spain in 1946 after travelling through Yugoslavia, Italy and Toulouse. Similarly 'Vladimiro', a veteran of action with Soviet partisans, travelled to France via Yugoslavia and Italy in the summer of 1945 and by early September 1945 was on his first underground visit to Spain.[42] At the end of February 1946 Manuel Taguena and other Spanish students at the Frunze Military Academy were sent, with other members of the Spanish battalion of the NKVD headed by Francisco Ortega, to Yugoslavia. There they were given Yugoslav army uniforms and joined a training group established in November 1944 as a direct consequence of Stalin's 'message' to the Spanish communists. Those with experience in the NKVD battalion were then marched clandestinely to Toulouse via a series of safe houses in Trieste and northern Italy, while the others stayed behind in Yugoslavia for further training in the experience of guerrilla warfare in Yugoslavia.[43]

Clear echoes of these Yugoslav connections could be seen as early as Ibarruri's speech to the April 1946 Plenum when she went out of her way to stress that Tito – 'that legendary hero who raised up his people in the struggle for independence and freedom' – had recognised Giral's government; she also made an overt analogy between what was happening in Spain and what was happening in Greece.[44] But it was not until July 1946 that it became clear to Ibarruri that this analogy with Greece was acceptable to Moscow. Determined to make her dissatisfaction with the communists' humiliating position in the government-in-exile known to Moscow, on 3 July 1946 she wrote to the controller of Radio Independent Spain in Moscow outlining her fury at what she saw as the manoeuvring of the PSOE and its British Labour Party allies in trying to discredit both the government-in-exile and the PCE. In particular she alleged that the so-called 'Colonel Padillo', broadcasting on the BBC, was none other than General Casado himself, responsible for blackening the name not only of the PCE but the Soviet Union. This letter, sent by 'special mail', was routinely read by the Department for Relations with Foreign Communist Parties and seen as important enough to be copied and forwarded by Suslov to Stalin, Molotov, Zhdanov and Beria. Suslov's proposal that *Izvestiya* should take up the campaign against the British policy towards Spain was endorsed.[45]

Unwittingly, Ibarruri's letter arrived just at the moment when Stalin was considering founding a new Communist International under Yugoslav leadership.[46] That the West had failed the 'test' on Spain was made clear in *Pravda* on 1 July 1946, when the UN

Security Council's decision simply to keep Spain 'on its agenda' was denounced in the following terms:

> Our press has long maintained that the Spanish Question in the Security Council has far outgrown its original framework and now not only touches on the fate of Spain, but the question of the UN itself. ... The English and U.S. delegates did all they could to reduce the competence of the Security Council, the UN body responsible for maintaining international peace. ... The issue is not so much about limiting the activities of the UN, but of turning this young and developing organisation into a political weapon of just one group of states.

Stalin had abandoned cooperation with the Allies for confrontation and Ibarruri was one of the first to find out.

Over the summer of 1946, the PCE moved rapidly back to its favoured policy of the 'popular front from below'. On 15 August 1946, the PCE Central Committee dropped its campaign to transform the AFD into the core of resistance activity in Spain and called instead for the creation of a Central Council of Resistance (CCR): the AFD would continue to exist, but added to it would be other resistance organisations like the officers' organisation AFARE, the guerrilla formations, the Union of Free Intellectuals, youth organisations, and Basque and Catalan organisations. Such a council would be directly subordinated to the government-in-exile, but control of all activity in Spain would be in the hands of this *Unión Nacional*-style resistance council.[47] No more overt calls for unity 'from below' could be imagined, and the parallel with war-time Yugoslavia where Tito's partisans had controlled the resistance leaving an impotent government-in-exile to languish in London was never stated but was clear to all. By autumn 1946 the PCE was prepared to say in public what it had long held to be the case: there would be no international solution to the problem of Spain, only internal struggle within Spain could break the log-jam.

Because Spain was again on the agenda of the UN, the PCE back-pedalled on this demand somewhat until January 1947, when the failure of the UN to take up the issue of confronting Franco brought down the Giral government-in-exile. When the new socialist-led government of Rudolfo Llopis was formed on 10 February 1947 it declared 'the Spanish question has entered a new phase which demands closer unity with anti-Franco elements within the country and the creation of a government on a broader base, possibly to include rightist elements'. The communists were wary of the latter, the intention to get support from countries who had not yet given it – a clear reference to the West – but the ambition to unite within one resistance organisation all the anti-fascist resistance forces and to make that organisation the representative of the government-in-exile within Spain suited them perfectly.[48]

This commitment to resistance persuaded the communists to remain in the government, but the Party did not support the government-in-exile *per se*; its true concern was to revive the campaign for a CCR. The real focus of PCE activity from January 1947 onwards was action within Spain, and in particular guerrilla struggle, and since no guerrilla units were represented in the AFD, it would have to be supplanted by the CCR.[49] So that no Party member was unaware of the true attitude towards the government-in-exile, from February 1947 both Ibarruri and Carrillo routinely described the correct policy of the Party as being one of *Unión Nacional*. Ibarruri's speech to the Party Plenum, 19 to 22 March 1947, constantly repeated the slogan *Unión Nacional* and described in detail the guerrilla struggle: Franco had launched a counter-attack over the spring and summer of 1946, but to no avail, and the movement had survived to the end of 1946 and spring of 1947 'more ready for battle and more closely linked to the peasants than before'; if in 1945 there had been 29 actions per month, in 1946 the average had been 37 and in 1947 it was already 40. These operations were now offensive not just defensive.[50] The May strikes in Bilbao were a godsend to the communists, for they appeared to support the principle claim of the Party that, despite everything Franco did, resistance was possible. More than that, the communists claimed that in taking the path of action and organising their strike the people of Bilbao had involved a local *Junta de Resistencia*, confirming this as the correct line and highlighting once again the need for a CCR, a task made more acute since Basque organisations were not represented in the AFD.[51]

From June 1947 onwards, far more often than not, reports of guerrilla actions in Spain began to appear on the front page of *Mundo Obrero*; this would be the case until February 1948. Just as the Greek Communist Party was in 1947 falling more and more under the ideological sway of the Yugoslav example, so too did the PCE. In this regard the Spanish military delegation in Yugoslavia which had arrived in February 1946 was particularly active. One of its leaders, Manuel Taguena, argued that on arriving in Yugoslavia he had been optimistic that in this new socialist country the 'errors' of the Soviet model could be avoided, while Radio Belgrade's Spanish service – headed by José Sevil, the official PCE representative in Yugoslavia –

argued consistently that Yugoslavia was the model for socialism, and communist parties should orientate themselves on the Yugoslav example. At all levels the Spanish in Yugoslavia were told the same message, follow and learn from the Yugoslav example. Thus a Yugoslav general told them in 1946: 'the people who free themselves from capitalism tomorrow will go the Yugoslav way, and not follow the October Revolution; the Yugoslav experience is closer to the conditions that will pertain in Spain, more than that, they constitute a new way to build socialism which corresponds to the new historic epoch.' Velko Vlahovic, Head of the Department for Relations with Foreign Communist Parties, made clear to them that, while for foreign policy reasons the Yugoslavs could not boast it to the world, they were the ones prepared to help them. Equally, Tito had declared in March 1946 at a reception attended by the Spanish delegation, that no partisan movement had been victorious which had not secured for itself a liberated base within the country concerned; this pronouncement had then been repeated to the delegation on numerous occasions.[52] Developing a liberated area became the partisans' most cherished ambition and the Yugoslavs were closely involved in plans to establish such a free territory in spring 1947.[53]

From July 1947 onwards, determined efforts were made to escalate the partisan war and work within the government-in-exile was abandoned. On 24 July 1947, Ibarruri criticised Llopis in a speech in Toulouse for not doing enough to construct the CCR,[54] then after the Departmental Conference of Llopis's Socialist Party had sided with Prieto at the end of July, the communist minister Uribe resigned on 6 August 1947. In July *Mundo Obrero* began a regular series of reports from the Levante guerrillas, followed by a second series which began in September and continued into October. The line was clear: having withstood government offensives in March and May 1947, the Levante guerrillas were by the autumn battling to survive the third offensive of the year, but were doing so successfully.[55] When the PCE held an assembly in Paris on 21 September 1947 to weigh up the consequences of the collapse of the Llopis government-in-exile, the key speech by Antonio Mije went out of its way to praise the shining example of Tito and denounced the AFD as 'inspired by the British Intelligence Service'.[56]

Given the PCE's close links with the Yugoslavs at this time, it was not difficult for the Party to adapt to the new Yugoslav-inspired rhetoric of the Cominform, established at the end of September 1947 – although it was disappointed at not being invited to attend the founding meeting.[57] On 23 October 1947 *Mundo Obrero* seized on the Cominform's criticism of the French and Italian Communist Parties, that they had succumbed to 'the danger of underestimating their own forces'; this, the PCE weekly stated with truth, the Spanish communists had never done. After the Cominform meeting the PCE's obsession with the Levante guerrillas became greater than ever: articles in *Mundo Obrero* in November argued that guerrilla actions were up from 67 per month in 1946 to 77 per month in 1947 and that even reactionary journals like the *Economist* had been forced to cover them; and resistance committees were springing up like mushrooms after the rain.[58] The only adjustment the Cominform required of the PCE was that it drop the call for a new government-in-exile. After talks in Moscow on 10 November 1947 between Uribe and representatives of the Bolshevik Party Central Committee,[59] talk of a new 'firm' government-in-exile began to be dropped: on 11 December 1947 *Mundo Obrero* noted that henceforth popular fronts should be developed on the Yugoslav model and in Spain that meant constructing unity around councils of resistance; on 15 January 1948 *Mundo Obrero* announced that, since the government-in-exile was clearly not going to form the CCR, the initiative must come 'from below', from inside Spain. Finally, on 3 March 1948 *Mundo Obrero* made clear that, even outside Spain, any future government-in-exile should be accountable to a popular front, the so-called National, Republican and Democratic Front.

At the start of 1948 the PCE held out the prospect of an escalation of the partisan war: guerrilla actions, it hoped, could soon be coordinated with strike action, strike action which would divert pressure from the guerrillas and enable them to regroup; the whole struggle would then enter a new higher phase.[60] It was in this context of rising expectations, alongside continuing bitter repression from Franco's security forces, that the PCE decided to turn to the Yugoslavs for a dramatic increase in military support. On 11 February 1948 Lister and Carrillo left Paris for Belgrade on a mission to ask for substantial aid in a massive expansion of guerrilla action, including air support for parachute drops to the guerrillas of Levante. In Belgrade they were received by Tito, Rankovic, Djilas and Kardelj, but arrived just at the moment when Tito's break with Stalin was imminent; the Yugoslavs feared a provocation, asked if the Russians had been consulted, and when they learned they had not, sent the Spanish delegation on a propaganda tour coming up with a string of 'technical' reasons why such help could not be forthcoming.[61]

From February 1948 the prominence given to guerrilla stories in *Mundo Obrero* rapidly declined. The Party continued to campaign for a CCR[62] and in May 1948 the Levante guerrillas duly issued an appeal for the creation of a CCR, calling all local councils of resistance, trade unions, parties, women's groups, and youth groups – the classic ingredients of the 'popular front from below' – to attend a founding meeting.[63] But this appeal was issued into a vacuum. There were scarcely any guerrilla actions in Levante to report and *Mundo Obrero* published instead a detailed series of reports from its correspondent's visit to Levante the previous year.[64] The Yugoslavs' expulsion from the Cominform in June 1948 made the situation even worse. In September 1948 *Mundo Obrero* started to serialise Lenin's 1906 pamphlet *On Guerrilla Warfare*, clearly trying to make the point that not only Tito had favoured partisan warfare;[65] but the writing was on the wall. Before the CCR could be set up, Stalin intervened to stop the partisan operations. In September 1948 Ibarruri and Carrillo met Stalin who advised ending the guerrilla struggle and suggested that, modelling themselves on Stalin's own experience of the trade unions in Tsarist Russia, the PCE should concentrate on infiltrating the workers organisations tolerated by Franco.[66]

In the international climate of 1948 Stalin was quite prepared to expand communism into the parts of Central Europe where he had a sphere of interest; thus February 1948 saw the Czechoslovak coup and the start of the final phase of the absorption of Hungary. Confronting the West's sphere of influence was another matter. When his dispute with the Yugoslavs began in February 1948 Stalin made clear that he had severe doubts as to whether the Greek Civil War could be won; at the same time he spoke warmly of Mao Tse-tung's partisans in China.[67] Checked in the West, Stalin came to believe in the last years of his life that 'imperialism' could best be countered in the East. In such a scenario Spain played no role and Stalin's commitment to Spain fell victim to the 'eastward turn' brought on by his dispute with Tito.

Left to themselves, the Spanish communists would never have abandoned the policy of *Unión Nacional*. They did so with reluctance when Stalin decided to make the question of Spain part of the 'test' the Allies needed to pass to prove that there would be no return to the diplomacy of the 1930s. When the Allies failed the 'test', the Spanish communists found they had the support of Zhdanov and Suslov and hastened to resume the policy of *Unión Nacional*, readopting it with such gusto that they threw themselves into the arms of the Yugoslavs. They were thus uniquely exposed when the Yugoslavs were expelled from the Cominform.

Notes

1. Future scholars might like to know that much of the work for this article was conducted in Moscow in April 1996. Unlike a year earlier, access to archival material was frustrated by a new government circular on reclassifying documents which meant that much relevant material was not made available. The Russian Centre for the Preservation and Study of Documents Relating to Contemporary History (RTsKhIDNI) holds in Fond 17 Opus 128 the documents of the International Department of the Bolshevik Party Central Committee. There is much information on Spain, but because many of the files (ed. khr. in Russian) contain material in which the Spanish communist leaders make libelous statements about each other and people who are still alive, these files were closed during my visit. Thus ed. khr. 798, which contains key files on the work of 'Scientific Institute 205' and 'the speeding up of personnel transfers to Spain' also contained much of Hernández's critique of the PCE and the Soviet Union and was withheld on those grounds.
2. See my 'Stalin's Wartime Vision of the Post-War World' in *Diplomacy and Statecraft* 7, no. 1, 1996: 73-96.
3. E. Lister, *Asídestruyó Carrillo el PCE*, Barcelona, 1983, p. 28.
4. For the invasion, see D.W. Pike, *Jours de gloire: Jours de Honte*, Paris, 1984, pp. 120-30; for Carrillo, see S. Carrillo, *Dialogue on Spain*, London, 1976, pp. 93-5 and F. Claudin, *Santiago Carrillo: Crónica de un Secretario General*, Barcelona, 1983, p. 79.
5. Carrillo, *Dialogue*, pp. 93-4; RTsKhIDNI f. 17, o 128, ed. khr. 41.
6. See my 'The Cominform: Tito's International?', *Historical Journal* 35, no. 3, 1992: 641-663.
7. RTsKhIDNI f. 17, o 128, ed. khr. 41, l. 11.
8. Pike, *Jours*, p. 85.
9. J. Borras, *Política de los exiliados españoles, 1944-50*, Châtillon-sous-Bagneux, 1976, p. 168; H. Heine *La oposición política al Franquismo: de 1939 a 1952*, Barcelona, 1983, p. 161.
10. RTsKhIDNI f. 17. o 128, ed. khr. 50 – see p. 26 of issue number 4 of this secret 'Bulletin on Foreign Affairs' issued to all members of the Bolshevik Party Central Committee.
11. Borras, *Exiliados españoles*, p. 172.
12. L. Woodward, *British Foreign Policy in the Second World War*, London, 1975, vol. IV, pp. 28-34; K. Hamilton, *Non-intervention Revisited: Great Britain, the UN and Franco's Spain in 1946*, London (FCO Occasional Paper), 1995, p. 48. See also the contribution of Quasim Ahmad to this present volume.
13. *Pravda*, 4 February 1945.
14. E. Lister, *Basta*, Madrid, 1978, p. 182.
15. Pike, *Jours*, p. 144.
16. Heine, *Oposición política*, p. 228.
17. V. Mastny, *Russia's Road to the Cold War*, New York, 1979, p. 293.
18. *Pravda*, 5 August 1945.
19. Heine, *Oposición política*, p. 168; *Keesings Contemporary Archives* 1943-6, p. 7419.
20. *Pravda*, 22 August 1945. See Quasim Ahmad's contribution to this present volume.
21. *Pravda*, 24 and 26 August 1945.
22. Pike, *Jours*, p. 150.

23. *Pravda*, 30 November 1945.
24. For the attitude of the United States, see FRUS 1945, vol. V, pp. 701-4; for the rallies, see *Pravda*, 13 January 1946.
25. The work of the Moscow Conference has been written about in detail by W. O. McCagg in his *Stalin Embattled, 1943-8*, Detroit, 1978. He was influenced in turn by the work of V.L. Israelyan in *Mezhdunarodnye otnosheniye i vneshnaya politika Sovetskogo Soyuza 1945-49*, ed G.A. Deborin, Moscow 1958, who used the *Pravda* editorial of 28 December as a theme for his argument that the Soviet Union was always willing to compromise, leaving the West responsible for the Cold War. McCagg's book is enormously stimulating: I have interpreted things rather differently in the detail, but have no hesitation in pointing to *Stalin Embattled* for illuminating the dramatic change in Soviet foreign policy early in 1946.
26. RTsKhIDNI f. 17, o 3, 29 December 1945. Unfortunately, the detail surrounding the decision is kept in a 'special folder'; all such 'special folders' – the majority of which relate to matters relation to security and the judiciary (i.e. executions) – were being reclassified in April 1996.
27. *Pravda*, 19 January 1946.
28. FRUS 1946, vol. VI, pp. 696-709. See also Boris Liedtke's contribution to this present volume.
29. *Pravda*, 10 February 1946. I interpret this speech rather differently from McCagg, see *Stalin Embattled*, p. 217.
30. *Pravda*, 8 February 1946.
31. FRUS 1946, vol. V, p. 1033.
32. *Pravda*, 9 March 1946.
33. RTsKhIDNI f. 17, o 3, 13 April 1946.
34. *Pravda*, 20 April 1946.
35. RTsKhIDNI f. 17, o 128, ed. khr. 965, l. 106.
36. FRUS 1945, vol. V, p. 703.
37. The long negotiations to enable the communists to join the government-in-exile are summarised in some detail in RTsKhIDNI f. 17, o 128 ed. khr. 965, ll. 8-20; what is clear, though rarely stated, is that the communists constantly had to back down on their demand that, rather than enlarging his existing government, a completely new government should be formed. Ibarruri's speech to the April Plenum is in RTsKhIDNI f 17, o 128, ed khr. 965, ll. 106-142; for the acceptance of Giral's terms, see l. 112.
38. Ibid., l. 112.
39. Ibid., l. 17.
40. Ibid., l. 120.
41. A. Ulunyan, *Kommunisticheskaya Partiya Gretsii*, Moscow, 1994, vol. III, pp. 177-9; P.Stavrakis, *Moscow and Greek Communism, 1944-49*, Ithaca, 1989, p. 144.
42. E. Pons Prades, *Guerrillas españolas, 1936-1960*, Barcelona, 1977, pp. 25 and 145.
43. M. Taguena, *Testimonio de dos guerras*, Mexico City, 1973, pp. 512-55.
44. RTsKhIDNI f. 17, o 128, ed. khr. 965, l. 120; it is interesting that when preparing this text for publication, the Soviet editor put a line through all references to Tito.
45. The letter is in RTsKhIDNI f. 17, o 128, ed. khr. 163, ll. 9-11; Suslov's response is in ed. khr. 965, l. 173.

46. V. Dedijer, *Novi prilozi za biografiju Josipa Broza Tita*, Belgrade, 1984, vol. III, p. 271.

47. *Mundo Obrero*, 11 July 1946, and elaborated more fully 22 May 1947.

48. RTsKhIDNI f. 17, o 128, ed. khr. 110, l. 20, l. 188.

49. *Mundo Obrero*, 6 February 1947.

50. RTsKhIDNI f. 17, o 128, ed. khr. 1100, l. 148.

51. *Mundo Obrero*, 15 and 22 May 1947.

52. For Taguena and the role of Sevil, see Taguena, *Testimonio*, pp. 512 and 524; the other information in this paragraph comes from the tendentious report to Moscow on the delegation's activities after it had been withdrawn from Yugoslavia in summer 1948, see RTsKhIDNI f. 17, o 128, ed. khr. 494, ll. 6, 8, 30, 31.

53. Pike, *Jours*, p. 141, citing E. Comin Colomer, *La Republica en exilio*, Barcelona, 1957, pp. 412-13.

54. *Mundo Obrero*, 24 July 1947.

55. Ibid., 18 September 1947.

56. Ibid., 25 September 1947.

57. RTsKhIDNI f. 17, o 128, ed. khr. 1100, l. 284.

58. *Mundo Obrero*, 6, 13 and 27 November 1947.

59. Uribe, accompanied by Fernando Claudin, arrived in Moscow on 9 November on a visit the primary purpose of which was the situation among the Spanish emigration in the Soviet Union. Since, however, they were criticised for not taking on board the decisions of the Cominform meeting, it is clear that broader issues were discussed. See RTsKhIDNI f. 17, o 128, ed. khr. 1100, l. 287.

60. *Mundo Obrero*, 15 January 1948.

61. Carrillo, *Dialogue*, p. 96; Lister, *Asi*, p. 53.

62. See, for example, *Mundo Obrero*, 26 February and 7 March 1948.

63. Ibid., 27 May 1948.

64. These appeared in the paper regularly from May until the middle of August 1948.

65. Ibid., 9 and 16 September 1948.

66. Carrillo, *Dialogue*, p. 98; Lister, *Asi*, p. 54.

67. M. Djilas, *Conversations with Stalin*, Harmondsworth, 1969, pp. 140-1.

13

Compromising with the Dictatorship

U.S.-Spanish Relations in the Late 1940s and Early 1950s

Boris N. Liedtke (Singapore)

THE political and diplomatic relations between the United States and Spain during the Cold War provide a gripping story, in particular because of the implications the relationship entailed for both countries: in the case of the U.S. for the development of its Cold War policy, in the case of Spain for the survival of the Franco dictatorship. This article provides an analysis of this important relationship focusing in particular on the changing attitudes of U.S. policy-makers in Washington. In the aftermath of the Second World War, the U.S. position towards the Franco dictatorship was hostile. This account shows the slow abandonment of this hostility and the eventual adoption of a more cynical approach by the Republican administration under President Dwight D. Eisenhower. In chronological terms, the analysis takes us from the end of the Second World War up to the signing in 1953 of the military and economic agreements between the United States and Spain which marked the welcoming of Franco's regime into the international community.

Ever since 1953, large sections of the Spanish political establishment and the left-wing opposition have argued that Franco bought these agreements at the cost of national sovereignty. In return, the

Spanish dictator ensured the survival of his regime by eliminating possible foreign support for democratic forces and by obtaining sufficient economic aid to keep the Spanish economy afloat. On the other side of the Atlantic, the Eisenhower administration was criticised for compromising its democratic values by entering into a superfluous agreement with a fascist dictator.[1]

Arguably, global changes in technology, warfare and the geopolitical balance meant that Washington not only had to rise to its global responsibilities, but had to abandon its previously idealistic approach to world affairs. In this respect, the U.S. compromise with the Franco dictatorship was the first in a series of realpolitical decisions which defined U.S. cold war policy for decades. Similar to compromising its moral values by entering agreements with Franco, the U.S. would be willing to make policy decisions that assured victory against the Soviet Union though sometimes ran counter to democratic values. In the context of Cold War History, the American change of policy towards the Franco dictatorship deserves close scrutiny.

With the liberation of Europe by the Allies the nightmare of fascist dictatorships appeared to be over. Yet, most of the Iberian peninsula was still dominated by a totalitarian regime of General Franco. Spain's past provided diplomats and politicians with enough material to justify either isolation from or integration into the Western defence structure. Consequently, two contradictory versions of Spain's recent history were formulated. Those favouring isolation of the Franco regime saw it as another fascist system, created through the help of the Axis and totalitarian in its form. On the other hand, those favouring integration of Spain into the Western structure tried to prove that Franco's association with Hitler was not what it seemed, but had, in fact, constituted a diplomatic success for the Spanish dictator. Francoist mythmakers claimed that the Spanish Caudillo had never been willing to help Hitler in his struggle against the Allies, alleging that the military and economic support which Hitler received from Franco had been wrung out of him. In exchange the Spanish dictator was able to guarantee Spain's neutrality.[2] The meeting at Hendaye in October 1940 between the two dictators had been disappointing for both, but Francoists projected it as a clever success for the Spanish dictator. Franco himself promoted this argument wholeheartedly; after all, his position would have improved considerably if his country had been welcomed by the international community.[3]

However, during the last days of the war, President Franklin D. Roosevelt made his antipathy towards the Spanish regime known.

Liberals across Western Europe and the U.S. had good reasons to expect that following the defeat of the fascist powers in Italy and Germany, General Francisco Franco would meet a similar fate. Initially, the Roosevelt and later the Truman administration seemed eager to demonstrate their disapproval of the political structure of the Spanish regime as well as its cordial relations with Nazi Germany. In various press conferences, President Harry S. Truman reiterated his dislike of Franco. He publicly acknowledged that Spain's government had been founded with the help of Nazi Germany and Fascist Italy during one of the bloodiest civil wars of this century.[4] As a result, it came as no surprise that the three major Western powers, France, Britain and the USA condemned Spain in a tripartite statement issued in early 1946. Nor was it surprising that the Mediterranean country was excluded from the UN. After some discussions in the UN, which were initiated and strongly supported by communist countries, UNGA recommended to all nations the immediate withdrawal of their ambassadors from Spain.[5] From then onwards and during the following four years most countries only maintained limited diplomatic relations with Spain.[6]

As the international community in general and Truman in particular publicly voiced their opposition to Franco, military planners in the U.S. armed services identified Spain as a useful ally. Her strategic geographic position at the south-western tip of the European continent, guarding the entrance to the Mediterranean, as well as the Pyrenees, a natural protection against an invading army from the north, made her a valuable partner in a potential European conflict. Spain's geopolitical importance was further enhanced by the country's wealth of raw materials and her relatively large standing army. From a military point of view, Spain had too many assets to be ignored, and to be left isolated, let alone alienated. As a result, a number of military studies restated the strategic importance of Spain and encouraged successive administrations to enter into close relations with Franco's regime.[7] However, during the years immediately after the Second World War, little attention was being paid to these military interests. Only as relations with the Soviet Union deteriorated did these gain importance.

At the Yalta conference in February 1945, it became already obvious that the Atlantic Charter was representative of Western war aims only. The Soviet Union was pursuing other goals. Despite several attempts by Western diplomats and politicians to find a compromise, the trend towards a permanently divided Europe became unavoidable. Churchill's famous speech at Fulton, Missouri,[8]

George Kennan's 'long telegram' from Moscow[9] and the chilly atmosphere throughout the Paris Conference of 1946, were clear indications that the two superpowers were pursuing different aims, which appeared impossible to reconcile.

Throughout the year 1947, the situation in Europe deteriorated considerably. On top of the economic hardship and the increasing dollar gap experienced by nearly all European states, the Soviet Union moved from the defensive creation of satellite states to an aggressive challenge of countries outside central Europe. When Britain announced that it could no longer support the Greek government and had to withdraw its occupying forces, alarm bells went off in Washington. The crisis culminated in Truman's message to Congress on 12 March 1947.[10] The division of the world into a bipolar order could no longer be denied and Truman outlined his doctrine in a vague and indeterminate commitment to the free part of the world. The same year this commitment was expanded into the Marshall Plan to save Europe from economic and political disaster. As far as Spain was concerned, the consequence was clear. If the country was to receive any aid, Franco either had to go or make far-reaching changes to his regime.

At the same time, neither the U.S. nor the British government saw any viable alternative to Franco. The monarchists had been divided by the Law of Succession, transforming Spain into a monarchy without a monarch. The Republican government-in-exile was divided internally over a number of issues, including its relation towards the far left. Most important of all, however, was the unwillingness of London and Washington to risk instability in Spain out of fear that this might lead to an increase of communist activities in France and Italy.[11]

In the meantime, the Joint Chiefs of Staff decided that it was time to change U.S. foreign policy towards Spain and to initiate cordial military relations with Franco. Nowhere else was this more apparent than in 'Drumbeat', a study concluded in August 1947. Even though it was not the first of its nature, it constituted the clearest indication of military interests in Spain. The study concluded that, from a military point of view, the United States should furnish economic aid to Spain as soon as feasible.[12] Shortly afterwards, and based on military recommendations, the Policy Planning Staff, headed by George Kennan, decided that it was in the national interest to modify U.S. policy towards Spain.[13]

Before the end of the year, the National Security Council, headed by President Truman and consisting of representatives from the

Defense and State Department, acted on Kennan's recommendation.[14] The past approach to isolate Franco was not only abandoned but severely criticised. Washington gave instructions to work towards a normalisation of U.S.-Spanish relations, both political and economic. As a direct result, the United States relaxed restrictive measures on commerce, eliminated tariffs on a variety of exports and generally encouraged private trade with and financial assistance for Spain. At the same time, U.S. delegates at the UN were instructed to oppose any further measures which could adversely affect Spain. Officially, the change of policy was justified by arguing that ostracising Spain had failed to weaken Franco's regime. With hindsight, however, and in view of the context of the military studies, it must be concluded that the real motives had more to do with the deteriorating relationship with the Soviet Union.

The years 1948 and 1949 confirmed that a bipolar balance of power had become reality. Czechoslovakia, one of the most advanced industrial states in Eastern Europe, fell to a communist coup. The Soviet delegates decided to walk out of the Allied Control Council, the body officially charged with governing Germany, causing that country to remain divided for over forty years. Even more shocking for Washington was the success of the communist revolution in China. In the same year U.S. military strategists detected to their horror that the Soviet Union had successfully detonated an atomic bomb, breaking America's monopoly on nuclear arms.

Throughout this period, Spain relentlessly tried to exploit the deteriorating relations between the two superpowers by lobbying for military and economic assistance and against the UN resolution. Essential for these efforts was the appointment of José Félix Lequerica as inspector of the Spanish embassy in Washington. Under his guidance a Spanish lobby was formed in Congress which was supported by catholics, commercially oriented Representatives, warmongers, anti-communists, and those who simply wanted to exploit the issue for political reasons.[15] The influence of this lobby on U.S. relations with Spain should not be underestimated. Again and again it brought up the Spanish issue in the U.S. Congress and on several occasions it came close to forcing the U.S. Administration to allocate funds to Spain against the wishes of the White House.[16] In the end, though, it was only in the context of an overall change of policy towards the Soviet Union that the Truman Administration considered a revision of its attitude towards the Franco dictatorship.

During the first half of 1950, a series of discussions were conducted at the highest level in Washington concerning relations with

Spain. As these went on, a consensus emerged that the necessary steps should be taken to assure the full cooperation of the Spanish regime in case of war with the Soviet Union.[17] On the one hand, it was feared that during a conflict in Europe, Franco might decide to remain neutral; on the other that the price he would demand for his participation would be too high. Throughout these discussions, the necessity to invest in Spain's infrastructure was highlighted. If the U.S. military wanted to make use of installations in Spain, these had to be improved urgently. New roads, airfields, port facilities and pipelines had to be constructed. A joke in Congress made fun of Spain's best defence being her appalling infrastructure which was bound to slow down any advancing army. As a result of the urgency to make use of Spain's resources, relations with Madrid had to be improved. While it was acknowledged that possible objections by France and Britain could not be ignored, every effort was to be made to overcome these and to help Spain improve her relations with other European countries.[18]

With the outbreak of the Korean War in 1950, the necessity to exploit Spain's military potential became even more pressing. For the first time since the end of the Spanish Civil War, the U.S. Export and Import Bank earmarked specific funds for projects in Spain. The UN decided to withdraw its recommendation made in 1946 and Britain and the USA promptly appointed ambassadors to Madrid. At the same time discussions were initiated by the Department of Defense on a further revision of relations with Spain. Over the following twelve months, the State Department and the Pentagon engaged in talks over the Spanish question. The latter saw no point in further delaying military agreements. The State Department, on the other hand, was concerned about the possible negative repercussions this might have on relations with other allies in Europe. Above all, France felt that any U.S.-Spanish military agreement would prove that U.S. troops planned to withdraw from central Europe in case of an attack by the Soviet Union. The USA had to make it clear that a defence of Europe was not only possible, but was also strategically desirable. The remilitarisation of Germany supported America's commitment and ability to defend NATO against a Soviet invasion.[19]

As these diplomatic concerns were discussed, the National Security Council finally issued another policy paper, in June 1951, on relations towards Spain.[20] The changes were dramatic. Diplomatic and political considerations were no longer to hinder the development of Spain's military potential. While it was recognised that it would be advantageous to integrate Spain into NATO, opposition by France and Britain to direct U.S. military agreements with Spain were bluntly ignored. The previously idealistic approach by the USA towards foreign affairs was abandoned for a classical policy of *Realpolitik*. Despite Franco's dictatorship and the repression of fundamental liberties under his regime, Washington did not even attempt to explain or justify its new approach in words other than those previously used by European statesmen of the nineteenth century. Political or military concerns by other NATO countries were insufficient to delay military negotiations.

In a press conference, Truman stated that his disapproval of Spain's human rights record should not override the conviction of U.S. military planners.[21] Without delay, the President authorised a mission by Admiral Forrest Sherman, the Chief of Naval Operations, to hold preliminary talks with General Franco and high-level Spanish officers in Madrid. These talks went extremely well and the press speculated that agreements could be signed within months.[22] Above all Sherman established cordial relations with Franco and General Juan Vigón Sueirodiaz. However, shortly after leaving Madrid, Admiral Sherman suffered a heart attack and died. Even though this delayed the talks somewhat, the U.S. was able to send two study teams in order to establish the requirements of the Spanish economy and to decide which locations were the most appropriate for U.S. military installations.

The economic mission under Dr Sidney Sufrin, an academic at Syracuse University, was a disaster. Sufrin failed to free his team from the influence of INI. The Spanish bureaucrats followed him everywhere, making it impossible to gather independent economic material. As a result Sufrin had to rely heavily on studies previously compiled by the State Department. At the same time, he handled the complicated situation clumsily, causing several conflicts between his team and the U.S. embassy.[23]

The military mission on the other hand was more successful. It was clearly established that the Pyrenees provided a useful natural defence against an invading Red Army, allowing the U.S. to maintain a foothold on the continent from which to liberate Europe. While it was already accepted that the Iberian peninsula was extremely useful for air force and naval bases, the exact location of these had not been established. The military mission under Air Force General James Spry had received instructions to survey existing facilities which might meet U.S. requirements. After inspecting a series of sites, the group decided that it was more beneficial to construct new facilities at strategic locations rather than compromise by expanding existing airfields and ports. Given the appalling infrastructure of Spain at the time and the enormous supply requirements of a modern airforce, it became clear that the sites were determined above all by logistical considerations. As a result, a large number of bases were located near the coast or communication hubs. Unfortunately this meant that in many cases they were situated near major Spanish cities. Naturally, these bases were strategic bombing targets for an enemy airforce and their proximity to population centres endangered civilian life. While the study group acknowledged this, the issue was not considered important enough to use facilities elsewhere.[24]

Once the two reports had been received in Washington, they were analysed by a number of governmental agencies and shortly afterwards two negotiation teams were sent to Spain to meet with their counterparts. The more important one was a military team under General Kissner who had previously been involved in the base negotiations with Portugal. The economic mission, headed by Mr Train, included a number of officials from the State Department. The Spanish military team was headed by General Juan Vigón while the economic team reported to the Spanish Minister of Commerce Manuel Arburúa de la Miyar.

Over the following eighteen months, the two sides were engaged in negotiations. The development of these can be divided into three phases. During the initial phase, from April to December 1952, the two sides familiarised themselves with each other's demands. The U.S. team wanted to obtain several airforce bases in Spain, notably at Torrejón, near Madrid, in the southern area of Cadiz-Seville-Malaga, and near Zaragossa, as well as a naval base at Rota, near Cadiz. The airforce bases were strategically situated to support an attack on the Soviet Union while remaining outside the reach of the Red Army. The naval base was to become the headquarters of the Sixth Fleet, operating in the Mediterranean and of enormous strategic importance. In return the USA was willing to grant military and economic aid.[25] Generally speaking, Spain was willing to grant these bases but wanted to be assured that, in case of war, sufficient forces together with the necessary equipment were under Spanish command to guarantee the defence of the country against an invading force. This inferred that the United States had to rebuild the Spanish armed forces into a modern army – a task which would have put considerable strain on U.S. military stockpiles. Alternatively, the USA could guarantee Spain's defence by way of a treaty similar to the commitment given to NATO. As it turned out, the U.S. Administration decided to do the latter. By the end of 1952, it appeared that the two sides would come to an agreement. Then almost out of the blue, Franco decided to withdraw all concessions made by the Spanish negotiators.

In a note, the Spanish dictator inextricably linked the utilisation of military facilities on Spanish soil with sufficient military equipment for Spain's armed forces to guarantee an independent national defence. This concept became known as 'parallel development' of the military facilities and Spain's national defence capabilities. At the same time it was made clear that under no circumstances was Spain willing to allow the U.S. to use military bases without prior consultation. During the second phase of the negotiations, from December 1952 to June of the following year, the two sides engaged in diplomatic bluff and counterbluff. Neither of the two was willing to give in to demands made by the other and several times the talks were on the brink of breaking up.[26]

In the final phase of the negotiations, the two sides decided to find an acceptable compromise. Spain's demand of a 'parallel development' was partly fulfilled by a U.S. guarantee to defend Spain against an attack by any foreign power. Even though such a commitment theoretically required approval by Congress, Truman and his legal advisers considered that the permanent stationing of troops in Spain was sufficient to guarantee a defence of the bases, of the infrastructure necessary to maintain them and, implicitly, of Spain itself.[27] On the other issue, it was decided that prior consultation would take place in all circumstances apart from a Soviet sneak attack on Europe. Under such circumstances the facilities could be used immediately and Spain merely had to be informed. It is highly questionable whether Spain had the choice of remaining neutral in such a conflict even without the agreements. In order to avoid domestic criticism against the Franco dictatorship, the U.S. Government was willing to sign a secret agreement which guaranteed it this right. This was in the interest of the Spanish regime which thus hoped to maintain the perception of full sovereign control over its foreign policy.

These compromises were sufficient for the Spanish regime to go ahead with the agreements. On 26 September 1953 the two sides signed three official and one secret agreement. In return for granting facilities, Spain obtained military aid worth around $600 million (U.S.) and economic aid of almost $500 million (U.S.). However, the actual figures are less important than the fact that through these agreements Spain was welcomed back to the international community. Before the end of the year, France, Germany, Italy and Great Britain had resumed military cooperation with Spain. At the same time financial institutions felt comfortable enough to grant credits to Spain's industry. Over the next ten years more than $1 billion (U.S.) worth of credits were approved by private credit institutions in the USA alone. In addition, $500 million (U.S.) came from the U.S. Export and Import Bank. To a considerable extent, these credits together with growing commercial activities and foreign investments help to explain the economic growth Spain experienced during the following years.[28]

Clearly, the Franco regime benefited both economically and politically from these agreements, thus helping the dictatorship to remain in power for another twenty-two years. At the same time, however, it was one of the first steps of the dictatorship towards loosening its grip on power and thus marked the end of the period of the 'first Francoism'.

For the United States it was the first of a series of far-reaching compromises justified by the necessities of the Cold War. Despite these agreements and the establishment of the military bases during the late 1950s, the U.S. maintained a respectful distance in relations with Spain until the death of Franco. Even though all Republican Presidents from 1953 to 1975 visited Madrid and even John F. Kennedy and Lyndon B. Johnson paid lip-service to Franco, it was only during and after the transition to democracy in Spain that close and friendly relations were established between the two countries.

Notes

1. *New York Times*, 27 September 1953; *New Republic*, 27 September 1953.
2. Spanish Embassy Washington, *Report on Spain*, Washington, 1946, p. 1.
3. *La Vanguardia Española*, 2 October 1943.
4. PPUS (Harry S. Truman 1945), Washington, 1961, doc.107.
5. See also Quasim Ahmad's contribution to this present volume. A.J. Lleonart y Anselem, 'España y la ONU: La cuestión Española 1945-1950', *Revista de Política Internacional* 152, 1977: 310-89.
6. See José Luis Neila's contribution to this present volume.
7. S.T. Ross and D.A. Rosenberg (eds), *American Plans for War against the Soviet Union 1945-1950*, New York, 1990, vol. 5 (1947), pp. 7, 27 and 76-7, 'Drumbeat', 'Mediterranean', 'Broiler'; ibid., vol. 7 (1948), 'Crankshaft'.
8. Winston S. Churchill, 'The Sinews of Peace', 5 March 1946, in *Winston S. Churchill: His Complete Speeches 1897-1963*, ed. J.R. Rodes, New York, 1974, pp. 7285ff.

9. George Kennan, 'Long Telegram', 22 February 1946, in FRUS 1946, Washington, 1969, vol. VI, p. 687.

10. PPUS (Harry S. Truman 1947), Washington, 1963, p. 178.

11. NA, Military Branch, CCS 092, Spain (4-19-46), sec. 1-8, 15 March 1946, *Possible Developments*, JIC memo 242.

12. Ross and Rosenberg (eds), *American Plans*, vol. 5 (1947), pp. 3-39.

13. NA, Military Branch, CCS 092, Spain (4-19-46), sec. 1-8, 24 October 1947, PPS/12, U.S. policy toward Spain. See also Quasim Ahmad's contribution to this present volume.

14. NA, Civil Branch, NSC 3, U.S. policy toward Spain, 5 December 1947.

15. Theodore J. Lowi, 'Bases in Spain', in *American Civil – Military Decisions; A Book of Case Studies*, ed. Harold Stein, Birmingham, Ala, 1963, pp. 679ff.

16. Foreign Assistance Act of 1948, House, Senate, Joint Congressional Conference Committee, 1948.

17. NA, Civil Branch, NSC 72, secretary of state, 8 June 1950.

18. Ibid.

19. NA, Military Branch, U.S. JCS, CCS 092, Spain (4-19-46), Sec. 1-8, memo, 13 December 1950.

20. NA, Civil Branch, NSC 72/6, revision by senior NSC staff of NSC 72/5, 27 June 1951.

21. PPUS (Harry S. Truman 1951), Washington, 1963, 19 July 1951.

22. *New York Times*, 18 and 19 July 1951.

23. NA, Civil Branch, 59D108, Sufrin diary, part 6, 25 October 1951.

24. NA, Military Branch, CCS 092, Spain (4-19-46), sec. 1-8, 31 October 1951, report by the JMST (Spain); NA, Civil Branch, 64D563, U.S. embassy (Madrid) to Department of State, 2 November 1951.

25. NA, Military Branch, CD 091.3, Spain 1952, terms of reference for the Joint U.S. Military Group (Spain), 22 March 1952.

26. FRUS 1952-1954, vol. VI, Washington, 1988, 1923, Chargé Jones to Department of State, 27 March 1953.

27. FRUS 1952-1954, vol. VI, Washington, 1988, 1959, memo secretary of state to Bonbright, 25 September 1953.

28. Stanford Research Institute, *Las inversiones norteamericanas en España*, Barcelona, 1972.

14

The Foreign Policy Administration of Franco's Spain

From Isolation to International Realignment (1945-1957)

José Luis Neila Hernández

(Universidad Autónoma, Madrid)

ALTHOUGH Spain's foreign policy administration has been increasingly recognised as an essential factor in any examination of the decision-making process in the country's foreign policy, it remains nonetheless a little studied subject. Yet, its study is indispensable for a proper understanding of Spain's foreign policy throughout the last two centuries.[1]

Monographic studies have approached this subject from various viewpoints: some are of an interdisciplinary nature, for instance the results of the first study conferences on the Foreign State Service held in 1985 in the Diplomatic School;[2] other studies have a diplomatic slant;[3] others again provide a jurisprudential standpoint;[4] while, finally, studies, such as those of Carlos Fernández Espeso and José Martínez Cardós on the first State Secretariat and the State Ministry, adopt a legal-historical perspective.[5] A general, purely historical study of Spain's foreign policy administration, however, has not yet been attempted. Up to now research has focused on specific aspects of Spain's foreign policy administration such as the administration of foreign economic policy,[6] the foreign such as the administration of foreign economic policy,[6] the foreign policy administration during the political transition,[7] the diplomatic service,[8] and the Diplomatic School.[9] In addition, the subject has also been analysed, in varying degrees, as a complementary aspect to general studies on Spain's foreign policy.[10] In recent research on more specific aspects of the latter, greater importance has also been given to foreign policy administration.[11]

Before turning our attention to the matter in hand, the study of Franco's Spain foreign policy administration during the years of ostracism and subsequent international realignment, the object of analysis needs to be defined first. If we apply Manuel Espadas Burgos's definition of foreign policy as a 'set of lines of action of one State in its relations with other States or with other international institutions',[12] the State appears as the main actor in foreign policy. It therefore follows that the State's international position and its own nature and resources will determine its foreign policy. In drawing up and carrying out this policy the foreign policy administration plays a central role as an integral part of the state administration, in terms of running public affairs within the context of foreign interactions. Its field of action is therefore a complex and singular one within the whole Administration. Such a conclusion may be drawn from the words of Aurelio Guaita:

> As for its material content, its prime concern (diplomacy) aside, foreign policy administration also includes cultural, economic, legal and charitable ends among its objectives, i.e., all the goals of the domestic administration, from which it differs not in content (fundamentally the same), but rather in legal-territorial factors (international).[13]

In studying the foreign policy and foreign administration of Franco's Spain, from the setting up of the new international postwar order until the start of Spain's partial incorporation into it, two different contexts must be considered: first the international system and the ever-changing position of Franco's Spain within it; and secondly the domestic system, since the political-institutional nature of the Franco regime will be an essential determining factor of the principles, objectives and means of Spanish foreign policy.

International and Domestic Factors in the Study of the Foreign Policy Administration of the Franco Regime in the 1940s and 1950s

Both contexts have been considered in the ongoing debate over whether or not a true foreign policy did in fact exist. From among the many opinions expressed, those of A. Viñas and J.M. Armero deserve to be highlighted. According to the former 'the Franco regime carried out an international policy strictly tailored to its needs,' and steeped in pragmatism to win 'from international relations important concessions of legitimisation for the regime'.[14] The latter defined Franco's foreign policy as a 'drawn-out game of adaptations to changes in the worldwide political arena, with the purpose of hanging onto power'.[15] This short-sighted foreign policy, aimed at the regime's political survival, determined the development of the foreign policy administration itself.

Spain's foreign policy during the Second World War, swinging from neutrality to nonbelligerency, placed Spain on the sidelines of the new, post-war international order. In the eyes of the victors and of exiled Spaniards, Franco's Spain was a vestige of fascism. The support given to Franco by Hitler and Mussolini during the Spanish Civil War and the progressively more fascist character of the regime and its foreign policy during much of the World War compromised its position *vis-à-vis* the creation of a new international order. The short-term result was the isolation of Spain from the new international system. 'The Spanish question' was a problem brought up at the Potsdam conference, and it would later be dealt with by the UNGA, culminating in Resolution 39 (I) of December 1946, according to which Spain was to be excluded from all international organisations and conferences linked to the UN, and all accredited ambassadors in Madrid were to be withdrawn.[16] By the end of 1946 only Argentina, Portugal, the Dominican Republic and the Holy See still maintained ambassadors in Madrid. Nonetheless, international pressure was not telling enough to jeopardise the survival of the regime owing to internal divisions among the exiled Spanish opposition and the divergent attitudes among the victorious allies.[17]

At any rate, being ostracised by the international community geared Spain's foreign policy towards the ultimate goal of survival. And it was precisely towards international acceptance that all the efforts of a pragmatic and opportunist foreign policy were directed. At the same time, this acted as a smoke-screen strategy to conceal the regime's real political and ideological nature, which at no time ceased to be basically authoritarian.

As part of its strategy of winning acceptance from the international community, Franco's regime, in the opinion of Antonio Moreno, took steps to avoid 'being, in the first place, essentially challenged abroad. Secondly, it trod the difficult tight rope of aligning itself socially and economically with the West without adopting their ideological and political forms.'[18] Essential factors in this process were the changes which occurred in the aftermath of the war, specifically the dichotomised world that arose from the Cold War. The regime took advantage of these circumstances to realign itself with the West, making much of its anti-communism and strategic geographical position. At the same time, the lack of official relations with the Western powers was offset by a policy of seeking foreign relations with Latin American and Arab countries, and Portugal. In these, the regime emphasised cultural activities in view of its limitations in the political and economic field.

This partial readmission into the international system widened Spain's foreign policy agenda, not only because of the exigencies arising from bilateral relations but also because of the problems and challenges posed by multilateral diplomacy. This process of international readmission began to take shape in the early fifties. Normalisation of bilateral relations picked up speed after UNGA, in the session of 4 November 1950, approved the possibility of the return of ambassadors and the entry of Spain into international organisations. Between 1950 and 1953 Spain normalised diplomatic relations with countries in Western Europe, the United States and Canada.[19] A qualitative leap in this process occurred in 1953 with the signing of a Concordat with the Holy See (on 27 August) and the Hispanic-American agreements of 26 September. On a multilateral level normalisation got off the ground with Spain's admission to the FAO on 10 November 1950, to UNESCO two years later, to the UN on 15 December 1955, and to the IMF and the World Bank in 1958. But Franco's Spain never achieved full international acceptance nor complete realignment with the West, as a result of the intrinsic contradiction of striving to join a bloc whose values it did not completely share. From this point of view the survival of the regime led to profound contradictions in its international position and within Spanish society itself.

The ideological-political nature of the regime and its institutional structure, as well as its development, had a marked influence on its foreign policy. Throughout the Civil War the rebels had to improvise power structures as the struggle progressed. Once victory was within their grasp, a process of 'normalising' the legal framework was begun. The institutional pillars of the new State were also established. The new political-institutional set-up embodied the political and ideological values and views of the conservative-reactionary coalition while simultaneously bolstering the legitimised hegemony of the military victory.[20] In the early post-Civil War period the regime became steadily more fascist, stimulated by the euphoria of the military triumph, the dynamism of the FET and the JONS and the unstoppable advance of the Axis troops in the first years of the Second World War.[21]

The privileged position of the Falange, which never achieved hegemony owing to Franco's policy of balancing out the various factions of the conservative coalition, underwent some changes as the fortunes of war began to tilt towards the Allies. The regime began a cosmetic operation to make itself more acceptable to the eventual victors. This process, signified by the return to neutrality in October 1943 and the withdrawal of the Blue Division, intensified throughout 1945 with the promulgation of the *Fuero de los Españoles* (Spaniards' Charter of Rights) of 13 July, the *Ley de Referendum Nacional* (National Referendum Act) and the *Ley de Sucesión en la Jefatura del Estado* (Law of Succession to the State Leadership) of 26 July 1947.

National catholicism became the new standard bearer of the chameleonic strategy of the regime. Its authoritarian essence was not altered while the balance struck by Franco between the factions of the conservative coalition was maintained. At this juncture Franco acted with consummate caution, allowing only unavoidable changes to neutralise his monarchist opposition at home and play for time with his enemies abroad. To that end he chose to resist international ostracism until such time as the natural antagonism between the communist and capitalist blocs finally came to a head.[22]

In the political-institutional structure, both at the time when the regime was becoming more fascist and in the subsequent reversal of this process, General Franco was always the cornerstone of the system. During the dictatorship, 'foreign policy was essentially a governmental undertaking defined, drawn up and put into practice within the State apparatus'.[23] Thus, Franco himself played a large part in running this policy. Under his personal supervision as Head of State the main lines of Spain's foreign policy were drawn up and put into practice. In the words of Juan Carlos Jiménez:

> [this] authoritarian, personalized [structure] conferred a special importance on the Head of State as definer of foreign policy, since there is no

doubt that the essential elements of his thought and his very way of exercising the functions of government had a very profound effect on the foreign policy carried out.[24]

This key role lasted throughout the regime though it tended to diminish somewhat from 1953 onwards as he left daily government affairs in the hands of others.[25] This decline became even more marked as the health of the dictator deteriorated, and the running of foreign affairs became ever more complex.

So much is true. But not even in an authoritarian regime can the study of foreign policy be focused exclusively on the part played by the dictator; rather must it take in the State as a whole. Likewise, in the study of the decision-making process, the State must be considered not as an abstract, single and rational body in defence of national interests, but rather as the result of interactions between organisations and a wide range of political and social agents. From this viewpoint, states Viñas, the model of a bureaucratic policy 'introduces a wide range of agents with varying opinions and different views on the line to be taken in any given circumstances or on how to solve a specific problem. [These agents] compete between themselves to try and swing governmental actions and decisions their way.'[26]

Governmental action, he goes on, is the 'product of an internal, complex and silent political game, obeying written and unwritten rules and carried out within the bureaucracy and the highest levels of political management'. In the opinion of Marlis G. Steinert, it is essential to understand the legal and institutional structures in order to be able to identify the part played by bureaucrats, experts and pressure groups. The cohesion of the decision-making team should also be taken into account, taking as points of departure their values and common images, which may have an influence on the decision-making process.[27] Yet, Steinert's judgement holds true only in a context of political and administrative stability and continuity, and of a defined constitutional set up. Strictly speaking, the bureaucratic model of foreign policy is applicable only in a democratic system, such as in Western Europe, wherein 'a diminution of the presidential role is assumed and also a reassessment of the governmental apparatus charged with the drawing-up and execution of foreign policy',[28] and where control mechanisms, public opinion and pressure groups play an important part in its development.

Any study of the bureaucracy and development of the foreign policy of Franco's Spain will therefore have to be undertaken with the authoritarian essence of the State in mind. Starting from the consideration that the State, in 'trying to conserve or reestablish the social order, is in fact perpetuating the specific domination structure of the country, by institutionalizing the hegemony of the ruling classes',[29] the State of Franco's regime must then be understood as the structure of domination established by the conservative coalition that triumphed in the Civil War.

General Franco, it should not be forgotten, stood at the very pinnacle of the political system and played a crucial role in the decision-making process. The survival of the regime was due in part to the willingness of the dictator to bring together very diverse conflicting interests. As a result Franco's governments were usually coalitions, reflecting the balance between the different forces making up the limited pluralism of the regime. Franco granted a certain freedom of action to government members in their respective areas, always reserving for himself the most important decisions. Ministers, in the absence of political parties, did not dispose of any other effective support mechanisms than the departments they were in charge of and the particular strand of regime forces they identified themselves with. Interdepartmental conflicts were continually cropping up, which obviously affected the foreign policy administration of the State. Ministers were very wary of possible interference by other departments in the field of action of their ministry.

The organisation of the bureaucracy is therefore a basic element of the study of Spanish policy during the Franco regime. Indeed, the percentage of government employees who formed part of Franco's political personnel is higher than that of democratic regimes and than that of Spanish regimes before Franco's dictatorship.[30]

In the political-institutional set-up of the regime, the most influential department, under the Head of State, was the Government Presidency. Its most outstanding figure was without doubt Admiral Luis Carrero Blanco, Franco's right-hand man, with whom there was a perfect political and ideological understanding. Subsecretary of the Presidency from May 1941, he was promoted to the rank of minister by the decree of 19 July 1951. He remained in that post until June 1973 when he was appointed President of the Government.[31] He played an important part in drawing up the objectives of foreign policy and in the promotion of certain persons and groups within the regime to take charge of fundamental areas of the state's activities.

The specific department for running foreign policy is the Ministry for Foreign Affairs (MAE), headed in the period under consideration by Alberto Martín Artajo. He was appointed on 20 July 1945 and remained in the post until 1957. In the opinion of Florentino Portero, his promotion to MAE at that delicate juncture was one of the most significant 'gestures' of the new image that Franco wished to give to his regime. He was one of the outstanding figures of political catholicism at home. With his appointment:

> Franco brought to the Ministry for Foreign Affairs a man with a image of relative independence from the regime, in the hope of winning the support of European Christian Democracy and of the Vatican, with whom Artajo maintained smooth relations. It was one more element in the change-of-image operation by means of which Franco hoped to overcome the foreseeable tensions of the postwar world.[32]

His work as Minister for Foreign Affairs was rather that of Franco's secretary than that of an authentic administrator of foreign policy.[33] In this respect Franco led Martín Artajo to believe that he could force him, Franco, to liberalise the regime, fully aware that his statements to democratic governments would thereby ring more true. Franco thus exploited the minister to give his regime a face more acceptable to the international community.[34]

The political-bureaucratic administration for running foreign policy was subordinated to the latter's ups and downs and to the future of the State itself. The foreign policy administration therefore shared the essential traits of the state administration during Franco's regime, though it obviously also had its own peculiarities. In this respect two traits should be underlined: the primacy of the 'informal procedures' in the bureaucracy; and the 'patrimonialization' of the administration.

In the first place the bureaucratic 'bedlam' of Franco's regime, a substitute for its lack of constitutional principles, gave rise to the primacy of informal procedures. The regime was characterised by a practice of 'shrouding in red tape the identity of those who really took the decisions. Except for decisions of high political responsibility taken by the highest echelons of the State, it is generally difficult to distinguish between the persons, services and organisations that really took part in decision-making processes.'[35]

The second trait was the 'patrimonialization' of the Administration. In setting up the new State and generating a new bureaucracy tailor-made for it, the personnel available and those newly recruited were individuals who supported the regime; this had the double aim of rewarding them for their services and guaranteeing their affinity to the regime. The Administration, assures Alejandro Nieto, became a recruiting service feeding off the National Movement. It was thus reduced to 'war booty, and the vanquishers did not have the least commitment to setting up a minimally efficient system.'[36] This pattern was maintained throughout the period 1939-1957, although a gradual generational change set in throughout the 1950s. This new generation was characterised more by its technocratic training than its strict ideological loyalty to the regime.

The foreign policy administration had certain peculiarities arising from its functional structure and its powers. Other particular factors were its sociological composition and the particular demands of members of the diplomatic service as the élite body of the Administration, specialised, though not exclusively, in those functions. Nonetheless, the progressively more complex nature of the foreign policy administration tended to favour its becoming more expert and the incorporation of experts from other departments. A debate thus began about this process of modernisation and its adaptation to the new international order, limited during the Franco regime to its narrow scope for manoeuvre a consequence of the maintenance of its authoritarian essence.

The Foreign Policy Administration between Ostracism and International Readmission

Three main factors need to be emphasised in an examination of the foreign policy administration during the Franco regime: first, the peculiarities of the foreign policy administration; secondly, the nature and development of its functional structure; and lastly, the breakdown in the unity of foreign action as a result of the underlying problem of modernisation and updating the foreign policy administration.

The foreign policy administration institutionally embodies the wide range of interactions between domestic and foreign policy. This is a trait that no doubt alerts us to its peculiarities. Reflecting on the foreign service, Nieto distinguishes a series of peculiarities, from amongst which we will stress those that are applicable to the Spain of General Franco. These are as follows: its scattered destinations; its organic and functional heterogeneity – by virtue of the great number of services that have to be covered and the different character that the offices may have in each country or destination; linguistic variety; its standardisation with foreign and international systems; the particularly intense application of international and foreign law; 'identification with the State', as a result of the character its various bodies have in representing the state; its functional variety which makes the foreign policy administration 'a State

Administration on a smaller scale' and undoubtedly affects the unity of foreign action; its organic variety, seen in the wide range of diplomatic missions, permanent representations, delegations, consular offices and, above all, the complex network of organisations, services and institutions dependent on other departments; and, finally, the tradition and even the inertia of so secular a state function as diplomacy.[37] This whole set of traits became steadily more perceptible in Franco's dictatorship as progress was made in the 'normalisation' of its international position and foreign relations.

To all this must be added, from a sociological point of view, the fact that the members of the diplomatic corps maintained their loyalty to the system throughout the regime, but, in contrast to other élite corps, without normally holding important posts in the rest of the administration – except in the Trade Ministry. According to Nieto, Franco felt a certain distrust of professional diplomats 'exposed to the contamination of forms of behaviour and attitudes emanating from abroad'. Furthermore, many diplomats were convinced monarchists and had exercised their profession during the reign of Alfonso XIII, though they had subsequently been filtered out through a purification process during the Civil War. Nonetheless, throughout the history of the regime the Spanish government employees most connected with the outside world tried to 'stimulate a certain institutional liberalisation; although continually thwarted, these attempts show certain fractures in the regime, which, from the very start, was much less monolithic than is usually claimed'.[38]

Before turning to the second factor, the nature and development of the functional structure of the Spanish foreign policy administration during Franco's regime, certain points need clarification. The structure of the foreign policy administration has been summarised by Jesús Nuñez Hernández as follows:

> All international relations of the State are mainly governed by the 'ad hoc' Ministry, that is, the Ministry for Foreign Affairs. There exists therefore a 'central' Department responsible for this type of relations, and this Department will have to coordinate relations having a similar purpose stemming from other ministries. Secondly, there is, in each country with which diplomatic relations are maintained, a set of services and organisations presided over, run by and even embodied in the ambassador. Besides the Central Administration, therefore, there are other organisations exterior to it.[39]

A distinction can therefore be made between internal or central organisations of foreign policy administration and external or peripheral ones. The former obviously include MAE, plus the departments coordinated by it and the institutional administration, whose affairs transcend national boundaries. The latter are located outside the country. As far as Spain's representation in other countries – the bilateral channel – is concerned, the following distinctions can be made: central organisations, which have powers throughout the whole territory, such as embassies, missions and diverse annexes; and peripheral organisations, with powers in a limited part of the territory of the country in question, such as consulates and offices with special powers. In international organisations – the multilateral channel – representations will be set up to deal with the varied agenda of questions arising in international forums.

The central organisations of the foreign policy administration, and especially MAE, were gradually created in line with the establishment of the State under Franco's regime. Subsequently, they were continually adapted to different international circumstances. In the provisional government structures set up by the rebels from the beginning of the Civil War, direct control of international affairs was bestowed by the Order of 30 July 1936 on a diplomatic cabinet dependent on the National Defence Council and later on the Secretariat of Foreign Affairs and the diplomatic cabinet of the Head of State, run by Antonio Sangróniz y Castro, as stipulated by the Act of 1 October 1936.

The first attempt to create a more solid administrative structure for the new State, but without in any way being definitive, was laid down in the Act of 30 January 1938. Eleven ministries, including that of Foreign Affairs, and all dependent on the Vice-presidency of the Government, were set up with the purpose of creating a 'stable, orderly and efficient Government'.[40] Franco's Ministry for Foreign Affairs was eventually brought into being by the Decree of 16 February 1938 and its services were grouped together in a subsecretariat and two National Services Central Offices: that of Politics and Treaties and that of Administration.[41] The structure bore a certain resemblance to that of the former State Ministry of 1935 and remained relatively unaltered until well into the fifties, there being little overlap with other bureaucracies.[42]

The structure of the ministry underwent hardly any changes during the reform of the Central Administration undertaken at the end of the Civil War by the Act of 8 August 1939.[43] The office holder from the moment of its creation was General Francisco Gómez Jordana y Souza. According to Rosa Pardo, whose work is essential reading in any study of the development of MAE between

1939 and 1945, Jordana favoured a military style and facilitated the access to higher posts of government employees he had already known in north Africa, many of them with monarchist and catholic leanings.[44] This trend did not change significantly with the arrival of Juan Beigbeder Atienza at the ministry. During the period that Ramón Serrano Suñer held office, Spanish diplomacy became steeped in falangist language while attempts were made to improve budgetary and human resources in order to normalise completely the diplomatic function – witness the Decree of 6 December 1941 inviting applications to enter the diplomatic corps.

It was not until Jordana returned to the Ministry in September 1942, however, that a new restructuring of the department organisation was carried out, within the context of his policy of giving Spanish diplomacy less of a falange content and returning it to the 'bureaucratic normality' altered by his predecessor.[45] Indeed, the Decree of 16 October 1942 restructured MAE as one subsecretariat and three directorates: the General Directorate of Foreign Policy, under which came the sections of Europe, Overseas and Asia, Press, Passports and Cultural Relations; the General Directorate of Economic Policy, responsible for trade treaties and Spanish foreign trade; and the Directorate of General Affairs, for running administrative and legal affairs. On 7 November 1942, the Diplomatic School was set up with the task of training successful applicants to the corps. According to Alberto Martín Artajo, the author of this was Jordana. During José Félix de Lequerica y Erquiza's brief stint at the ministry, the organisation of MAE was completed with the creation of the Directorate of America on 9 November 1944.

Throughout those years instruments were re-established and created to boost Spain's international presence through less formal channels than diplomatic ones. Included amongst these were those of a propagandistic nature. Some were organisations dependent on MAE, such as the Cultural Relations Council, re-established by Decree on 16 February 1938 and reorganised on 5 June 1945 with its functions already defined back in 1926, and the Pious Works Board, set up on 3 June 1940. Others were autonomous state bodies, in which the Minister for Foreign Affairs played an important role, for example the Higher Missions Council set up on 5 March 1940 and the Hispanic Council (*Consejo de la Hispanidad*) created on 2 November of the same year.

The arrival of Alberto Martín Artajo at MAE on 20 July 1945 brought a shake-up designed to meet the adverse international situation, although the measures taken by Franco – as Florentino

Portero points out – did not involve any great change in Spanish foreign policy.[46] The activity of the new ministry and the circumstances and resources for action in the international field were reflected in the new ministerial set-up and its subsequent development.

The Act of 31 December 1945, reorganising MAE's services, was thought to be the ideal opportunity for undertaking an internal change to 'increase its efficiency', given the circumstances under which Spanish policy had developed in recent years.[47] In the new structure the subsecretariat continued to act as head of the different services and the number of general directorates was increased. In first place was the General Directorate of Foreign Policy, including the geographical groupings of Europe, the Holy See, Latin America, Africa and the Near East, Philippines and the Far East, and thematic Directorates – General Agreements. Next came the General Directorate of Economic Policy, which became more important as MAE took on more responsibility for economic and trade affairs under the overall self-sufficiency policy. A General Directorate of Cultural Relations was created as traditional political and economic channels silted up and cultural channels thereby increased in importance. Lastly, the General Directorate of the Interior was introduced.

International ostracism left MAE with precious little work to do, so other channels of action were promoted such as the cultural, with the purpose of maintaining and increasing international support for the regime. In this context, Moreno maintains that 'the misnamed "informal diplomacy" offered enormous possibilities, in the light of the blockage or severe restriction of traditional diplomatic channels'.[48] Within this overall approach various cultural instruments of political penetration were developed, such as the Hispanic Culture Institute replacing the Hispanic Council in the 1945 reform, the European Documentation and Information Centre of 1953 and the Hispanic-Arab Cultural Institute of 1954.

As Spain slowly gained readmittance into the international community from the late 1940s onwards, the instruments of the foreign policy administration were progressively adapted to the new demands arising from the growth of bilateral relations and the return of multilateral ones. In relation to the former, certain readjustments are to be observed in the ministerial structure, such as the creation of the General Directorate of Consular Affairs by Decree of 16 February 1949, together with progressive modifications in the General Directorate of Cultural Relations in January 1948 and especially on 2 April 1951. As a result two directorates were created: one for cultural policy, broken down into geographical sectors (Europe, Latin America and Philippines and the Arab World) and one for operative services. Activity increased in the different services of MAE owing to the 'normalisation' of foreign relations, and was further boosted from the 1950s onwards by new relations with those states which were emerging from the process of decolonisation. As for the economic side, the creation of the Ministry of Trade, motivated by the formation of the new Government in July 1951, had a notable effect on the General Directorate of Economic Policy, although it was not until 1957 that meaningful changes were produced in the regime's running of economic affairs.

But without doubt one of the great novelties in the structure of MAE was the creation of instruments to deal with the activity of international organisations. This also increased interaction and conflicts between other departments of the state administration. Participation in the first international bodies dependent on the UN from the early 1950s and full membership of the UN in 1955 led to the setting up by Order of 2 April 1951 of an International Organisations' Section in the General Directorate of Cultural Relations. By an Order of 4 April of the same year the General Directorate of Foreign Policy was reorganised, a Directorate of International Political Organisations and another of Agreements and International Political Conferences and Treaty Register were formed.[49] Finally, with Fernando María Castiella at the helm of MAE, the section of International Organisations was raised to the status of General Directorate in order to centralise and channel the activities of the services of the state administration in international forums.

The regulations of the diplomatic corps were also adapted, both to the new administrative situation of the government employees of the civil state administration regulated by the Act of 15 July 1954, and to the circumstances of the new international situation. Thus the new general bye-laws of 15 July 1955 reflected the new technocratic slant of the Administration and defined the diplomatic corps in article 1 as 'the special Professional Corps of the State responsible for the Foreign Service of the Nation, in Spanish Representations abroad and in International Organisations, without prejudice to the functions bestowed by law on special services'.[50]

Peripheral organisations of the foreign policy administration also suffered initially from international ostracism, and likewise experienced a slow normalisation thereafter that translated into a higher rate of activity and an increase in the resources and personnel of the Foreign Service. Figures on the peripheral network directly dependent on the Ministry are conclusive in this respect: in 1945 there were 40 embassies and legations, 26 general consulates and 56 consulates; by 1950 the number had risen to 47 embassies and legations, 31 general consulates and 66 consulates; and by 1962 there were 60 diplomatic missions, 46 general consulates and 48 career consulates.[51] To all this must be added the incorporation of Spanish representatives into international organisations.

The development of the foreign policy administration, and specifically that of MAE, leads us to the third and last factor: the breakdown of a unified foreign action. This was not a new problem but it did emerge definitively in Spain in the 1950s. It is what Marcel Merle has defined as the 'dismemberment of the Executive' and Angel Ballesteros as the 'dispersal of the unity of foreign action'.[52] In this process 'the prime, ineluctable principle of the unity of State action came up against the centrifugal impulses of each Department', which wanted to impose its own functional and bureaucratic criteria.[53]

The problem was not new; it had arisen in the interwar period during Spain's participation in the League of Nations. The Ministry for Foreign Affairs, like its forerunner the State Ministry, tried to maintain the principle of unity of foreign action by insisting on the protagonism of the department itself. Witness the Order of 9 November 1948 of the Government Presidency, requiring an advance report from MAE on those questions that could have international repercussions. When this problem first came to the fore in the 1950s, the universality and centralisation of high-level foreign policy was

> the unquestioned and unquestionable domain of the Ministry for Foreign Affairs. Yet, the damming up of its own activity led to a natural overflowing into other more or less connected areas, even when this meant invading the territory of other departments to a greater extent than was strictly necessary according to the sacrosanct principle of the 'unity of action of the State', duly laid down by law.[54]

There were two sides to this process of a breakdown in the unity of foreign action: the authoritarian nature of the State and its working mechanisms on the one hand, and on the other the effects resulting from the gradual adaptation to multilateral relations, as one additional aspect of the process of the international readmission of Spain.

In the first place the authoritarian nature of the State and its development, together with the already mentioned lack of constitutional definition of the regime, and likewise the patrimonialization of the administration, all had an effect on the unity of foreign

action. In the most fascist phase of the regime the duplication of the
state administration of the Party, and specifically the foreign service
of the National Delegation of the Falange, produced frequent interference in foreign policy administration. Such interference reached
its peak while Serrano Suñer held office in MAE, especially concerning propaganda activity, but declined following the return of
Jordana to the Department.[55] More persistent throughout the
regime was the interference of the military bureaucracy – the ministries of the three forces and the General Staff – in law and order
problems which became evident in the pacts with the United
States. In addition, MAE had to deal with interference from the
Government Presidency, for instance, in the handling of the
Morocco question, and from the catholic hierarchy in relations with
the Vatican and, of course, in the negotiation of the Concordat.[56]

A typical case illustrating this breakdown in the unity of foreign
action has been presented by Angel Viñas: the handling of economic
affairs and foreign trade. During the self-sufficiency period the subordination of economics to politics made it indispensable for the
ministry confronting the international boycott to control the instruments of foreign action. To this end, and following the approach of
Navasqüés, the Subsecretariat of Foreign Economy and Trade was
set up in 1947. In technical matters, it depended jointly on MAE
and the Ministry of Industry and Trade, in administrative matters on
the latter only. Later, with the creation of the Ministry of Trade in
1951, the slow dismantling of the self-sufficiency policy and the
approximation to Western economic models, the privileged position
of MAE was gradually undermined, a process which accelerated
after the passing of the Stabilisation Plan in 1959 and the disappearance of the aforementioned Subsecretariat.[57]

This dispersion in the unity of foreign action became greater as
the international readmission of Spain progressed, and was especially
favoured by its incorporation into international organisations from
the 1950s onwards. Indeed, the multilateralisation of international
relations had very profound effects on the foreign policy administration. Incorporation into international organisations created a real situation to which the administration thereafter was forced to adapt.
The wide range of activities carried out within these international
organisations intensified the dispersion in the unity of foreign action,
since the operative departments in question tended to take on direct
responsibility for matters related to their sphere of influence abroad.
These departments tended to: participate in the representation function *vis-à-vis* international organisations, intervene directly in nego-

tiating processes, take on directly the liaison functions with their opposite numbers abroad and the secretaries of international organisations, and increase their presence in the foreign network. What this all added up to, therefore, was a process of division in the drawing up and execution of foreign policy and the creation of international services in the main ministries involved, thereby lowering 'the action profiles of the Ministries of Foreign Affairs'.

In response, the foreign policy administration initiated 'a progressive specialisation of services and human resources, and the consequent intervention of operative bodies and services of the Administration outside the Diplomatic Corps, into the areas of economics, trade, defence, culture and information'.[58] All this, as already pointed out, contributed towards increasing bureaucratic tensions between operative departments and MAE, as the latter tried to hang on to its traditional powers. It should not be forgotten that Spain's membership of the UN and associated organisations gave rise to the creation of instruments in the Ministry to centralise and coordinate the work in those international forums. It was precisely in this context that the International Civil Servants' School was created in late 1955, in which an important role was played by Antonio de Luna, Professor of International Law. In a note on the creation of this school sent by de Luna to Martín Artajo on 16 June 1953 he warned of the new situation arising from multilateral diplomacy and distinguished in its management between: the 'Political Ministry' for everything related to foreign policy, this being MAE; and the 'Operative Ministries', which were those carrying out, within the national organisation, general plans on an international scale.[59] The result of this process was a heightening of bureaucratic tensions between MAE and the operative ministries and a progressive deterioration of the principle of unity of foreign action, which became even more marked as a wave of technocratization swept through the State from the late 1950s onwards.

By way of conclusion, we wish to underline first the greater interest which has lately been taken by Spanish historians in the functional aspects of foreign policy and specifically the foreign policy administration. Analysing the foreign policy administration from a historical perspective allows us to reconstruct the operative organisation through which foreign action was drawn up, planned and executed, and the changes to which this was subjected through time. Secondly, the configuration of the foreign policy administration, as a means of defending national interests and channelling efforts to achieve foreign policy objectives, depends on two fundamental variables: the nature and circumstances of the international scene; and the nature of the State of which the foreign policy administration is part, as one component more of the state administrative structure.

The adverse international circumstances Spain was faced with from the end of the Second World War to the start of the partial normalisation of its foreign relations in the 1950s had a substantial effect on its foreign policy administration. The switch from international ostracism to Spain's inclusion in the international system led to modifications in the foreign policy administration, not only in terms of the amount of work it had to do, but also in terms of its very philosophy, determined by the greater complexity and interdependence of the international system in which multilateral relations had become a basic element. In this sense the debate sparked off within the State on its foreign policy administration reflected many of the problems that had already arisen in the Spain of the inter-war years.

On the other hand the nature of the State, and in particular its political-ideological basis and the foreign policy guidelines laid down by the regime, substantially determined the structure, resources and methods of the foreign policy administration. The authoritarianism of the regime, the balance struck between the various factions of the conservative coalition and the patrimonialization of the Administration had an obvious effect on the foreign policy administration. In the process of setting up the new State and its subsequent development the foreign policy administration underwent a profound transformation resulting from the dispersion of the unity of foreign action. Fierce, underlying inter-bureaucratic tensions then broke out, and not a few contradictions in the running of foreign affairs. This structural problem came to a head in the 1950s, as a result of the beginning of Spain's admittance into the international system and the changes taking place within the regime, without ever altering its authoritarian essence.

Notes

1. See P. Martínez Lillo, 'La historia de las relaciones internacionales', *Boletín de la Asociación de Historia Contemporánea* 1, 1996: 5.
2. See *Documentación Administrativa* 205, 1985.
3. A. Ballesteros, *La técnica de la política exterior*, Mendoza, 1995.
4. J. Nuñez Hernández, *La función consular en el Derecho Español*, Madrid, 1980.

5. C. Fernández Espeso and J. Martínez Cardós, *Primera Secretaría de Estado. Ministerio de Estado. Disposiciones Orgánicas (1705-1936)*, Madrid, 1972.
6. A. Viñas, 'La Administración de la política económica exterior en España, 1936-1979', *Cuadernos Económicos de I.C.E.* 13, 1980: 159-247.
7. A. Moreno, 'La Administración exterior en la transición de la política exterior española (1975-1986)', in *Historia de la transición y consolidación democrática en España*, eds several authors, Madrid, 1995, vol. 2, pp. 235-50.
8. A subject dealt with in *Documentación Administrativa* 205, 1985; and M. Casanova, 'El ingreso en la carrera diplomática durante la II República', *Cuadernos de la Escuela Diplomática* 1, 1988, Madrid, pp. 129-38; B. Lozano, 'Pasado, presente y futuro de la carrera diplomática', *Documentación Administrativa* 210-11, 1987: 307-42.
9. M.A. Ochoa Brun, 'La Escuela Diplomática: pasado y presente', *Cuadernos de la Escuela Diplomática* 1, 1988, 5-13; L.E. Togores and J.L. Neila (under the direction of José Martínez Cardós), *La Escuela Diplomática; cincuenta años de servicio al Estado (1942-1992)*, Madrid, 1993.
10. R. Gillespie, F. Rodrigo and J. Story, *Las relaciones exteriores de la España democrática*, Madrid, 1995; J.C. Pereira, *Introducción al estudio de la política exterior española (siglos XIX y XX)*, Madrid, 1983; B. Pollack and G. Hunter, *The Paradox of Spanish Foreign Policy. Spain's International Relations from Franco to Democracy*, New York, 1987.
11. Such is the case in recent publications by L. Delgado, *Imperio de papel; Acción cultural y política exterior durante el primer franquismo*, Madrid, 1992; J.C. Jiménez, *El ocaso de la amistad entre las dictaduras ibéricas, 1955-1968*, Mérida, 1996; R. Pardo, *Con Franco hacia el Imperio; La política exterior española en América Latina, 1939-1945*, Madrid, 1995; J.C. Pereira and A. Cervantes, *Relaciones diplomáticas entre España y América*, Madrid, 1992; F. Quintana, *España en Europa, 1931-1936; Del compromiso por la paz a la huida de la guerra*, Madrid, 1993; and of the doctoral theses of A. Moreno, 'Actitud y reacción de España ante Europa; Franquismo y construcción europea', (PhD Diss., University of Madrid, 1995); N. Tabanera, 'Las relaciones entre España e Hispanoamérica durante la IIª República española, 1931-1939; La acción diplomática republicana' (PhD Diss., University of Madrid, 1990); L. Togores Sanchez, 'La acción exterior de España en Extremo Oriente (1830-1885)'((PhD Diss., University of Madrid, 1990); J.L. Neila, 'España república mediterránea, seguridad colectiva y defensa nacional (1931-1936)' (Ph.D. diss., University of Madrid, 1994).
12. M. Espadas Burgos, *Franquismo y política exterior*, Madrid, 1987, p. 13.
13. A. Guaita, *Derecho administrativo especial*, Zaragoza, 1965, vol. 1, pp. 45-6, quoted in J.M. Paz Agueras 'El servicio exterior y la protección de los intereses de los nacionales en el extranjero', *Documentación Administrativa* 205, 1985: 130. J. Núñez Hernández distinguishes four main missions in foreign policy administration: negotiating, representing, informing and protecting; Núñez Hernández, *Función consular*, pp. 12-13.
14. A. Viñas, 'La política exterior española en el franquismo', *Cuenta y Razón* 6, 1982, pp. 62-3.
15. J.M. Armero, *La política exterior de Franco*, Barcelona, 1978, p. 69.
16. See Quasim Ahmad's contribution to this present volume; see also F. Portero *Franco aislado; La cuestión española (1945-1950)*, Madrid, 1989; A.J. Lleonart y Anselem, *España y la ONU*, 4 vols, Madrid, 1978, 1983, 1985 and 1991.

17. See again Quasim Ahmad's contribution to this present volume; A. Marquina, *España en la política de seguridad occidental, 1939-1986*, Madrid, 1986, pp. 145-59; several authors, *Historia de España; España actual. España y el mundo (1939-1975)*, Madrid, 1996, pp. 460-2.

18. Moreno, 'Administración exterior', p. 237.

19. In 1950 Ireland normalised diplomatic relations with Spain. In 1951 Belgium, Denmark, the United States, France, Greece, Holland, Italy, Luxembourg, Norway, the United Kingdom and Sweden did likewise followed by the Federal Republic of Germany in 1952 and Canada in 1953.

20. See J.L. Neila, 'La articulación del Estado franquista en la posguerra civil; la reorganización de la Administración exterior y la creación de la Escuela Diplomática (1939-1945)', in *II Encuentro de investigadores del franquismo; Alicante, 11, 12, y 13 de mayo de 1995*, Alicante and Valencia, 1995, p. 171.

21. For a theoretical reflection on this process of making the regime progressively more fascist, see I. Saz Campos, 'El Franquismo: ¿Régimen autoritorio o dictadura fascista?', in *El Régimen de Franco (1936-1975); Congreso internacional*, eds J. Tusell, S. Sueiro, J.M. Marín, M. Casanova, Madrid, 1993, vol. 1, pp. 193-8.

22. See P. Preston, *Franco; 'Caudillo de España'*, Barcelona, 1994, pp. 666-7.

23. Viñas, 'Política exterior', p. 63.

24. Jiménez, *Ocaso* , p. 11.

25. Preston, *Franco*, p. 783.

26. Viñas, 'Administración', p. 161.

27. M.G. Steinert, 'La décision en matière de politique extérieur: un essai sur l'utilisation de théories pour l'étude des relations internationales', in *Enieux et puissance. Hommages à Jean-Baptiste Duroselle*, eds several authors, Paris, 1986, pp. 73-4; see also Pardo, *Con Franco*, pp. 15-16.

28. C. Arenal, 'La posición exterior de España', in *Transición política y consolidación democrática. España (1975-1986)*, ed. R. Cotarelo, Madrid, 1992, pp. 395-6. The question is approached from a similar standpoint in Pollack and Hunter, *Paradox*, p. 106.

29. R. Bañon Martínez, 'Burocracia, burócratas y poder político', *Información Comercial Española* 522, 1977: 37.

30. See Viñas, 'Administración', 169-71.

31. See Jiménez, *Ocaso* , p. 12.

32. Portero *Franco aislado*, p. 106.

33. Ibid., p. 110.

34. Preston, *Franco*, p. 672

35. Moreno, 'Administración exterior', pp. 237-8.

36. A. Nieto, 'De la República a la Democracia: la Administración española del franquismo', *Revista de Derecho Administrativo* 11, 1976: 569-72; Togores and Neila, *Escuela Diplomática*, pp. 130-1 and 192.

37. A. Nieto, 'Selección y perfeccionamiento del personal del Servicio Exterior', *Documentación Administrativa* 205, 1985: 165-9.

38. A. Viñas, *Guerra, Dinero y Dictadura; Ayuda fascista y autarquía en la España de Franco*, Barcelona, 1984, p. 299.

39. Núñez Hernández, *Función consular*, pp. 13-14.

40. The ten resulting ministries were: Justice, National Defence, Public Order, Home Office, Treasury, Industry and Trade, Agriculture, National Education, Public Works and Trade Union Action and Organisation.

41. The National Services of Politics and Treaties included the sections: Europe, Overseas and Asia, Cultural Relations, Legal Affairs and Actions, and Holy See and Pious Works; and the National Administration Services those of Personnel and General Affairs, Accounts and Financing, and Records, Files and Libraries.

42. Viñas, 'Política exterior', p. 66.

43. The Act abolished the Government Vice-presidency and set up the following ministerial framework: Foreign Affairs, Home Office, Army, Navy, Air Force, Justice, Treasury, Industry and Trade, Agriculture, National Education, Public Works and Employment.

44. See Pardo, *Con Franco*, pp. 83-5 and 93.

45. Ibid., pp. 270 and 275.

46. Portero *Franco aislado*, pp. 104-105.

47. See Pereira and Cervantes, *Relaciones diplomáticas*, pp. 100-101.

48. A. Moreno, 'El Centro Europeo de Documentación e Información. Un intento fallido de aproximación a Europa', in *El régimen de Franco (1936-1975). Congreso internacional*, eds J. Tusell et al., Madrid, 1993, vol. 2, p. 461.

49. The other Directorates and Services were: European Political Affairs; American Political Affairs; Political Affairs of the Arab World, Near and Middle East and Africa; Political Affairs of the Philippines and Far East; Relations with the Holy See and Foreign Passports Service; *Boletín Oficial del Estado*, 12 April 1951.

50. MAE, *Reglamento orgánico de la Carrera Diplomática, passed by Decree 15 July 1955*, Madrid 1955, 7. See also B. Lozano, 'Pasado', 325-326; and Togores and Neila, *Escuela Diplomática*, pp. 194-5.

51. Figures taken from AMAE, in *Representantes de España en el Extranjero*, Madrid, January 1945 and August 1950; and from Pereira and Cervantes, *Relaciones diplomáticas*, p. 109.

52. See *Libro Blanco sobre la Administración Exterior del Estado*, Madrid, Government Presidency, 1986, vol. 1, p. 9; Moreno, 'Administración exterior', p. 240; Ballesteros, *Técnica*, p. 109.

53. A. Nieto, 'Selección y perfeccionamiento', 168.

54. Viñas, 'Administración', 200.

55. Pardo, *Con Franco*, pp. 253, 270 and 275.

56. See Viñas, 'Política exterior', pp. 67-8.

57. Viñas, 'Administración', 184-200

58. Moreno, 'Administración exterior', p. 242; idem, 'La ruptura de la unidad de acción exterior en el caso español y las organizaciones regionales europeas', in *La Historia de las Relaciones Internacionales; una visión desde España*, ed. Comisión Española de las Relaciones Internacionales, Madrid, 1996, pp. 430-44.

59. See Togores and Neila, *Escuela Diplomática*, pp. 224-5.

15

Franco's Dreams of Autarky Shattered

Foreign Policy Aspects in the Run-up to the 1959 Change in Spanish Economic Strategy[1]

Angel Viñas (Universidad Complutense, Madrid)

Introduction

THE efforts of such a long-lasting regime as General Franco's to define its interaction with the international environment are bound to have gone through different phases and to have fluctuated in accordance with different tactical requirements. However, after the Second World War the regime's overriding strategic aims did not substantially change. These aims were basically two. First of all there was the overarching objective to erode the consequences of the regime's 'original sin', i.e., the association with the fascist powers which dated from the beginning of the Spanish Civil War. As a sort of functional corollary, this objective also involved the need to neutralise external instability factors which might constrain to an intolerable degree the regime's room for manoeuvre. The second objective was no less important: it involved the systematic whipping-up of domestic political allegiance to the leadership because of its skilfulness in navigating the international arena where anti-Spanish conspiracies were believed to abound.

In meeting their two strategic aims, Spanish decision-makers undoubtedly expected to bestow additional legitimacy on the *Caudillo* and the peculiar political institutions of the dictatorship. It is, therefore, not illogical that, when confronted with the end of the road for the economic strategies followed during the first two decades of the regime's existence, a *volte-face* was carried out in 1959. The stabilisation and liberalisation policies then introduced began the opening up of the Spanish economy to the international division of labour. They also sounded the death-knell of the autarkic chimera dear to General Franco and his immediate entourage.

One of the most important foundations of the Spanish economic development of the 1960s – the golden age of expansion for Western capitalism – was the opening up of the economy. It is no exaggeration to assert that the change in economic strategies was critical for the regime's evolution in that it paved the way for vast social and economic changes. The dictatorship successfully built upon them in search of new elements of legitimacy which became intimately associated with high rates of economic growth and the experience of increases of wealth although these increases were unevenly distributed across the social and geographical divide.

A summary understanding of the ideas of General Franco and his loyal entourage in the run-up to the 1959 *volte-face* is essential to comprehend some of the serious obstacles which had to be overcome. In fact, one can speak of a 'first' and a 'second' Francoism, separated by the critical 1959 operation.[2] Although, on closer analysis, policies and policy outcomes show considerable differences between the 1940s and 1950s, the first two decades can be considered as a period in which economic policy was carried out in a rather homogeneous framework. Autarky, subordination of economic life to political and ideological chimeras, and exacerbated government controls over every aspect of economic life were presented in a permanent apotheosis of nationalism as the ideal of economic policy and of state policy *tout court*.

The Stabilisation and Liberalisation Plan of 1959 has been exhaustively studied as an exercise in economic policy making.[3] While this approach is undoubtedly correct because it was, after all, an economic operation, the *volte-face* was also based on a complex set of foreign policy perceptions and linkages. The main thrust of this article is to show that any attempt to endow General Franco or his immediate entourage with far-reaching foresight in foreign or economic policies – where according to the regime's panegyrists resounding successes were achieved – is either propaganda or an outcome of flawed analyses.[4]

Franco had high-blown dreams for making Spain as self-sufficient as possible. These dreams of autarky were held right up to the 1959 operation. They had to be shattered and Franco had to be helped in spite of himself. The United States, in particular, rescued Franco from the cul-de-sac into which his original economic strategies had led Spain. If, though ruled by Franco, Spain changed so much in the 1960s and 1970s, this was not necessarily because of his enlightened thinking, but essentially in spite of the ideas he had harboured throughout the twenty most unpleasant years of his long regime. Finally, the outcome of the *volte-face* vindicated the main strategic projections of the U.S. Government.

The U.S. Connection and the Decision for Multilateral Diplomacy

The 1953 agreements with the United States were undoubtedly the key achievement of all foreign policy efforts under Franco.[5] Obviously, the U.S. connection secured for the Spanish regime vitally needed accommodation with the pre-eminent Western power. It led to the admission of Spain into the UN in 1955, albeit in a package deal which benefited many other candidate countries. The connection also underscored the view that, although democracy was preferable to dictatorship in Spain, the United States saw more merit in using the country's geostrategic location than in maintaining the Franco regime in relative isolation or at arms' length, as many western European democracies were still prone to do.

The connection provided the Spanish regime with other kinds of breathing space. U.S. economic assistance was granted to Spain. This assistance has generally been overrated, but it did ease balance of payments constraints and led to a certain degree of modernisation in a wide range of production and distribution activities. Without such assistance, the run-up to the 1959 operation would have been much more difficult. No less importantly perhaps, the agreements with the U.S. lifted the thick clouds which had darkened foreign policy experiences. What the regime pretentiously called 'the siege' was the extremely disheartening realisation that Spain, in the absence of the U.S. embrace, might need some more years until it could become *salonfähig* in the international arena.

Once the U.S. connection was established, reformist high officials in Spain would argue in favour of giving strong attention to multilateral diplomacy, particularly in the economic area. This was considered a better venue for strengthening Spain's external position, at least in Europe, than the continuous strain to improve bilateral relationships at whatever cost. Two major experiences must have heavily supported this foreign policy reorientation. The first one had to do with the bitter realisation that the U.S. connection failed to provide the inordinate amounts of economic support that the regime had hoped for. Given this collapse in expectations, the argument was soon advanced that Spain had incurred very high security costs for which the economic rewards were not commensurate. In 1955 and 1956 a certain frustration with the economic fallout of the U.S. embrace was detectable in the higher echelons of the Spanish regime. It therefore made sense to explore other venues.

The second experience related to the attractiveness of a *rapprochement* with the OEEC. This was potentially a ground-breaking change as well. It was energetically pursued by some high officials in the Ministries of Commerce and Foreign Affairs. The reason was that a substantial part of those external commercial relations which the autarkic strategy had not been able to eliminate altogether was maintained with western European countries. However, within the thick network of commercial and financial agreements bilateral deficits could not be covered by using any positive bilateral surpluses that had been achieved. Hence, Spanish room for manoeuvre had become extremely constrained. Multilateral compensation was an interesting alternative approach.

In January 1955, Spain negotiated its full participation in some of the OEEC's working groups. This arrangement was fairly soon understood to allow for Spanish participation in many other groups, albeit in the capacity of an observer. Already in June 1955 Spanish diplomats such as Jaime Argüelles were defending how convenient it would be for Spain to become a formal member of the OEEC. It was recognised that this would imply devising a new international economic strategy, even if this was at odds with the foundations of the very policy carried out until then. The recommendations also acknowledged that there would be a need to adopt the OEEC's Code of Liberalisation and to participate, albeit with all imaginable restrictions, in the European Payments Union and its mechanisms for payments multilateralisation.[6] However, two major events militated against pursuing this reorientation further. The first had to do with the inability of the Spanish Government to obtain economic assistance from the United States to cushion the effects of such intended changes. A formal request by the then Spanish Foreign Minister, Alberto Martín Artajo, to the U.S. ambassador on 31 August, 1956 fell on deaf ears.[7]

Furthermore, when unusually severe frost conditions resulted in the collapse of Spanish agricultural exports, in particular of the citrus fruit crop, one of the mainstays of Spanish sales abroad, critically scarce foreign currency holdings had to be reallocated. The possibility of using some of these holdings to cushion the effect of a rapprochement with the OEEC disappeared into thin air.

This notwithstanding, it must be categorically stated that no far-reaching reorientation in external economic relations was on the cards at that juncture. It is true that within the regime's bureaucracy some circles had been espousing ideas in favour of developing external economic relations far beyond the limits which the autarkic foundations of the Spanish grand strategy allowed. However, the complex web of political, institutional, economic and psychological obstacles to opening up the economy to foreign influence remained too strong to be cut. The quest for self-sufficiency was still very active. Elaborate systems of quotas, import and export licensing and multiple exchange rates shackled the economy. The Government was too interventionist, uncoordinated and incompetent to contemplate an alternative global strategy.

Franco and Carrero Blanco in an Autarkic Time-Warp

On 25 February 1957, a new cabinet took office. As Paul Preston has stated, the reshuffle 'was to be one of the great watersheds of Franco's political career. It marked the beginning of his transition from active politician to symbolic figurehead. The details were worked out in close collaboration with Carrero Blanco whose influence was growing by the day'.[8] Franco's transition was to take yet some more time. In 1957, the all-powerful *Caudillo* gave evidence that his economic ideas had not changed substantially over time.

The composition of the new cabinet represented a further emasculation of the Falange and included some new ministers who would eventually toll the bell for the autarkic dreams. Two of them (Mariano Navarro Rubio in Finances and Professor Alberto Ullastres in Commerce) were Opus Dei members. Fernando María Castiella (former Falangist, former ambassador and astute weather-vane) went to Foreign Affairs. All would be assisted by a group of modern-thinking high officials with a similar outlook.[9] Among these, some thought in basically economic terms. Others were more sensitive to foreign policy considerations. Many had become exposed to the challenge of the permanent interaction and coordination with U.S. officials. Others simply saw no future in the continuance of past policies.

The 'domestic' ministries – Industry, Agriculture, Public Works – and agencies such as the INI had very different perspectives and would do battle against the economic reformists. The INI, in particular, under Juan Antonio Suanzes, remained wedded to past strategies.[10] Nonetheless, just before the 1957 reshuffle, it was clear that some of the ministers who would later be dropped (Alberto Martin Artajo in Foreign Affairs, Manuel Arburúa in Commerce) had become deeply interested in exploring new venues in international economic policy. They were not prepared to accept concrete commitments in terms of economic liberalisation, but had sent up to the cabinet a strong sense of the need for economic change.[11]

The fundamental philosophies of both General Franco and Admiral Carrero Blanco provided a very strong barrier to the opening up of the economy. Their beliefs had permeated policy making for many years and had led to a complex interlocking of vested interests, arbitrary regulations and official auto-complacency which stifled any sense of economic rationality. 'Stone Age economics' (Tortella) easily mixed with 'perverse rationality': Franco and his entourage were convinced that any let-up in economic policy might lead to requests for liberalisation in the political or institutional areas.[12]

Whatever merits may be attributed to the Spanish dictator, one which should be underlined time and again is the consistency in his basic economic beliefs. Throughout the years, from the experiences of the Civil War and the post-war bungled reconstruction up to his moment of glory in his secure relationship with the United States, General Franco adhered to a vision of what the proper course for Spain should be, not only in political and institutional terms, but also in economic grand strategy. He put that vision forward in a great number of public statements and speeches. Obviously one could argue that such statements involved an important element of rhetoric or declaratory policy and were not necessarily indicative of the *Caudillo*'s true intentions and strategies. Since other authors have analysed Franco's public statements as a heuristic means to approach whatever his beliefs may have been,[13] the reasoning which follows will be based solely on Franco's views as expressed in documents which were not intended to be made public.

The first document is dated 9 October 1939. It was an internal memorandum to his ministers in which Franco clearly stated his ideas and suggestions on how to deal with Spanish economic problems in the period of post-war reconstruction.[14] According to the *Caudillo*, the critical problem of the Spanish economy was the balance-of-trade deficit. The policies to follow should therefore be predicated upon the need to eliminate all unnecessary imports, to reduce to the greatest possible extent all foreign goods which could be replaced by domestic ones and, finally, to expand exports, if necessary with the help of substantial subsidies. These ideas were justified by one simple reason: imports meant foreign exchange outflows and these outflows would enrich the economies of the exporting countries. General Franco also commented upon the major categories of imported goods. They were all – he stated – agricultural (cotton and other natural fibres, tobacco, rubber, dry goods, oil seeds, eggs, wood, and cereals) and should therefore be produced domestically. Transforming other Spanish natural resources would lead to the production in Spain of oil, chemicals and steel. Spain, to put it simply, could and should substantially decrease its dependency on purchases abroad. This would have a favourable impact on military preparedness and on job creation.

General Franco's drivelling nonsense was coloured by an extremely narrow hyper-nationalist outlook. This grew out of the belief that the Spanish economy could develop a very high degree of self-sufficiency and, in so doing, drastically curtail Spanish external vulnerabilities. Writing in poor language and arguing in a childish way, the dictator left no doubt about the firmness of his convictions. Autarky was the strategy necessary to transform and industrialise the Spanish economy.[15] Spain had to be forced to produce everything needed, regardless of costs or competition. As a political choice, the economy had to be cut off from the outside world. A few weeks later, the Industrial Laws of 24 October and 24 November, 1939, showed that General Franco's ideas were effectively translated into legislation.

All this is well-known. However, some Spanish authors have suggested that the autarkic orientation of Spanish economic policy under Franco was a reaction to the world war situation and to the political isolation of the regime in the post-war environment. A slightly more sophisticated interpretation is to present Spanish economic policies since 1939 as a mere extension of the import-substituting strategies of the pre-Civil War period, even looking for foundations in the protectionist approaches of the outgoing nineteenth century. None of this holds water.

It could, of course, be argued that whatever beliefs General Franco may have had in 1939, or later, on how to handle the Spanish economy and to relate to the international environment would perhaps have changed by 1957, given his long experience by then in policy making. This hypothesis must, however, be refuted on the basis of new documentary evidence. Although it is generally admitted that the dictator was not in favour of the 1959 *volte-face* and had to be persuaded with great difficulty by his reformist ministers, private evidence about his actual beliefs in the run-up to that operation has not been forthcoming until recently.[16] This evidence has been found in the minutes of the meetings of the *Comisión Delegada del Gobierno para Asuntos Económicos*, a sort of inner cabinet composed of the ministers responsible for economic matters.

The work of another inner cabinet on 'constitutional' reform (*Comisión Delegada del Gobierno para el Estudio de las Leyes Fundamentales*) has been somewhat illuminated, while no light has been shed on the impact of the economic inner cabinet. The first formal meeting of the new body took place on 15 March 1957. It was deemed so important that General Franco felt compelled to give his new ministers a wide-ranging presentation about his economic ideas, beliefs and strategies. To my knowledge, neither Navarro Rubio nor Ullastres nor any other minister of the 1957 cabinet has ever made any reference to the *Caudillo*'s musings.[17] This is regrettable because the critical single element for the success of the 1959 *volte-face* was, obviously, General Franco's consent. Ullastres himself has so far kept his own counsel.[18] Navarro Rubio, on the other hand, indicated a long time ago that he was able to convince the Caudillo by appealing to his exalted sense of patriotism.

Whatever the circumstances and the reasoning which led to General Franco's grudging acceptance of the 1959 operation, one thing can be empirically tested: the nature of his ideas to deal with Spanish economic problems in 1957, i.e., when the hardest reconstruction years lay in the past and the regime was publicly basking in the warmth of the U.S. embrace. General Franco's presentation to his inner cabinet did not contain any trace of self-enlightenment. A cursory comparison between his views in 1957 and 1939 shows that his basic beliefs, ideas, and strategies had scarcely changed in almost twenty years, if at all.

One of the arguments used in the presentation convinced, however, the present writer that General Franco still had an excellent memory. After the Civil War German experts had identified possibilities for linking as intimately as possible the economies of the Third Reich and Spain. Since Germany was highly dependent on imports of natural rubber which could easily be interrupted, the Germans were on the lookout for *ersatz* productions. They came across some rubbery plants called *guayules* which grow in southern Spain and recommended their cultivation.[19] Almost twenty years later General Franco expounded before his ministers the practicalities enshrined in the systematic cultivation of *guayule* as a means for cutting down imports of rubber and tyres which were a drain on the balance of trade. Continuous industrialisation based on Spanish mineral and agricultural resources was the key strategy which should be adhered to.

Some days after this presentation, on 19 March, Franco gave *New York Times* readers a lesson in comparative economic history. He alluded to the economic difficulties of other European countries which had in the past exploited their colonial empires. This was coming to an end and their future would not be rosy any longer. Such was not the case of Spain. Spain, he boldly stated, had been living for more than half a century on its own resources and faced a

> far brighter horizon: the possibilities offered by an immense domestic market to accommodate increases in domestic production; vast opportunities for industrialisation and for the transformation of natural resources. There are unlimited possibilities for increasing domestic output via application of modern technologies and by taking advantage of a perfect balance in natural wealth. How many countries must envy the possibilities which Spain's future contains!

he said waxing almost lyrical. However, if the public utterances of 1939 had led to a legislative outcome, this would not happen in 1957. Spain, and the international environment, had changed too much for that.

The consistency of views held by the Spanish dictator[20] can also be tested on the basis of additional documentary evidence generated by his most immediate entourage. Sometime in 1957 Admiral Carrero Blanco, as powerful Minister in charge of the Presidency's office, distributed among the government departments a long memorandum entitled *Introduction to the Study of a Coordinated Plan for Increasing Domestic Output*. There is no discernible disparity between the basic ideas contained therein and the public or private statements on the autarkic strategy made by Franco himself. According to Carrero Blanco, the first objective of Spanish economic policy was to increase domestic output by all means. Foreign trade was to be shunned to the largest extent possible. The optimal situation would be reached when the absolutely unavoidable imports would be capital goods only. The earliest possible elimination of purchases of consumption goods abroad should be the alpha and omega of an intelligent economic policy.[21]

When Carrero Blanco drafted his memorandum some of the despised western European democracies had already concluded the

Treaty of Rome under which the European Economic Community was established. Although, in July 1957, an interdepartmental committee was created to analyse the possible repercussions for Spain, there is no doubt that the two most powerful men in the regime lived in a time-warp of their own making. This time-warp is easily explained. Franco and his most reliable *apparatchiki* saw in the international environment an arena full of dangers and entrapments. Their relationship with the outside world was deeply neurotic. They had too often experienced how external vulnerabilities constrained their room for manoeuvre. Furthermore, they believed that Spain, 'their' Spain, was targeted by redoubtable evil forces. The defunct fascist powers had, according to their own mythology, contended with the Jews, plutocratic capitalism, and decadent democracies. Franco had his own personal 'bestiarium' to which he frequently referred in public: communism, socialism, freemasonry, liberalism – the Jews having conveniently gone backstage after 1945.

It is, of course, tempting to contemplate such obsessions as a mere dialectical device to justify repression at home. However, it is likely that Franco himself believed what he said about the encirclement of Spain by dark and powerful international forces. Fortunately, Admiral Carrero Blanco can again be used as a proxy to illuminate some of the ideological spectacles through which Franco himself and much of his entourage contemplated the international scene. In their view, Spain remained encircled and the best way to interact with the international environment was simply to reduce as far as possible her dependency upon it. Militarily, this was not possible (although Carrero Blanco for a moment thought that the facilities extended to the USA should be curtailed). Economically, it was highly desirable. Retrenchment and watchful vigilance were, in any case, the keywords. To strike a positive balance, in terms of imperviousness to international influences, was the highest goal.

On 21 February 1961, Carrero Blanco wrote to Foreign Minister Castiella in connection with the implementation of the agreements with the U.S. and gave him what he undoubtedly considered to be a lesson in world politics. Three powerful *Internationales* ruled the world, he stated, the communists, the socialists and the freemasons. All three were interested in the spread of democratic regimes. It was under conditions of democracy that those *Internationales* could most easily exert their nefarious influence. Although they pursued very different ultimate goals, all of them coincided in their desire to get rid of regimes like the Spanish one, that is, a regime which was catholic, anti-socialist, anti-communist, anti-capitalist and rabidly independent [*sic*].[22]

The thrust towards economic and institutional change had therefore to overcome such deeply rooted ideological approaches and preconceptions.

The Acceleration of Franco's Learning Curve

The private and public utterances made by General Franco in 1957 on the merits of the autarkic orientation of his regime's economic grand strategy were, in fact, a swan-song. Throughout that year, General Franco accelerated his absorption of modern economic thinking. This learning process can be tested empirically. Three illustrations should suffice.

The first can be found in the meeting, on 20 December 1957, between General Franco and the U.S. Secretary of State, John Foster Dulles. Although the conversation dealt with military and strategic developments in Europe and north Africa, the Spanish dictator raised the perennial issue of the insufficiency of U.S. economic aid to Spain and said that his Government was not satisfied. He indicated that Spain had not been included in the Marshall Plan (as if at that time the regime's stance would have made it possible) and finally concluded that Spain, as a result, 'now finds it impossible to compete with other countries because it has no modern industrial plant'.[23] It is therefore obvious that some elements of economic rationality had begun to penetrate General Franco's thinking by the end of 1957.

The second illustration of this learning process had to do with the accession to the Bretton Woods institutions. Just before the crucial governmental reshuffle of 1957, policy advisers within the regime had already drawn attention to the need to assess the advantages and disadvantages of IMF membership.[24] After the cabinet reshuffle the idea was picked up. In June 1957, Professor Sarda visited the IMF. Other groups of reformist-minded officials followed in August. The U.S. International Cooperation Administration was told that the Spanish Government was seriously considering applying for membership. In September, diplomat José Miguel Ruiz-Morales saw in the accession to the Bretton Woods institutions the final breach of the international siege to which the Spanish regime had been subjected since 1946. It would be, he said, the triumphal crowning of the Spanish reinsertion in the community of nations.[25]

In October a U.S. progress report on Spain, approved by the President, stated that Spanish officials had shown interest in joining the IMF, the IBRD and the IFC. It was recalled that Spain was also cooperating fully with OEEC groups with a view to achieving closer association. On the U.S. side, policies were geared towards inducing positive action by the Spanish Government for stabilising and liberalising the economy. Economic developments appeared critical. In U.S. opinion, demonstrations by labour, students and other political opposition groups in Spain would not constitute a political threat to the regime as long as the deterioration of the economic situation could be averted. Since political stability would be helpful for implementing the 1953 agreements – after all a paramount U.S. objective – there is no wonder that Spain's opening towards the IMF was encouraged.[26]

In January 1958 the Spanish ambassador in Washington formally raised the issue. Although his language was suitably vague, after verbal clarifications the IMF understood it to be a formal application. The U.S. Government decisively supported the Spanish *démarche*. On 14 April, the IMF Executive Board formally approved the application. In September, 1958, Spain became a member of both the IMF and the World Bank. At that time foreign exchange holdings were very low. The proud Spanish regime had to negotiate a bank loan of up to $12 million (U.S.) with the Chase Manhattan Bank, the First National City Bank and the Manufacturers' Trust to pay for the Spanish subscriptions to the two Bretton Woods institutions.

The third illustration of General Franco's acceleration in learning is to be found in the *rapprochement* towards the OEEC which was intensified with the critical encouragement of the U.S. Government. At the same time as the application for IMF membership was tabled, the regime scored an important success: the OEEC agreed to accept Spain as an associate member. All this implied that in the future foreign experts would study Spanish economic problems and policy making from the analytical and political framework prevalent in the most important Western international economic organisations and agencies. They would add their weight to the advice and prodding provided by the U.S. Government itself.

International experts in particular would strengthen the hand of those reformist Spanish high officials who were trying to disseminate a minimum of economic rationality. That such officials stood a good chance of success can be demonstrated by analysing the bureaucratic outcome of the Carrero Blanco memorandum. A year and a half later, that primitive approach had been transmuted into a decree which formally approved an investment programme. This programme acknowledged the need for the Spanish economy to adjust to the transformations which were taking place in the international economic environment. It was also recognised that rapid increases of domestic output and national income required ever increasing imports of foreign goods. Although the investment programme became obsolete, once the Stabilisation Plan was adopted, the gulf between this decree and the 1939 legislative outcome of Franco's appalling ideas is evident. The time for autarky had passed.

The chances of success for the reformist officials were also increased because the continuation of the policies of the past had become discredited. In 1957 and 1958 the new cabinet, which had unified multiple exchange rates and devalued the peseta, had to contend with a drastic deterioration in the balance of payments. Hence, multiple exchange rates were reintroduced. Old interventionist instruments were resuscitated with a vengeance. Nevertheless, slowly but unstoppably foreign exchange holdings started vanishing. The analysts of the State Department were aware of the ambiguity of the reform process. By mid-1958 they speculated that:

> although the Spanish authorities will probably endeavor to do some of the things that American officials have been urging upon them, and although they may be forced by economic necessity to relax certain controls, they are likely to stop short of carrying out many of the major recommended reforms. For these would require a fundamental reorientation of Spanish economic policy and philosophy involving a radical change in the psychology of the Spanish business community as well as Spanish officialdom.

The conclusion was that, with exports static and investment resources being inefficiently allocated, the Spanish government had become 'highly and dangerously dependent upon the United States'. It was 'doubtful that Spain will be able to stand on its own by 1963, unless there is a fundamental reorientation of Spanish economic policy'. Critically, the State Department analysts assessed that 'when the United States ceases to subsidise the Spanish economy, the real troubles of the regime will probably begin'.[27]

A year later, in June 1959, the Acting Secretary of State, Douglas Dillon, reported to President Eisenhower on the rationale of the strategy which the United States had followed in order to help Spain.

1. The basic idea was to take Spain out of the cocoon of isolationism. Dillon indicated that U.S. policies in Spain had been 'the catalysts of its present evolution into the modern society of nations'.

2. Realisation of the danger of identifying U.S. policies with the continuance of General Franco and his regime. According to Dillon, the U.S. had sought to underline the benefits which the Spanish people as a whole, whatever their political beliefs, could derive from U.S. aid.
3. Recognition of the value of Spanish participation in international organisations. The U.S. had been instrumental in ensuring admission to the UN. It had also encouraged membership of the Bretton Woods institutions and of the OEEC.
4. However, U.S. support had been unable to overcome reticence on the part of certain western European countries towards Spanish membership of NATO.

Dillon stated very clearly that the purpose of all these efforts was to europeanise Spain, 'and to establish and nurture as many bonds as possible between the Spanish people and the Western world'. For the U.S. Government the ending of Spain's isolation offered the best hope that the change 'which seems inevitable sooner or later' would be evolutionary rather than revolutionary.[28]

There is little to add to this clear-sighted presentation of U.S. policies towards Spain, particularly when they are compared with the obsessions of Franco and Carrero Blanco. The Spanish regime was being helped in spite of its leaders. For this to be done, the U.S. observers had to cut through the rhetoric of the dictatorship. In August 1958, they recalled that Spanish foreign policy was basically a compromise among the major groups who supported Franco and who did not entirely agree on what course that policy should take. In the last analysis, however, Franco decided what policy was to be followed. The State Department officials foresaw that Spain would probably become more closely integrated with western Europe and its regional and political arrangements and that the ties with the United States would be firmly maintained. They were right. The basic thrust would be contained in the *volte-face* of 1959.

Foreign Assistance for the Change in Strategy

U.S. enticements were a necessary, though not sufficient, condition for the carrying out of the 1959 operation. Three additional factors would make the change of strategy virtually unstoppable:

1. The continuance of past policies was at odds with the new foreign policy position attained by the Spanish regime.

2. By 1958 a critical intellectual and institutional mass had been reached for devising a strategic alternative.
3. The balance of payments position had reached an intolerable crisis and the foreign exchange reserves were exhausted. Technically, by 1959 the Franco regime had got itself into a situation of virtual bankruptcy.

The combined additional impact of those three factors, as relayed by the reformist ministers, was too much for General Franco. When confronted with the imminent collapse of Spanish international payments, he reluctantly conceded defeat.

The first factor can be easily illustrated: on 30 January 1959, the economic inner cabinet discussed a forthcoming IMF mission. IEME, a subsidiary organ of the Ministry of Commerce, had written to the IMF requesting that the mission also consider a plan to allow for a more intense Spanish participation in the European organisations. On 11 February, Foreign Minister Castiella warned Carrero Blanco that the mission would carry out a critical assessment of the Spanish economic situation in order to suggest the necessary measures to adopt. A new global economic policy was on the cards. The IMF and the OEEC connection had created a completely new situation.

The second factor was illustrated by the intellectual and technical poverty displayed by the enemies of reform. Even Suanzes had to recognise that the 'rational and progressive liberalisation of Spanish merchandise flows' could be a positive development to tackle the balance of payments problem. Meanwhile, *Información Comercial Española* and the reformist economists increased their intellectual effort in favour of change. The IMF mission gave the modernising Spanish officials immense encouragement. Gabriel Ferras, director of the European Department, drafted the first version of a memorandum in his Madrid hotel. It was extremely respectful of the policies pursued since the end of the Civil War. It also provided a rationale for the change of strategy which the Spanish government was being asked to carry out. By the end of February 1959, the outline of the stabilisation and liberalisation plan had also been drafted.

The third factor generated a dynamic of its own: IEME reported that reserves were minus $66 million (U.S.). Furthermore, short-term debts amounted to $145 million (U.S.). Impending payments for the authorised imports in 1959 were estimated at $108 million (U.S.). This dismal situation at the end of February would worsen even more with the passing of time. As Navarro Rubio has indicated in his not always reliable memoirs, General Franco was at a loss.[29]

Some ideas were proposed in the corridors of power to deal with such an extreme situation, but they came to nothing. The U.S.-IMF-OEEC connection did. In July 1959, the Spanish ambassador to Washington discussed the forthcoming measures with the State Department. One U.S. official indicated that two months earlier he would not have believed that Spain could arrange credits with private banks to the extent that was going to be the case. The participation of private banks would give strong signals about confidence in the Spanish programme, even more so than the funds provided by the U.S. Government.[30]

The *volte-face*, announced on 20 July 1959, implied a combination of measures: devaluation of the peseta, introduction of a single exchange rate, a programme of monetary and fiscal restraint, a liberalisation of price controls and trade restrictions. Later on, a new customs duty system and a certain liberalisation of foreign investment were added.[31] The IMF and a consortium of twelve U.S. private banks provided $75 million (U.S.) in drawing facilities and $68 million (U.S.) in loans and credits respectively. Spain was admitted to full membership of the OEEC and was granted an additional $100 million (U.S.) credit from the European Monetary Fund. Bilateral debts with OEEC governments were consolidated to the amount of $45 million (U.S.). However, the U.S. Government did not give any specific, programme-targeted assistance. Within the implementation of the 1953 agreements, up to $130 million (U.S.) were made available.

On 31 August, Castiella met in London with President Eisenhower. He was fulsome in expressing Spanish gratitude, in particular for U.S. political and moral support. He ingratiatingly underlined that 'Spain was the most anti-Communist country in the world'. The Americans seemed happy.[32]

Conclusions: Franco and Two Defining Movements in the International Environment, 1936–1959

No reflection on Spain in an international context between 1936 and 1959, the years of the 'first Francoism', can be concluded without underlining a fundamental paradox. The Spanish dictatorship maintained throughout those years an exalted rhetoric of unenlightened and primitive nationalism. At its head, General Franco persistently adhered to a strategy of few but selective contacts with the international environment. The overbearing need to undermine the 'siege', without giving up the political and institutional essence of the regime, led to the strategic realignment enshrined in the 1953 agreements with the U.S.. However, mistrust of the international arena and Franco's sheer inability to cast off his own ideological shackles provided for continuous retrenchment. The Spanish economy was condemned to recurrent balance of payments crises.

Ideological drivel notwithstanding, the Spanish dictatorship could not operate independently of the international context. In the heady days of fascist expansion, the military, political, and diplomatic support given to General Franco by the Axis powers was a critical element in ensuring his victory in the Civil War. This was the first defining movement in the international arena with which Franco became intimate. The Cold War, as the defining phenomenon of the post-war world, and not Franco's alleged supernatural foresight, was the critical element behind the 1953 agreements. As U.S. diplomatic documents make clear, the Americans liked Spain's strategic location more than the Spanish regime and tried, albeit without much success, to disassociate the defence of their own long-term interests from any crude manifestation of support for the dictatorship.[33] Massive Francoist indoctrination and propaganda prevented the Spanish public from perceiving that attempt at disassociation. On the other hand President Eisenhower's visit to General Franco in 1959 enhanced the U.S. connection as a major prop for the regime.

Finally, direct and indirect U.S. assistance in the intellectual, political, and diplomatic fields was one of the key factors which dynamised Spanish pursuit of economic reform after the 1953 agreements. The opening up of the economy meant that foreign capital goods and foreign consumption goods gradually put Spanish production and consumption patterns more in line with the western European context. Foreign investors began to invest, although cautiously, in Spain. More importantly perhaps, many Spaniards realized that the authoritarian methods of economic policy making and the autarkic stranglehold which Franco's dreams had imposed upon the Spanish economy and society had been a dismal failure.

Some of Franco's primitive economic beliefs were shaped during the interaction with Hitler's Germany. It is therefore interesting to underscore the belated nexus between the U.S.-led crusade against fascism in Europe, the U.S.-led acceptance of the enduring Spanish regime and the U.S.-inspired policies which would finally assist

General Franco in overcoming the intellectual and political collapse of some of his most tenaciously held personal beliefs.[34]

Notes

1. This article is lovingly dedicated to my children Laura and Daniel for whom this story will be ancient history.
2. Gabriel Tortella, *El desarrollo de la España contemporánea. Historia económica de los siglos XIX y XX*, Madrid, 1994, pp. 204 and 385-6, also supports this dichotomy.
3. See, *inter alia*, Juan Sarda, 'El Banco de España, 1931-1962', in *El Banco de España; Una historia económica*, Madrid, 1970; Manuel-Jesus González, *La económica política del franquismo (1940-1970); Dirigismo, mercado y planificación*, Madrid, 1979; Joaquín Muns, *Historia de las relaciones entre España y el Fondo Monetario Internacional, 1958-1982*, Madrid, 1986; Manuel Varela, 'El Plan de Estabilización como yo lo recuerdo', *Información Comercial Española*, August-September 1984: 41-55; Enrique Fuentes Quintana, 'El Plan de Estabilización Economica de 1959, veinticinco años después', *Información Comercial Española*, August-September 1984: 25-40. On the basis of Spanish archival evidence: Angel Viñas, Julio Viñuela, Fernando Eguidazu, Carlos Fernández Pulgar y Senen Florensa, *Política comercial exterior en España, 1931-1975*, Madrid, 1979.
4. For a shining example of latter day Francoist propaganda see Fundación Nacional Francisco Franco, *El legado de Franco*, Madrid, 1992.
5. On the agreements see Boris Liedtke's contribution to this present volume.
6. See AMAE R5332 for much documentation on all of these aspects.
7. AMAE R5883/E4. It has not been reproduced in FRUS.
8. Preston, *Franco*, London, 1993, p. 665.
9. Varela became technical General-Secretary in the Ministry of Commerce. Professor Fuentes Quintana was Head of the Research Department and editor of the influential monthly *Información Comercial Española*, the mouthpiece of all economists longing for change. Some of the very distinguished names in later Spanish economic policymaking (foremost Luis Angel Rojo, currently Governor of the Bank of Spain) became rapidly involved in the operation. In the Bank of Spain, Professor Sarda was Head of Research at that time. In the Ministry of Finance Juan Antonio Ortiz Garcia became the technical General-Secretary.
10. Alfonso Ballestero, *Juan Antonio Suanzes, 1891-1977. La política industrial de la posguerra*, LID, 1993. Suanzes was one of Franco's most trusted cronies and had twice been Minister for Industry and Trade. He launched enormous industrial projects in the 1950s; for an excellent overview see Francisco Comin, 'Sector público y crecimiento económico en la dictadura de Franco', *AYER* 21, 1996.
11. See Viñas et al., *Política comercial*, pp. 861ff., for documentary evidence from AMAE and IEME. Experts from an OEEC working group had gone to Madrid in January 1957 and sounded out Spanish interest for commercial and financial liberalisation.
12. This insight has been described by one of the most outstanding protagonists of the 1959 operation as follows: 'The major difficulty did not lie in the economy. Quite the contrary. Notwithstanding the defence that some people, in certain institutions, put up in favour of the previous economic system, I hold that the

great fear – and rightly so – was that economic liberalisation would be inexorably followed by political liberalisation, albeit not immediately. Nobody wanted to speculate about the depth of that political liberalisation but most of the establishment certainly did not wish it'. Varela, 'El Plan de Estabilización', 45.

13. See, for instance, Carlos Velasco, 'Las pintorescas ideas económicas de Franco', *Historia 16*, May 1983.

14. The document entitled 'Fundamentals and Directives for a Plan for the Reorganisation of our Economy in Harmony with our National Reconstruction' was discovered by Javier Tusell, in the private archive of one of the non-economic ministers who entered the cabinet in August 1939. Tusell who did not identify the minister concerned, published the document with an interesting commentary, 'La autarquía cuartelera. Las ideas económicas de Franco a partir de un documento inédito', *Historia 16*, Nov. 1985. Preston, *Franco*, pp. 344-5, has situated Franco's appallingly simplistic and forthrightly stupid ideas in the context of the terrible shortages which Spain was undergoing at the time.

15. Many of the ideas, and occasionally complete paragraphs, of that memorandum had already been used by Franco in a famous speech on 5 June 1939 before the Falangist National Council. Although in his public rhetoric Franco often changed course and juggled with perfectly contradictory themes, there are certain beliefs which he adhered to with gusto.

16. In Viñas et al., *Política comercial*, pp. 990 and 993-4, we speculated about the content of the minutes of the meetings of the Council of Ministers (in both their usual and restricted formats). We underscored that it had not been possible for us to find statements designed for the enlightenment of the cabinet only.

17. Unfortunately, at the moment of writing, I do not have Franco's presentation before me. I photocopied it some years ago from the files of the *Comisión Delegada* in the APG I was, however, so struck by it that I did not forget the basic argument. Javier Tusell, *Carrero, la eminencia gris del régimen de Franco*, Madrid, 1993, pp. 256ff., came across the statement later and mentioned it without realising its importance. He indicates as source (APG) series SG, box 072, file 10.

18. Fuentes Quintana deplored Ullastres's silence as a crucial lacuna in all attempts at reconstructing the 1959 operation. He also considered it to be unlikely that Ullastres would break that self-imposed silence, which later interviews have not essentially impaired. One trivial anecdote may help hypothesise about his reasons. Before 1959, Ullastres used to refer elliptically to Franco as 'ese señor'. One day, in the early 1960s, he startled one of his most trusted aides when, overnight and without explanation, he began to refer to Franco as the *Caudillo*.

19. That Franco in 1957 specifically remembered the *guayule* case is simply extraordinary. In studies by Spanish historians the best and most detailed analysis of German-Spanish economic relations during World War II is Rafael García Pérez, *Franquismo y Tercer Reich*, Madrid, 1994. Not surprisingly *guayule* is not mentioned.

20. The consistency between private and public utterances in 1957 can also be explained by the fact that, by then, Franco must have had many reasons to feel great satisfaction. He had achieved victory in his efforts to replace foreign with Spanish goods! Later statistical estimates would show that the share of domestic goods in the total supply of consumption goods, which had been 77 percent in 1941, went up to 94.4 percent in 1958. In the case of capital goods the respective shares were 33 and 71. All sectors considered, overall shares were 74 and 86 percent respectively. By 1958, Spaniards therefore massively used or

consumed Spanish products. Hence, Spanish vulnerabilities, according to Franco's quaint theories, ought to have substantially decreased. However, unfortunately for the theories and fortunately for most Spaniards, this was not the case.

21. Carrero Blanco's memorandum in APG SG 4/115/57. It has now become commonplace to refer to it; see for example Tusell, *Carrero*, pp. 259ff. Needless to say that no pro-Francoist economist (there are still some) or pro-Francoist writer on foreign policy (there are more) bother to interpret such documents.

22. See AMAE R 12028/E2 for the 'lesson' given to Castiella. Tusell, *Carrero*, pp. 301ff., has also commented on it while highlighting Carrero Blanco's consistency of views throughout the years.

23. FRUS 1955-1957, vol. XXVII, doc. 207, p. 596.

24. For documentary evidence see APG SG 1/8, records of the Director-General of IEME, file IMF, Spain's accession.

25. AMAE, R 5332/E6.

26. FRUS 1955-1957, doc. 205, pp. 585-6.

27. FRUS 1958-1960, vol. VII/ 2, doc. 309, pp. 718-20.

28. Ibid., doc. 312, p. 728. This policy towards Spain fitted easily into the more general goal of supporting western European integration via the implementation of the Rome Treaty and the strengthening of the OEEC. See Pascaline Winand, *Eisenhower, Kennedy, and the United States of Europe*, New York, 1993, in particular chap. 5.

29. Preston has elaborated on Franco's perplexity. Viñas et al., *Política comercial*, pp. 1022 and 1116f., contains a summary of some inconsistencies in Navarro Rubio's recollections.

30. FRUS 1958-1960, doc. 313, p. 732.

31. One of the reasons given by Franco in the early fifties to explain his opposition to foreign direct investment was his experience with German economic penetration in the Civil War years.

32. FRUS 1958-1960, doc. 315, p. 735. Since Castiella possibly considered the Americans to be particularly gullible, he said, in a subsequent meeting with the secretary of state, that he expected to receive U.S. support for retrieving $600 million in 510 tons of gold sent by the Republican government to the Soviet Union during the Civil War. The gold would, he claimed, greatly assist Spanish economic recovery.

33. See Boris Liedtke's contribution to this present volume.

34. See Preston, *Franco*, pp. 682 and 785, for a similar scathing criticism: 'The economic boom – so assiduously claimed by his propagandists as the greatest achievement – was, like wartime neutrality, little to do with Franco.'

Select Bibliography

Ahmad, Q. *Britain, Franco Spain and the Cold War 1945-1950.* Kuala Lumpur, 1995.

Alexander, M.S. *The Republic in Danger. General Maurice Gamelin and the politics of French defence, 1933-1940.* Cambridge, 1993.

Alexander, M.S. and Graham, H. (eds). *The French and Spanish Popular Fronts: Comparative Perspectives.* Cambridge, 1989.

Alpert, M. *A New International History of the Spanish Civil War.* London, 1994.

Alvarez del Vayo, J. *The Last Optimist.* London, 1950.

Areilza, J.M. and Castiella, F.M. *Reivindicaciones de España.* 2nd edn, Madrid, 1941.

Armero, J.M. *La política exterior de Franco.* Barcelona, 1978.

Badia, G. et al. *Les barbelés de l'exil.* Grenoble, 1979.

Ballestero, A. *Juan Antonio Suanzes, 1891-1977; La política industrial de la posguerra.* Madrid, 1993.

———. *La técnica de la política exterior.* Mendoza, 1995.

Blinkhorn, M. *Democracy and Civil War in Spain, 1931-1939.* London, 1988.

Bolloten, B. *The Spanish Revolution: The Left and the Struggle for Power during the Civil War.* Chapel Hill, NC, 1979.

Boor, Jakim [pseudonym of Francisco Franco Bahamonde]. *Masonería.* Madrid, 1952.

Borrás Llop, J. *Política de los exiliados españoles, 1944-50.* Châtillon-sous-Bagneux, 1976.

———. *Francia ante la guerra civil española: burguesia, interés nacional e interés de clase.* Madrid, 1981.

Brome, V. *The International Brigades, Spain 1936-1937.* London, 1965.

Broué, P. *Staline et la révolution: le cas espagnol (1936-1939).* Paris, 1993.

Burdick, C.B. *Germany's Military Strategy and Spain in World War II*. Syracuse, NY, 1968.

Cantalupo, R. *Fu la Spagna. Ambasciata presso Franco. Febbraio-Aprile 1937*. Milan, 1948.

Carr, E.H. *The Comintern and the Spanish Civil War*. London, 1984.

Carr, R. *The Spanish Tragedy*. London, 1977.

Carrillo, S. *Dialogue on Spain*. London, 1976.

Cattell, D.T. *Soviet Diplomacy and the Spanish Civil War*. Berkeley, 1957.

Claudin, F. *Santiago Carrillo: Crónica de un Secretario General*. Barcelona, 1983.

Colton, J. *Léon Blum: Humanist in politics*. Durham NC, 1987.

Corta, D. de. *Le rôle de l'Attaché militaire français pendant la guerre civile espagnole*. Paris, 1981.

Courtois, S. Peschanski, D. and Rayski, A. *Le sang de l'étranger. Les immigrés de la MOI dans la Résistance*. Paris, 1989.

Coverdale, J. *Italian Intervention in the Spanish Civil War*. Princeton, 1975.

Crozier, B. *Franco: A Biographical History*. London, 1967.

Delgado, L. *Imperio de papel; Acción cultural y política exterior durante el primer franquismo*. Madrid, 1992.

Delperrie de Bayac, J. *Histoire du Front Populaire*. Paris, 1972.

Detwiler, D.S. *Hitler, Franco und Gibraltar: Die Frage des spanischen Eintritts in den zweiten Weltkrieg*. Wiesbaden, 1962.

Doussinague, J.M. *España tenía razón (1939-1945)*. Madrid, 1949.

Dreifort, J. *Yvon Delbos at the Quai d'Orsay: French Foreign Policy during the Popular Front*. Kansas, 1973.

Duroselle, J.B. *La politique étrangère de la France. La décadence, 1932-1939*. Paris, 1979.

Edwards, J. *The British Government and the Spanish Civil War*. London, 1979.

Espadas Burgos, M. *Franquismo y política exterior*. Madrid, 1987.

Fernández Santander, C. *Tensiones militares durante el franquismo*, Barcelona, 1985.

Franco Bahamonde, F. *Textos de doctrina política: palabras y escritos de 1945 a 1950*. Madrid, 1951.

Fyrth, J. *The Signal was Spain: The Aid Spain Movement in Britain, 1936-1939*. London, 1986.

García Pérez, R. *Franquismo y Tercer Reich*. Madrid, 1994.

Goda, N.J.W. *Tomorrow the World: Hitler, Northwest Africa, and the Path toward America*. College Station, TX, 1998.

González, M.-J. *La económica politica del franquismo (1940-1970); Dirigismo, mercado y planificación.* Madrid, 1979.

Graham, H.E. *Socialism and War. The Spanish Socialist Party in power and crisis, 1936-1939.* Cambridge, 1991.

Hamilton, K. *Non-intervention Revisited: Great Britain, the UN and Franco's Spain in 1946.* London (FCO Occasional Paper), 1995.

Haslam, J. *The Soviet Union and the Struggle for Collective Security in Europe, 1933-1939.* London, 1984.

Heine, H. *La oposición política al Franquismo: de 1939 a 1952.* Barcelona, 1983.

———. 'Political Opposition to the Franco Regime between 1939-1952', PhD thesis, University of London, 1981.

Hills, G. *Rock of Contention: A History of Gibraltar.* London, 1974.

Hoare, S. *Ambassador on Special Mission.* London, 1946.

Hoisington, W.A. *The Casablanca Connection. French Colonial Policy, 1936-1943.* Chapel Hill, NC, 1984.

International Editorial Board. *International Solidarity with the Spanish Republic, 1936-1939.* Moscow, 1975.

Jackson, G. *The Spanish Republic and the Civil War, 1931-1939.* Princeton, 1965.

Jackson, J. *The Popular Front in France, 1934-1938: Defending Democracy.* Cambridge, 1988.

Jiménez, J.C. *El ocaso de la amistad entre las dictaduras ibéricas, 1955-1968.* Mérida, 1996.

Knox, M. *Mussolini Unleashed 1939-1941: Politics and Strategy in Fascist Italy's Last War.* Cambridge and New York, 1982.

Lachadenède, R. Sabatier de. *La Marine française et la guerre d'Espagne.* Vincennes, 1993.

Landis, A. *Spain: The Unfinished Revolution.* New York, 1972.

Laroche, G. *On les nommait des étrangers; les immigrés dans la Résistance.* Paris, 1965.

Lefranc, G. *Histoire du Front Populaire.* Paris, 1970.

Leitz, C. *Economic Relations between Nazi Germany and Franco's Spain.* Oxford, 1996.

Livian. M. *Le Parti Socialiste et l'immigration. Le gouvernement Blum. La main d'oeuvre immigrée, et les réfugiés politiques, 1920-1940.* Paris, 1982.

Lister, E. *Basta.* Madrid, 1978.

———. *Así destruyó Carrillo el PCE.* Barcelona, 1983.

Lleonart y Anselem, A.J. *España y la ONU.* 4 vols, Madrid, 1978, 1983, 1985 and 1991.

López Rodó, L. *La larga marcha hacia la monarquía.* Barcelona, 1977.

Maisky, I. *Spanish Notebooks.* London, 1966.

Marquina, A. *España en la política de seguridad occidental, 1939-1986.* Madrid, 1986.

Martínez Parilla, J. *Las fuerzas armadas francesas ante la guerra civil Española (1936-1939).* Madrid, 1987.

Milza, O. *Les Français devant l'immigration.* Brussels, 1988.

Moradiellos, E. *La perfidia de Albión. El gobierno británico y la guerra civil española.* Madrid, 1996.

Moreno, A. 'Actitud y reacción de España ante Europa; Franquismo y construcción europea', unpublished PhD thesis, University of Madrid, 1995.

Morrow, F. *Revolution and Counter-Revolution in Spain.* London, 1963.

Muns, J. *Historia de las relaciones entre España y el Fondo Monetario Internacional, 1958-1982.* Madrid, 1986.

Neila, J.L. 'España república mediterránea, seguridad colectiva y defensa nacional (1931-1936)', unpublished PhD thesis, University of Madrid, 1994.

Nuñez Hernández, J. *La función consular en el Derecho Español.* Madrid, 1980.

Pardo, R. *Con Franco hacia el Imperio; La política exterior española en América Latina, 1939-1945.* Madrid, 1995.

Payne, S.G. *The Spanish Revolution.* London, 1970.

Pereira, J.C. and Cervantes, A. *Relaciones diplomáticas entre España y América.* Madrid, 1992.

Peterson, M. *Both Sides of the Curtain.* London, 1950.

Piétri, F. *Mes années d'Espagne 1940-1948.* Paris, 1954.

Pike, D.W. *Vae Victis! Los republicanos españoles refugiados en Francia, 1939-1944.* Paris, 1969.

———. *Les Français et la Guerre d'Espagne, 1936-1939.* Paris, 1975.

———. *Jours de gloire: Jours de Honte.* Paris, 1984.

Pollack, B. and Hunter, G. *The Paradox of Spanish Foreign Policy. Spain's International Relations from Franco to Democracy.* New York, 1987.

Pons Prades, E. *Guerrillas españolas, 1936-1960.* Barcelona, 1977.

Pons, S. *Stalin e la guerra inevitable, 1936-1941.* Turin, 1995.

Portero, F. *Franco aislado: la cuestión española (1945-1950).* Madrid, 1989.

Pratt, L.W. *East of Malta, West of Suez. Britain's Mediterranean Crisis, 1936-1939.* Cambridge, 1975.

Preston, P. *Franco: A Biography.* London, 1993.

Preston, P. and Smyth, D. *Spain and the EEC and NATO.* London, 1984.

Quintana, F. *España en Europa, 1931-1936; Del compromiso por la paz a la huida de la guerra.* Madrid, 1993.

Rafaneau-Boj, M.-C. *Odyssée pour la liberté. Les camps des prisonniers espagnols, 1939-1945.* Paris, 1993.

Rémond, R. and Bourdin, J. *Edouard Daladier. Chef de gouvernement.* Paris, 1977.

Roberts, G. *The Unholy Alliance: Stalin's Pact with Hitler.* London, 1989.

———. *The Soviet Union and the Origins of the Second World War.* London, 1995.

Ruhl, K.-J. *Spanien im Zweiten Weltkrieg: Franco, die Falange und das "Dritte Reich".* Hamburg, 1975.

Ruiz Holst, M. *Neutralität oder Kriegsbeteiligung? Die deutschspanischen Verhandlungen im Jahre 1940.* Pfaffenweiler, 1986.

Sagnes, J. and Caucanas, S. (eds). *Les Français et la Guerre d'Espagne. Actes du Colloque de Perpignan.* Perpignan, 1990.

Saña, H. *El franquismo sin mitos: conversaciones con Serrano Suñer.* Barcelona, 1981.

Sandoval, J. and Azcarate, M. *Spain 1936-1939.* London, 1963.

Saz, I. *Mussolini contra la Segunda República.* Valencia, 1986.

Schor, R. *L'Opinion française et les étrangers, 1919-1939.* Paris, 1985.

Séguéla, M. *Pétain-Franco. Les secréts d'une alliance.* Paris, 1992.

Serrano Suñer, R. *Entre Hendaya y Gibraltar.* Madrid, 1947.

———. *Memorias: Entre el silencio y la propaganda. La historia como fue.* Barcelona, 1987.

Shirinya, K.K. *Strategiya i Taktika Kominterna v Borbe Protiv Fashizma i Voiny (1934-1939).* Moscow, 1979.

Smyth, D. *Diplomacy and Strategy of Survival: British Policy and Franco's Spain, 1940-41.* Cambridge, 1986.

Stanford Research Institute. *Las inversiones norteamericanas en España.* Barcelona, 1972.

Stein, L. *Beyond Death and Exile: The Spanish Republicans in France, 1939-1955.* Cambridge, MA, 1975.

Stone, G. *The Oldest Ally: Britain and the Portuguese Connection, 1936-1941.* Woodbridge, 1994.

Tabanera, N. 'Las relaciones entre España e Hispanoamérica durante la II^a República española, 1931-1939; La acción diplomática republicana', unpublished PhD thesis, University of Madrid, 1990.

Taguena, M. *Testimonio de dos guerras*. Mexico City, 1973.

Terrón Montero, J. *La prensa de España durante el régimen de Franco*. Madrid, 1981.

Thomas, H. *The Spanish Civil War*. rev. edn, London, 1965, 3rd edn. London, 1977.

Thomas, M. *Britain, France and Appeasement. Anglo-French Relations in the Popular Front Era*. Oxford, 1996.

Togores, L.E. and Neila, J.L. (under the direction of José Martínez Cardós). *La Escuela Diplomática; cincuenta años de servicio al Estado (1942-1992)*. Madrid, 1993.

Tortella, G. *El desarrollo de la España contemporánea. Historia económica de los siglos XIX y XX*. Madrid, 1994.

Trotsky, L. *The Spanish Revolution (1931-39)*. New York, 1973.

Tusell, J. *Franco y los católicos: la política interior española entre 1945 y 1957*. Madrid, 1984.

———. *Carrero. La eminencia gris del régimen de Franco*. Madrid, 1993.

Tusell, J. and García Queipo de Llano, G. *Franco y Mussolini: la política española durante la segunda guerra mundial*. Barcelona, 1985.

Viñas, A. *Guerra, Dinero y Dictadura; Ayuda fascista y autarquía en la España de Franco*. Barcelona, 1984.

Viñas, A. Viñuela, J. Eguidazu, F. Pulgar-Fernández, C. Forensa, S. *Política comercial exterior en España, 1931-1975*. 2 vols, Madrid, 1979.

Whealey, R.H. *Hitler and Spain. The Nazi Role in the Spanish Civil War*. Lexington, 1989.

Young, R.J. *In Command of France: French Foreign Policy and Military Planning, 1933-1940*. Cambridge, MA, 1978.

Abendroth, H.-H. 'Deutschland, Frankreich und der spanische Bürgerkrieg, 1936-1939', in *Deutschland und Frankreich, 1936-1939*, eds Klaus Hildebrand and Karl Ferdinand Werner. Munich, 1981.

Bernecker, W.L. 'Neutralität wider Willen: Spaniens verhinderter Kriegseintritt', in *Kriegsausbruch 1939: Beteiligte, Betroffene, Neutrale*, eds H. Altrichter and J. Becker. Munich, 1989, pp. 153-77.

Bloch, C. 'Les relations franco-allemandes et la politique des puissances pendant la guerre d'Espagne', in *Deutschland und Frankreich, 1936-1939*, eds Klaus Hildebrand and Karl Ferdinand Werner. Munich, 1981.

Burdick, C. '"Moro": the Resupply of German Submarines in Spain, 1939-1942', *Central European History* 3, no.3, 1970: 256-83.

Caron, V. 'The Missed Opportunity: French Refugee Policy in Wartime, 1939-40', *Historical Reflections/Reflexions Historiques* 22, no. 1, 1996: 117-57.

Carreras, A. 'Depresión económica y cambio estructural durante el decenio bélico (1936-1945)', in *El primer franquismo: España durante la segunda guerra mundial*, ed. J.L. Garcia Delgado. Madrid, 1989.

Clarence-Smith, G. 'The Impact of the Spanish Civil War and the Second World War on Portuguese and Spanish Africa', *Journal of African History* 26, 1985.

Comin, F. 'Sector público y crecimiento económico en la dictadura de Franco', *AYER* 21, 1996.

Fuentes Quintana, E. 'El Plan de Estabilización Economica de 1959, veinticinco años después', *Información Comercial Española*, August-September 1984: 25-40.

Goda, N.J.W. 'Hitler's Demand for Casablanca in 1940: Incident or Policy?', *International History Review* XVI, no. 3, 1994: 491-510.

Haslam, J. 'The Comintern and the Origins of the Popular Front', *Historical Journal* 26, no.3, 1979: 673-91.

Halstead, C. 'Aborted Imperialism, Spain's Occupation of Tangier, 1940-1945', *Iberian Studies* 7, no. 2, 1978: 53-71.

Koerner, F. 'Les répercussions de la guerre d'Espagne en Oranie (1936-1939)', *Revue d'histoire moderne et contemporaine* 22, no. 3, 1975.

Leitz, C. 'Nazi Germany's Struggle for Spanish Wolfram during the Second World War', *European History Quarterly* 25, 1995: 71-92.

———. 'Nazi Germany's Intervention in the Spanish Civil War and the Foundation of HISMA/ROWAK', in *The Republic Besieged: Civil War in Spain 1936-1939*, eds P. Preston and A.L. Mackenzie. Edinburgh, 1996, pp. 53-86.

Lleonart y Anselem, A.J. 'España y la ONU: La cuestión Española 1945-1950', *Revista de Política Internacional* 152, 1977: 310-89.

Lowi, T.J. 'Bases in Spain', in *American Civil-Military Decisions; A Book of Case Studies*, ed. H. Stein. Birmingham, Ala, 1963.

Maga, T.P. 'Closing the Door: the French Government and refugee policy, 1933-1939', *French Historical Studies* XII, no. 3, 1982: 424-42.

Meshcheryakov, M.T. 'Sovetskii Souz i Antifashistskaya Voina Ispanskogo Naroda (1936-1939gg.)', *Istoriya SSSR*, January 1988.

———. 'Kommunisticheskaya Partiya Ispanii i Komintern'. *Novaya i Noveishaya Istoriya* 5, 1991.

———. 'SSSR i Grazhdanskaya Voina v Ispanii'. *Otechestvennaya Istoriya* 3, 1993.

Moradiellos, E. 'The Origins of British Non-Intervention in the Spanish Civil War: Anglo-Spanish Relations in Early 1936', *European History Quarterly* 21, no. 3, 1991: 339-64.

———. 'Appeasement and Non-Intervention: British Policy during the Spanish Civil War', in *Britain and the Threat to Stability in Europe, 1918-1945*, eds P. Catterall and C.J. Morris. London, 1993.

———. 'The Gentle General: The Official British Perception of General Franco during the Spanish Civil War', in *The Republic Besieged: Civil War in Spain 1936-1939*, eds P. Preston and A.L. Mackenzie. Edinburgh, 1996, pp. 1-20.

Munholland, J.K. 'The Daladier government and the "Red Scare" of 1938-1940', in *Proceedings of the Tenth Annual Meeting of the Western Society for French History (14-16 October 1982)*, ed. J.F. Sweets. Lawrence, KA, 1984, pp. 495-506.

Neila, J.L. 'La articulación del Estado franquista en la posguerra civil; la reorganización de la Administración exterior y la creación de la Escuela Diplomática (1939-1945)', in *II Encuentro de investigadores del franquismo; Alicante, 11, 12, y 13 de mayo de 1995*. Alicante and Valencia, 1995.

Nieto, A. 'De la República a la Democracia: la Administración española del franquismo', *Revista de Derecho Administrativo* 11, 1976.

Preston, P. 'Franco and Hitler: The Myth of Hendaye 1940'. *Contemporary European History* 1, no. 1, 1992: 1-16.

———. 'Franco and the Axis Temptation', in Paul Preston, *The Politics of Revenge; Fascism and the military in twentieth-century Spain*. London, 1995, pp. 60-71.

———. 'Mussolini's Spanish Adventure: From Limited Risk to War', in *The Republic Besieged: Civil War in Spain 1936-1939*, eds P. Preston and A.L. Mackenzie. Edinburgh, 1996, pp. 21-52.

Renouvin, P. 'La Politique extérieure du premier gouvernement Léon Blum', in *Léon Blum: Chef du gouvernement*, eds R. Rémond and P. Renouvin. 2nd edn, Paris, 1981.

Roberts, G. 'Collective Security and the Origins of the People's Front', in *Britain, Fascism and the Popular Front*, ed. J. Fyrth. London, 1985.

Sarda, J. 'El Banco de España, 1931-1962', in *El Banco de España; Una historia económica*. Madrid, 1970.

Saz Campos, I. 'El Franquismo: ¿Régimen autoritorio o dictadura fascista?', in *El Régimen de Franco (1936-1975); Congreso internacional*, eds J. Tusell, S. Sueiro, J.M. Marín. M. Casanova. Madrid, 1993.

Smyth, D. 'Reflex Reaction: Germany and the Onset of the Spanish Civil War', in *Revolution and War in Spain, 1931-1939*, ed. P. Preston. London, 1984, pp. 243-65.

———. 'The Politics of Asylum, Juan Negrín and the British Government in 1940', in *Diplomacy and Intelligence during the Second World War: Essays in Honour of F.S. Hinsley*, ed. R. Langhorne. Cambridge, 1984.

———. '"We are with you": Solidarity and Self-Interest in Soviet Policy towards Republican Spain, 1936-1939', in *Radicals, Rebels & Establishments*, ed. P.J. Corish. Belfast, 1985. (Revised and expanded version in *The Republic Besieged: Civil War in Spain 1936-1939*, eds P. Preston and A.L. Mackenzie. Edinburgh, 1996, pp. 87-106.)

———. 'The Moor and the Money-lender: Politics and Profits in Anglo-German Relations with Francoist Spain 1936-1940', in *Von der Konkurrenz zur Rivalität: Das britische-deutsche Verhältnis in den Ländern der europäischen Peripherie 1919-1939*, ed. M.-L. Recker. Stuttgart, 1986.

———. 'Screening "Torch": Allied Counter-Intelligence and the Spanish Threat to the Secrecy of the Allied Invasion of French North Africa in November, 1942', *Intelligence and National Security* 4, no. 2, 1989.

———. 'The Despatch of the Spanish Blue Division to the Russian Front: Reasons and Repercussions', *European History Quarterly* 24, no. 4, 1994: 537-53.

Stone, G. 'Britain, France and the Spanish Problem, 1936-1939', in *Decisions and Diplomacy: Essays in Twentieth Century International History*, eds D. Richardson and G. Stone. London, 1995.

———. 'Britain. Non-Intervention and the Spanish Civil War', *European Studies Review* 9, no.1, 1979.

———. 'The European Great Powers and the Spanish Civil War, 1936-1939', in *Paths to War: New Essays on the Origins of the*

Second World War, eds R. Boyce and E.M. Robertson. London, 1989, pp. 199-232.

―――. 'Britain, France and Franco's Spain in the Aftermath of the Spanish Civil War', *Diplomacy and Statecraft* 6, no. 2, 1995: 373-407.

Swain, G. 'The Cominform: Tito's International?', *Historical Journal* 35, no. 3, 1992: 641-663.

―――. 'Stalin's Wartime Vision of the Post-War World', *Diplomacy and Statecraft* 7, no. 1, 1996: 73-96.

Thomas, M. 'Plans and Problems of the Armée de l'Air in the Defence of French North Africa before the fall of France', *French History* 7, no. 4, 1993.

Tusell, J. 'La autarquía cuartelera. Las ideas económicas de Franco a partir de un documento inédito', *Historia 16*, November 1985.

Varela, M. 'El Plan de Estabilización como yo lo recuerdo', *Información Comercial Española*, August-September 1984: 41-55.

Velasco, C. 'Las pintorescas ideas económicas de Franco', *Historia 16*, May 1983.

Viñas, A. 'Gold, the Soviet Union and the Spanish Civil War', *European Studies Review* 9, 1979: 105-28.

―――. 'La Administración de la política económica exterior en España, 1936-1979', *Cuadernos Económicos de I.C.E.* 13, 1980: 159-247.

―――. 'La política exterior española en el franquismo', *Cuenta y Razón* 6, 1982.

―――. 'Las relaciones hispano-franceses, el Gobierno Daladier y la crise de Munich', in *Españoles y franceses en la primera mitad des siglo XX*. Madrid, 1986.

Whealey, R.H. 'Foreign Intervention in the Spanish Civil War', in *The Republic and the Civil War in Spain*, ed. R. Carr. London, 1971, pp. 213-38.